ARAB MIGRANT COMMUNITIES IN THE GCC

ZAHRA BABAR

(*Editor*)

Arab Migrant Communities in the GCC

Center *for* International *and* Regional Studies

OXFORD
UNIVERSITY PRESS

OXFORD
UNIVERSITY PRESS

Oxford University Press is a department of the
University of Oxford. It furthers the University's objective
of excellence in research, scholarship, and education
by publishing worldwide.

Oxford   New York
Auckland   Cape Town   Dar es Salaam   Hong Kong   Karachi
Kuala Lumpur   Madrid   Melbourne   Mexico City   Nairobi
New Delhi   Shanghai   Taipei   Toronto

With offices in
Argentina   Austria   Brazil   Chile   Czech Republic   France   Greece
Guatemala   Hungary   Italy   Japan   Poland   Portugal   Singapore
South Korea   Switzerland   Thailand   Turkey   Ukraine   Vietnam

Oxford is a registered trade mark of Oxford University Press
in the UK and certain other countries.

Published in the United States of America by
Oxford University Press
198 Madison Avenue, New York, NY 10016

Copyright © Zahra Babar 2017

All rights reserved. No part of this publication may be reproduced,
stored in a retrieval system, or transmitted, in any form or by any means,
without the prior permission in writing of Oxford University Press,
or as expressly permitted by law, by license, or under terms agreed with
the appropriate reproduction rights organization. Inquiries concerning
reproduction outside the scope of the above should be sent to the
Rights Department, Oxford University Press, at the address above.

You must not circulate this work in any other form
and you must impose this same condition on any acquirer.

Library of Congress Cataloging-in-Publication Data is available
Zahra Babar.
Arab Migrant Communities in the GCC.
ISBN: 9780190608873

Printed in India on acid-free paper

CONTENTS

Acknowledgements vii
Contributors ix
List of Tables and Figures xvii

1. Introduction   *Zahra Babar*   1
2. Working for the Neighbours: Arab Migrants in Qatar
                                                  Zahra Babar   19
3. Arab Migrant Teachers in the United Arab Emirates and Qatar: Challenges and Opportunities
                Natasha Ridge, Soha Shami and *Susan Kippels*   39
4. The Model Immigrant: Second Generation Hadramis in Kuwait and the Legacy of a 'Good Reputation'   *Abdullah Alajmi*   65
5. The Egyptian 'Invasion' of Kuwait: Navigating Possibilities among the Impossible   *Abbie Taylor, Nada Soudy* and *Susan Martin*   85
6. The 'Other Arab' and Gulf Citizens: Mutual Accommodation of Palestinians in the UAE in Historical Context   *Manal A. Jamal*   111
7. Yemeni Irregular Migrants in the Kingdom of Saudi Arabia and the Implications of Large Scale Return: An Analysis of Yemeni Migrants Returning from Saudi Arabia
                            Harry Cook and *Michael Newson*   133
8. An Emerging Trend in Arab Migration: Highly Skilled Arab Females in the GCC Countries   *Françoise De Bel-Air*   169
9. Highly Skilled Lebanese Transnational Migrants: A Kuwait Perspective   *Garret Maher*   197

CONTENTS

10. Sport Labour Migrant Communities from the Maghreb in the GCC *Mahfoud Amara* 217
11. Attitudes of Students in the GCC Region towards the Arab Spring: A Case Study of Students in the UAE
    George Naufal, Ismail Genc, and *Carlos Vargas-Silva* 235

Appendix: Survey of Students' Attitudes in the GCC Towards the Arab Spring (November 2013) 247

Notes 251
Index 297

ACKNOWLEDGEMENTS

This volume emerged as the result of a grant-driven research initiative undertaken between 2012 and 2014 by the Center for International and Regional Studies (CIRS) at Georgetown University in Qatar. From the very early stages of this project a number of scholars provided their intellectual input in crafting this study of Arab migrant communities in the GCC. Grateful acknowledgement goes to the participants of the two working groups that were held in Doha, in particular to Mohammad Al-Waqfi, Sulayman Khalaf, Heba Nassar, Ramzi Nasser, Ganesh Seshan, Nasra Shah, and Paul Tacon. My own two chapters in this volume benefited significantly from the intellectual and practical input of my colleagues at the CIRS, without whom the task of editing this volume would have been impossible. For all their encouragement and assistance, I would like to offer a heartfelt thanks to Haya Al-Noaimi, Misba Bhatti, Matthew Buehler, Nerida Child Dimasi, Islam Hassan, Mehran Kamrava, Dionysis Markakis, Suzi Mirgani, Dwaa Osman, Nadia Talpur, and Elizabeth Wanucha. Barb Gillis, who is no longer physically with us at CIRS, is missed greatly each and every day. My two student research assistants, Hazim Ali and Umber Latafat, provided me with invaluable support in multiple ways, but I owe them a particular debt of gratitude for sorting out the data into decipherable charts and figures. I would also like to thank officials at Qatar's Ministry of Labour and Social Affairs for providing me with access to the data that makes Chapter 2 of this volume possible. Finally, grateful acknowledgement goes also to the Qatar Foundation for its support of such research endeavours.

From my birth, my parents, Maryam and Bashir Khan Babar, dragged me to all corners of the earth, and thus deserve a good portion of the blame for my enduring fascination with questions of mobility, alienation, and the search for roots and belonging. For that and for many other reasons, I dedicate this volume to them.

Zahra Babar

CONTRIBUTORS

Abdullah Alajmi is Professor of the Department of General Studies and also Assistant Director of Academic Affairs at the Arab Open University in Kuwait. He is an anthropologist whose research interests include ethnohistory, economic culture, development, migration, sociolinguistics, and the problematics of ethnographic interpretation. While completing his Master's degree in the US, he examined the production of Bedouin Nabat poetry in Kuwait as a politico-cultural practice in relation to state politics. While completing his MSc and PhD at the London School of Economics, he carried out ethnographic research among Yemeni immigrants in Kuwait, focusing particularly on the Hadrami service in the domestic sphere of Kuwaiti households.

Mahfoud Amara is Assistant Professor in Sport Management and Policy at the College of Arts and Sciences at Qatar University. Prior to joining Qatar University, from 2004 until 2015, he was Assistant Professor in Sport Policy and Management and Deputy Director of the Centre for Olympic Studies and Research in the School of Sport, Exercise and Health Sciences, at Loughborough University. His research interests focus on sport business, culture, and politics in Arab and Muslim contexts. He has published on the politics of the Pan-Arab Games, sport in colonial and post-colonial contexts, sport and the business of media broadcasting, the sport and modernization debate, and sport development and development through sport. His other research interests include sport, multiculturalism and intercultural dialogue, including the provision of sport for ethnic minorities, sport and social inclusion, and sport and integration. Dr. Amara has carried out research for a range of national and international bodies including the British Academy, the European Commission, and UNESCO. He was a member of an external

CONTRIBUTORS

assessment panel of the BBC's regional sports coverage in 2007, and has been invited to speak on his research at a number of national and international conferences, particularly in relation to sport in the Middle East and North African region, and on sport and multiculturalism debates in Europe. In 2012, he published a book entitled *Sport Politics and Society in the Arab World*, (Palgrave Macmillan). He has also served as co-editor with Alberto Testa of *Sport in Islam and in Muslim Communities* (Routledge, 2015).

Zahra Babar is Associate Director for Research at the Center for International and Regional Studies, Georgetown University in Qatar. Previously, she served with the International Labor Organization and the United Nations Development Programme. Her current research interests include rural development, Gulf migration and labour policies, citizenship in the Persian Gulf states, and GCC regional integration. Her recent publications include: with Andrew Gardner, 'Circular Migration in the Gulf States', *Impact of Circular Migration on Human, Political and Civil Rights: A Global Perspective*, eds. Carlota Sole et al (Springer, 2016); with Dwaa Osman, 'Women, Work, and the Weak State: A Case Study of Pakistan and Sudan', *Fragile Politics: Weak States in the Greater Middle East*, ed. Mehran Kamrava (Hurst/Oxford University Press, 2016), 'Population, Power, and Distributional Politics in Qatar', *Journal of Arabian Studies* (Vol. 5, Issue 2, 2015), and 'The Cost of Belonging: Citizenship Construction in the State of Qatar', *Middle East Journal* (Vol. 68, No. 3, 2014). She has co-edited, with Mehran Kamrava, *Migrant Labor in the Persian Gulf* (Hurst/Columbia University, 2012) and, with Suzi Mirgani, *Food Security in the Middle East* (Hurst/Oxford University Press, 2014).

Harry Cook is Data Management and Research Specialist for IOM (International Organization for Migration)'s Migrant Assistance Division at IOM Headquarters in Geneva. He serves as the Organization's primary reference point for data on human trafficking and vulnerable migrants, developing standard operating procedures, policies, tools, and technology solutions for the collection, management, and analysis of such data. He was previously Research Officer for IOM's Regional Office for the Middle East and North Africa, responsible for research into migration trends and related issues in the region and their impact on development and humanitarian objectives. Harry has an MSc in Comparative Political Economy from the London School of Economics and Political Science, and a BA in Philosophy from King's College London.

Françoise De Bel-Air is a researcher and consultant based in Paris, France. A social demographer by training, she specialises in the political demography of

CONTRIBUTORS

Arab countries and has published extensively on her areas of research. She is currently the Scientific Coordinator for the demography module of the Gulf Labor Markets and Migration Program with the Gulf Research Center in Geneva and Dubai, and the Migration Policy Centre of the European University Institute in Florence, Italy. She has previously served as part-time Professor at the Migration Policy Centre, and was for several years Research Fellow and Programme Manager at the French Institute for the Near East in Amman, Jordan.

Ismail Genc is currently Professor of Economics and the head of the Economics Department at the American University of Sharjah. He previously served as Associate Professor at the University of Idaho, and as Vice President of the Southwestern Economics Association. He currently sits on various editorial boards, and provides testimonies to policy- and decision-makers in industry and governmental bodies. His expertise is broadly in applied monetary economics, economic development, and remittances, and his work has appeared in a number of academic journals and books.

Manal A. Jamal is Associate Professor of Political Science at James Madison University in Harrisonburg, Virginia. Her most recent publications have appeared in *Comparative Political Studies, British Journal of Middle Eastern Studies, International Feminist Journal of Politics,* and *International Migration Review,* as well as in a number of edited volumes. She recently completed her first book, and is beginning a second, multi-year project. In her first book, *Democracy Promotion in Distorted Times,* which draws on research for which she won the Best Fieldwork Award (Comparative Democratization section) of the American Political Science Association, she examined the impact of the political settlements and the mediating role of Western donor assistance on political movements and emergent civil society groups in El Salvador and the Palestinian territories, culminating in Hamas' 2006 election victory and the political aftermath that transpired. In her new project, *The Arab Uprisings & Movement Mobilization in Cross Regional Perspective,* she evaluates the political-economic determinants of social movement organisation that led to these moments of upheaval in Egypt and Tunisia, compared to their predecessors in Latin America, such as in Argentina, Brazil, and Chile.

Susan Kippels is a Research Fellow at the Sheikh Saud bin Saqr Al Qasimi Foundation for Policy Research. She previously conducted research for UNICEF, undertook advocacy work with an international NGO in Uganda, and managed a private sector business in Lebanon. With UNICEF, she

CONTRIBUTORS

researched non-formal education strategies as well as early learning in emergency contexts. Her current research interests include philanthropy and education, private education in the Gulf, and Arab migrant teachers. Susan holds a dual Bachelor's degree in Economics and Arabic from the University of Notre Dame as well as a Master's degree in International Education Policy from the Harvard Graduate School of Education.

Garret Maher has worked in the higher education sector for more than a decade. He joined the University of Exeter in February 2016, as Assistant Head of International Partnerships with a key focus on the wider European Region. Previously he worked at the University of Warwick to advance international links in Central Asia; as a lecturer at the National University of Ireland, Galway; and as Assistant Professor of Geography at Gulf University for Sciences and Technology in Kuwait. He has also worked as a private research consultant in Dubai, has led research operations in Brazil, Ireland, the USA, the UAE, Kuwait, and Lebanon, and has published in a number of highly ranked journals. He received his PhD in Geography, and his BA, from the National University of Ireland, Galway, and his Master's Degree from University College Dublin.

Susan Martin is the Donald G. Herzberg Professor Emeritus in the School of Foreign Service at Georgetown University. She previously served as the Director of Georgetown's Institute for the Study of International Migration. She currently serves as the Chair of the Thematic Working Group on Environmental Change and Migration for the Knowledge Partnership in Migration and Development (KNOMAD) at the World Bank. Before coming to Georgetown, she served as the Executive Director of the U.S. Commission on Immigration Reform, established by legislation to advise Congress and the President on US immigration and refugee policy. Her most recent book publications include *International Migration: Evolving Trends from the Early Twentieth Century to the Present*; *Migration and Humanitarian Crises: Causes, Consequences and Responses* and *A Nation of Immigrants*. She received her MA and PhD in the History of American Civilization from the University of Pennsylvania, and previously taught at Brandeis University and the University of Pennsylvania.

George Naufal is Senior Research Associate at the Public Policy Research Institute at Texas A & M University and Research Fellow at the Institute of Labor Economics (IZA). Previously he was the technical director at Timberlake Consultants in London. He was also Assistant/Associate

CONTRIBUTORS

Professor of Economics at The American University of Sharjah (2007 to 2014) in the United Arab Emirates. His primary research focuses on the Middle East and North Africa region with an emphasis on the Gulf countries. He has served as a consultant on issues related to the Middle East and has published on expats and the labour force in the GCC.

Michael Newson is currently based in Vienna as IOM's Labour Mobility and Human Development Specialist for South Eastern & Eastern Europe and Central Asia Region. From 2012 to 2016 he held the same position in the Middle East North Africa Region at IOM's Regional Office in Cairo. He provides technical support, policy expertise, capacity building, and training to governments, IOM officials, and other relevant stakeholders throughout the MENA region. Michael has previously worked with IOM in Bogotá and Mauritius, focusing on the development and implementation of labour migration programmes, and has served as Senior Policy Advisor in the Labor Market and Immigration Division of the Government of British Columbia in Canada, where he focused on policy issues relating to both temporary foreign workers and permanent economic immigration streams. Michael holds an MA in Social and Political Philosophy from York University in Toronto and an MBA from the Warwick Business School at the University of Warwick in the UK.

Natasha Ridge is currently Executive Director of the Sheikh Saud bin Saqr Al Qasimi Foundation for Policy Research. She previously served as Acting Director of Research at the Dubai School of Government. Natasha's latest research focuses on the role and impact of Arab father involvement, philanthropy and education, and access and equity in the Gulf education sector. She wrote a book entitled *Education and the Reverse Gender Divide in the Gulf States: Embracing the Global, Ignoring the Local* and has a number of other publications, including chapters for the World Education Yearbook, the Emirates Centre for Strategic Studies and UNESCO and working papers for the Dubai School of Government and the Al Qasimi Foundation. Natasha holds a Doctorate of Education in International Education Policy from Columbia University and a Master's in International and Community Development from Deakin University, Australia.

Soha Shami previously worked as a Research Associate at the Sheikh Saud bin Saqr Al Qasimi Foundation for Policy Research, where she conducted qualitative and quantitative education research on secondary school male dropouts in the UAE, gender and education in the GCC, the role of Arab fathers, and

CONTRIBUTORS

teachers in the UAE. Prior to joining the Foundation, she was a teaching assistant in the Economics Department at the American University of Sharjah (AUS), where she employed her background in economics to assist in teaching coursework to undergraduate students. She also conducted qualitative market research and consumer studies in the UAE and Qatar for The Nielsen Company. Soha holds a Bachelor's degree in economics from the AUS with a minor in International Studies, and her background includes economic policy, labour economics, and development. She is currently pursuing an MSc in Economics for Development at the University of Oxford.

Nada Soudy is a Senior Associate at Teach For All in Qatar, supporting the network's partner engagement and growth efforts in the Middle East and North Africa. Previously, she was a Research Associate and Project Manager at Carnegie Mellon University in Qatar, undertaking an education project that targeted different populations, including migrant workers in Qatar. Her interest in Arab migration is inspired by her own experience as an Egyptian born and raised in Qatar after her parents migrated to Qatar in the eighties. Nada recently obtained her MA in Arab Studies from Georgetown University. She conducted qualitative research on Egyptians living in the US and in Qatar for her MA thesis and recently published an article entitled 'Home and belonging: a comparative study of 1.5 and second-generation Egyptian "expatriates" in Qatar and "immigrants" in the U.S.' in the *Journal of Ethnic and Migration Studies*. After graduation, she spent the summer working as a Research Assistant at the Institute for the Study of International Migration at Georgetown University on a project focusing on Egyptians in Kuwait.

Abbie Taylor is a graduate of the Center for Contemporary Arab Studies and co-authored her chapter in this volume while working as a Research Associate at Georgetown University's Institute for the Study of International Migration. During her time at Georgetown, her research focused on the Levant, where she contributed to efforts to advocate for displaced Iraqis, Palestinians and Syrians, focusing on the histories and trajectories of both refugees and neighbouring host populations, as well as perceptions of the future and prospects of return among those displaced. The research on Egyptians in Kuwait served as a continuation of her interest in the experiences of both Arab migrants and host communities within the broader sphere of Arab intra-regional migration.

Carlos Vargas-Silva is Senior Researcher at the Center on Migration, Policy, and Society and a member of the Migration Observatory team at the University of Oxford. He primarily works on the labour markets cluster. He

CONTRIBUTORS

previously served as a consultant on migration-related projects for several international and policy agencies including the Asian Development Bank, the European Commission, the Inter-American Development Bank, the World Bank, the UK Home Office, and the United Nations University. His research interests include the economic impact of immigration on migrant-receiving countries and the link between migration, including forced migration, and economic development in migrant-sending countries. He is also Associate Editor of the *Migration Studies* journal.

LIST OF TABLES AND FIGURES

Tables

Table 1.1:	National and foreign populations in the GCC (by most recent year available)	2
Table 1.2:	Total Arab migrant populations in the GCC region (% of total population)	3
Table 1.3:	Arab expatriate populations in the GCC region	3
Table 2.1:	Arab dependants in Qatar	30
Table 4.1:	Cost comparison of a typical immigrant's income and expenses	79
Table 4.2:	Breakdown of typical marriage expenses	80
Table 7.1:	Education level indicated by respondents	148
Table 7.2:	Occupation of respondents	149
Table 7.3:	Occupation of employed respondents	150
Table 7.4:	Indicated communities of return of respondents	152
Table 7.5:	Duration of stay in Saudi Arabia by governorate of return	153
Table 7.6:	Expected livelihood strategy of respondents by governorate of return (percentage)	155
Table 7.7:	Education level of respondents by governorate of return	156
Table 7.8:	Amount of monthly remittances to Yemen	157
Table 7.9:	Amount of monthly remittances to Yemen by non-short-stayer respondents	158
Table 7.10:	Remittances value cross-tabulated with respondents' level of education	159
Table 7.11:	Remittance value correlated with duration of stay in Saudi Arabia	159

LIST OF TABLES AND FIGURES

Table 7.12: Differential regional impact of *nitaqat* policy changes — 162
Table 8.1: Highly skilled, employed and total (15–64 years) populations (Bahrain, 2010; Kuwait, 2012) — 176
Table 8.2: Non-Kuwaiti population by sex, migration status and country or region of citizenship of holder (December 2012) — 179
Table 8.3: Distribution of respondents to the survey residing in the Gulf States by country of current residence in the Gulf and sex (Summer 2012) — 181
Table 8.4: Highest university degree obtained by respondents in Lebanon and abroad (Summer 2012) — 183
Table 9.1: Profile of Kuwait interviewees' monthly earnings — 204
Table 10.1: Professional football players of Maghrebi origin playing in GCC clubs — 225
Table 11.1: Descriptive statistics of students — 238
Table 11.2: Country of birth and passport usage (%) — 240
Table 11.3: Preferred location to raise children — 241
Table 11.4: Proxies for religiousness — 242
Table 11.5: Correlation matrix among religiousness proxies — 242
Table 11.6: Mean and standard deviation of responses, by country of birth — 243
Table 11.7: Mean and standard deviation of responses by religiousness — 244

Figures

Figure 2.1: Qatar's population breakdown (1990–2010) — 25
Figure 2.2: Qatari labour force breakdown (2013) — 28
Figure 2.3: Arab nationalities as a percentage of non-local Arabs in the labour force — 29
Figure 2.4: Arab nationalities as a percentage of total Arab residents — 29
Figure 2.5: Labour force sectoral breakdown: education (by country of origin) — 32
Figure 2.6: Labour force sectoral breakdown: finance and insurance activities (by country of origin) — 33
Figure 2.7: Labour force sectoral breakdown: legal and law enforcement activities (by country of origin) — 33
Figure 2.8: Labour force sectoral breakdown: managerial and administrative services (by country of origin) — 33

LIST OF TABLES AND FIGURES

Figure 2.9: Labour force sectoral breakdown: media and journalism (by country of origin) — 34

Figure 2.10: Labour force sectoral breakdown: professional and technical activities (by country of origin) — 34

Figure 2.11: Occupation of non-local Arabs in Qatari labour force — 35

Figure 2.12: Resident Arabs vs. other resident nationalities — 36

Figure 2.13: Expatriate Arabs vs. other expatriate nationalities — 36

Figure 3.1: UAE–Arab migrant educators by nationality—male (2008) — 48

Figure 3.2: Qatar–Arab migrant educators by nationality—male and female (2013) — 49

Figure 3.3: Push and pull factors — 53

Figure 3.4: Challenges of teaching experiences in the UAE and Qatar — 55

Figure 3.5: Factors that encourage teachers to stay in UAE/Qatar — 56

Figure 3.6: World cloud of the ninety-one most frequently used words in interviews — 57

Figure 7.1: Percentage of total respondents by length of stay reported in Saudi Arabia, over time — 144

Figure 7.2: Number of respondents by age (in years) — 146

Figure 8.1: Arab employed population by main occupation group and sex (Bahrain, 2010; Kuwait, 2012) — 177

Figure 8.2: Respondents' marital status by sex (2012) — 182

Figure 8.3: Respondents' field of education by sex (2012) — 184

Figure 8.4: Main economic occupation of respondents, by sex (2012) — 185

Figure 8.5: Respondents' professional status, by sex (2012) — 186

Figure 8.6: Ownership of the company employing respondents (2012) — 187

Figure 8.7: Size of the company employing respondents (2012) — 188

Figure 8.8: Respondents' first job in the Gulf: recruitment channels, by sex (2012) — 189

Figure 8.9: Reasons for leaving Lebanon, by sex (2012) — 192

1

INTRODUCTION

Zahra Babar

Increasingly, the cross-border mobility of people and international migration has become a central and dynamic hallmark of human existence. While migration is by no means a recent phenomenon, present-day migratory experiences are increasingly informed by national and international policy settings, and by the needs of the global labour market. In contemporary times, the six Gulf Cooperation Council (GCC) member states of Bahrain, Kuwait, Oman, Qatar, Saudi Arabia, and the United Arab Emirates (UAE) have emerged as the third-largest hub of international labour migration.

This migration has attracted increasing journalistic attention and a growing body of scholarship from academics.[1] What has gone almost completely unnoticed, however, is the regional, intra-Arab aspect of the phenomenon. Migration into the Gulf region from other Arab countries by far outdates more recent, and comparatively more temporary, migratory patterns from South and South-East Asia, and Western Europe. Not only are Arab migratory patterns into the Gulf comparatively and qualitatively different from other similar patterns, the historical setting within which they have unfolded, the processes through which they have taken place, and their economic, sociological, and political consequences have all been different. This book examines the dynamics involved in the emergence of Arab migrant communities in the Gulf region, focusing specifically on how they came about, their overall sociological compositions and economic profiles, and the causes, processes, and consequences of their interactions with and integration within their host countries.

Table 1.1: National and foreign populations in the GCC (by most recent year available)

GCC states[2]	Year	Nationals	Foreigners	Total population
Bahrain	2013	614,830	638,361	1,253,191
Kuwait	2011	1,089,969	1,975,881	3,065,850
Oman	2014	2,260,705	1,732,188	3,992,893
Qatar*	2013	177,666	1,592,608	1,770,274
Saudi Arabia	2007	17,493,364	6,487,470	23,980,834
UAE	2005	825,495	3,280,932	4,106,427

* In Qatar the only publicly available data on population states for those '15 years and above', so this total does not include minors under the age of 15.

The Middle East displays high levels of inequality, where countries with very different economic, political, and social resources live side by side.[3] Over the past fifty years, the primary marker differentiating the developmental conditions amongst Middle Eastern states has been the natural endowment, or lack thereof, of petroleum resources. The difference in economic strength between neighbouring states has had a profound impact on the dynamics of intra-regional migration. Migration has largely been from the less wealthy states of the Arab world to the small sheikhdoms of the Gulf. The particular demographic features and economic needs of the states of the GCC have facilitated this pattern of migration.

From the middle of the twentieth century, and with staggering rapidity, petroleum-derived wealth transformed the six GCC states from some of the poorest countries within the region to some of the wealthiest in the world.[4] These conditions stood in clear contrast to the non-oil Arab states, where rapidly increasing youth populations, limited local opportunities, statist policies, and stagnant economic development placed increasing pressure on the absorptive capacity of domestic labour markets. As a consequence, in the non-oil states labour out-migration evolved into a critical lifeline for individuals seeking economic traction, as well as policymakers concerned with providing employment opportunities for their citizens.[5] The wealthier GCC states, whose burgeoning development agendas outstripped local labour supplies, served as a natural regional draw for labour migrants from within the Arab world.

Table 1.2: Total Arab migrant populations in the GCC region (% of total population)[6]

Country	Year	
	1995	2004
Bahrain	12	15
Kuwait	33	30
Oman	11	6
Qatar	21	19
Saudi Arabia	30	33
UAE	10	13

Table 1.3: Arab expatriate populations in the GCC region[7]

Country of origin	Bahrain 2002	Kuwait 2004	Oman 2003	Qatar 2004	Saudi Arabia 2002	UAE 2004
Egypt	30,000	260,000	30,000	35,000	900,000	140,000
Yemen	–	–	–	–	800,000	60,000
Sudan	–	–	–	–	250,000	30,000
Jordan/Palestine	20,000	50,000	–	50,000	260,000	110,000
Syria	–	100,000	–	–	100,000	–
Bidoon (stateless)	–	80,000	–	–	–	–

As is the case in other parts of the world, particular structural push and pull factors have prompted migration within the Middle East. In addition to these existing structural factors, the region has seen its share of cyclical patterns of regional migration resulting from economic crises, conflict and war.[8] While the economic push factors in the Arab labour-sending countries have not radically changed, the numbers of Arab migrants present in the Gulf have significantly decreased.[9] Although substantive and detailed data is limited, scholars agree that the ethnic and national composition of the GCC expatriate work force has changed dramatically. In the 1960s and 1970s the bulk of the foreign work force was Arab, but gradually Asian workers replaced Arabs. In 1975, 72 per cent of the GCC expatriate workforce were Arabs. By 1985 this had decreased to 56 percent, and by 2009 this figure had further dropped to 23 percent.[10] Asians are now estimated to constitute more than double the number of Arab expatriates in the GCC's labour force.[11] Some estimates suggest that in the private sector workers not of Arab origin comprise 96 per cent of Qatar's work force, 98 per cent of the UAE's, and 90 per cent of Kuwait's.[12]

Economic and political factors have shaped historic patterns of migration to the Gulf, and led to the transition from a predominantly Arab expatriate labour force to one that is more 'Asianised' and international. Although reliable data is not readily available, figures suggest that about 2.4 million Arab foreign workers are present in the GCC,[13] and Arab migrants contribute US$33 billion in remittances to their homelands on an annual basis.[14] Despite the transition in the Gulf's expatriate labour force, the continued employment opportunities provided to Arab migrants in the GCC are still of vital importance, particularly because the Middle East is once again in the throes of high levels of instability and conflict. While the Gulf may not be amenable to hosting refugee populations from neighbouring Arab states, the desire of Arab workers to find employment in the GCC can only have increased as a result of the violence and warfare they are experiencing at home.

Intraregional mobility: economic drivers

During the 1960s, Arab policymakers attempted to lay down the foundations for a common understanding of how to manage intraregional mobility, emphasizing that doing so would increase regional economic integration.[15] Several protocols were put forward, including the Arab Economic Unity Agreement of 1964 and the Arab Agreement for Mobility of Arab Labour No. 2 of 1967. A lack of consensus and limited political will on managing regional mobility was demonstrated by the two agreements only being ratified by fourteen countries, none of them GCC members.[16] Historically, GCC labour-receiving countries have considered pan-Arab market solutions not to be in alignment with their interests, and non-oil Arab states have primarily driven efforts to develop a unified regional agreement on labour mobility. While there are indications that during the 1960s the Gulf states attempted to develop migration policies sensitive to the pan-Arabist sentiments of the time, and original policies were worded in ways that privileged the hiring of Arabs, in reality these were never broadly implemented.[17]

As part of their socialist ruling bargains, many non-oil Arab states began investing heavily in education from the 1950s, but these efforts were more

INTRODUCTION

successful in expanding access to rather than quality of education.[18] The end result was that a greater number of young people across the Arab world obtained secondary and tertiary education, but lacked the fundamental skills to match the needs of the labour market.[19] In addition, the continuously increasing population levels and the stream of young people entering the job market led to a situation where, despite economic growth in the non-oil countries, simply not enough jobs were available in the domestic sector.[20]

While Arab-origin migrants were present in the GCC states in earlier decades, the real wave of intraregional labour migration occurred in the 1970s—particularly after 1973—when astronomical increases in oil revenues led to unprecedented infrastructural development in all of the GCC states.[21] With small local populations unable to meet the ensuing labour demands, the region was a natural draw for Arabs from neighbouring countries with less robust economies and large numbers of the educated unemployed. Egypt, Jordan, Syria, and Yemen emerged as the four countries with the highest numbers of their citizens working in the Gulf.[22] By the middle of the 1970s there were 1.4 million Egyptians working in the Gulf region, and by 1983 the figure had reached 2.9 million.[23] By 1980 almost 300,000 Jordanians (approximately 30 per cent of the Jordanian labour force) were employed in the GCC.[24] Yemen also served as a key exporter of its citizenry, particularly to Saudi Arabia, and in the 1980s it was estimated that close to 1 million Yemenis were living and working in one of the six oil states of the Gulf.[25]

In addition to the changes in the number of Arab migrants, there have been historic transitions in the skills and qualifications of Arab expatriates present in the Gulf, and the way that they have been integrated into the GCC's labour markets. During the 1950s and 1960s the bulk of Arab workers in the region were skilled workers, engaged primarily in professions such as medicine, education and engineering. But by the 1970s this had changed, and Arab workers were visible throughout the labour market, including in less-skilled and lower-paying jobs.[26] Migration policy has not only been implemented in the GCC states to restrict people's entry, it has also been used by Arab states interested in controlling their citizens' exit. When Egypt lifted restrictions on emigration in 1973, many more Egyptians began seeking jobs in the GCC. In the 1960s, the majority of Egyptians working in the Gulf came from educated, white-collar, professional backgrounds. But by the 1970s, with changes in emigration policy, a massive wave of unskilled Egyptian migrants began to populate the region.[27] Post-1980s, with the influx of cheaper Asian labour to compete for jobs at the lower end of the Gulf labour market, the pattern of Arab migration to the region changed again.[28]

From the 1980s onwards, several Arab states began facing increasing rates of unemployment. Economic growth and development and the expansion of national labour markets were unable to keep pace with rapid increases in population size.[29] Onn Winckler has suggested that these states began to suffer from 'structural unemployment', partially as a result of demographic factors.[30] These factors included the pressures of sustaining societies where the majority of the population was young and below working age, a very low female participation rate in the labour force, dramatic increases in educational attainment levels, and public-sector employment offering 'early retirement' opportunities.[31] Despite implementing ambitious economic reforms and restructuring programmes, many of the non-oil Arab states continued to experience high levels of unemployment and limited opportunities for upward economic mobility for their middle classes.[32] While these adverse economic circumstances were apparent several decades ago, in recent years they have been magnified. Today, across the region those who struggle the most to find employment are the young, educated segment of the population who are new entrants to the labour market. As a result, many of the Arabs working in the Gulf currently are younger, educated people who were unable to find occupation in their own countries.[33]

The benefit for the non-oil Arab states of sending their citizens to work in the GCC—in addition to the successful, productive employment of their nationals—was most visible in the flows of financial remittances that sent infusions of foreign currency back home, along with the increasing levels of development aid that the GCC states provided. However, the disastrous impact on the non-oil Arab states when the oil market collapsed in the 1980s showed that the relationship between labour-sending and -receiving states was at best tenuous and came with costs, risks, and vulnerabilities.

With the collapse of oil prices in the mid-1980s, the economic trajectories for the Gulf states changed dramatically and the demand for Arab labour significantly declined. The then largest Arab exporters of labour—Egypt, Jordan, Syria and Yemen—faced the most immediate negative consequences of this development.[34] The shift from the mid-1980s onwards, when the GCC states began to increasingly seek and rely on cheaper workers from less developed Asian countries, showed that there was no such thing as regional solidarity when it came to economic pragmatism.

The decrease in Arab workers' presence in GCC countries has occurred because of the implementation of labour migration policies based on the economic, political and security concerns of the Gulf states. The argument of economic rationality is that the expansion of the regional private sector, the increasing integration of the Gulf into the global economy, and the success of neo-liberal economic policies, which predicate the logic of seeking cheaper sources of labour, have all curtailed the regional demand for Arab workers. Arab economists and policymakers from the non-oil states have long suggested—and continue to suggest—that the Middle East is best served if it is conceived of as a single unit, where different parts offer different strengths to complement and stabilise one another.[35] Such analysis encourages a regional approach to managing labour needs, and suggests that the current domination of the Gulf labour force by Asian workers has negative consequences for the political economies of all the Arab states. In line with this, Arab neighbours urge GCC states to actively work to replace Asian migrant workers with Arab ones.

Despite ebbs and flows over time, remittances and labour mobility continue to play a significant role in relations between the GCC states and their neighbours, and this will remain so despite the decline in the overall number of Arab migrants present in the region.[36] Intra-regional remittance flows to the Arab labour-exporting states from the resource-rich states have outpaced trade-related flows.[37] Remittances from the Gulf have provided a vital economic lifeline to the less economically robust Middle Eastern countries. For example, in 2007 more than half of remittances received in Egypt came from GCC countries.[38] Egypt, Morocco and Lebanon today are the three largest receivers of workers' remittances in the Arab world, while the four countries that provide the largest numbers of Arab workers to GCC countries are Egypt, Jordan, Lebanon, and Syria. Saudi Arabia remains the largest single source of remittances from the GCC region to Arab states.

Intraregional mobility: political factors

Economic considerations have not been the sole determinative factor to affect Arab migration to the Gulf. This of course reinforces what the existing literature on migration has already told us: although applying an economic lens is critical to studying migration, economics alone is not enough to understand migration in any context.[39] As early as the 1960s, Gulf governments were uneasy with the potential threat posed by hosting large numbers of non-national Arabs.[40] This threat was not one that derived from Gulf governments' economic concerns, but primarily stemmed from their political qualms.[41] Following Iraq's invasion of Kuwait in the 1990s, it became quite clear that labour migration policies were not immune to political events, and in fact were directly shaped by them. During

7

and after the First Gulf War of 1991, almost 2 million non-GCC Arabs were either expelled or voluntarily left the Gulf, which had an enduring impact on the pattern of intraregional migration.[42]

During the First Gulf War, several of the Arab labour-sending states with high numbers of their citizens present in GCC countries either supported Saddam Hussein and Iraq's Kuwait campaign, or expressed neutrality. The GCC states' response to this perceived disloyalty was immediate and effective. Jordan, which had not expressed outright support for the Kuwaiti cause, saw more than 200,000 of its citizens summarily ejected from Kuwait and neighbouring GCC states.[43] The Palestine Liberation Organization adopted a similar position during the Iraqi occupation, which resulted in the same consequences for Palestinians living and working in the Gulf.[44] In 1965 Palestinians had comprised 30 per cent of the foreign population in Kuwait but following the Gulf War, 150,000 Palestinians were summarily expelled from the country.[45] The Yemeni government also faced similar consequences over its lack of support for the Kuwaiti regime and the other GCC states, and as a result 800,000 to 900,000 Yemenis were expelled from Saudi Arabia alone. On the other hand, Syria, by way of implicit thanks for its support of the anti-Iraq coalition, benefitted by seeing an increase in the numbers of its citizens present in the GCC region after the war.

The polarising consequence of Iraq's invasion of Kuwait was undoubtedly one of the most important political events to affect the region's demography. However, while the invasion may have served as a catalyst, the gradual departure of Arabs from the Gulf labour market was not the result of one causal event. Beginning in the 1970s the GCC region steadily tilted in the direction of Asian migrants, not only for the economic benefits of the cheaper labour they offered, but also because politically, culturally and socially Asians were perceived by GCC policymakers to be more amenable to short-term labour recruitment, and easier to socially and culturally segregate from the rest of the population. Due to their cultural differences, GCC policymakers considered Asians to have less of a chance of achieving assimilation and integration with the host population, and that they would leave less of a diasporic footprint, and have less of a moral right to or interest in permanent settlement and citizenship.

In addition to the First Gulf War, the Arab world has seen its share of mass movements because of political and social upheavals. The current political turmoil in the Middle East has reinvigorated older political and security concerns of the GCC states, and will certainly have repercussions on Arab intraregional mobility. The GCC states are not signatories to the 1951 Geneva

INTRODUCTION

Refugee Convention and have no official framework for managing or accepting refugees or asylum seekers. As of 2015, 2 million Syrian refugees are hosted in the Middle East, primarily by five countries: Turkey, Jordan, Iraq, Lebanon, and Egypt. None of the GCC states has expressed a desire to play a role in hosting refugees of current crises. The conflict currently playing out in Yemen is certain to create a new cadre of internally displaced people pressing against the borders of yet another fractured Middle Eastern state.

The reconfiguration of the ethnic and national composition of the GCC labour force has been a gradual process and a result of economic and political factors. Over time, the region has moved from being dominated by high numbers of non-national Arab migrants to contemporary circumstances where a far greater number of non-Arabs make up the workforce. While the configuration of different nationalities and ethnicities present in each of the GCC states is continuously changing, the bulk of migrants working and living in the Gulf today come from South and South-East Asia. The notion that intra-regional Arab labour migration has supported and promoted sustained social, political, cultural and economic regional integration is clearly questionable. While intraregional labour migration has benefitted both Arab labour-sending and -receiving states, it has flourished more as a result of the national interests of states on either side of the migration divide, rather than as a result of an active effort to promote Arab solidarity. Much as we see in other parts of the world, the national interests of a particular state at a given historic moment dictate migration policies in sending and receiving Arab states.

Gulf migration in comparative perspective

The study of migration in the GCC region has provided us with a richer understanding of how patterns of movement have developed in this sub-region of the Middle East. Among other things, the emerging literature on this topic has deepened our understanding of the conditions and lived experiences of migrants living in the Gulf states; focused our attention on the challenges of local labour governance practices such as the *kafala* (sponsorship system); and explored some of the deeper societal dynamics and tensions around migration that have developed in the GCC context.[46] However, despite the increasing empirical work being produced, a trend persists in theoretical literature of treating conditions in the Gulf as exceptional, as though the patterns of regional migration, the policymaking mechanisms in place, and the particular vulnerabilities of Gulf migrants are somehow unique to the region. The Gulf's story of migration is all too frequently seen through the lenses of oil flows and repressive regimes, and this limited view allows for little comparative perspective and robs us of analytical depth.

Much of the story of Gulf migration in fact reflects broader global trends, and can be compared with what occurs in other parts of the world that are similarly struggling with the challenges of managing migration. While the Gulf region has increasingly become a site of contestation over accepted rights and norms for migrants, this is but one site in what is in fact a globalised struggle. While much of the discussion in the GCC region appears to centre on regional specificities and focuses on the particularly egregious nature of local practices of migration management, the attention that Gulf governments are receiving is very closely tied to and informed by debates that are equally relevant elsewhere. At the most fundamental level, the implementation of national immigration policies by all states often inherently clashes with migrants' basic human rights. Broader rights for migrants, such as rights to integration and inclusion, are being contested and challenged in many parts of the world. The rising popularity of temporary worker programmes—which share a marked similarity with the *kafala*—in the historic migration hubs of North America and Europe indicates that, worldwide, states are showing a noticeable preference for meeting labour-market shortages without offering permanent settlement.[47] Increasingly, researchers on Gulf migration are pointing out that migrants in the Gulf are far from a homogeneous group, and that their particular conditions and exposures to vulnerability reflect differences in class, gender and income levels.[48] Targeted migration policies and practices, which separate out skilled and sought-after international workers from lower-income, less-skilled migrants, is also not a phenomenon unique to the Gulf.[49] The era of globalisation, which has allowed an increasing number of the skilled and highly skilled to take up international occupations and in essence become 'transnational' migrants, has simultaneously led to a proliferation of policies that ease the settlement of 'more desirable' migrants, while increasing restrictions and limitations on unskilled workers populating jobs in the lower strata of the labour market.[50] Furthermore, in addition to income, skill and gender levels, the migration experience in the GCC region is also informed by migrants' particular ethnic, linguistic and national identity affiliations.[51] Focusing on Arab communities in the region allows us not only to explore not only how culture and ethnicity are entwined with migration in the Gulf, but also to contribute to the broader global understanding of migration.

The research that was undertaken for the chapters that follow is neither based on a single a priori hypothesis nor on a series of interlinking hypotheses.

INTRODUCTION

Rather, the goal is to present readers with a series of cross-disciplinary studies that provide a deeper, empirically based understanding of a phenomenon that has gone largely neglected in the study of the Gulf region, namely the persistent presence of an Arab expatriate community. Within the literature on regional migration acknowledgement is growing that it is not only the markers of class and income, but also ethnicity, nationality, language, religion and culture that shape and inform the migration experience. It is thus even more of an imperative to study sub-national and ethnic foreign communities in the Gulf, so as to gain a more nuanced understanding of processes and experiences of regional migration. Additionally, and as discussed in the previous paragraphs, the different chapter contributions in this volume, when read as a whole, push against prevailing assumptions about the Gulf's exceptionalism in terms of labour migration.

In this volume

Sensitivities in some of the GCC states regarding the public disclosure of information on their demographic conditions mean that simply obtaining accurate numbers of Arab-origin migrants present in the region has been a persistent challenge. The absence of adequate data on the region's Arab migrant communities has meant that in-depth studies that examine various aspects of Arab migrants' lives in the Gulf are almost non-existent. This volume partly addresses this gap in the literature by providing empirically rich analyses on Arab migrant communities in the GCC. The chapters that follow use multi-disciplinary views to provide us with original material on the historic and contemporary dynamics of Arab migration to the Gulf, and unravel how the particular social and cultural practices of Arab migrants have interacted with the host states. Among other things, specific contributions allow us to consider the particular socio-economic and political factors that have historically shaped the character of the Arab migratory experience; the sorts of work opportunities that Arab migrants have sought in the region; what their work conditions and lived experiences have been; and whether we can discern any patterns of socio-cultural integration for Arab non-nationals.

Given that across the GCC region we know that the vast numbers of migrants occupying lower-income and less-skilled jobs in the construction and service sectors originate from Asia, can we say that Arab migrant workers tend to be more visible in medium- or high-skilled occupations? Chapter Two focuses on addressing this particular question through a review of the Arab expatriate labour force in Qatar, and provides us with original data from Qatar's Ministry of Labour. Data provided in the chapter shows that the number of Arab migrants present in Qatar is far lower than previous work has suggested. Additionally, the analysis of Arab migrants' integration into the Qatari national labour market bolsters the argument that Arab migrants for the most part tend to occupy positions in sectors that are at higher income and skill levels than their Asian counterparts'.

Historically, Egypt has provided the Gulf with a trained workforce that has served as the backbone in certain critical sectors such as education, healthcare and the judiciary. Despite the transition in the region's workforce and the move to a less costly, Asianised labour pool, many Egyptians continue to work in the Gulf's education sector. In Chapter Three, Natasha Ridge, Soha Shami and Susan Kippels explore the dynamics of skilled Arab migrants through a sectoral analysis of their integration into the education sectors in the UAE and Qatar. Through this comparative case study, Chapter Three unravels anxieties and challenges Arab migrant teachers face in GCC countries, and also provides us with a deeper understanding of how their motivations and reasons for working in the Gulf differ from other expatriate teachers in the Gulf. Zahra Babar's and Ridge, Shami and Kippels' chapters underscore that skilled Arab workers dominate particular sectors and may continue to do so in the future, a reflection perhaps of the particular linguistic and ethno-cultural abilities required to do certain jobs in the Gulf.

What are the overall living, employment and residential conditions and status of long-term Arab migrants in Gulf states? The Yemeni, Egyptian and Palestinian communities in the GCC are assumed to be into their third generation and have left a diasporic presence in the region, despite restrictive policymaking mechanisms designed to curtail pathways to assimilation and long-term settlement. Have there been naturalisation tracks for these migrants, and if so, what is the form of citizenship access that they may benefit from? Despite the obvious need to expand their domestic labour forces, the GCC states have been extremely reluctant to extend naturalised citizenship, even to their Arab neighbours.[52] Several chapters in the volume address the enduring presence of certain Arab migrant communities in the Gulf. Abdullah Alajami examines the experiences of migrants in Kuwait who come from the Hadramaut region of Yemen. He suggests that this historically embedded migratory pattern developed as a result of individual- and household-level economically motivated decision-making, but was also buttressed by congenial and fraternal social relations that existed between Yemen and Kuwait. He

INTRODUCTION

also discusses the role that Hadramis have historically occupied as domestic workers in Kuwaiti households, and how over time this solidified relationships of dependency between Hadrami migrants and their Kuwaiti *mu'azzibs*.[53] Through extensive ethnographic fieldwork in Kuwait, Alajmi draws attention to the challenges that exist for younger Hadramis, and the difference in their levels of satisfaction compared to their parents who worked in Kuwaiti households before them. Younger or second-generation Hadrami migrants in Kuwait feel burdened with having to uphold an image of serving as Kuwait's 'model minority', and struggle with the inheritance of the reputation assigned to them of being good, 'loyal' workers.

Chapter Five is also set in Kuwait, but focuses on the largest Arab migrant community in that country, the Egyptians. Egyptians in Kuwait number almost half a million, making them the second-largest migrant community in Kuwait after the Indians. Abbie Taylor, Nada Soudy and Susan Martin draw on a robust pool of interviews with Egyptians and Kuwaitis, and discuss ways that these two communities interact with one another in the social, economic and political spheres. The authors also explore the ways that Egyptians have navigated the complex system of migration rules and regulations that exist in Kuwait. While for the most part the legal environment around migration governance in the Gulf is meant to ensure that migrants remain strictly temporary in nature, clearly a large number of the Egyptians present in Kuwait have been able to work around the obstacles of bureaucracy. As the interviews in the chapter suggest, Egyptians use various means to gain entry into Kuwait, and once there, despite the restrictive visa laws and contractual agreements girding the foreign population in the country, many achieve a state of 'permanent temporariness' and do so with greater success than most other foreign workers. However, as Taylor, Soudy and Martin point out, this enduring temporariness that Egyptians in Kuwait experience is akin to being in a state of limbo and creates a deep-rooted sense of angst and insecurity. Considering the sustained political turmoil and uncertainty in contemporary Egypt, the anxieties of long-standing Egyptian communities in Kuwait who have no access to citizenship in the host state can only grow worse.

If the Egyptians in Kuwait and other parts of the Gulf are currently feeling insecure, the Palestinian diaspora community has carried the weight of its far deeper anxieties for many decades more. In Chapter Six, Manal A. Jamal provides us with a historic review of the conditions of Palestinians in the UAE. What little exists in the literature on Palestinians in the GCC region has largely drawn attention to their presence in Kuwait and how the First Gulf

War affected them.⁵⁴ Jamal reminds us that, despite Gulf governments historically being perceived as more open to receiving Arab migrants, in fact Palestinians have never found themselves easily accommodated anywhere in the region. One of the interesting findings of Jamal's research is that—similar to the case of the Hadramis in Yemen—a generational divide exists when it comes to the integration and socialisation of Palestinians in the Emirates. Younger Palestinians in the UAE appear to have a different sense of themselves in relation to the state, to other migrant communities, to Emirati citizens, and to the world in general compared to their parents before them. A second critical point in the chapter is in its discussion of naturalisation laws and access to citizenship rights in the UAE, given the particular salience that statelessness holds for Palestinians. For Palestinians in the Emirates, the class and income divide has led to very different outcomes, and a dissimilar sense of anxieties around their residency status. More skilled, professional Palestinians, even if long-term residents in the UAE, are principally interested in acquiring citizenship from a third country, such as the US, Canada or Australia, even if they are planning to continue to work and reside in the Emirates. For lower-income and less-skilled Palestinians the situation is considerably different, and they are more likely to be left vulnerable and exposed to the whims of the Emirati state and its strict controls over migrants' rights to residency.

Yemen remains forever the poor step-child of the Arabian Peninsula. The country's annual population growth is close to 3.5 per cent, and a large majority of the 22 million people who live there are under the age of 25. The current civil war and threat of a total collapse of the state will have dire consequences for the entire region. Chapter Seven examines the migration chain that has historically persisted between Yemen and the Kingdom of Saudi Arabia. Despite occasionally problematic political relations between the two states, Saudi Arabia has for decades served as one of the primary employment destinations for Yemenis. Given the vastly different economic conditions and resources of the two neighbours, it is hardly surprising that the Saudi labour market has lured so many Yemenis across the border for the past forty-five years or so. Harry Cook and Michael Newson offer rich empirical detail in their chapter, drawing principally on a survey set of almost 35,000 interviews conducted by officials of the International Organization for Migration at the Saudi Arabia–Yemen border between 2013 and 2014. One of the important insights the authors provide is in their discussion of the effect of out-migration on Yemen. The chapter also provides a robust case study of how remittances have a profound impact on development trajectories in a non-oil Arab coun-

INTRODUCTION

try relying on the export of labour. While the remittance flows from Saudi Arabia have been critical for Yemen's foreign currency reserves and for the dependent family members of migrants in the sending state, the out-migration of able-bodied men has had a direct—and apparently often negative—impact on Yemen. Not only has it led to an over-dependency on remittances, but, as this chapter argues, the Yemeni agricultural sector has suffered as a result of loss of farm labour, and a very rapid pace of urbanisation has taken place across the country, which has adversely affected the entire Yemeni labour market. The chapter's originality lies also in its focus on irregular labour migration—a phenomenon that is seldom discussed in the context of the GCC region. As the chapter shows, irregular migration is just as much of an issue in the Gulf as elsewhere. Saudi Arabia's implementation of the *nitaqat* law, meant to put an end to migrants working illegally in the Kingdom, has resulted in the deportation of thousands of irregular workers—many of whom are of Yemeni origin. As Newson and Cook point out, the large number of deported Yemeni migrants who stated that they planned to return to Saudi Arabia for employment as soon as possible indicates that access to the Saudi labour market is critical for vulnerable low-income communities in Yemen. These migrants are willing to put themselves at considerable risk just for the opportunity to obtain employment in the Kingdom.

In addition to irregular workers, another group of migrants often placed in the high-risk category are women. Much work has already been done that highlights the particular vulnerabilities that female migrants in the Gulf are exposed to, with the principal focus often being either on low-income female domestic workers, female dependants accompanying their spouses to the Gulf, or else women who have been trafficked to the region to work in the illicit sex industry.[55] This over-arching focus on women as victims of abuse and/or trafficking has elided other ways that women are choosing to migrate to the Gulf and taking up an occupation. Additionally, the emphasis has mostly been on studying the experiences of Asian female migrants, and very little work has looked at the growing trend among skilled Arab women who are migrating to the GCC region. In Chapter Eight, Françoise De Bel-Air discredits the notion that it is only Arab men who are seeking opportunities to work in the Gulf by providing a rich dataset reviewing skilled Arab female migrants and their integration into the region's labour force. De Bel-Air emphasizes a common theme running through several of the accounts in this volume: that nationality as a marker is important in terms of how one is integrated into the Gulf's labour market. Arab migrants, whether female or male, cannot easily be subsumed into a single categorisation and defined as merely 'Arab'; their country of origin appears to correlate with the job sectors they may be absorbed into. Moreover, De Bel-Air stresses, for Arab expatriates residing and working in the Gulf, the migratory experience is informed more by their education and skill levels than their gender.

Chapter Nine draws us into an even more focused case study on how nationality and skill level influence the success of particular migrant communities in the GCC region. Here, Garret Maher focuses on highly skilled Lebanese migrants in Kuwait. Lebanon continues to be the Arab world's largest exporter of its own people proportionate to its overall population. With almost two-thirds of the global Lebanese population living outside Lebanon, it is a country that boasts one of the world's largest diaspora and migrant communities. As Maher states, from about the 1970s onwards increasing numbers of Lebanese began to conceive of the Gulf as an attractive migration destination. This pattern of migration from Lebanon to the Gulf was driven by conflict and war within Lebanon, as well as by the lure of burgeoning economic opportunities in the oil states. Through a series of qualitative interviews with Lebanese nationals either residing in Kuwait or migrant returnees back in Lebanon, Maher provides in-depth, nuanced insights into what this migration experience has been like. The chapter discusses the motivations expressed by a small group of skilled Lebanese who migrated to Kuwait. It provides information on their remittance behaviour—financial and social—and also parses issues of identity and 'integration' for this group of migrants. Based on discussions with his interlocutors, Maher posits that Kuwait continues to be a preferred migration destination for highly skilled Lebanese for a number of reasons. The Gulf state offers these migrants the opportunity to earn high incomes, live in a relatively safe and stable country, and also feel culturally affiliated through their shared Arabian heritage. Kuwait's proximity to Lebanon is an added bonus for those Lebanese who wish to regularly return home and maintain their connections to their family and country. Despite being quite content with their life in Kuwait, Maher's research does not suggest that the Lebanese, by virtue of being Arabs, are somehow able to interact with Kuwaiti nationals with greater ease than other migrants. Engagement with nationals appears to be limited, and most of those interviewed perceived strong cultural differences between the Lebanese and Kuwaitis.

The literature on migration has pointed out that it is not uncommon for certain groups of migrants who originate from the same sending country—or even a sub-region of a sending country—to cluster together in certain economic niches or employment sectors in a migrant receiving state.[56] Migration chains are formed when a few migrants first arrive and establish themselves in a particular employment sector, and then assist in providing information and recruiting support to their compatriots back home.[57] In Chapter Ten, Mahfoud Amara examines the emergence of a new trend in out-migration from the Maghreb to the GCC region. In the Gulf, the sports industry has increasingly become a significant employment sub-sector. Several of the GCC states, and the UAE and Qatar in particular, are rapidly developing their sports industries as part of their overall developmental agenda. Qatar and the UAE have become destination countries for sports labour migration from the Maghreb. Amara explores this pattern of Maghreb–Gulf migration by focusing on three sub-components of the sports sectors: football players, elite sports' developers, and those employed in sports media. The chapter provides original, empirical data on a new and unexplored sub-area of regional migration.

Beginning in December 2010, many countries in the Middle East were affected by what has been called the Arab Spring, and a burgeoning body of new academic literature on this phenomenon has emerged. The final chapter in the volume presents new empirical research on the Arab Spring by exploring the attitudes of Arab migrant residents in the UAE, and trying to discern their responses towards the turmoil across the region. George Naufal, Ismail Genc and Carlos Vargas-Silva seek to explore what the Arab Spring meant to Arab migrant communities in the Gulf. The authors focus their research on Arab-origin university students based in the UAE, the rationale being that young people played an integral role across the region in the Arab uprisings, and gauging the attitude of Arab young people resident in the Gulf would provide insights on how these migrants engaged with the political realm. Naufal, Genc and Vargas-Silva provide detailed empirical survey results, the first of which is that mostly Arab migrant students in the UAE approved of the revolts that occurred across the Middle East. Egyptian students in particular were euphoric about the events in Egypt in 2011, although perhaps the survey results indicated that particular time when the students were polled. Many of the students surveyed responded that the Arab Spring was about people standing up to dictators and against corruption, and were not inclined to suggest that the revolts had been prompted by Western interference.

Together, the contributions in this volume help unpick assumptions about the Gulf's and the Arab world's exceptionalism, insofar as the study of global migration is concerned. The same broader dynamics that undergird the causes, processes, and consequences of migration elsewhere in the world are at work in the Gulf region. Vast economic disparities, chronic political instability, linguistic and cultural affinities, and a jealous guarding of finite economic and citizenship benefits inform push and pull factors and integration possibilities in the Gulf region as they do elsewhere in the world. Scholarship continues to enrich our understanding of the phenomenon of labour migration in the Gulf. This book takes that understanding one step further, shedding light on one specific, and until now largely understudied, community of migrants in the region.

2

WORKING FOR THE NEIGHBOURS

ARAB MIGRANTS IN QATAR

Zahra Babar

Introduction

This chapter examines Arab-origin migration to Qatar, reviewing how the state has negotiated the entry and control of 'alien' Arabs. It examines the evolution and transformation of patterns of migration to the Gulf Cooperation Council (GCC) region and assesses policies GCC states have adopted to better manage their regional labour markets and control the flow of foreigners. Particular attention is given to scrutinising how and why Qatar has become more selective and politicised in negotiating labour migration, and how this has affected the Arab expatriate population. Articles within the Labour Law of Qatar privilege Arab workers, yet the drive for less-skilled workers who are willing to accept lower wages has led to an increasing reliance on migrants from less-developed countries further afield. The forces and factors driving regional migration have become more complex over time, and traditional explanations for the motivations, attraction, and selection of migrants are no longer sufficient in the study of migration to the Gulf. Qatar, which in the past decade has emerged as one of the Middle East's fastest-growing economies, provides a sound case study for discussing some of the emerging dynamics of regional labour migration.

The empirical focus of this chapter is on the original data it provides on Arab migrants present in Qatar's expatriate work force. Empirically based analysis of the stocks and flows of Arab migrants to the GCC is often limited by the lack of accurate data, and data that does exist is in many cases outdated, scattered and unreliable. The chapter concludes by assessing the emerging dynamics and future direction of policy within Qatar, and how this will affect intraregional labour mobility.

The regional policy context

Economic necessities as well as perceptions of political constraints and security concerns have shaped GCC states' policies for managing migration. Regional integration and free-flowing circulation of labour have not been established. Meanwhile, pan-Arab labour agreements have been unsuccessful in the past, and there is little interest in pursuing such strategies now.[1] None of the GCC countries is signatory to the Arab labour mobility protocols, and the Arab League's Mobility Agreement of 1975 was never effectively established, illustrating the obvious differences between how labour-exporting and -receiving states view intraregional labour mobility. Several of the GCC states have articulated policies that provide for the preferential hiring of Arabs over other nationalities. In reality, however, these policies have not been broadly implemented.[2]

Many scholars have widely discussed the structural peculiarities of the GCC region's labour market.[3] In essence, the region operates a dual labour market, one of which consists of citizens employed in the public sector, with the other comprising the foreign labour force that primarily works in the private sector. With a burgeoning and increasingly educated youth population and the addition of women to the workplace, all of the GCC states have been grappling with the issue of unemployed citizenry. The six member states—Bahrain, Kuwait, Oman, Qatar, Saudi Arabia and the United Arab Emirates (UAE)—show wide variances in how they are tackling the issue of ensuring employment for their nationals, but all agree that it is an issue of utmost national importance. Some of the GCC states with smaller citizen populations, healthy balance sheets, and large-scale development plans, such as Qatar, have largely managed to cope by expanding the employment of nationals in the public sector, albeit with an awareness that this can at best serve as a short- to medium-term solution. Other states, such as Saudi Arabia, face a far more critical situation, with increasing numbers of unemployed or underemployed citizens.

Each of the six GCC states has instituted affirmative action policies supporting the 'nationalisation' of their workforce. These nationalisation programmes, in essence, establish preferential hiring practices for Gulf citizen workers over foreign workers. These GCC-wide efforts to replace the foreign labour force with national ones have been met with varying degrees of success.[4] Nationalisation efforts have been motivated by the states' interest in curtailing dependency on foreign workers, and also the need to expand employment opportunities for citizens, particularly in the private sector. Among other things, GCC governments have imposed industry-wide, quota-based employment targets for nationals; introduced wage subsidies for private-sector employers hiring citizen workers; and placed quota restrictions on the hiring of foreigners in certain occupational categories.[5] Nationalisation policies have been more vigorously implemented in some GCC states and less forcefully in others. In 2013, Saudi Arabia's Ministry of Labour galvanised nationalisation efforts by implementing the *nitaqat* law, which appears to have had a significant impact on the 'Saudi-isation' of the Kingdom's workforce.[6] Despite evidence of successful implementation of programmes to enhance the employment of citizens in a few of the GCC states, the flow of migrant workers into the region has continued, particularly of those brought in to occupy the lower tiers of the job market.[7]

Scholars have suggested that nationalisation programmes across the GCC region have had a higher impact on curtailing the employment of Arab expatriates than on other migrant communities.[8] The argument is that GCC nationalisation policies have not dramatically transformed regional private-sector labour markets, but have in fact been more broadly successful in altering access of foreigners to public-sector markets. Nationalisation policies have had a direct impact on the Arab migrant population that used to be engaged in public-sector occupations, because they have gradually been replaced by skilled and educated nationals.

Evolution of the Gulf's labour source: the shift to the east

Information on the ethnic breakdown of the Gulf's foreign populations is extremely hard to come by, and poor data collection in sending and receiving

Arab states means that obtaining comprehensive data on the different Arab nationalities present in the GCC region is not always possible.[9] However, data that has been collected shows that in the Gulf Asians and Arabs have dominated the foreign component of the labour force.[10] Maurice Girgis has argued that a variety of economic factors have determined the shift to an 'Asianised' labour market in the Gulf. The principal reason for the transition has been wage differentials between sending Asian and Arab states, with Asian workers being willing to come to the Gulf at lower salary levels than their Arab counterparts. A secondary reason for the shift has been the compatibility between jobs in demand in the Gulf and the employment interests of foreigners seeking work opportunities. Arab foreign workers historically were more likely to be engaged in categories of employment that Gulf nationals now occupy, such as jobs in the public sector or in administration. According to Girgis, Asian migrants to the GCC region have largely been employed in different sectors and occupations compared to nationals and Arabs.[11] Arab migrants have tended to be employed in white-collar jobs and worked in the private as well as public sectors. Over time, they have come into competition with newly trained cadres of Gulf nationals entering the labour market, because of their shared skills. Currently, the vast number of jobs in lower tiers of the regional labour market, such as in construction or the domestic sector, can more easily be filled by Asian migrant workers. A third motivation for Gulf states to move towards preferring Asian workers over Arab expatriates has centred on the issue of family unification. Arab migrants to the Gulf have shown a preference for migrating with their families, while Asian workers appear more willing to migrate as single workers. Arab workers have been much more inclined to migrate to the Gulf with their spouses and dependants, and in doing so added significantly to the GCC population stock. Arabs have also tended to stay in the Gulf for longer periods than Asian migrants, and conformed less to the short-duration, temporary pattern of migration that the GCC policymakers have increasingly sought.[12] This longer-term, diasporic presence of Arabs has been of growing political concern to all the GCC states, because longer durations of stay begin to raise uncomfortable questions on the rights of migrants in terms of integration, participation and permanent settlement.

GCC leaders have consistently viewed political and social inclusion of Arab migrants as an unappealing proposition, which has also had an impact on regional migration policies. During the 1950s and 1960s Arab migrants were thought to bring with them pan-Arabist, socialist and other politically 'destabilising' ideologies, which threatened the legitimacy of the Gulf monarchies and challenged the notion of an exclusive Gulf nationalism.[13] One of the outcomes of this unease that Gulf rulers felt, with the influx of many Arabs from neighbouring states, was that pathways to GCC state citizenship began to be progressively curtailed.[14] Increasingly, legal regimes and carefully crafted nationality laws were established, designed to ensure that nationality in the GCC region became a protected domain. The growth of welfare states across the region in the 1970s further increased the need to tighten citizenship and naturalisation regulations. The inherent threat that Arab non-nationals posed to the domain of Gulf citizenship was seen as greater than the threat posed by Asian migrants, and GCC states began to adopt strict legal structures to limit who could and could not be a GCC citizen.

Detailed data on the comparative educational and skill levels of Arab and Asian migrants to the GCC region is scant, inconsistent or altogether absent. A few of the studies that have been carried out indicate that Arab migrants in the Gulf have higher levels of education than their Asian counterparts.[15] Khaled El Sayad Hassan, in his case study on Kuwait, points out that 40 per cent of Arabs working in Kuwait in 2010 were engaged in highly skilled occupations, while most Asian migrants worked in lower-income and less-skilled jobs.[16] The greatest dichotomy, however, was where nationality and gender aligned: almost 80 per cent of Arab women migrants in Kuwait were in highly skilled jobs, whereas only 10 per cent of Asian women were engaged in such positions.[17]

It must also be pointed out that existing demographic conditions in the Gulf have not merely resulted from the natural expansion of neo-liberal economics or traditional labour supply and demand factors. Demographic conditions in the GCC region have arisen due to particular choices that policymakers and citizens have made.[18] These states have chosen to follow a particular development trajectory, which has created labour needs of a magnitude that could never be sourced from local populations. The demography also reflects the choices of citizens, who for decades have shown a marked preference for public-sector occupations, which invariably come with better pay, shorter hours, and a more flexible and supportive work environment that allows for more family time and leisure activities. Many nationals in the Gulf will not consider low-paying or low-status jobs, and their choices not to do so have had an impact on countries' demographic make-up. The employee sponsorship system itself creates a mechanism whereby profit generation or income accrual result merely from being a citizen.[19] In the GCC region, market needs do not entirely determine labour policies; as scholars have noted, the policies and practices around labour migration are actually far more political in nature. Mohammed Dito has suggested that labour migration policies in the Gulf are conscious, state-driven choices of ensuring the efficacy of the rentier bargain between state and citizen, and stressed that a clear linkage exists between perceptions of 'citizenship rights' and the importation of cheap, foreign labour.[20]

The GCC states have operated labour migration policies that artfully balance economic expediency, political concerns and security interests, which may emerge at particular moments in time. Labour migration to the region, it can be argued, has served to alter the balance of power within the Arab world. Whereas, historically, the power brokers and regional leadership consisted of countries such as Iraq, Syria and Egypt, this balance has shifted on multiple levels to tilt in favour of the GCC countries.[21] Labour migration diplomacy and determining who gets to send citizens to occupy lucrative jobs in the Gulf has been part of the subtle exertion of power that GCC states have used over their Arab neighbours.

Arabs in a Gulf labour market: a case study of Qatar

With vast hydrocarbon resources at its disposal, Qatar has seen extraordinary growth in per capita income. However, the improved standard of living for citizens has come at a price, as an ever growing development agenda has led to increased dependency on imported labour. In 1970 the population of Qatar was deemed to be around 111,000 people; currently it is estimated at more than fifteen times that amount at 1.8 million.[22] As Figure 2.1 shows, this growth has been a direct result of the expansion of the migrant stock in the national population. While the economic downturn of the 1990s temporarily stemmed the influx of labour migrants, and saw a marginal increase in the percentage of nationals versus migrants in Qatar's total population, since the turn of the century the number of migrants has steadily increased. Currently, the percentage of foreigners in relation to nationals in Qatar's population stands at a historic apex.

In 2007 the active labour force in Qatar was 831,886 people, consisting of 768,292 non-nationals and just 63,594 Qataris.[23] According to the Qatar Statistics Authority,[24] by the middle of 2013 the country's labour force had grown by more than an additional 600,000 people to 1,465,949.[25] While the number of Qatari citizens engaged in the national labour force grew to 84,895 by 2013, foreigners occupied 1,381,729 jobs.[26] The expectation is that by 2017 the population will need to grow to a total of 2.4 million to meet projected

Figure 2.1: Qatar's population breakdown (1990–2010)

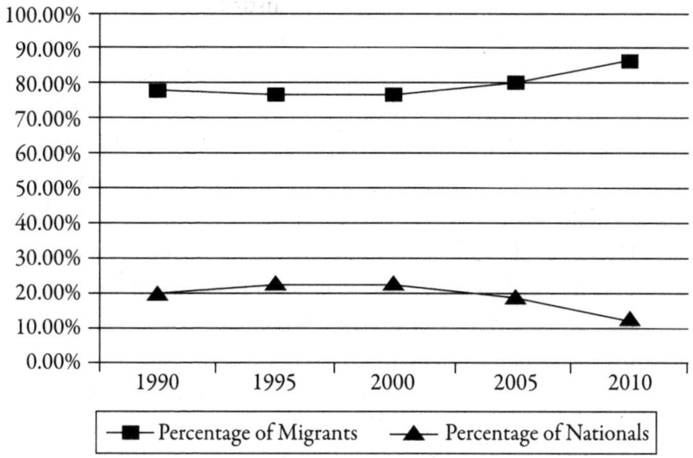

Year	Population	Migrant Total	National %	National Total
1990	467,000	369,397	20.9	97,603
1995	526,000	406,072	22.8	119,928
2000	617,000	470,771	23.7	146,229
2005	885,000	717,425	19.5	172,575
2010	1,508,000	1,304,420	13.5	203,580

Source: United Nations Department of Economic and Social Affairs.

labour market needs. Foreign workers, who dominate the national labour force, range from large cadres of lower-income migrants, who occupy jobs in the construction sector, to smaller numbers of the skilled and highly skilled working in technical and professional fields. As elsewhere in the GCC region, the national labour market in Qatar is highly segmented, with nationals predominantly occupying positions in the public sector, while the private sector is almost entirely composed of foreign workers. Anticipated development needs combined with segmentation of the labour market, which places nationals in public-sector jobs and non-nationals in the private sector, means that for the foreseeable future Qatar will continue to rely on importing labour regardless of the demographic pressures that result.

Broader, strategic development plans for the state are embedded in the notion of creating a knowledge economy.[27] Efforts towards this have driven up the need to bring in a range of skilled and highly skilled foreign workers to populate jobs in higher education, scientific institutions, and the technology sector. Official statements suggest that as Qatar's plans to establish a knowledge-based economy bear fruit, the labour market will move towards greater numbers of skilled workers and fewer numbers of the low-skilled. Policy documents acknowledge that in the short term many foreign workers will still be needed for positions in construction and associated infrastructural development sectors. The longer-term goal presented in the guiding Qatar National Vision 2030 policy document seeks to change the qualitative nature of the foreign workforce in Qatar, to make it more appealing and attractive to the highly skilled, and to perhaps seek ways of retaining them for longer durations within the national labour market.[28]

Despite this, Qatar does not see itself as a destination for permanent settlement, and national discussions around the country's labour market challenges stress the aspiration to build a citizen workforce, and thereby lighten the dependency on foreign labour. Until that goal can be achieved, however, the guiding principle on migration management is one that strives to ensure that the large, foreign workforce that currently dominates the national labour market remains strictly temporary in nature. Policies such as the *kafala* or sponsorship system ensure that these flows of foreign labour remain temporary in nature, and that pathways to permanent settlement remain virtually non-existent.[29]

Obtaining data on the national and ethnic compositions of Qatar's migrant population has been a particular challenge for academics and researchers. Data availability, accessibility and reliability have limited researchers' attempts to assess the dynamics of national labour migration. Many breakdowns of national-ethnic compositions of Qatar's migrant population are at best 'guesstimates'. Data on migrants disaggregated by nationality and further broken down by age, gender, income and education levels, and labour-market integration is largely unavailable.

Time-based data showing breakdowns of the Arab expatriate presence in Qatar by nationality is almost completely absent, making a historically nuanced and dynamic understanding of the ebb and flow of Arab migrants to the state impossible. The Arab Labor Organization provided data in 2007 that stated that 40 per cent of Qatar's non-national population was Arab—a much higher percentage than in other GCC labour markets.[30] There is no information on how Arab migrants in Qatar have been integrated into the national labour market, what sorts of jobs they were previously engaged in, and what their lived experiences have been. Figures suggest that in 2002 35,000 Egyptians and 50,000 Jordanians and Palestinians were living and working in Qatar.[31] Published data for the same time frame on the numbers or occupations of other Arab nationalities in Qatar is unavailable.[32] In the absence of data, one must assume that the conditions of the national labour market have historically replicated the pattern present across the Arabian Peninsula. One assumes that in Qatar in the 1960s and 1970s the majority of the foreign workforce was most likely of Arab origin, but that over decades the national-ethnic composition transitioned to the predominantly non-Arab one that we see today.

Qatar has adopted a measured approach when it comes to meeting its labour needs from within the broader geographic context of the Middle East. Qatar's decision-makers, like their GCC counterparts, have had no interest in promoting a regional labour market where their labour deficiencies are served predominantly by the more populous Arab states. Qatar's labour relations with its Arab neighbours have been managed on a strictly bilateral basis, rooted in and formalised by labour agreements that it has signed with eleven states in the region. Qatar's first labour agreement with an Arab state was signed with Egypt in 1974, and in 1981 similar agreements were drawn up and signed with Sudan, Somalia, Tunisia and Morocco.[33] Between 1997 and 2012, Qatar signed additional labour protocols with Lebanon, Jordan, Djibouti, Mauritania, Yemen and Syria. These agreements, which were signed between the Qatari Ministry of Labour and its counterparts in Arab labour-sending states, primarily serve to create overarching cooperative mechanisms that facilitate procedures for procuring labour from among Arab neighbours. Among other stipulations, the agreements include specific details on the rights and duties of foreign workers, in accordance with existing Qatari labour laws.

While economics has clearly been a vital dynamic propelling Qatar to increasingly move beyond the Arab world to draw its pool of labour from the cheaper supplying states of Asia, political and security interests have also played a role. Supplementary protocols to the initial labour agreements drawn up between Qatar and Arab labour-supplying countries were subsequently adopted, specifically to insert clauses providing for the expulsion of Arab foreign workers if their presence in Qatar was perceived to be a threat to Qatar's national security interests. For example, the additional protocol signed between Qatar and Morocco states:

> The Government of Qatar may undertake actions to return any number of Moroccan workers if it is proved that their stay in Qatar conflicts with the public

interest of the State or its national security, and that is, without infringement of the rights accrued to them under the contracts entered with them or under the labour law in the State of Qatar.[34]

As of 2012, Qatar's Ministry of Labour has undertaken more active attempts at collecting and compiling data in relation to labour force participation of the foreign workforce, including data that provides a breakdown of foreign workers corresponding to their nationality of origin.[35] The Ministry of Labour data came from workers' contracts and sponsorship arrangements—the ministry vets and approves these official documents. Data on nationality is not disseminated in the public domain, nor is it openly or easily accessible, and public sensitivity to disclosure of such breakdowns is considerable. Based on data the Ministry of Labour shared directly with the author, the total number of foreigners engaged in Qatar's labour force in the last quarter of 2013 was 1,144,518.[36] Of this total, 146,498 people were classified as foreign Arab workers, and Arab migrants comprised 13.6 per cent of the total number of foreign workers.[37] Based on the ministry's data, 87 per cent of the foreign workforce in Qatar originated from outside the Arab world.

The Ministry of Labour data indicated that in 2013 foreign Arab workers in Qatar were a diverse group, originating from twenty different Arab countries. However, for the purpose of this paper the data will focus on the six countries that send the largest numbers of workers. As Figure 2.2 shows, Arab migrants as a whole make up 13 per cent of the national labour force, Qatari citizens make up 7 per cent, and over 80 per cent of the labour force originates from outside the Arab world. The three Arab labour-supplying states that provide the bulk of Arab workers to Qatar are Egypt, Syria, and Sudan. Citizens of these three coun-

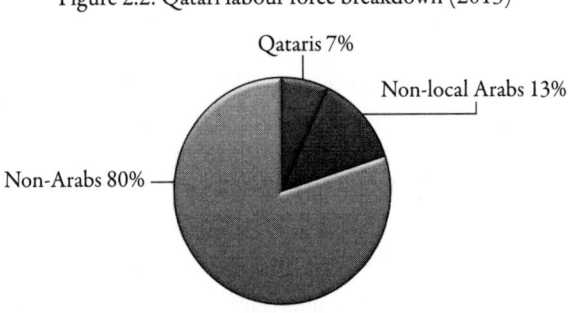

Figure 2.2: Qatari labour force breakdown (2013)

Source: Ministry of Labour.

Figure 2.3: Arab nationalities as a percentage of non-local Arabs in the labour force

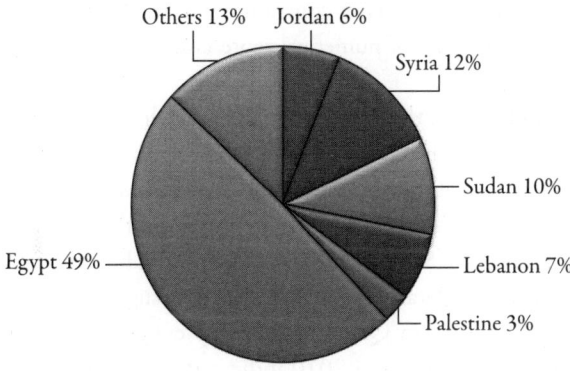

Source: Ministry of Labour.

tries numerically dominate the Arab migrant presence in Qatar, and when combined make up 72 per cent of the Arab community.

As Figures 2.2–2.4 show, Egyptians make up 7 per cent of the foreign workforce in Qatar, 43 per cent of the Arab expatriate population, and 49 per cent of the Arab expatriate labour force. Syrians make up almost 2 per cent of the foreign workforce, 11 per cent of the Arab expatriate population, and 12 per cent of the Arab expatriate labour force. Sudanese comprise 1.3 per cent of the foreign workforce, 11 per cent of the Arab expatriate population, and

Figure 2.4: Arab nationalities as a percentage of total Arab residents

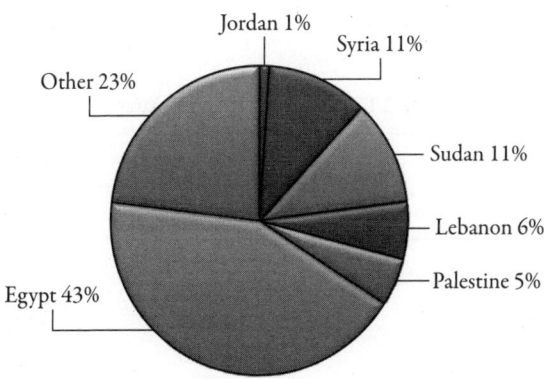

Source: Ministry of Labour.

10 per cent of the Arab expatriate labour force. Following Egypt, Syria and Sudan, the next three Arab states contributing to the Arab expatriate workforce in descending order of numerical representation are Lebanon, Jordan, and Palestine.

As one would expect, the data shows a very small number of non-Qatari GCC citizens working in Qatar. Despite GCC-wide free mobility arrangements that allow ease of travel and residence for GCC state citizens, research has shown that GCC nationals prefer to remain in their home country.[38] While small numbers of Saudis, Emiratis, Omanis, and Bahrainis are indicated as being active in the Qatari labour force, the data suggests that not a single Kuwaiti national works in Qatar. However, previous data that the Qatar Statistics Authority released in 2010 indicated a much higher number of GCC nationals (including Kuwaitis) employed in the country, with a total of 5,799 reported as being active in the Qatari labour force.[39] The discrepancy in figures is most likely related to differences in data collection methodology between different agencies. As previously mentioned, the Ministry of Labour tracks the participation of non-nationals in the labour force through sponsorship arrangements and labour contracts, which the ministry reviews and approves. The statistics authority's data collection is based primarily on interviews and workplace- or household-level surveys. Given that GCC state nationals are not required to obtain sponsorship to work or reside in Qatar, their presence in the country may go undocumented by the Ministry of Labour. GCC state citizens may have informal contractual arrangements in place, be self-employed or work with a Qatari business partner, or be married to a Qatari citizen. Their actual numbers are therefore likely to be higher than the Ministry of Labour's data reflects.[40]

Table 2.1: Arab dependants in Qatar[41]

Dependant	Total number of Arab dependants	
	Percentage	Number
Child	33.24	44,955.11
Student	29.38	39,723.87
Home-caretaker/housewife	37.38	50,550.02[42]
Total	100.00	135,229

Source: Ministry of Labour.

While 52 per cent of resident Arabs in Qatar—approximately 146,000 people—are active in the national labour force, according to the Ministry of Labour the total population of Arabs residing in Qatar is 281,728. As shown in Table 2.2, 48 per cent of the Arab expatriate population—135,229 people—are non-working dependants consisting of children, students, and housewives.

Corresponding data from the Ministry of Labour shows that out of the combined Asian and Arab expatriate population a much lower total of 18 per cent are non-working dependants.[43] This data reinforces and provides empirical validation of previous scholarship, which has suggested that Arabs are more likely to migrate to the GCC region with their families and spouses. Given that the GCC labour-receiving states are reluctant to add to their overall population stocks and prefer to have their labour market needs met without an incremental increase in demographic pressure, a choice of Asian labour migrants appears to be more aligned with state and societal interests.

Additionally, the high percentage of dependants among the Arab migrant population indicates that Arab workers' salary structures and integration into the workforce may differ greatly from Asian workers. Under current Qatari immigration law, foreign workers can only apply for family residency visas if they earn a minimum monthly salary of US$2,746 or 10,000 Qatari riyals. If they earn less than this amount, foreign workers are not permitted to apply for visas that would allow their spouses and children to accompany them for the duration of their stay in Qatar. Linking monthly salary levels to family visas prevents the hundreds of thousands of low-income migrant workers who populate the lower tiers of the labour market in Qatar from bringing their dependants into the country. Low-income workers, who on average may earn between US$200 and US$300 a month, fall far outside the eligibility criteria.[44]

Since 2012 the Ministry of Labour has collated data on occupation by workers' nationality. Arab expatriate workers occupy positions across a range of different sectors, without showing a clear trend towards occupation in any single sector. However, the data shows variations in how different Arab nationals are integrated into the workforce, and appears to suggest that Arabs and Asians do not necessarily occupy the same tiers of the foreign labour force.

While Egyptians, who make up the bulk of the expatriate Arab populace, are present in relatively high numbers across many different occupational sectors, in descending order they occupy jobs in managerial and administrative sectors, professional, scientific and technical activities, and services.[45] Sudanese expatriates in Qatar principally work in professional, scientific and technical activities, followed by the managerial and administrative sectors, and then law enforcement and legal services.[46] Syrians are for the most part employed in the mining, construction, and manufacturing sectors, professional, scientific and technical activities, and domestic, social and public services. Jordanians in Qatar mostly work in professional, scientific and technical areas, service sectors, managerial and administrative occupations, and education. The top three sectors employing Lebanese in Qatar are the managerial and administrative sectors, professional, scientific and technical sectors, and finance and insurance.[47] Palestinians work predominantly in service sectors, managerial and administrative sectors, and professional, scientific and technical fields.[48]

Jordanians only make up 6 per cent of the expatriate Arab workforce, yet they occupy 17 per cent of jobs in the education sector that are occupied by Arabs. Lebanese only make up 7 per cent of the expatriate Arab workforce, but occupy 13 per cent of jobs in finance and insurance. Egyptians make up 49 per cent of the Arab expatriate workforce, but take up 60 per cent of all the jobs occupied by Arab migrants in the law and legal enforcement professions. In managerial and administrative occupations, as well as in the fields of media and journalism, the Lebanese and Jordanians in Qatar are disproportionally represented and show high levels of participation.

The majority of foreign workers present in Qatar populate lower-income and less-skilled occupations in the mining, construction, and manufacturing sectors—over 700,000 migrant workers are employed in these sectors. Out of the Arab states only two, Egypt and Syria, have sizeable numbers of their citizens working in mining, construction and manufacturing; 8,682 Egyptians and 3,037 Syrians work for these sectors. Arab migrants from 17 non-GCC states combined occupy only 14,144, or just over 2 per cent of the jobs occu-

Figure 2.5: Labour force sectoral breakdown: education (by country of origin)

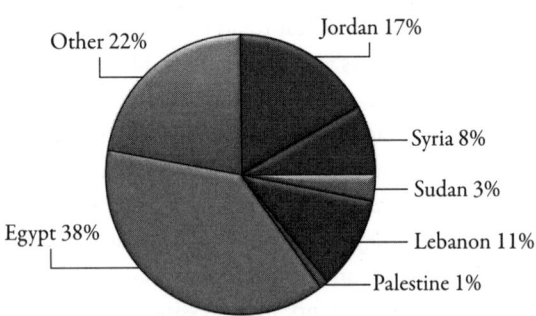

Source: Ministry of Labour.

Figure 2.6: Labour force sectoral breakdown: finance and insurance activities (by country of origin)

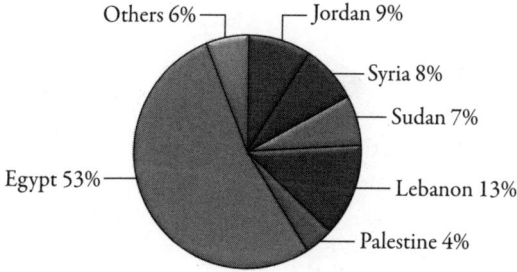

Source: Ministry of Labour.

Figure 2.7: Labour force sectoral breakdown: legal and law enforcement activities (by country of origin)

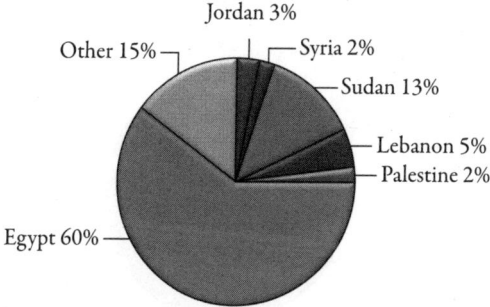

Source: Ministry of Labour.

Figure 2.8: Labour force sectoral breakdown: managerial and administrative services (by country of origin)

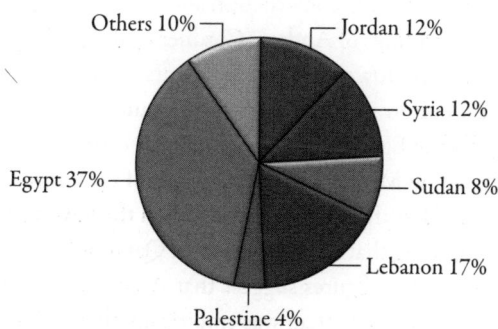

Source: Ministry of Labour.

Figure 2.9: Labour force sectoral breakdown: media and journalism (by country of origin)

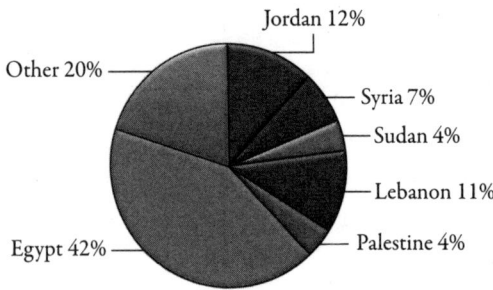

Source: Ministry of Labour.

Figure 2.10: Labour force sectoral breakdown: professional and technical activities (by country of origin)

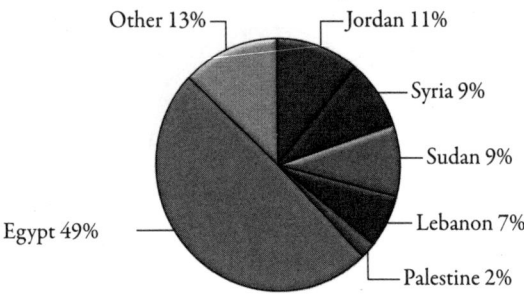

Source: Ministry of Labour.

pied by foreigners in mining, construction and manufacturing. This corroborates the empirical findings of Andrew Gardner et al., whose quantitative and qualitative sample of lower-income migrants in Qatar showed only a 3 per cent participation rate of Egyptian migrants in the lower tier of the labour force,[49] despite Egyptians making up 7 per cent of the total expatriate labour force. Based on Ministry of Labour data, of the entire Arab expatriate workforce in Qatar, less than 10 per cent work in the lowest-income sectors.

While not proposing that Arab migrants in Qatar only work in skilled and highly skilled jobs, these figures suggest that Arabs occupy proportionately higher numbers of these jobs than was empirically shown. In Figure 2.11 the lightest colour bar (Other) represents occupational sectors that would historically have been considered low- to low-medium-skilled in broadly defined terms, while the other six colour bars represent a combination of categories of employment more usually considered skilled to highly skilled. Except for the Syrian population, the other five countries represented in Figure 2.11 show almost 45–50 per cent of their nationals engaged in skilled occupations. Lebanese and Jordanians in fact show significantly higher levels than that, with 88 per cent of the Jordanian population and 81 per cent of the Lebanese working in skilled or highly skilled positions in Qatar.

For comparative purposes, in Figure 2.12 occupation levels in three high-skill sectors—education, finance and insurance, and professional/scientific and technical activities—have been selected to show how Arabs from different countries are integrated into the Qatari workforce. While obviously these three sectors are significantly smaller (in terms of total numbers employed) the results are quite startling.[50] Arabs comprise only 12 per cent of the foreign Qatari labour force, yet make up more than 20 per cent of jobs in the educational sector, more than 95 per cent of finance and insurance jobs, and over 89 per cent of the jobs in professional, scientific and technical fields.

In the absence of comparative timescale data on earlier national-ethnic compositions in the expatriate labour force, this data only allows us to draw

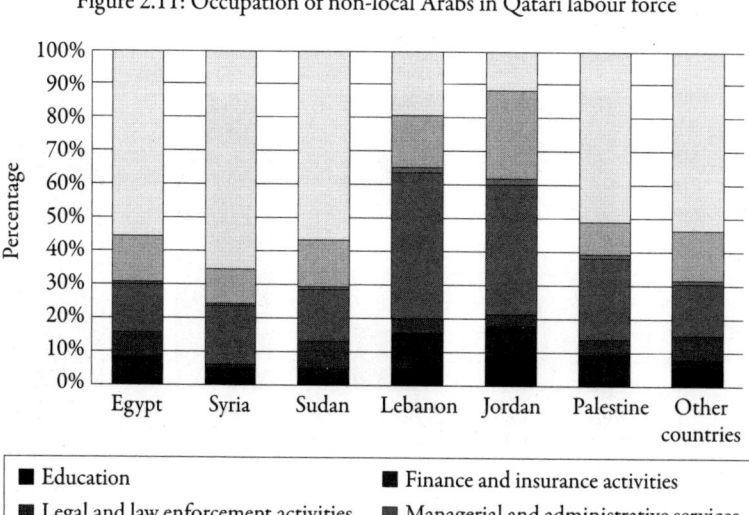

Figure 2.11: Occupation of non-local Arabs in Qatari labour force

Figure 2.12: Resident Arabs vs. other resident nationalities

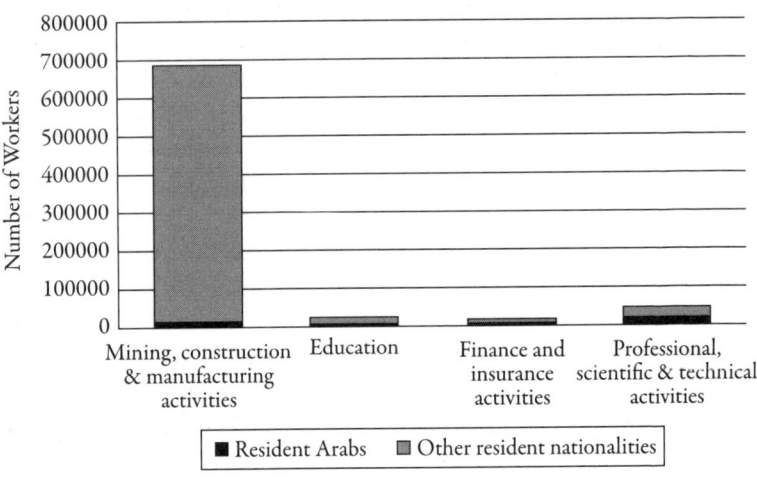

Source: Ministry of Labour.

Figure 2.13: Expatriate Arabs vs. other expatriate nationalities

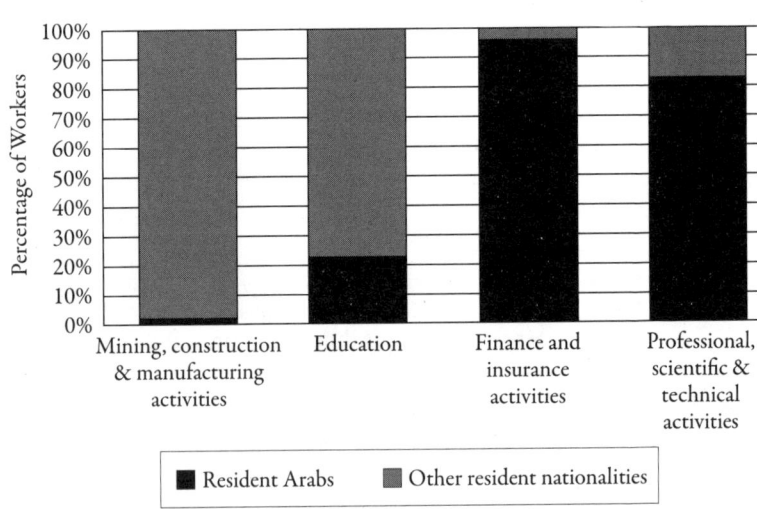

Source: Ministry of Labour.

the general conclusion that gradually, as elsewhere in the region, Asian migrants have replaced Arabs in lower-income jobs in Qatar.

Concluding thoughts

The data presented in this chapter allows us to come to two principal conclusions. The first is that the Arab component of the foreign workforce in Qatar is significantly lower than was previously assumed. The driving forces for this shift away from Arab labour in Qatar are undoubtedly similar to what has prompted other GCC states to move towards employing Asian workers: they can be brought in quickly and cheaply to meet the nation's labour needs, and create less of a pressure point in terms of demands for greater rights to integration and participation. Given that Qatar's labour market is among the most heavily dependent (in the GCC region) on foreign workers, the compulsion to ensure that these foreigners leave less of a diasporic footprint might be even greater. Arabs, who prefer to migrate with their families, tend to stay for longer durations, and have greater cultural and linguistic affinities to the local population, undoubtedly present more of a challenge for the state.

The second contribution of this research is its demonstration that Arab migrants in Qatar tend to cluster in certain tiers of the labour market, and are more heavily represented in particular employment categories. As other scholars have stressed, nationality and ethnicity have a determinative role in the migration process in Qatar, not only in terms of how migrants from different countries of origin may be integrated into the labour market, but also in how they experience living and working in the country.[51] For example, Egyptians in Qatar working in lower-income sectors may pay higher fees to labour brokers, but when occupying the same tier of jobs as Asians they are paid higher salaries, are more likely than Asians to have their salaries paid to them on time, appear to have fewer problems with their living and working conditions, and generally have a more positive experience living and working in Qatar.[52]

If nationality and ethnicity are intertwined with how migrants integrate into Qatar's labour force at the lower end of the scale, and also on their qualitative experiences while working in the country, one can stretch the argument to assume that this will also be true for the medium and higher ends of the labour market. A general interpretation of the data provided in this paper is that in percentage terms Arab migrants tend to occupy positions in sectors that are possibly at higher income and skill levels than their Asian counterparts. The causal reasons for this variation may well be cultural and linguistic skills and abilities that Arab migrants bring to those positions. Policymakers consistently refer to the need for Qatar to recruit and retain highly trained and skilled migrants, and have also discussed how to amend immigration laws to attract more skilled workers. This is significant because if Qatar is indeed to transition to a knowledge-based economy, the chances are that the need to hire and retain skilled Arab expatriates, who occupy a substantial portion of jobs in these particular sectors in the country today, will increase.

3

ARAB MIGRANT TEACHERS IN THE UNITED ARAB EMIRATES AND QATAR

CHALLENGES AND OPPORTUNITIES

Natasha Ridge, Soha Shami and *Susan Kippels*

Introduction

The discovery of oil in the mid-twentieth century in the countries of the Gulf Cooperation Council (GCC), as described in the introduction to this volume, marked the beginning of rapid economic development across the region.[1] This in effect transformed the oil-rich countries of the GCC from desolate outposts in the Middle East to thriving metropolitan communities in a matter of decades. The new-found wealth also affected their relations with neighbouring countries, taking the countries of the Gulf from being recipients of aid to donors of aid. This rapid development placed the GCC countries in the midst of a new demographic challenge, unlike the rest of the Middle East region, which was brought about by the need for vast numbers of migrant workers to build infrastructure and fill middle management and administrative roles in the public and private sectors. But it also translated into benefits for Arabs from nearby countries such as Egypt, Syria, and Jordan, who were recruited to provide much of the assistance needed in the creation of public sector institutions in the newly wealthy countries, because of their common language and comparatively better education. In time, however, the need for Arabic speakers from outside the Gulf declined across the public sector, with the exception of education.

The expansion of the public education sector and mass building of schools required large numbers of teachers. Given that the GCC countries themselves had no teacher training programmes before the 1960s,[2] these teachers had to come from neighbouring Arab countries. While in the wider public sector, as populations have become more educated nationals have filled many positions, the education sector has been unable to attract nationals in sufficient numbers. This is largely due to lower salary levels and associated lack of prestige, and the sector has continued to depend on migrant labour.[3] Given their common language, most GCC countries continue to use significant numbers of Arab expatriates as teachers in government schools.[4] In the United Arab Emirates (UAE), 90 per cent of teachers in boys' government schools and 20 per cent in girls' government schools were expatriate Arabs, as of the academic year 2010/11.[5] In Qatar, expatriate Arabs comprised approximately 87 per cent of teachers in all government schools in 2013.[6]

Despite their contribution to national development in the above countries, Arab expatriate teachers as a unique migrant population are not well-studied. The lack of research on this population gives rise to larger questions about the factors that attract them to the region, what keeps them there, and the implications for national education systems that depend heavily on them. Wider research on the use of migrant teachers elsewhere indicates that, similar to other migrant groups, teachers encounter personal, professional, and institutional barriers that affect their practice in schools. National policies related to the recruitment of migrant teachers, therefore, need to take these factors into account to improve the quality of national education systems. In the words of Ransford Smith, deputy secretary-general of the Commonwealth Secretariat, and Arnaldo Nhavoto, director of the UNESCO International Institute for Capacity Building in Africa, 'It is critically important to provide frameworks that protect teachers and to acknowledge that, formally recognized and properly supported, these same teachers can present an important resource for recipient countries to educate children.'[7]

In this chapter, we examine the case of Arab migrant teachers working in the UAE and Qatar through educational and institutional lenses. The first half of the chapter reviews existing literature, provides a brief history of Arab migration to the GCC, and outlines some of the challenges Arab migrant teachers in the UAE and Qatar encounter. The second half details our research on this issue, which identifies issues related to contractual agreements, employment experiences, and the integration of Arab migrant teachers in both countries. The chapter concludes by exploring the possible ramifications of the current working environment of Arab migrant teachers for schools and students, and the wider development of countries in the GCC region.

Migration to the GCC region

Gulf nations are described as blessed twice: firstly by the discovery of hydrocarbon resources and secondly by convenient access to the migrant pipeline from nearby countries.[8] Dependency on temporary foreign workers in the GCC region has steadily increased. In the 1970s expatriate workers and their families were estimated to be between 800,000 and 1.25 million people.[9] By 1985 the number of migrant workers in the region had increased almost fourfold to 4.4 million.[10] And by 2008 the number of expatriates exceeded 10.6 million in the GCC countries, with foreigners comprising 85 per cent of the workforce in the UAE and 92.5 per cent of the workforce in Qatar.[11]

The majority of Arab migrants in the receiving GCC nations are from Egypt, Yemen, Palestine, Jordan, Sudan, and Syria.[12] Referred to as the 'Temporary Migration Phenomenon,' Arab migrants in the UAE and Qatar are typically treated as transitory residents who will ultimately be replaced by qualified nationals in the future.[13]

Arab migration to the GCC countries was initially high after the Second World War, when a large number of non-Gulf Arabs moved to the region during the 1950s and 1960s seeking work.[14] Following the oil boom post-1973, Arab migration further intensified and became an important aspect of the development plans of the GCC ruling families. Arab migrants contributed the labour needed to support rapid development and modernisation.[15]

At the same time, however, large numbers of non-Arab migrants came to the region, primarily from South Asia.[16] Fearing cultural degradation as a result of these non-Arab foreigners, GCC governments made multiple public declarations that they would prioritise Arab migrants over other foreign workers from places such as South Asia.[17] These declarations led to agreements made at the Arab Labor Organization in 1968 and the Arab League in 1975, as well as the Arab Declaration of Principles on the Movement of Manpower in 1984. Individual countries, such as the UAE, also created specific procedures to prioritise Arabs over other migrant workers. For example, in 1980 the UAE introduced policies that mandated that a minimum of 30 per cent of the workforce should be from Arab countries and, in turn, signed official recruiting agreements with countries including Morocco, Sudan and Tunisia.[18] Similarly, in 1974, Qatar made a pact with Egypt to hire 9,000 Egyptians on an annual basis.[19] Over time, though, these agreements faded away and were not implemented rigorously, leaving Arab migrants to deal with the consequences of unemployment and uncertainty.[20]

A key part of the tacit bargain that the ruling families in GCC countries made with Arab migrant workers was that they would be 'apolitical' and 'transient' while contributing the labour required for national growth.[21] However, despite these hopes, Arab migrants also brought with them political ideologies from their countries of origin. In particular, Egyptians, Palestinians and Yemenis arrived with strong ideas about socialism and Arab nationalism.[22] These ideologies caused anxiety in host countries and some governments faced strikes and demonstrations led by expatriate Arab workers.[23] For example, Arab migrants were heavily involved with strikes and protests in Kuwait, particularly those related to the Suez Crisis in 1956, the United Arab Republic in 1959, and the war in Israel in 1967.[24] In 1967, non-Gulf Arabs in Saudi Arabia also participated in anti-government demonstrations.[25] The feeling of insecurity that arose from contrasting political ideas was one of the factors that contributed to the changes in Arab migrants' positions that occurred during the late 1970s.

Therefore, while official policy in the 1970s encouraged Arab migration to the GCC region, many Gulf nationals were beginning to see Arab migrants as a demographic, political and cultural threat. Nationals reportedly began to isolate themselves from former non-Gulf Arab allies to reduce potential threats to the ruling families.[26] At the same time, GCC labour policies were changing as nations introduced labour indigenisation policies to reduce dependence on foreign labour.[27] Other sanctioned policies included stricter regulation of the issuing of visas, deportations, indirect taxes that raised the cost of living for migrants, and nationalisation of workforces through quota systems.[28] A decline in oil revenues in the 1980s led to a decreased number of projects and a fall in the demand for foreign labour.[29] The First Gulf War in 1991 also led to the displacement of approximately 2 million Arab migrants from the GCC region—including 1 million Yemenis, 200,000 Jordanians, 158,000 Egyptians, and 150,000 Palestinians—who were eventually largely replaced by South Asians.[30] This was a major turning point in Arab migration in the region, as expatriate Arabs from nations that supported Iraq were deported to their countries of origin in large numbers.[31]

Since the 1970s, the proportion of Arab migrants among the foreign population in the UAE and Qatar has declined. In 1975, the Arab share of the foreign population in the UAE was estimated to be 26 per cent of the population, but by 2002 it had dropped to 13 per cent.[32] In Qatar, the percentage of Arabs in the foreign population fell from 33 per cent in 1975 to 19 per cent in 2002,[33] and to 13 per cent in 2013.[34] However, while there has been a reduction in the percentage of Arab migrants there has also been an overarching shift in migrant workforce demographics from Arab to Asian workers in the GCC region. Part of the attraction of Asian migrants is that they are perceived to arrive without conflicting ideologies, and to be more willing to work longer days for lower wages and in less than ideal conditions.

In the education sector, however, even with this shift away from Arab migrant workers in general, non-Gulf Arabs still account for a significant percentage of the teacher workforce. The reasons behind this are explored later in the chapter. Teacher migration, however, is not a phenomenon unique to the GCC region and it is important to situate this discussion in a global context.

Patterns and trends in global teacher migration

Globally, studies on teacher migration have offered insights on a number of factors that have been found to contribute to teachers' decisions to leave their home countries to pursue opportunities abroad. The earliest studies primarily investigated economic motivations behind migration trends. E.G. Ravenstein theorised that economic factors such as better pay and career opportunities dominated people's choices with regards to the decision to migrate, irrespective of their industry.[35] However, studies that specifically explore teacher migration in developing countries are relatively new.[36]

Teacher migration studies say that in addition to economic motivations, a combination of non-economic push and pull factors exist that encourage teachers to move across the globe. In a study conducted in Fiji, nearly one-third of all emigrants between 1987 and 2001 were teachers.[37] Political instability, discrimination, and land rights issues were cited as being the most significant factors contributing to the teachers' decision to migrate. Other push factors included a lack of opportunities for continuing education, and poor training facilities and conditions. The loss of such a large portion of an already diminished highly skilled workforce was reported to have had serious consequences for the economy of Fiji, with an estimated loss of F$4.6 million (US$2.5 million) in 2001 alone.

In South Africa, Sandhana Manik found that teachers are pushed out of their country because of dissatisfaction with national education systems, and are pulled towards other countries, in particular to the United Kingdom (UK), to what they perceive to be better career opportunities (or 'greener pastures').[38] However, Manik also found that within a year of migration to the UK, many were pushed back to South Africa after being exposed to a demanding work environment with poorly behaved students and social alienation, among other factors.[39]

Rashmi Sharmah found that the reasons for teacher migration in India were similar to those in Fiji and South Africa.[40] Despite an internal shortage of teachers, Indian teachers migrate to developing and developed countries to further their professional development and expose themselves to careers internationally. They are pushed out of India as a result of low salaries, corruption, and social issues. While respondents in the study indicated an awareness of the loss to India as a result of the teacher brain drain, the importance they placed on personal satisfaction trumped everything else. Indian teachers were also found to seek permanent migration, in contrast with teachers from South Africa.

While such studies have examined teacher migration in other parts of the world, then, the phenomenon of teacher migration to the Gulf in particular is unexplored. The remainder of this chapter will examine the case of Arab teacher migration to the UAE and Qatar.

Teacher migration to the UAE and Qatar

The UAE and Qatar have made advances in terms of access and quality of education, from minimal access in the 1950s to comprehensive coverage by the mid-1970s.[41] Given rapidly expanding education sector needs, demand for teachers in the two countries has continually exceeded domestic supply over the past 40 years.[42] Attempts have been made to increase national participation in the teaching workforces, but shortages have persisted because of alternative opportunities for nationals in other higher-paying sectors.[43]

The numbers of students in both countries have increased dramatically over the past decade. By way of illustration, in 2002 in the UAE approximately 585,098 students were enrolled in the public and private K-12 school system; by 2013 the number had increased by 66 per cent to 969,538.[44] The number of students in Qatar increased to an even greater degree from 69,666 students in 2001[45] to 167,739 students in 2011,[46] an increase of 141 per cent.

The overriding pull factor to the UAE and Qatar for Arab migrant teachers, according to the literature, is the promise of higher salaries.[47] In some cases, promised salaries do not materialise and migrants are left in debt and legally bound by contracts with employers who hold their passports.[48] But in other scenarios the hope of greater earnings is realised. For example, in the late mid-1980s a local teacher in Syria could earn roughly US$1,800 a year, but after he moved to the Gulf his annual income from teaching and private tutoring was approximately US$29,000, allowing him to save US$10,000 a year.[49] As expatriate Arab teachers in the UAE and Qatar are frequently male and typically the sole wage earner for their families,[50] the perceived ability to earn more and thus be able to send sizeable remittances back to their country of origin is a key attraction. These GCC country remittances have helped sustain the economy of the Palestinian territories and are also said to have strengthened the development of other countries such as Egypt and Yemen.[51]

A number of push factors encourage Arab teachers to leave their home countries. These may include lack of economic prospects in national education labour markets or political factors. Regional conflict also results in unemployment and other difficulties that may force teachers to leave their country.[52] Naufal describes how twenty-eight wars took place in non-Gulf Arab countries between the Second World War and the 2010 Arab Spring.[53] This is in contrast to very few conflicts in the GCC countries, which have remained

---

The role of Egypt in the development of education systems in the UAE and Qatar

Egyptian teachers have historically played a particularly important role in the education systems of the UAE and Qatar. While their numbers are decreasing as a percentage of the workforce, Egypt has been the largest exporter of teachers to the Middle East over the past four decades.[54]

Historically, Egyptian teachers went to the UAE and Qatar as contract workers hired through the Egyptian Ministry of Education. They were moved through a government-to-government circular labour migration programme.[55] In 1993 formal opportunities to join secondment programmes declined when many GCC education ministries, such as

Qatar's, stopped requesting teachers.⁵⁶ The decreased demand led the number of teachers in the secondment programme to fall from almost 30,000 in the mid-1980s to fewer than 2,000 in 2006/07.⁵⁷ Most Egyptian teachers independently move to the GCC through the private education market and seek jobs themselves or work with an employment broker.⁵⁸

The so-called 'Egyptianisation' of local culture and dialects through the education field has concerned some Emiratis and Qataris,⁵⁹ with a *Gulf News* editorial writing:

> It is a sad but established fact that the UAE's secondary schools are not good enough for the modern world. It is clear that the country's educational pioneers in the 1960s and 1970s had the herculean task of building an entire educational network from nothing. They did a heroic job, but by importing teachers en masse from Egypt, they rebuilt the problems of the Egyptian state system here, with a whole generation of Emiratis learning their secondary studies by rote without being taught to think for themselves or value independence of mind.⁶⁰

Therefore, while the role and influence of Egypt in the GCC region has declined since the 1960s and 1970s, a strong Egyptian presence remains in the education sector in the UAE and Qatar. Remnants of the Egyptian curriculum are in both national curricula, but more influential is the continuing presence of large numbers of Egyptian teachers who work in both countries.

comparatively stable and thus offer another plausible reason why Arabs continue to migrate to the UAE and Qatar for employment.

Challenges to Arab migrant teachers

While teaching in the UAE and Qatar, Arab migrant teachers face numerous challenges. Some studies have found that they may be poorly incentivised to creatively engage students in the classroom because of their uncertain work environment—annual contract renewals often create prolonged states of apprehension.⁶¹ Sulayman Khalaf and Saad Alkobaisi refer to this as the 'insecurity syndrome.'⁶² A lack of job security in both countries means that Arab migrant teachers fail to fully engage with the system out of fear of losing their jobs.⁶³

To supplement their salaries, teachers in Qatar and the UAE often seek a second source of income through private tutoring.[64] Teachers bring a culture and tradition of private tutoring from their home countries[65] as a way to generate additional income.[66] While this may have originated in a situation in which they received low salaries, some Arab migrant teachers have said that even if their salaries were 100,000 AED (US$27,700) a month, they would continue to tutor[67] because it is part of their identity. Given that private tutoring is highly sought after by parents to supplement regular classes, teachers are easily able to find opportunities to teach outside of the school,[68] sometimes with students from their own classrooms.[69] Teachers' feelings of impermanence can cause them to focus on the present, pushing them to maximise their earnings through tutoring instead of considering the long-term repercussions for themselves and their students. Officially teachers in the UAE and Qatar are prohibited from getting paid for private lessons, but the rule is often ignored, and infrequently enforced. Another issue relating to the quality of Arab migrant teachers is that the countries from where these teachers tend to come do not have consistent teacher training standards and teaching is often viewed as the profession of last resort.[70] Arab migrant teachers have generally received less pedagogical training in comparison to their local counterparts in the UAE and Qatar.[71] Students in Arab migrants teachers' home countries do not score high on international tests, such as the Trends in International Mathematics and Science Study (TIMSS) and the Programme for International Student Assessment (PISA), and as a result many of the teachers originating from these countries are likely to suffer from the same knowledge gaps, which then affects their teaching.[72]

While there are many similarities with regards to the Arab migrant teachers working in the UAE and Qatar, each country is also unique in many aspects. The next section looks at the individual countries in more detail.

The case of the UAE

In the UAE there is a very clear gendered aspect to the Arab migrant teacher population, because the majority of these teachers working in the public school system are male. While historically migrant males and females accounted for the majority of teachers in government schools, the expansion of the national higher education sector has meant that Emirati women now account for over 80 per cent of female teachers. On the other hand, the reverse is true for Emirati men, who account for only 20 per cent of the male teacher workforce.[73] Currently, close to 100 per cent of primary school teachers in boys' and girls' primary schools are females. However, at the preparatory (mid-

Figure 3.1: UAE–Arab migrant educators by nationality—male (2008)*

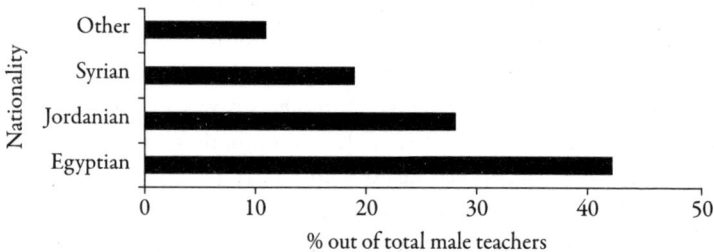

*Note: This data is only from the emirate of Ras Al Khaimah and only pertains to males. This was the only data available at the time of writing. The "Other" category includes Palestinians.

Source: Ridge, Natasha, 'Privileged and penalized: The education of boys in the United Arab Emirates', PhD diss., Columbia University, 2009, p. 68.

dle school) and secondary levels men teach boys and women teach girls. Anecdotally, using Emirati female teachers at preparatory-level boys' schools has been discussed,[74] but very few women, if any, occupy such roles.[75] At secondary level, gender and nationality segregation becomes much more defined, with girls being taught by Emirati women and boys being largely taught by expatriate Arab men.

As Figure 3.1 shows, Arab migrant teachers in the UAE largely come from Egypt, Syria, Jordan, and to a lesser extent Palestine.

Generally, working conditions for Arab migrant teachers are very different from those of national teachers. Their pay is approximately half that of their national counterparts, and this is combined with a very minimal chance of advancement or promotion.[76] As previously mentioned, many teachers in the UAE privately tutor outside of school hours. In a study conducted in the UAE, 83 per cent of tutors were men, and of the male tutors 94 per cent were Arab migrants, primarily from Egypt. In the same study, over half of male students in tutoring received lessons from their classroom teacher, and 70 per cent of students said that their teachers encouraged struggling students to take private lessons with them.[77]

The case of Qatar

The situation in Qatar regarding the use of Arab migrant teachers is even more pronounced than in the UAE because of a shortage of Qatari teachers. Non-

Qatari teachers account for 70 per cent of the total teacher population in Qatar,[78] of whom around 53 per cent are Arabs.[79] Similarly to the UAE, female teachers dominate the primary-school sector, making up 83 per cent of teaching staff, with their numbers falling to 59 per cent in preparatory schools and 57 per cent in secondary schools.[80] In a Supreme Education Council survey that excluded non-Arab expatriate community and embassy schools, non-Qatari Arab teachers were found to account for around 99 per cent of teachers in Arab private schools, 71 per cent in independent (government) schools, 28 per cent in semi-independent schools, and 29 per cent in international schools.[81]

Figure 3.2 shows that during 2013, the majority of Arab educators in Qatar were from Egypt, Jordan, Lebanon, and Syria.[82]

In summary, research on Arab migrant teachers working in the GCC region reveals pieces of a larger puzzle. Although we know about working conditions, salaries, and migration status, very little research has looked at the teachers themselves. Research, our own included, largely hypothesises these teachers' feelings and perceptions with regard to their status in their host countries. This study therefore gathered data from Arab migrant teachers to find out how they perceive their lives and employment in the UAE and Qatar. While the research has a naturally rights-based aspect, the benefit to host countries in understanding this specific population of teachers is very real,

Figure 3.2: Qatar–Arab migrant educators by nationality—male and female (2013)

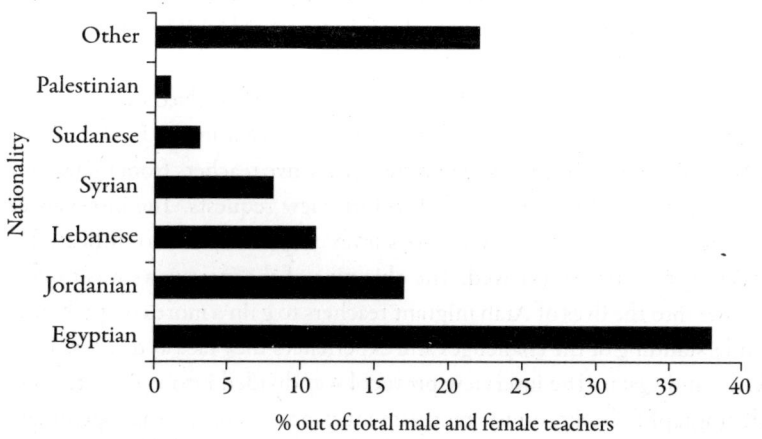

Source: Babar, 'Working for the Neighbors: Arab Migrants in Qatar', CIRS Monthly Dialogue lecture, 11 December 2013.

because they are responsible for educating the majority of Emirati/Qatari children and are therefore vital to future economic and social development.

Exploring Arab migrant teachers' perceptions in the UAE and Qatar

After examining regional and international literature on migrant teachers, this study defined the following three research questions to guide the data collection and analysis processes:

1. What are the characteristics of Arab migrant teachers in the UAE and Qatar?
2. What are the push and pull factors that bring and keep Arab teachers in the UAE and Qatar?
3. What are the implications of the current status of Arab migrant teachers in the UAE and Qatar for education systems in both countries?

To address these questions, the study employed a mixed-methods comparative approach that combined quantitative and qualitative components. In the first stage, a total of forty-eight teachers from the UAE and forty-three teachers from Qatar were convenience sampled[83] and completed a survey that explored their personal and professional characteristics, recruitment, compensation and benefits, integration, and overall experience in the UAE or Qatar. The survey instrument used in this stage of the study was adapted from the International Teacher Mobility Survey 2013 of the American Federation of Teachers' Educational Foundation.[84] Data from the survey was compiled and analysed with IBM's SPSS statistical software, using descriptive statistics, frequencies and cross-tabulations.

The second stage of the study was qualitative and involved in-depth interviews with seven Arab migrant teachers, five based in the UAE and two based in Qatar. While we hoped to interview five teachers from Qatar, only two teachers in Qatar responded to interview requests. The interviewees were selected from the twenty-six survey respondents who indicated an interest in being interviewed. The objective of the interviews was to delve deeper into the lives of Arab migrant teachers to gain a more comprehensive understanding of the challenges and experiences they face as teachers in the UAE and Qatar. The interview protocol was divided into eight categories: demographic background; recruitment process; contractual agreement; social and professional integration; working experience; academic freedom and collegiality; professional development; and future plans. Interviews lasting about an hour were conducted in Arabic, and were recorded after oral consent was given. Interviews were transcribed, translated into English, analysed, and broken down into themes using QSR International's NVivo quality data analysis software.[85]

Limitations

Given that this was an exploratory study, a number of limitations resulted from institutional barriers and the researchers' ability to access new research terrains. In the UAE and Qatar, respectively, respondents came from the emirate of Ras Al Khaimah and the city of Doha because of difficulties in accessing teachers in other locations. While the sample surveyed in the study was not nationally representative, it was representative of government-employed teachers. In the Qatar sample, a large number of Sudanese teachers took part, which arose from the use of convenience sampling—one of the researchers had a personal connection to the Sudanese community. Also, the majority of those surveyed, 77.6 per cent, were male due to the large gender differential of Arab migrant teachers in government schools in the UAE. The large percentage of males in the study is, however, roughly proportional to the actual percentage of male and female Arab expatriate teachers in the UAE and Qatar, and in that context is not considered problematic.

The data is also limited because it represents a cross-section of teachers for the year 2013. Longitudinal data is difficult to obtain in the UAE and Qatar, partially due to issues of access. Conducting a longitudinal study would give a more accurate portrayal of migrant teachers, their development, and responses to new policies across the years they spend in the UAE or Qatar. Finally, data was self-reported, which suggests that some responses may not have been entirely accurate, particularly when relating to issues of regulation, because teachers may have been fearful about giving a negative report. This fear may have also contributed to the difficulty in recruiting participants and the smaller sample size than initially hoped for.

Quantitative findings

The quantitative findings were largely consistent with existing research on migrant teacher populations; however, concerns over social and professional integration stood out as commonly shared views among the migrant Arab teacher populations in both countries. It should be noted that due to sample limitations, analysis was confined to descriptive statistics but still revealed meaningful results for further research.

Personal profile of Arab migrant teachers

Based on the survey results in the UAE and Qatar, the average age of migrant Arab teachers in both countries was around forty-six years old. Male teachers formed a majority of the Arab expatriate teachers surveyed (78 per cent). In terms of teachers' nationalities, most came from Egypt (39 per cent) followed by Jordan (22 per cent) and then Syria (18 per cent). Some 95 per cent of respondents reported that they were married at the time of survey distribution. Of these, 66 per cent had spouses who were also educated and had obtained a bachelor's degree. More spouses were employed in the UAE than in Qatar (59 per cent in the UAE vs. 44 per cent in Qatar). Of the spouses employed in the UAE, a greater number (69 per cent) also worked in education than did in Qatar (52 per cent). Each respondent also reported supporting around three to four children, with male teachers supporting a few more children on average than females.

Professional profile of Arab migrant teachers

With respect to teachers' professional characteristics, 60 per cent of respondents reported having a subject-specific bachelor's or master's degree, while only 33 per cent reported having a degree in education or teaching. Overall, male respondents reported higher levels of education than their female counterparts, with 82 per cent and 63 per cent, respectively, reporting having a bachelor's degree. An overwhelming majority of all teachers (89 per cent) had teaching experience prior to moving to their current position, with males being more experienced than females on average. On average, migrant teachers in the UAE had 20.5 years of teaching experience compared to those in Qatar who had taught for seventeen years. Correspondingly, in the UAE, around 76 per cent indicated that they had taught outside of their home countries for more than ten years, while only 54 per cent of teachers surveyed in Qatar had more than ten years' teaching experience outside of their home country.

Causes of migration: push and pull factors

The survey results indicated that 50 per cent of the Arab migrant teachers who participated in the survey perceived higher salaries in the UAE and Qatar to be the most important determining factor in their decision to migrate from their home countries (see Figure 3.3). Some 51 per cent of males, as opposed to 44 per cent of females, selected this factor. From a similar perspective, 38 per cent of respondents said that potentially adverse conditions in their home countries that fostered a 'need' to support family were the number one factor that drove or pushed them and their families to the UAE or Qatar: 42 per cent of males and 36 per cent of females selected this factor.

Nevertheless, income factors were not the only elements that were significant in attracting teachers. Another major pull factor underlying the decision to migrate was having greater access to opportunities for professional development. Approximately 30 per cent of teachers ranked training opportunities as the primary cause for their departure to the UAE or Qatar.

The process of migration

Many teachers applied for their current positions through a recruitment agency (46 per cent). However, when examined more closely, Arab migrant teachers working in the UAE primarily found their job by applying directly to a job advertisement (64 per cent), while in Qatar finding a teaching job

Figure 3.3: Push and pull factors

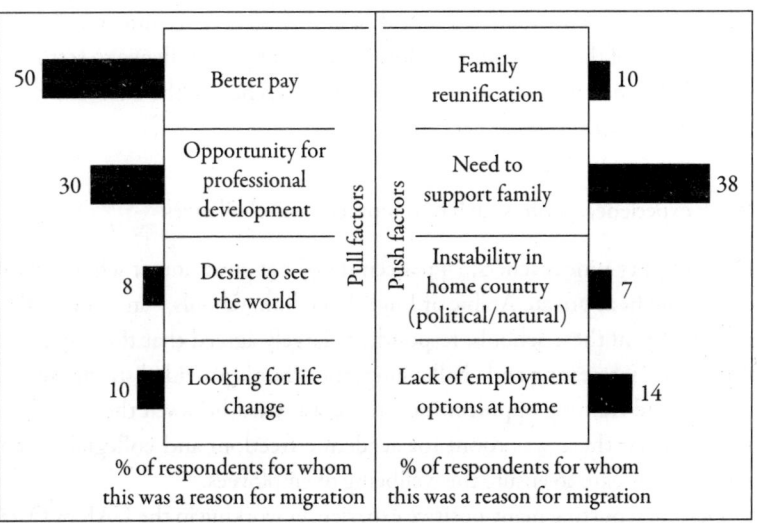

Source: Survey results.

through friends/relatives was the most common method (49 per cent). In Qatar, teachers also applied for advertised openings, with about one-third (30 per cent) of teachers finding their current job through that process. After a successful application, interview completion and selection, higher rates of ambiguity and unfilled contract obligations were reported in the UAE than in Qatar. In the UAE, 35 per cent of respondents said that the terms of their contracts were not clearly explained before signing, compared to less than 10 per cent in Qatar. Additionally, 23 per cent of participants in the UAE did not receive everything they were promised in their contracts compared to 10 per cent in Qatar.

Social integration

Approximately 84 per cent of teachers reported fitting in very well in the UAE or Qatar. According to the survey results, schools were an important factor in this process because they offered newcomers orientation programmes. However, contradicting this, 68 per cent reported alienation, 59 per cent housing problems, and 55 per cent job instability as challenges to settling in. Men reported housing and job instability to be a challenge more frequently than woman (37 per cent vs. 26 per cent), emphasising the male role as the primary wage-earners and supporters in Arab families. Consistent with this, men also said that housing support, contractual arrangements, and the possibility of permanent residency would help them feel more integrated in the social fabric of the host country. Housing was a bigger challenge to settling in in the UAE than in Qatar, with 65 per cent of teachers in the UAE citing it as a concern compared to 28 per cent in Qatar.

Work experience, professional development and challenges

Out of eighty-nine teachers, 74 per cent taught at government schools, while others taught at private Arabic or English medium schools.[87] In terms of their experiences in these schools, respondents largely agreed that their work was sufficiently interesting and challenging; the schools provided strong support systems and training opportunities; there was trust between the school and the teachers; there was room for academic freedom and collegiality; and schools took care to ensure the wellbeing of employees.

Despite reporting many positive experiences working in the UAE or Qatar, some teachers reported promotional, regulatory and classroom difficulties.

Figure 3.4: Challenges of teaching experiences in the UAE and Qatar*

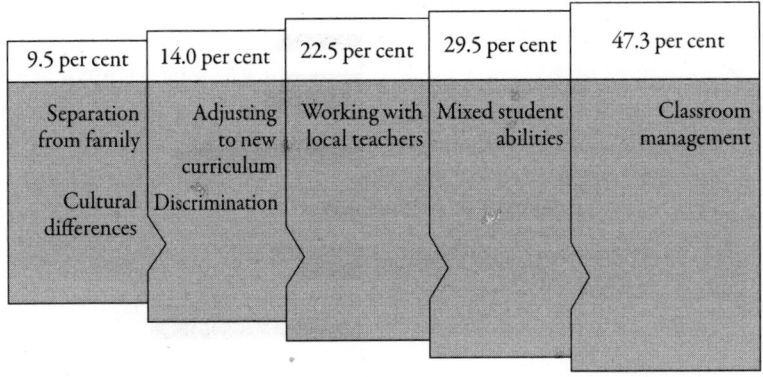

Source: Survey results.
*Some respondents selected more than one answer.

For example, only 41 per cent agreed or strongly agreed with the statement 'I am satisfied with the way promotions are given out.' Around 34 per cent were content about equality of salaries with colleagues. Some 39 per cent said that they needed to engage in external activities to supplement their wages, with private tutoring being the most popular means. Finally, teachers ranked the most important challenges to their teaching experience in the UAE and Qatar as being in the classroom (see Figure 3.4). Close to 50 per cent reported difficulties managing students and 30 per cent dealing with mixed-student abilities as the number one problem that they faced in their current position.[88]

Reflections and future plans

Reflecting on their jobs, teachers in Qatar reported higher levels of satisfaction than their UAE counterparts. In ranking overall levels of satisfaction with their job, 54 per cent in Qatar and 36 per cent in the UAE rated their satisfaction on a scale of one to five, with one representing the highest satisfaction and five the lowest. All respondents suggested that they would like to continue to teaching in the UAE or Qatar for at least one more year, with 52 per cent aiming to stay for more than ten years. Given a list of options about factors that would encourage them to stay longer, most teachers in the UAE said they would most prefer a wage increase (58 per cent), followed by more secure positions (42 per cent). This was in contrast to Qatar where teachers preferred

Figure 3.5: Factors that encourage teachers to stay in UAE/Qatar*

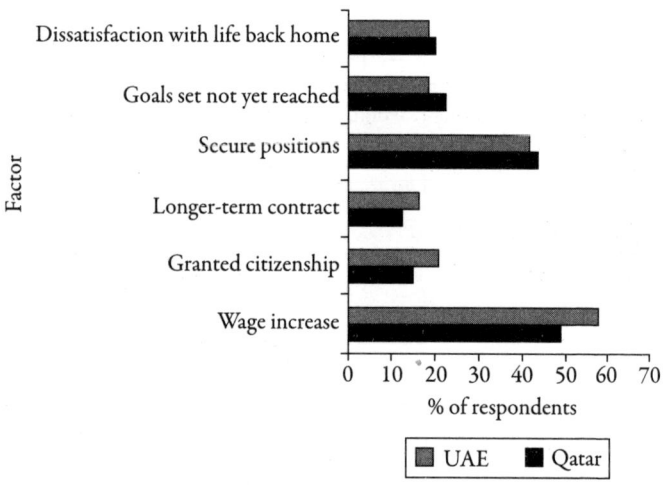

* Some respondents selected more than one answer.
Source: Survey results.

more secure positions (46 per cent) to a wage increase (40 per cent). This chapter will expand on some of the significant findings from this section and the implications for school systems in both countries.

Qualitative findings

Following quantitative data collection, seven of the surveyed teachers took part in in-depth interviews. The primary themes that emerged were commitment to the UAE and Qatar, motivation for migration, implications of current status of Arab migrant teachers for education, and the desire for recognition and permanency. These themes are also featured in the discussion section. Figure 3.6 illustrates the ninety-one words most frequently used[89] in the interviews. Among them were the words 'contract', 'salary', 'time', 'different' and 'moved'. The themes behind these words are explored in the following section.

Commitment to the UAE and Qatar

Out of the seven respondents randomly selected to take part in the interviews, all had lived in the UAE or Qatar for eighteen years or more, with the exception of one who had moved to Qatar around four years previously, because of political strife in his home country, Egypt. Most had a strong sense of commit-

Figure 3.6: Word cloud of the ninety-one most frequently used words in interviews

> activities administration always amount another anything asked back benefits came challenges changed children clear comfortable continue contract country courses curriculum **different** education Egypt environment evaluation everything exam example face factors family feel follow found friends grades help home hours IAT idea increase insurance interview job Jordan know locals long management ministry mostly moved need new now opportunities others outside parents per place plan position pressure principal private professional promotion provided responsibilities rules salary sometimes stay subject taught technology tell think tickets time tough tried university used visa way week workshops years

Source: Survey results.

ment to the UAE and Qatar, which they saw not just as temporary places of residence, but their homes. One respondent went so far as to invest in a house in the UAE, although he revealed at the end of the interview that he would be leaving the country to pursue a job in Qatar where he had received a better offer. This loyalty is depicted in the following respondent statements:

> I have lived here longer than I've lived in my home country. I don't know much about Egypt. I started my career in this country and I hope to continue it here.
>
> UAE respondent No. 1
>
> This is my twenty-second year teaching in the UAE. I have been here in the UAE since I was a child and this is the main reason why I am still here. Although I have properties in Syria, I only visit for one month every two to three years. I prefer the UAE over Syria because I feel closer to the UAE.
>
> UAE respondent No. 2
>
> I believe that someone's home is the place where they find harmony and safety and this is provided by this country.
>
> Qatar respondent No. 1

Motivations for migration: push and pull factors

As described in the quantitative findings section, respondents indicated that a mix of push and pull factors had contributed to their decision to move to the UAE or Qatar. The majority cited better pay and the need to support family as the primary reasons for moving. While the qualitative interview responses revealed a similar pull of higher salaries consistent with the quantitative findings, they placed greater emphasis on the UAE and Qatar as safe havens. Interviewees commonly reported that they were attracted by the safety and ease of life the UAE and Qatar offered, relative to their home countries. Responses from the interviews highlighting the importance of the safety factor are presented below.

> The UAE is a safe, secure, and sophisticated country with many services and benefits. I believe anyone who lives in UAE would like to stay here and never leave. (Pull factor.)
>
> UAE respondent No. 2
>
> [I moved here] largely because of the political problems that occurred some years back [in my home country]. I thought to myself it would be great if I had the opportunity to teach and live somewhere else. (Push factor.)
>
> Qatar respondent No. 2

Along with safety and comfort, two interviewees also revealed that professional development opportunities provided in the UAE and Qatar contributed to their decision to migrate to the region. They suggested that they were in search of opportunities to continue their education and also work.

Finally, respondents described their economic motivations for moving to the UAE and Qatar through the use of language including the words/phrases 'better jobs', 'convenient', 'good income', 'financial stability.' However, none of the respondents hesitated to suggest that while they received what they initially thought were decent salaries, they quickly became aware that their salaries were not enough to match the cost of living in the UAE and Qatar. Consequently, many found secondary sources of income such as private tutoring, teaching at adult education centres, and starting small businesses, which the survey findings also showed. Their thoughts are given below:

> I spend around three hours a day on external activities... Being a private teacher is not an easy or respectable thing... If the salary was better, no one would do private tutoring because everyone would like to lead comfortable lives.
>
> UAE respondent No. 3
>
> [Despite getting a salary raise,] the expenses have doubled... We do not have the security of health insurance for ourselves or our families. We are not even given a flight ticket. We are likely to spend a whole month's salary covering the cost of a normal child birth. That's why teachers are obligated to look for other alternative

forms of income and business. For example, tutoring is the number one option. Teachers who tutor dedicate at least three hours every evening to it.

UAE respondent No. 2

The educational implications of the status of Arab migrant teachers

When considering the implications of the current financial and work conditions of expatriate Arab teachers on the Emirati and Qatari education systems, the interviewees' reactions differed. Four out of seven noted how the mismatch between salaries and cost of living, high workload, and temporary visa status could lead to a negative impact on their quality of teaching. They felt that tutoring and an increasing workload, such as the continuous updating of work sample portfolios,[90] forced teachers to spend time on these activities that they would have otherwise spent on lesson-planning and grading. One UAE respondent explained that between his regular teaching obligations and private tutoring, around eleven to twelve hours a day, he had very little or no time to plan lessons. He shared the concern of another respondent about the amount of time teachers must spend on their teacher portfolios as part of mandatory annual teacher evaluations required by the education authorities.

> Everything... needs to be supported by photos and evidence. Classes, meeting with colleagues, and even trips... because at the end, we are evaluated on those photos... We don't have time to grade and provide feedback on [student] projects.
>
> UAE respondent 1

In addition to limited time dedicated to lesson-planning, interviewees also highlighted the negative implications of job insecurity that resulted from the temporary visa status. One respondent illustrated a true scenario of how teachers can be pushed into raising student grades by anywhere from 10–30 per cent for fear of losing their jobs.

> We have many teachers who moved to different schools because they were afraid of the principal... [One principal] asked me to help students cheat during their exams. I refused... so he spoke to [an Education Zone officer who] came and told me to do what he asked. [They] try to pressure the teachers sometimes... and some teachers will accept this because they are afraid of being moved or something.
>
> UAE respondent No. 3

One teacher commented that temporary status has meant being transferred to two schools within the span of a few months because an Emirati teacher was promised the original position. The respondent reported living in constant fear and therefore being unable to completely commit to the school or to students. The teacher reported that this is not only personally worrying, but also disruptive for students who will have to continue with a different teacher from mid-year.

> My students threw me a goodbye party and they asked me to stay. I would have loved to have stayed but it's not my call.
>
> UAE respondent No. 4

Interviewees in Qatar gave conflicting and vague responses with respect to the implications of their work status on education. On the one hand, while one respondent acknowledged being to some extent afraid of losing his job, he remarked that he did not see any impact on education. The other respondent in Qatar did not have any such fear:

> Having a yearly contract is worrying because you don't know if you're going to stay for the next year or get laid off. Having a five-year contract would bring teachers peace of mind because they would know that they aren't going anywhere. This fear would impact the person emotionally, but probably not their teaching.
>
> Qatar respondent No. 2

> There isn't any fear because [current] teachers [have a lot of] experience in education. It's difficult for the school to think about replacing these teachers because nowadays it's hard to find teachers with qualifications… Fresh graduates wouldn't have the upper hand in taking the position of a [more] experienced teacher.
>
> Qatar respondent No. 1

Desire for recognition and permanency

Overall, respondents reported a desire to be acknowledged for their efforts and commitment and to be rewarded accordingly. In Qatar, both teachers called for recognition of hours worked outside of regular hours:

> Any extra work from the teachers should be rewarded. If I have to teach an extra class or I have to work overtime, I should be paid for it. It is an incentive for the teacher.
>
> Qatar respondent No. 2

> Nowadays, [teaching responsibilities are increasing] and we are putting in a lot of time and effort. We should get something in exchange for our extra services and the overtime.
>
> Qatar respondent No. 1

In the UAE, all five respondents suggested that providing teachers with permanent residency would be beneficial for them and the country, given the dependency on Arab expatriate teachers.

The feeling of being secure and settled would encourage and motivate me as a teacher to create and produce more...A permanent residency would ease teachers' states of mind... [We] would feel more settled and the concern of being laid off and sent back home would be relieved.

UAE respondent No. 2

I wish it was possible for me to attain permanent residency. It would strengthen my commitment to the UAE and to my job, and allow me to earn a better salary and even provide higher education opportunities for my children in the UAE.

UAE respondent No. 4

Conclusion

Four important themes emerge from this study that deserve greater discussion. Firstly, Arab migrant teachers come to the Gulf with the hope of spending the greater part of their lives in the region, in contrast to literature on Western expatriate faculty in universities who appear to come to the region for short stints, categorised by David Chapman *et al.* as 'adventure seekers'.[91] The majority of Arab teachers had spent over ten years working in either the UAE or Qatar, and the majority also hoped to still be working for at least ten more years. Arab migrant teachers come to the Gulf with the intention of living and working there for significant periods of time. The respondents did not express a desire to return to their home countries any time in the near future. This is probably a result of a number of factors. Most recently the events of the Arab Spring have meant that for some teachers there is no home to return to. For others, continuing instability coupled with low salaries for teachers back home has also meant there is no desire to return. The qualitative findings highlighted that the UAE and Qatar offer political stability and safety relative to other non-Gulf Arab countries. Arab expatriate teachers who come from conflict-affected countries find comfort and safety in the UAE and Qatar. This is consistent with previous literature which emphasises the value of safety and availability of services as a factor in migration.[92]

Secondly, while economic motivation was the primary factor in teachers choosing to come to the UAE and Qatar, professional development and career opportunities were also highly important in their choice. This was particularly true for males, and around 28 per cent of teachers in the UAE and 33 per cent in Qatar ranked professional development opportunities as the draw to teach in the two countries. This is consistent with previous literature on international migration of Indian teachers where opportunities for professional development were found to be the single most important determining factor in the decision to migrate.[93] This desire for career progression and professional development indicates that for many of these teachers they have not simply come to the Gulf for monetary reasons, but as part of a career move whereby they not only make more money, but they also get a chance to improve their skills and to potentially rise through the ranks. If this does not happen, it could be reasonably hypothesised that these teachers will become demotivated and disengaged—especially with regard to promotion opportunities, with only 41 per cent of respondents currently satisfied with the existing process. Giving Arab migrant teachers the same opportunities as nationals for promotion and improvement could also have many positive effects on their motivation and engagement. This is in line with other literature which outlines the benefits of reward and recognition, both intrinsic and extrinsic, on job motivation and satisfaction in educational institutions.[94]

Thirdly, the precarious status of Arab migrant teachers as temporary workers may be creating perverse outcomes in the education sector, whereby they are highly invested in the present rather than the future, are therefore more incentivised to engage in additional income-generating activities, such as private tutoring, and do not hold national students to high standards, but rather take the path of least resistance. In a forthcoming paper by Chetan Dave, Natasha Ridge and Soha Shami, Arab migrant teachers were found to be less willing to take on risk, less patient, and less altruistic than their Emirati counterparts.[95] Migrant teachers' impatience was found to be negatively associated with student achievement.[96] This suggests that the temporary residence status of Arab migrant teachers results in distinct behavioural characteristics that in turn appear to result in poorer student achievement. This is consistent with a study by Ridge, which found that Arab migrant teachers were less likely to confront their students and more likely to encourage cheating and other detrimental behaviour to protect their jobs.[97] This follows other research showing that teachers without permanent contracts have less control over their individual working conditions within schools, which contributes to higher levels of anxiety about the future of their jobs and how much they can commit.[98]

Finally, Arab migrant teachers form a large, unique and integral part of national education systems in the UAE and Qatar. The benefits are real to host countries, national students and teachers alike in considering these teachers less as temporary workers and more as permanent residents. In the UAE and Qatar, Arab migrant teachers form a significant percentage of government school teachers. In the UAE they comprise 90 per cent of all male teachers, while in Qatar they account for 87 per cent of all teachers working in government schools. Given that the medium of instruction in state schools is Arabic, the UAE and Qatar will continue to need Arab migrant teachers for the foreseeable future and will also for the same reason be unable to switch to migrant teachers from non-Arab countries. This is especially true in the case of males, because national males have so many other career opportunities that it is highly unlikely that there will ever be an influx into the teaching profession. With this in mind, policymakers in the UAE and Qatar perhaps need to rethink their approach to Arab migrant teachers as a distinct and unique subgroup of Arab migrants working in these two countries.

The results of our study are consistent with literature on the economic motivation for migration.[99] Arab migrant teachers come to the Gulf to make money and, in turn, to provide more for their immediate and extended families. Arab migrants to the Gulf more generally form a unique and in many ways an indispensable part of the population because of their shared language, culture and, in most cases, religion. While governments in the Gulf may well be able to switch between geographical regions in terms of sourcing unskilled labour, demand for the services of Arab migrant teachers will always remain, largely because of the language factor. In the public education sector, in particular, this demand shows no sign of abating, due to a severe and increasing shortage of Gulf male teachers in general, and in Qatar a shortage of national female teachers as well. Current employment practices and policies relating to Arab migrant teachers are failing to achieve the kind of student results that the UAE and Qatar wish to see. In both countries, national students score poorly on international assessments such as PISA and TIMSS, with male students in particular, who are taught almost solely by Arab migrants, performing the worst. Much more research is needed on the impact of current employment policies for Arab migrant teachers on student achievement and engagement, and on how states can help these teachers to be more effective in the classroom. Without a rethinking of current practices there is little hope that the existing national educational challenges will disappear. Improving the status and conditions under which Arab migrant teachers work therefore has the potential to benefit not only the teachers themselves but also their students and thus the nations in which they work.

4

THE MODEL IMMIGRANT

SECOND GENERATION HADRAMIS IN KUWAIT AND THE LEGACY OF A 'GOOD REPUTATION'

Abdullah Alajmi[1]

Introduction

Migration is a social process in which dynamics including individual rationalisation, household economies, cultural practices, and the ethno-history of the receiving society interact to shape the character of the migratory experience. Previous studies of migration to the Gulf mainly examine broad and official levels of Asian labour migration as observed in the legal, economic, and political conditions that labourers find themselves subjected to. These studies emphasise analyses of the outcomes of regional economic disparities and states' labour policies and their impact on migration flow, settlement and sponsorship.[2] However, as a social process migration operates at different levels involving state–state relations, and family connections at both ends of the migration process, as well as at the individual level. Therefore, further research requires, among other things, an examination of how state structures and migration policies are 'segmented' by immigrants; that is, managed, appropriated, or even manipulated.³ The migration of Hadramis⁴ from South Yemen to Kuwait is individualistic, but has always been carried out through household structure, friendship and regional relations. The link between a Hadrami practice of dependency on the *mu'azzib*⁵ (a formal or informal sponsor) and migration flow is characteristic of this. Historically, a Hadrami domestic role in Kuwaiti houses has been performed through persistent practices of dependency. This chapter will examine how the socioeconomic path of domesticity and its history may have moulded the Hadrami migratory experience of the 'model minority' as we know it today. For this purpose, it reveals Hadrami daily performance and reproduction of practices of total dependency on Kuwait and Kuwaiti *mu'azzib* as sources of income and social security. While practices of dependency and 'good reputation' are preserved as a form of social capital by the first generation Hadramis, the chapter examines whether they continue to delineate the perception and expectations of the second generation immigrants in Kuwait.

The research used ethnographic fieldwork to expose the migratory experience in the daily lives and narratives of Arab immigrants in Kuwait. As shown below, ethnography has not been used systematically in scholarship on migration in relation to Kuwait. Literature on migration to the Gulf Cooperation Council (GCC) region has tended to focus on immigrants and their sending societies. Such a tendency has led scholars to neglect how receiving societies have, to varying degrees, interacted with and shaped each Arab migratory experience. Thus, this research departs from existing scholarship on migration to Kuwait by elaborating on the role the receiving society has historically played in shaping the economic aspirations and social inclusion of Arab immigrants. Furthermore, this research brings a new perspective to the migratory experience in Kuwait by analysing the interaction between two generations of Hadrami immigrants. Ample primary ethnographic data from both generations was crucial, because it allowed a close assessment of different individual and age perspectives simultaneously.

No systematic ethnographic studies of Arab immigrants in Kuwait previously existed in contemporary scholarship.⁶ Research on Arab migration has instead concentrated on labour economics and national policies. A limitation of this kind of research is its emphasis on the economic success of immigrant communities and security issues concerning Kuwaiti citizenship.⁷ The research has paid little attention to the role of the receiving society or patterns of local interaction with each immigrant community. However, other research has shown that Kuwaiti society and state policies in effect categorise each Arab population differently. Categorisation was based on elements such as the time of contact and length of the immigrant community's settlement, skills, cultural proximity, immigrants' attachment to one segment of Kuwaiti society or another, regional politics, and the size of the immigrant community.[8] However, similar categorisation of immigrants is common practice in all the GCC countries and beyond. Hadrami, or other Arab, migration to Kuwait is by no means exceptional, either in terms of how the state has segmented immigrants or the immigrants' adaptive mechanisms when reacting to shifting political, economic and demographic conditions in Kuwait and the Gulf.

Scholarship is almost silent on Yemeni, not to mention Hadrami, migration to Kuwait. Hadrami migration to Indonesia and Malaysia, and Tanzania, has received immense scholarly attention, particularly the so-called 'Hadrami successes' in politics and commerce in those countries.[9] Such scholarship has mainly focused on achievements of prominent figures such as Hadrami merchants and religious individuals, while overlooking the majority of immigrants coming from peasantry and poor backgrounds.[10] This focus on prominent Hadrami experience produced what I call a 'standard view' of Hadramis, or an established predisposition to view the Hadrami immigrants as universally successful. This has strongly influenced writing on the subject, which has led some to suggest that 'Wherever there was money to be made... Hadramis were there among the leaders', or '[w]herever they settled, Hadramis involved themselves in commerce, the means to acquire the best economic position.'[11] The experience of Hadramis in Kuwait refutes such interpretations. Research should therefore account for the significance of variations in the socioeconomic and cultural background of Hadrami immigrants and their role in shaping a migratory experience.

Fieldwork for the present study included two small-scale surveys. The first collected demographic characteristics of 108 respondents of different generations.[12] Among other things, immigrants were asked about their age, place of origin and work. For example, 57 per cent of all respondents were between eighteen and forty-five years old. Some 60 per cent of survey respondents worked as couriers, and 25 per cent as special servants and cashiers. A minority of 15 per cent worked as guards and drivers. The average salary was 200 Kuwaiti dinars, equivalent to 150,000 Yemeni rials (US$600). The second survey was an 'attitude survey' conducted among sixty-three young Hadramis from eight *'izbahs* (all-male residences) who came from different Hadrami villages. Here, issues of saving, marital status, personal objectives, sponsorship, and generational differences were investigated.[13] Since 2000, Kuwait's official census has divided general segments of foreign populations into Arabs and non-Arabs without specifying their regional backgrounds.[14] The Ministry of Interior holds more detailed data, particularly regarding population size and legalities, but it was not possible to access this.

In total, thirty-two in-depth interviews of second generation Hadramis took place, which enabled a deeper understanding of migration as a social process. Theodoros Iosifides and Deborah Sporton have emphasised the significance of immigrants' stories, reconstructing the intricate and dialectical interplay between individual action, meaning, and structural and systemic conditions, constraints and enablements. Migrants' stories as evidence and data are an inescapable part of the ethnographic representation of immigrants' social reality.[15]

Multi-generational fieldwork: opening narratives

Kuwaiti meta-cultural categorisation of different migrant groups has depicted Hadramis as loyal, humble and well behaved—a model minority. A significant part of my ethnographic research, therefore, considered the opinions of Kuwaitis among Hadrami workers, and senior Hadramis—the first generation or the *'uggal*—with whom I established connections during my first round of fieldwork in 2003. The 'multi-generational' nature of this unusual and challenging fieldwork involved analysing data from primarily two social and generational worlds. This permitted sufficient though opposing accounts of the Hadrami migratory experience, as seen by Hadramis of different generations.

Hierarchical seniority of the elders and the cultural norms regarding age and wisdom meant that the senior Hadramis' concerns and voices were more forceful than those of the second generation. For example, the senior Hadramis said that their children were 'spoiled' by the Kuwaiti lifestyle of 'buying things', or that the young people were looking for *rahah* (comfort jobs). Also, they thought that young Hadramis showed less gratitude to their *mu'azzib*,[16] or that they were not 'real' Hadramis. Young immigrants occasionally, though not openly, exchanged concerns with their fathers. Avoidance and respect characterised young people's communication with their fathers.[17]

However, several young Hadramis openly criticised their elders' views on almost all issues. They believed that the 'good' reputation of Hadramis in Kuwait, as the model of proper immigrant behaviour, stigmatised older Hadramis who always internalised Kuwaiti expectations.[18] Consequently, many Kuwaitis equate this depiction of Hadramis with 'success' and recognition of their social proximity to Kuwaitis compared to other Arabs working

THE MODEL IMMIGRANT

in Kuwait. The Hadramis' reputation for loyalty and obedience, unlike the reputations of other Arab workers in Kuwait, reflects one aspect of reality. But young Hadramis, such as Fayiz, do not accept these Kuwaiti or Hadrami portrayals. Fayiz thought depictions of this kind were not useful or sufficient:

> If we were successful then why were we excluded from Kuwaiti citizenship or employment opportunities?... When my father came here in the 1960s he did not do good to himself or to us... All he wanted then was the work of *rahah* (comfort) so he worked as *farrash* (a peon). My father had the same job for all his years in Kuwait. Our *'uggal* in the past had a simple rule: get the salary, send home monthly remittances, buy stuffs [sic.] from Kuwait, and when visiting home spend everything, come back and wait for the next salary... Kuwaitis admired our loyalty because we are peaceful and don't cause headaches like other foreigners... My father was *farrash* and I now [am] *mandub* (a courier) for the same *mu'azzib* family, what's the difference!... It's funny when I carry my father's image with me but I can't remove it. Can you delete your father's memory?! If I do, Kuwaitis won't.[19]

Fayiz arrived in 2002 to work as a guard in a business belonging to a prominent Kuwaiti family. He has a diploma in commercial studies, and he also drives and shops for his *mu'azzib* and performs other services for the family outside his original job. Fayiz came to the attention of the research while he was visiting his uncle in hospital. The uncle had worked in Kuwait until he fled in 1990, like thousands of Hadramis, following the Iraqi occupation of Kuwait.[20] Three weeks after his stay at the hospital, his uncle died and Fayiz had to complete all the paperwork for his burial in Kuwait. 'We can't afford to fly him home, or bring his six children here'. Fayiz was somewhat contemptuous about seeking help from the *mu'azzib* to transport his uncle's body for burial in Hadramawt:

> I don't talk to our *mu'azzib* directly on such matters. Only my father can, given his many years of service, but you know that my father had always been reluctant to ask for something like that... My father never asked for a raise for his salary which does not feed a chicken; not seven human beings at home! This is what I get from Kuwait like this: I am born to follow my father's track, I marry before age thirty, I work until I am sixty, if I am lucky I buy a house in Hadramawt in my seventies, after that I give my children the house and die... Kuwaitis say we do not beg or ask for money like others. They say we have dignity and honour, only good words... our situation now is like my grandfather's proverb: *aish telaggi elkobarah bilwajh alshuwam* (make-up cannot beautify an ugly bride).[21]

Other young Hadramis indicated analogous experiences dealing with the legacy and moral weight of good reputation in Kuwait. Fayiz performs extra services to the *mu'azzib* as a way of paying back a 'moral debt' and to protect his father's honour in front of other Hadramis. Within his community, this was part of Fayiz's familial obligations, without which he may not have been able to maintain good relations with his kin and friends in Hadramawt and in Kuwait.[22] In other words, young immigrants such as Fayiz struggle to maintain different forms of loyalties to their family and to their sponsor.

A result of such a position for second-generation Hadramis is the tension it generates between working parents and their working children. Yaslam reacted to the pressure of working closely with a Kuwaiti *mu'azzib* while living with his parents:

> What else do I expect to hear from my *mu'azzib* but words of appreciation, he said I am like his son; of course, we had always been loyal to our [Kuwaiti] families. I only seek my mother and father's happiness, for they taught me to serve without complaining. My father said this: 'You take what is advanced to you by those who enabled us to work, to receive medication... You should thank Allah you work for friends [Kuwaitis] who promised they will give you my place when I die'... Now you asked me why my father didn't make any fortune, didn't even build a house in Hadramawt?... You know why, because we are not Hadramis of Saudi Arabia or the UAE... We can't be like these Hadramis. I can't continue my education for if I do, who will serve my *mu'azzib* and take care of my father? Who will pay for sisters and aunts at home... We are used to being fed to suck on the milk of the 'Kuwaiti cow'... But in reality I see it like we inherit nothing but despair and the 'good reputation' of our father.[23]

Yaslam came to Kuwait in 2004 under visa article no. 20, designated for domestic servants, though he does not work in the house of his *mu'azzib*. He drives the family's children to school, shops for them, and serves coffee at his *mu'azzib*'s *diwaniyya* (men's room).[24] He lives at the back of the *mu'azzib*'s house with his father, who is elderly and is not expected to work. Yaslam is constantly struggling to please two different worlds in his daily life, a balance visible in the way he addresses both his real father and his *mu'azzib* as 'father'. Yaslam is aware of the burdens he is dealing with. Although he does not accept it as his destiny, he has no plans for the time when his biological father will no longer be around.

These narratives may not reflect the entire spectrum of the second generation's migratory experience in Kuwait. Nevertheless, every young Hadrami in the research had experienced tension, doubt, pressure, insecurity, rigid forms of dependency, or the perverseness of good reputation. These originated from three elements: long-standing dependency on an attachment to a Kuwaiti sponsor, Hadrami intergenerational differences, and familial needs. The experience of the new generation is centrally situated at the nexus of sponsor–family–generation. These three elements are social triads and form the basic levels of analysis of migration as a social process. At the sponsorship level, Hadrami immigrants deal with *kafala* (sponsorship) in relation to a *mu'azzib* in daily practices of dependency and domination. At the generational level, young Hadramis face problems of seniority, in which understandings of loyalty vary between parents and children. At the familial level, new immigrants live under constant pressure of demands and specific expectations from peers in Kuwait and at home.

Hadrami migration to Kuwait: the past in the present

Hadrami migration to Kuwait started in the late 1940s and reached a peak during the period between 1955 and 1970. Hundreds of teenagers and children of mainly Hadar origin (agrarian villagers) were sent by their families to work as servants (Kuwaiti dialect: sing. *siby*, pl. *sibyan*) in Kuwaiti houses.[25] Hundreds of Hadrami labourers travelled to Kuwait by boat from coastal towns of Hadramawt such as al-Hami and al-Shihr.[26] They travelled without legal documents because Kuwaiti merchants at the time granted permits for entrance, work and residence in Kuwait and made deals with Hadrami captains who were known to be active in human trafficking.[27] Usually, the labourers were accompanied by elders (pl. *'uggal*, sing. *'agil*), such as parents, family members or fellow villagers. Ashur remembered:

> There were about thirty to forty people from my village alone on the day of our departure in 1958, a dhow was waiting for us, and there were four of us who hadn't reached the age of ten... Other people boarded on the way and there were 100 of us on that small dhow, but we were accompanied by *'uggal*, who took care of us... My mother was praying and crying, on the road I also cried... I then realized that I was away, I was terrified ... I wanted my mother.[28]

Recruitment began once a dhow reached one of the *niq'ah* (old-style port),[29] at which point Hadrami labourers were taken to Kuwaiti homes or shops. Others had to wait in Hadrami *'izbah*s, which were required to have one or more of the *'uggal*, who played a critical role in controlling labourers' incomes, work destinations and the remittances that young immigrants saved or sent home. As a bachelors' house, the *'izbah* still exists today, though it is not as active as it was in the 1960s and 1970s, particularly in its recruitment function. However, one important element of the traditional *'izbah* that endures is the co-existence of different immigrant generations in one place. With intergenerational gaps, new meaning and functions were introduced into the *'izbah*, because as a social space it began to expose more clearly generational powers and familial hierarchies among individuals.

This movement may be termed 'house-to-house' migration because Hadramis who came to Kuwait in that period left their family home to perform domestic services in urban Kuwaiti households. Hadramis were swiftly absorbed into the Kuwaiti domestic sphere for several reasons. In the 1950s, Kuwaiti urban households experienced a dramatic shift caused by a sudden shortage of domestic servants. During that period the state implemented rapid urbanisation and socioeconomic transformations that required the recruitment of massive numbers of foreign labourers.[30] Hence, education and government employment had a very significant effect on Kuwaiti households. In 1966, Kuwait became the first Arab state in the Gulf to introduce mandatory schooling for boys and girls. Families that had traditionally depended on girls to perform domestic activities reacted to the shortage of servants by recruiting immigrants, mostly boy labourers, from regions such as Baluchistan and Oman.

Besides these shifts, the Kuwaiti nationality law of 1959 granted citizenship to disenfranchised local groups such as house slaves, the poor and various social segments, that previously had worked in urban homes.[31] These groups are still referred to as *sibyan* in the Kuwaiti context. Previously, they were seen as dependants attached to 'the house' and formed the most marginalised group in Kuwaiti society. However, citizenship granted these groups free education, housing, and government employment, thus giving them relative independence from the families they served. (Many still work for those households, and even bear the names of the families they first worked for.) It is in this context that Hadramis filled a gap in local domestic services.

Hadramis came when Kuwait's household patriarchy needed to preserve and reinforce volatile relations of dependency that the withdrawal of slaves and local dependent groups had endangered. Dependency relations were to be made prevalent because they indicated the strength of structural and consumptive values within the house. For Kuwaiti families, the introduction of new 'members' of the family (i.e. Hadrami servants) not only safeguarded normative Kuwaiti division of labour within the urban house, but also became a symbolic value in itself.[32]

The role that Hadramis had once performed in Kuwaiti domestic life, however, should not be considered either characteristic or eccentric of the whole Hadrami migratory experience. This is because the vast majority of Hadramis today no longer work in a household; though they continue to be sponsored by affluent and middle-class households, they serve no significant or palpable role in Kuwait's migration economy. Although the *siby* experience preserves a solid Hadrami migratory presence in Kuwait, it nonetheless leaves members

THE MODEL IMMIGRANT

of this group devoid of opportunities. Today, most Hadrami immigrants therefore do not capitalise on any activities other than their monthly income.

A Hadrami is employed because he is a character from the past who encapsulates special family memories related to growth, successful relations, the extension of house rules and generosity of the prosperous. This is perhaps why ordinary Kuwaitis imitate the well-off and recruit Hadramis as 'special servants' who usually perform tasks 'around the house' (meaning for the household), rather than in the house itself. For Kuwaiti sponsor families today, Hadramis are only important because they represent the continuity of past relations governed by foreign labour dependency on the household. 'He reminds me of my husband's days and smell of our house in the real Kuwait of the past.' These were the words of an old Kuwaiti woman at a Souk who was followed by a Hadrami teenager carrying her purchases. Kuwaitis are clearly nostalgic when they recall memories of the 'traditional' or 'authentic' Kuwaiti household. In these narratives, the presence of an old servant figure recalls Kuwaitis' portrayal of a 'healthy' and 'happy' family life in the past.

But Hadramis also exemplify the state's vision of migration, which is based on a paradoxical process of inclusion designed for the purpose of exclusion.[33] This process marks every aspect of Kuwaiti social and daily life in relation to foreigners. To many Kuwaitis the ability to include or exclude and differentiate between themselves and foreigners represents a mechanism of control over massive immigrant populations. This is a privilege of being a citizen. Hadramis embody this process more than any other Arab or non-Arab group in Kuwait, as described by Fahad, a forty-six-year old Kuwaiti businessman. Fahad described Hadramis who worked for his father before the 1990 war: 'They are so peaceful and non-economising, unlike our Lebanese and Egyptian employees who go behind our back for a second job... We respect Hadramis most because they don't want anything from Kuwait, ready to do anything whenever you need them...I wish all foreigners be like them.' In 2011, Fahad sponsored Umar, a Kuwaiti-born Hadrami, to work as his driver. Umar, who is twenty-six years old, lives in a room with two Indian servants at the rear of his *mu'azzib*'s house. Besides his mother and wife, Umar's close family are in Kuwait, hence, some Hadramis see him as privileged, although he described this perception as ironic and onerous. In the next section, Umar's relationship with the sponsor (*mu'azzib*) will be illustrated as the first element in the social triad of Hadrami migration: sponsor–family–generation.

The mu'azzib

A flaw in much research on *kafala* in the Gulf region is its focus on the rudimentary and broad aspects of migration. In this context, sponsorship is examined as a state institution with legal, political and economic apparatuses. Similarly, research on *kafala* in GCC countries has tended to be limited to official categories that standardise sponsorship as an institution and as a language. Sociohistorical and cultural dimensions of *kafala* in immigrants' daily practices in relation to their sponsors are under-researched. In Kuwait, these dimensions have always demarcated each migratory experience in a particular way, and made each immigrant community approach *kafala* differently.

Kafala is a social practice that has its roots in the peculiarities of the history of practice of power not only through exclusion, as attested by Anh Nga Longva, but also inclusion. The degree of exclusion and inclusion of each immigrant community determines its character, presence, mobility, proximity, adaptability, and even economic identity among Kuwaitis and other immigrant communities. Other determinants of its character are factors such as the social level at which immigrants are excluded or included, and how, why and when immigrants are excluded or included. Inclusion, the Hadrami case reveals, is not only achieved through legality of sponsorship, but through other social means as well. This phenomenon might be termed social sponsorship, a practice accentuated by the *mu'azzib*'s personal character.

To show the complexity of sponsorship, a distinction will be made here between the *kafil* (legal sponsor) and the *mu'azzib* (social sponsor). To Hadramis, not every *kafil* is a *mu'azzib*, because a *mu'azzib* may be a person who was simply their first or previous *kafil*. So although a Hadrami can only have one *kafil*, he may also be connected with one or, more uncommonly, two *mu'azzib*s. Generally, the *mu'azzib* is the *kafil* or a direct employer, but this research found that young Hadramis also occasionally referred to their *mu'azzib* when speaking of someone who was once their father's *kafil* or *mu'azzib*. In daily practices, a *mu'azzib* is not directly addressed with this label, but rather as, for example, 'father', 'uncle' or 'father of'. These familial and quasi-kinship terms enable inequalities between Hadramis and Kuwaiti sponsors, as well as dependency through social sponsorship, which is maintained regardless of the legal status of the relationship the Kuwaiti *mu'azzib*.

'The *kafil* dies, but the *mu'azzib*, never.'[34] This has become a common saying among both Hadrami generations, and Umar used them to describe his family's attachment to his sponsor Fahad. Hadramis rarely use the word *kafil*, and

THE MODEL IMMIGRANT

instead refer to the *kafīl* as a *mu'azzib*, while other Arab or non-Arab immigrants use the term *mu'azzib* less frequently. In Kuwait, the *mu'azzib* is a figure that is mostly referred to in familial contexts, indicating a hierarchical order of relationships among individuals. As a term and metaphor the figure of the *mu'azzib* has its roots in Hadar (urban) Kuwaiti values and patronage associations, namely in the position and power of a male head of a family or group of households.[35] People must be visibly dependent on the *mu'azzib* to express his power in local relationships. A *mu'azzib* may be seen as a symbolic figure who epitomises several authorities at once, and also as the holder of a social and moral position that even ordinary Kuwaitis may aspire to as a result of being a *kafīl*. Nowadays, a *mu'azzib* can be a boss at work, a shop owner, an old patron, or a legal *kafīl*. In the context of migration, he captures the power of official establishment, but always has control over others' activities and has power to order their lives.

Umar's father started working for Fahad's father—who died in 1997—in 1970, and although he is beyond the legal age for foreign residency in Kuwait, through *wastah* (favouritism) the *mu'azzib* has been able to extend his residency multiple times at the Ministry of Interior. Umar's father does not pay rent; he lives in a small apartment at the old house of his deceased *mu'azzib*, which has been divided into several rooms that are let to other immigrants. Umar sends money to his father, who also receives endorsements during Eid from the *mu'azzib* and other family members. With no specific duties to carry out, he visits Hadramawt twice a year and stays for at least two months at a time. It is quite depressing for Umar that his father should be travelling at that age, without a fixed purpose or timescale.

Umar's father's frequent visits home embody an emerging pattern of what might be termed the 'visiting-feeding' immigrant. This type of movement is prevalent among the elderly generation and ex-immigrants. After many years in Kuwait, these *uggal* become totally dependent on the country, not only as a source of income but also as a system of social security. Umar's father's return to Kuwait is explicitly made for specific reasons, such as for medication (*baghaina nit'afa*), to eat real food (*nakul rayyith*) and to be comfortable (*baghaina nirtah*). Umar's father must regularly visit his sponsor's office and house to show his gratitude and pay his respects, and to greet the children of his *mu'azzib*. To many, such a move is understood as repayment of a moral debt, for the 'generosity' of the Kuwaiti for sponsoring them.

> Fahad is the son of my old *mu'azzib*, I raised him, took him to school as a child, this is why he brought Umar here. He is in no obligation to receive me or extend my

75

residency, I don't clean his house or open the office door for him every day... And he wants me around with him because he is very kind, just like his father.[36]

To the *mu'azzib*, the presence of Umar's father around the house is an indication of the well-being of his family. It simultaneously maintains the father's legacy of caring for the family's dependants and asserts before peers of his class the continuation of male power in the family.

Umar's daily life is divided into two worlds, in which he struggles to satisfy the daily requests and instruction of his father and his *mu'azzib*. To do this, he needs to preserve the good reputation of his father and continue to be dependent on the goodwill of the *mu'azzib*. Umar described his conflicting needs:

> Always infuriating my head is what shall I do when my father is no longer alive?! I don't ask my father about that prediction, I know it will happen sooner or later, but my father keeps repeating 'stick to your *mu'azzib*' whenever I express a desire to continue education... It is this 'stick to your *mu'azzib*' that is killing me, it's like a 'shut up' if I just think of elevating my position and be more useful than a driver... I am sure our *mu'azzib* doesn't see me any good but a driver or a courier, I mean good only as a *siby*, as you know.[37]

Emotionally, Umar needs his father around, yet this only generates more uncertainty about his presence in Kuwait. Studies of second-generation immigrants have found their experiences to consist of relentless doubts and justifications of their presence in a foreign land.[38] In this context, Umar evidently remains an immigrant so long as he is situated within the realm and history of the relationship between his father and the Kuwaiti household. For this reason, he constantly raised doubts about the reasons for his migration, work and return after his father's death:

> I don't know why the *mu'azzib* would need me when my father passes away, he can have as many Egyptian drivers as he likes. If I stay here I will be a *siby* the rest of my life. If I leave what job shall I find [at] home? I'm used to Kuwait... I will not go anywhere.[39]

Hadramis rarely protest about the length of their working day. Kuwaiti labour law limits working hours to eight hours a day. But Umar was rather cynical: 'I am a driving-*siby* not a driver, they [Kuwaiti family] don't call me the *sayiq* (driver), they are proud to call me the *siby*, you know like the *siby* of old Kuwait'. Hadramis' working relationship with their *mu'azzibs* is often characterised by their availability and readiness to serve. The greater his availability, the more tasks Umar is given. This availability creates more attachment between him and the *mu'azzib*, but also puts more obligation on Umar to serve like a *siby*. His readiness has meant that Umar was prepared to take on additional tasks on top of his original job, such as pouring coffee and tea at his *mu'azzib*'s *diwaniyya* and driving guests and family members around at night well after his bed time.

The continuation of the *siby* lifestyle is reflected in Umar's daily activities. Every day, Umar wakes up at 5.00 am, drives children to their schools at different locations, and then goes back to take his *mu'azzib* to work at 8.00 am. There he is sometimes instructed to receive shipments from the airport, go to embassies to deal with family passports, or complete paperwork for his *mu'azzib* at government offices. Usually, Umar's working day exceeds 10 hours. In fact, his working hours, like his peers', are not specified or discussed with his *mu'azzib*. Umar's availability and readiness to serve is commended by the *mu'azzib* whenever Kuwaiti friends visit on Saturday nights. Here, Kuwaitis see how the 'father of the house' has embraced Umar and given him job out of 'generosity' and 'kindness,' but also because Umar symbolises the subjective memory of the 'house'.

> You think I need him? Of course... But why does he need me if there are four Philippinos inside the big house, another driver from India, and two other Indians and an Egyptian for the men's gathering?... When Kuwaitis come and see me they ask my *mu'azzib*: could you get me someone like Umar?! This is how my cousin Salim came here.[40]

Salim's experience sheds light on the second element of the social triad of Hadrami migration, the family.

The family

Dedication to family and kinship is vital in the context of migration, not only because it represents genealogical actualities, but also because it is an essential value around which young Hadramis organise their everyday lives. Although the vast majority of Hadramis in Kuwait assume bachelor lifestyles, second-generation Hadramis' obligations towards their families at home function as a resource and a constraint.[41] Salim, who is thirty years old, has worked as a courier for a Kuwaiti bank since 2010. He has a diploma in teaching. Although he works for the bank, he is closely attached to one Kuwaiti manager there. Salim's father worked as a *siby* at the manager's house from 1963, and in 1980 moved out of the house to work at the *mu'azzib*'s shops. Salim shares two rooms of an *'izbah* with five young Hadramis in the immigrant-populated slum area of *jilib al-shuyukh*. Every Friday night, others join him for a communal meal. Regular topics at their gatherings revolve around families and friends in Kuwait and at home. Perhaps the most depressing and time-consuming topic among *'izbah* inhabitants is the demands (*talabat*) family and friends at home make. They refer to demands as *qalaq* (headaches), which are normally expressed through a mobile text message or brief phone call. They may satisfy demands with remittances, either in the form of money transfers or shipments of goods and items. In either case, the Hadrami immigrants' salaries are severely dented. Immigrants returning to Kuwait from a visit home bring back with them written, often lengthy, lists of *talabat* that they are expected to satisfy.

Sending remittances not only maintains or strengthens social relations, but indicators such as the type, length, or authors of the *talabat* usually show an individual's level of success in his relations with kin and family members.[42] Providing remittances is also used to justify one's stay abroad, as Salim noted:

> Our people in Hadramawt think just because I work in Kuwait that I have millions, if I don't send them money they wouldn't greet me when I visit, or they would say: 'Here he comes, played in Kuwait and was relaxed like Kuwaitis and doesn't care about relatives'... I don't know how to satisfy everyone, they always ask for more, I think now they want me to stay here to work for them.[43]

Family relations influence migrants' movements and decisions about when to return, particularly if they have been unable to send remittances and to satisfy the pressure of demands from home. As the data shows, the marital status of second-generation Hadramis in Kuwait is determined by how they send remittances and hence interact with people at home. In this regard, second-generation immigrants may be divided into three categories. Firstly, those Hadramis who left their spouses behind and do not think of bringing them to Kuwait. Secondly, the minority of immigrants whose wives and children join them in Kuwait. And finally, young Hadramis such as Salim whose main motivation for migrating to Kuwait was as part of a marriage plan. The amount of remittances sent home does not differ from one category to another. For example, although Yemeni immigrants in Kuwait enrol their children in public schools at no costs, they have to cope with the rising prices and expenses of rent, larger amounts of food, children's medication, their wives' demands, and entertainment. The average income of second-generation Hadramis is 200 Kuwaiti dinars (150,000 Yemeni rials, or US$600), which makes a vast majority legally ineligible to bring over their wives.[44]

Balancing the flow of demands and maintaining family and kin relations is a complicated exercise. This is perhaps why Salim decided to return home permanently, although his monthly salary was 250 Kuwaiti dinars (190,000

THE MODEL IMMIGRANT

Yemeni rials, or US$750). With no capacity to save, his debt accumulated, which he mainly incurred to meet his family's *talabat*.[45] His decision to return was very difficult for him, yet his reasoning was clear: 'There my mother and friends can see that I am poor like them, I have nothing to hide, they will stop asking for Kuwaiti stuff and burdening me with expenses. I am happy now.' Salim returned home to be a teacher in the village. Comparing his Kuwaiti salary with his average teaching salary in the village (25,000 Yemeni rials, or US$60), his family and *'izbah* members sternly criticised him. However, for those immigrants who are similar to Salim in terms of age, income and educational qualifications, the decision to stay is equally difficult.[46] To illustrate the economic strain of being an immigrant, compare the average young Hadrami's monthly income (200 Kuwaiti dinars, or US$600) with Salim's monthly salary and expenses.

Table 4.1: Cost comparison of a typical immigrant's income and expenses

Category	Cost (in Kuwaiti dinars)[47]
Total income	250
Contribution to *'izbah* rent	30
Remittances (money and goods)	120
Phone calls	40
Personal expenses	30
Food	20
Total expenses	240
Total monthly savings	10

Besides these payments, Salim's plans to marry the following year may only be achievable by two means: firstly, with the *mu'azzib*'s assistance in the form of endorsements, which in most cases are not specified and merely cover tiny portions of an immigrant's marriage budget; or secondly, by borrowing money from family members or fellow immigrants, whom he would need to repay when he got a job after returning home.[48] Customarily, families share the following marriage expenses, which are standard among Hadrami immigrants. Hence, Salim's prospective expenditures are as follows.

Salim may not be able to collect his entire family share on his return if he has to depend on his salary alone. He knows that families at home will seriously review their decisions to marry their daughters to an empty-handed returnee.

> I will seek help from the people I used to send remittances to and care for when I was abroad, but I know I will one day depend on my father, although he doesn't talk

to me anymore because I am returning to home... He thinks I am a failure, he wants me to be like him.[49]

Table 4.2: Breakdown of typical marriage expenses

Husband's family's contribution	Cost (in Yemeni rials)
Room and furniture	150,000
Dowry (money and gold)	250,000
Men's wedding dinner	50,000
Wedding lunch	100,000
Entertainment for guests	50,000
Subhah[50]	100,000
Total	700,000
Wife's family's contribution	
Women's wedding lunch	100,000
Complement of dowry and gold	700,000
Luxuries and personal care items	150,000
Total	950,000

During his migration, Salim created new relationships, and in some cases reconstructed damaged ones, but his departure from Kuwait has damaged close family ties. Salim's father said to him, 'You lowered my face in front of our *mu'azzib* who gave you a job, and now you say you don't need him, let me see who will help you!' Ironically, for Salim to rebuild his relationship with his father he will need to show reliance on his father's support when he is home in order to legitimise his father's dependency on their *mu'azzib*. The fissure Salim's decision has created in his relationship with his father is somewhat atypical in this community, but the tensions between father and son or in young–older migrants' relationships are not uncommon, though they may be minimised or disguised in daily encounters. Nowadays, such tensions point to intergenerational differences concerning the meaning and prospects of migration for work within family and kin contexts.

The generation

Migration as a process and practice creates its own social realm and forms of association according to its context. Generational differences in the migration context have to be analysed through young immigrants' conceptualisation and enactment of the tensions and loyalties that exist between them and their parents. Generational differences may not be limited to age or experience, but must be defined as a 'kin relationship' that is peculiar to migration processes.[51] Seen as a special kin relationship, such differences offer important insights into intergenerational associations that illustrate the diversity of understanding, choices, and experiences of family and kin ties during migration. That young Hadramis such as Umar, Fayiz and Salim have little choice other than to realise their parents' wishes and the needs of family and kin is a consequence and expression of kin relationships that might not have developed at home.

The effect of kin relationships in commanding immigrants' lives can be seen in ordinary Hadrami situations where the dominant mode of conversation takes the form of short and intimate statements, gestures of disciplinary respect, and often silence. For example, in the attitude survey more than 85 per cent of young Hadramis described their fathers' experiences in Kuwait as successful. This was clearly negated by all second-generation Hadramis during interviews and daily interactions and when seniors were absent. Among young immigrants only, kin relationships and the tensions and allegiances they produce were the main subjects of conversation during the research process.

Success and dependency highlighted generational differences. Second-generation Hadramis in Kuwait are ashamed of their status compared to their compatriots in Saudi Arabia and the UAE, who became citizens and are ubiquitous in large-scale finance and state politics.[52] The degree of success or failure, as seen by most of the second generation, ensues from the migratory condition and roles their fathers developed and accepted during their years in Kuwait. Mubarak, aged thirty-seven, was born in Kuwait and fled with his family following the 1991 Gulf War.[53] His father is retired now, but he has visited Kuwait twice to receive medical attention and *raḥah* (comfort). Mubarak works as a cashier alongside his older brother Naser, aged forty-one, a courier for a prominent Kuwaiti financier. Mubarak's description of success highlighted the tension that shapes intergenerational relationships resulting from migration:

> I eat, sleep, and spin in shopping malls, like Kuwaitis and Hadramis in UAE, but I don't ride a land cruiser, I don't have citizenship or a house...When I visit my village in the summer and meet with Salah coming from Dubai with lots of money and a four-wheel [drive] Lexus, and soon he opens his family house in the village for visitors for lunch and dinner every day, I feel lowered and try to hide like a woman from others until I return to Kuwait, where no one is higher than you, we are all

couriers... The education I got from my father before coming here is to thank Allah for what we have, and thank Kuwait for our refuge and sustenance.[54]

Senior Hadramis, particularly those who could secure a place for their children in the same household they once worked for, perceive success in a different way. Among elders, the relationship with the *mu'azzib* characterises success. Someone is successful if his dependency (elders would say 'friendship' or 'relationship') was strong enough to become a kind of capital and a lifelong source of income and security. During his visit to Kuwait, Mubarak's father was asked what advice he would give to his sons and other young Hadramis: 'Be aware of where you are and who you work for and show courtesy and be loyal to those [Kuwaiti *kafil* or *mu'azzib*] who helped you always carry money [income] in your pockets.' Not only elders see success in terms of dependency on and proximity to the *mu'azzib*. Mubarak's brother's understanding of his choices in Kuwait and his success were clearly influenced by their father's advice: 'When your *mu'azzib* always needs you, when you are cherished by him (*tan'az*), isn't that good friendship? When he doesn't need money from me but he gives [it to] me, this is because I am good and respectful... I see this [as] success, what else do I need in life?'[55] This view of success may explain why Hadramis have mostly positioned themselves close to powerful people in Kuwait, while being excluded from the means of power itself. To old Hadrami immigrants this could be the most effective approach to migration to Kuwait and their greatest moral achievement. To second-generation immigrants, however, this is exactly what has discouraged mobilising, saving, future planning, and any serious attempt to achieve Kuwaiti citizenship.

Old relations of dependence transcended the political and social boundaries between Kuwait and Hadramawt. Mubarak described how old people such as his father and father-in-law, all retired immigrants, are now totally dependent on Kuwait as their only means of livelihood and source of income. The dependency of these ex-immigrants illustrates the persistence of migration as a lifestyle even in retirement.[56] Mubarak compared his migratory experience to the pattern of Hadrami dependency: 'Our fathers threw us in a situation like you are digging a hole into rock-solid ground for many years thinking you are building a shelter, but you discover one day that you were slowly digging your own grave.'[57]

Most of the second generation acknowledged that their families and kin depended on their income. A problem for the second-generation immigrants is that their families and kin expect the flow of remittances either in cash or goods to be constant. However, some Hadramis in Kuwait were anxious not only about the continuation of remittances, but also about the future of their own presence as immigrants in Kuwait. In other words, the issue of income security as related to the political future of Kuwait is noticeably becoming a disturbing issue for both Hadrami generations.

Kuwait's history of territorial insecurity has had cruel effects on its massive immigrant population.[58] The elimination of Kuwait as a state during the Iraqi occupation in 1990 made young Hadramis doubtful about the political prospects of Kuwait as a secure source of income. Hence, somebody such as Mubarak defines security as better working conditions and freedom to change one's occupation. Similarly, for others like Mubarak one form of compensation for living in an insecure place is increased income that allows the accumulation of savings and building a house at home as quickly as possible. While the majority of second-generation Hadramis surveyed did not have entrepreneurial skills—'like the Palestinians and the Lebanese'[59]—most wished to improve their working conditions to pursue either education or another job. Mubarak expressed his expectations and frustrations about his working conditions:

> I don't want to spend my life as a cashier, what is my qualification but that the *mu'azzib* trusts us [Hadramis] not to steal his money... I know our *mu'azzib* doesn't trust other Arabs who manage his office, they are not as loyal as we are, but their salaries increase and their children follow their track, they don't remain as cashiers, only one or two years and the *mu'azzib* gives them promotions to become my supervisors... Trust is good but trust doesn't make you money.[60]

Comparative migratory cases reflected intergenerational differences in convictions and worldviews regarding social upward mobility and uncertainty about the future.[61] Interviewees said that if they express a desire to elevate their position or even to change their *kafil*, their endeavours are disregarded and described as *'ayb* (disgrace) for betraying their *mu'azzib*. Other *'uggal* ridicule their children's desire for upward mobility, arguing that they cannot tolerate heavy work responsibilities and risks as other Arab employees can. Very few immigrants have seriously attempted to challenge the kin relationships in terms of loyalties to the *mu'azzib* or adherence to instructions. Mubarak unhappily commented, 'We are stuck here, I bet you will find me as I am ten years from now, if you see an opportunity up there your closest kin will drag you down.'

As a form of migratory kin relationships, Hadrami intergenerational differences inform each generation's perspective on success and dependency. Thus, while *'uggal* see these as intertwined in a positive relationship, second-generation Hadramis view dependency as an obstacle to individual upward mobility; it therefore contrasts with their understanding of success as promotion and wealth in migration. The gap between the practical realities of migration and second-generation Hadramis' aspiration for success is wide. For young Hadramis such as Mubarak, success is to be like a 'real' Hadrami, or a 'Saudi-Hadrami'.

Conclusion

For many years, and throughout the *mu'azzib* attachment, first-generation Hadramis internalised hierarchical inequalities between locals and foreigners. For Kuwaiti *mu'azzibs*, their relations with Hadrami dependants are the ideal in comparison to relations with all other immigrants. The image of Hadramis as 'the best people' is sustained in Kuwaiti public life and social memory by affluent and ordinary Kuwaiti families. This, however, does not mean that old immigrants were totally passive in the process. Continuities of the domestic role and dependency practice perpetuate each other but also maintain a Hadrami presence in Kuwait regardless of the actual economic roles Hadramis fulfil. The research has shown how the concept of the 'model immigrant' has profound effects on the lives of the new generation of Hadramis in their relations with the *mu'azzib*, their families and their fathers. Unrelenting Kuwaiti and Hadrami seniors' expectations about their behaviour and mobility compared to other Arab and non-Arab immigrants shatter young Hadramis' aspirations. Many young Hadramis attempt to disengage from the image and practices their fathers developed during years of attachment to and reliance on Kuwaiti connections for their basic livelihoods. Yet ethnography and anecdotal narratives reveal an inauspicious reality for second-generation Hadramis. Young Hadramis' daily activities in Kuwait and their aspirations for individual self-sufficiency can only be achieved by maintaining a difficult balance between the elements of the social triad, and by managing, or perhaps preserving, the legacy of a good reputation.

5

THE EGYPTIAN 'INVASION' OF KUWAIT

NAVIGATING POSSIBILITIES AMONG THE IMPOSSIBLE

Abbie Taylor, Nada Soudy and *Susan Martin*[1]

Introduction

It was almost three in the afternoon on a Friday when we decided to go to an area located west of Kuwait City where we discovered a microcosm of the Egyptian capital, with crowds of people and traffic jams, the atmosphere and the landmarks as if it were Cairo....

The newspaper article entitled 'Khaitan: Cairo in Kuwait' from which this excerpt is taken depicts a working-class area with small businesses, shops and popular coffeehouses (*'ahwas*) in a transnational space that is, according to the author, 'overcome' by thousands of Egyptians—the majority of them men from Upper Egypt.[2]

Elsewhere, throughout the bustling residential and commercial areas of Hawally and Salmiya, working- and middle-class Egyptians, Jordanians, Lebanese, Syrians and Indians are found living alone or with their families in apartment blocks. Many of these buildings employ an Egyptian security guard, or *bawwab*, as Egyptians and often Kuwaitis and others refer to them. Since the construction of Saint Mark's Coptic Orthodox Church in Hawally, more members of its congregation—the vast majority of them Egyptians—are vying to move into the area. Small businesses and restaurants run by non-Kuwaitis nestle among shopping malls and restaurant chains, including a 'Cairo Pharmacy' and 'Tahrir Square Restaurant' in one street. While Kuwaitis live in these neighbourhoods, most others appear to pass in and out, taking trips to malls and restaurants, or looking for specific goods to buy from reputable dealers in electronics, sweets and tobacco among other things. The quieter residential areas of Jabriya and Salwa, close to Hawally and Salmiya, are home to Kuwaitis and a smaller number of Egyptians, among other wealthier expatriates. Other parts of Kuwait City include affluent residential areas that appear to be inhabited by Kuwaitis only—or in stark contrast—places such as Jleeb Shuyoukh, portrayed in the media as a crime-ridden ghetto, an ugly reality of society, and host to large numbers of Asian expatriates and *bidoon* (stateless Arabs who claim Kuwaiti nationality).[3]

The phrase 'Egyptians are everywhere' is not uncommon in Kuwait, and when asked, people may guess that the number of Egyptians is double the government estimate of 1 million, or 'equal to the number of Kuwaitis'. Jokes exist among Kuwaitis around what one described as the 'Egyptian invasion of Kuwait', while Egyptians for their part quip that 'between every Kuwaiti and Egyptian in Kuwait, there is another Egyptian'.

Numbers provide a point of entry into this study of Egyptians in Kuwait, as with other studies of Arab and non-Arab migrant communities in the Gulf. Egyptian consular statistics from 2012 suggest that some 480,000 Egyptians live in Kuwait.[4] For the same year, according to the Kuwaiti Ministry of Interior's General Administration for Immigration, almost half a million (456,000) Egyptians reside in the city—a slight increase from 453,000 in the previous year—and work in a variety of occupations. Egyptians constitute the largest Arab expatriate community in Kuwait, and the second-largest non-Kuwaiti population after some 653,000 Indian migrants.[5] Together, these communities make up more than half of the number of migrants, which in turn constitutes almost two-thirds of the total population of Kuwait. Egyptians comprise around 15 per cent of the total population, while Kuwaitis make up 35.5 per cent—1,089,969 people, according to the 2011 census.[6]

Egyptians are woven into Kuwait's landscape and have been for decades. By virtue of their omnipresence and lived investment in the country, Egyptians are heavily reliant on and intrinsic to Kuwait, its citizenry and its various forms of social, political and economic production. In this chapter, drawing on extensive interviews with Egyptians and Kuwaitis, we explore three main questions: How has Egyptian migration to Kuwait changed over time? In what ways do Egyptian expatriates and their Kuwaiti hosts perceive and interact with one another against official ideology, and within the time limits placed on migrants' lives in Kuwait? And what, if any, are the implications of political and socio-economic instability in Egypt on the well-being and migration trajectories of Egyptians in Kuwait? In response to these questions, our findings encourage adaptations within the parameters of existing state responses to inter-regional migration that could reduce longstanding human insecurities among Arab migrants in Kuwait, which have been exacerbated since the start of the Arab uprisings in 2011.

Implicit throughout the chapter is the framing paradox identified by Neha Vora in her study of the Indian diaspora in Dubai: namely, how Egyptians, as 'impossible citizens' suspended in a state of 'permanent temporariness', experience, narrate and negotiate their existence in Kuwait.[7] In making sense of these intricacies, in particular how Egyptians manipulate and are manipulated by the structures in which they find themselves, we also draw on Attiya Ahmad's 'Beyond Labour: Foreign Residents in the Persian Gulf States'. This analytical lens, which extends beyond the limitations and obfuscations of labour and economic concerns, focuses on 'historical inter-regional relations and contemporary forms of socio-political belonging'. Such an approach thus highlights the various forms and processes of the 'production of space' that are visible in the everyday lives of Egyptian expatriates and their Kuwaiti hosts at sites of exclusion and inclusion, respectively.[8]

Our micro-level analysis erodes somewhat the notion of Gulf 'exceptionalism', as alluded to in the introduction of this volume. In common with other international migrants, Egyptians find themselves at the mercy of national migration policies that are based more on domestic political and economic expediency than on the rights of migrants themselves. Yet, as in other parts of the world, individuals show varying degrees of adaptability and resourcefulness after turning to mobility as a means by which to live out their lives and achieve certain milestones. Although not exceptional to the Gulf region, the timing of this study, conducted in 2013 during a period of political and socio-economic turbulence in Egypt, makes it an acute example of how the divergence of national migration policies and individual aspirations can foster conditions under which the isolation of 'otherness', thwarted ambition, uncertainty and fear over premature return colour people's everyday lives.[9]

Following a brief review of the research methodology, this chapter begins by narrating the 'Egyptianisation' of inter-regional Arab migration to Kuwait in the twentieth century, describing how migration opportunities, which the Egyptian state sponsored, laid the foundations for an evolving but enduring legacy of temporary migration to Kuwait. From this we discern that Egyptian migration to Kuwait escaped, though not entirely unscathed, from the de-Arabisation of labour amid shifting regional alignments and increasing wealth disparity. After exploring the logics and informal structures of governance within Kuwait today, we then show how Egyptians navigate a degree of social and economic mobility in Kuwait, though these negotiations rarely succeed in eroding prejudices or extending existential time limits placed on their lives in Kuwait.

Methodology

The research on which this study is based includes interviews conducted with Egyptians and Kuwaitis who were known to key informants identified within our personal and professional networks. Additionally, during fieldwork in August and September 2013, we convened group discussions with Egyptians, participated in Egyptian and Kuwaiti social gatherings, and attended meetings with experts and officials. Egyptian and Kuwaiti students living in Kuwait were among the key informants. We also recruited these students and trained them in basic methods and ethics to conduct anonymous interviews with a cross-section of men and women of varying socio-economic backgrounds, migration histories and occupations within their own networks and daily routines.

Overall, a total of fifty interviews were conducted (ten with Kuwaitis and forty with Egyptians) in cafés, homes, and places of work, depending on the preferred location of the participant.[10] Of the Egyptians interviewed, twenty-five were men and fifteen women, with half the participants (twenty) describing themselves as 'single' or 'divorced', while the others were married with spouses in Kuwait or Egypt. Participants ranged in age from twenty to sixty-two years old, and while the majority of interviewees (twenty-nine) were born in Egypt, eleven were second- or third-generation Egyptians born in Kuwait. Places of origin among Egyptian participants—or parents of participants in the case of second-generation Egyptians—extended across rural and urban areas of Egypt, with fourteen interviewees coming from around Cairo, ten from Sohag and Asyut in Upper Egypt, six from Alexandria, three from Giza, three from Sharqiya, and four from Tanta and Mansoura in the governorates of Gharbiya and Dakhliya, respectively. Of the forty Egyptian interviewees, twenty-six had received or were studying for a Bachelor degree or higher in Egypt or Kuwait, six had attained a high school diploma, six had completed middle school, one had finished primary school, and one described himself as illiterate and never having received formal schooling.[11] In terms of employment in Kuwait, eighteen worked in highly skilled occupations in engineering, education, medicine, banking, sales, accountancy, and public sector administration; four were university students; ten were employed in skilled occupations as receptionists, secretaries, journalists and shopkeepers; and eight worked in low-skill occupations as waiters, plumbers, taxi drivers, security guards, or janitorial staff.[12] Kuwaitis interviewed were closer in age (between nineteen and thirty-five) due to the snowball sample method of recruitment. Of the six male and four female participants, five of those interviewed were university students in Kuwait, three had their own businesses, one worked in banking, and one was a lawyer.

An enduring and evolving presence

Developing Kuwait

In July 2013, two days after Mohammed Morsi had been ousted and five days before Kuwait seized this window of geo-political opportunity to pledge a congratulatory US$4 billion aid package to Egypt as it relapsed into military-backed rule, the Kuwaiti ambassador to Egypt was pictured presenting the Egyptian Scientific Academy with a rare historic document. It detailed correspondence between an Egyptian academic and a Kuwaiti donor to the academy in 1911 and self-proclaimed 'lover of Egypt', and was offered as a symbol of the longstanding ties between the two 'brotherly' nations.[13]

The history of exchange between the two countries precedes independence, dating back to the late nineteenth century when Kuwaiti students began arriving in Egypt to receive their education. In the 1930s, after deadly outbreaks of tuberculosis and smallpox that killed more than 4,000 people in the busy port town of Kuwait City, the authorities launched a free health system for every citizen, which stipulated the need to call on the expertise of hundreds of foreign doctors, particularly from Egypt but also from Iraq, Syria and Palestine, to provide medical care.[14] Newly established Kuwaiti courts also enforced laws borrowed from Egypt in particular, recruiting Egyptian legal experts to lead the legal reform process, along with Palestinian and Jordanian civil servants for assistance in the construction of fledgling government establishments.[15]

This early Egyptian migration to Kuwait, initiated by a passage of expert pioneers tasked with accelerating the social, economic and spatial production of Kuwait, expanded under Gamal Abdel Nasser's promulgation of pan-Arabism. Along these lines, the 1950s saw the arrival of education professionals sent by the Egyptian government, which coincided with Kuwait's ambitious development strategy. Recalling her father's memories of secondary school, a Kuwaiti woman described a young Egyptian man who used to memorise Nasser's speeches before standing on a balcony to recite them to crowds of cheering Kuwaiti students in the school courtyard. When the Kuwaiti authorities established a number of new schools in the hope that such facilities would transform Kuwait into a Middle Eastern hub for education, it was to Egypt that they applied for teachers and expert educational advisers, on salaries paid by the Egyptian government, while the majority of Kuwaitis who attended university continued to travel to Egypt for their higher education.[16]

This largely unprecedented economic opportunity afforded middle-class Egyptians the chance to work abroad in positions of relative power and influence for 'socially accepted' purposes that the state legitimised and encouraged.[17] Amid widespread Arab nationalist fervour, Egyptians came from a firmly established state that was, ideologically speaking, what many others aspired to achieve in their vision of a great Arab nation, but one that was only just beginning to realise the potential domestic and foreign policy gains of exporting its population.

While a relatively small number of Egyptians were among those instrumental in the initial phase of 'laying the foundations' for basic infrastructure and development in the lead-up to Kuwaiti independence, larger numbers of Jordanians and Palestinians, Lebanese and Iranians constituted the majority of the 247,000 non-Kuwaitis in 1965.[18] Indeed, the non-Kuwaitis were the perceived target of attempts to balance demographics and demand for development that began in the 1960s. These efforts on the part of the Kuwaiti authorities were enshrined in the Alien Residence Law and the Nationality Law of 1959, in addition to the Labour Law of 1964 and further decrees in the late 1960s. A major objective and indeed a lingering dichotomy in Kuwaiti policy, according to Sharon Stanton Russell, was the need to achieve essential economic growth by continuing to allow the relatively free import of labour, counterbalanced by the ruling family's desire to maintain stability. Russell goes on to observe that this balance was considered possible through control of entry, internal movement, and the rights and employment of aliens by way of work and residence permits, on the one hand; and, on the other, the strengthening of Kuwait's foreign policy of neutrality and reciprocity, facilitating visa waivers for friendly Arab states—most notably a large influx of Palestinians and Jordanians following the 1967 war and Israeli occupation.[19] However, as an article published in the Kuwaiti magazine *Al Siyasah* indicated, Kuwaitis were uneasy about the paradoxical presence of non-Kuwaitis:

> The head of Section is a Kuwaiti... but who runs the section?
> The speech is made by a Kuwaiti... but who writes the speech?
> The press is run by Kuwaiti editors... but who writes the pieces?
> The water is drunk by Kuwaitis... but who produces the water?
> The schools are for Kuwaiti students... but who teaches the Kuwaitis?
> The Members of Parliament are Kuwaitis... but who are the parliamentary experts?[20]

Amid public pressure at the end of the 1960s, the authorities' attempts to rein in immigration exposed non-Kuwaitis to higher living costs and placed their residency in Kuwait at the mercy of a Kuwaiti employer and sponsor through the universal establishment of a sponsorship system (*kafala*). Other restrictions precluded non-Kuwaiti ownership of industrial and financial institutions, and imposed stricter deportation provisions.

The attraction of oil wealth

When Egypt endured significant losses after the 1967 Arab–Israeli war, it was to Kuwait—alongside Saudi Arabia and Libya—that Nasser turned for financial support to alleviate the economic fallout from the war. In return, he shifted his political rhetoric from that of a champion of Arab radicalism to that of leader of the anti-Zionist movement until his death in 1970.[21] It was in this context of growing regional tumult and wealth disparity that more Egyptians from all rungs of society began to travel to the Gulf—a trend that continues to play out to this day.

In the early 1970s, with quadrupling oil revenues in the Gulf, the Egyptian government under Anwar Sadat's *infitah* (opening up) established migration (permanent and temporary) as a right in the constitution.[22] Certain administrative and bureaucratic restrictions on migration were also lifted, including restrictions on military conscription, exit visas and passport-processing, in a bid to ease the burden of a growing population on the Egyptian public sector during a protracted period of stagnation in economic growth.[23] Simultaneously, the Kuwaiti development plan from 1976/77 to 1981/82 enshrined the state's hunger to make strides as a nation by giving greater priority to increasing manpower by importing new migrants.[24] By the time of the 1975 census in Kuwait, the number of Egyptians had increased from 11,021 ten years previously to 60,534, as a burgeoning and malleable Egyptian expatriate workforce began assimilating into all areas of economic activity, in particular emerging areas of building and construction through private-sector contracts, as well as bilateral agreements between the Egyptian and Kuwaiti governments.[25]

The impact of these incoming migrants from lower-skilled professions was clearly visible. In 1985, four years after Sadat institutionalised emigration through the establishment of the Ministry of State for Emigration Affairs, the number of Egyptians in Kuwait was estimated to be more than 160,000, while the number of work permits issued to other Arabs, namely Palestinians and Jordanians, declined.[26] These newly arrived Egyptians, sharing a far greater variety of educational and socio-economic characteristics than the existing elite, also brought with them new social institutions and cultural symbols of 'Egyptianness', which they imprinted on the Kuwaiti landscape. Popular Egyptian restaurants and coffee shops appeared in Kuwait, many of them visible today, and unlike the earlier period, the presence of ordinary Egyptian workers in public places became a common sight.[27]

By early 1990, an unofficial report from the International Labour Organization (ILO) estimated that there were 215,000 Egyptians in Kuwait, 180,000 of whom were active in the labour force.[28] Conditions for migration to Kuwait in the 1980s were less favourable than in the previous decades due to a combination of an economic downturn, the ebb of Arab nationalism and increasing demand for cheaper labour from Asia, security concerns and heightened attempts to institutionalise and implement 'Kuwaitisation' policies.[29] But this did not stem the flow of Egyptian workers, whose government for the most part was more favourably aligned politically and economically with Kuwait than others in the region.[30] More importantly, Egyptians were willing to do jobs that Kuwaitis were not, and able to do those that many were not yet qualified to take, for lower wages than other expatriate populations would have demanded.

Post-invasion opportunity

The Iraqi invasion of Kuwait in August 1990 increased fears among Kuwaitis of domestic and regional insecurity, and fundamentally altered the make-up of the non-Kuwaiti population, particularly among Arab expatriates across the region.

It also 'emboldened' the Kuwaiti authorities to make it more explicit that immigration policies must prioritise national security, in addition to further decreasing benefits and raising living costs for expatriates, increasing restrictions on family reunification, and minimising the length of residency in Kuwait, as well as preventing integration and settlement.[31] Another practice following the invasion, though less systematic and articulated in policy, was more consideration for the need to control the balance and diversity of the expatriate population, based on ethnicity and nationality.[32]

Two months into the Iraqi occupation in October 1990, an estimated 1.6 million people—almost sixty per cent of the total population—fled Kuwait, with the Iraqi invasion achieving, at least temporarily, what restrictive migration policies had previously failed to do.[33] As some 158,000 Egyptian expatriates left the country, assisted through evacuations or in some cases fleeing in their cars across the desert until they reached Egypt, tens of thousands of Egyptian troops arrived in Kuwait to fight on the front lines alongside Coalition forces in Operation Desert Storm.[34] There is little doubt that the Egyptian decision to support Kuwait during the war was tied to the need for economic stability. Supporting Iraq would have cost Egypt its ability to secure labour contracts for Egyptians in Kuwait and Saudi Arabia, another popular destination for Egyptians, in addition to US financial assistance following the Camp David Accords.[35] It would also have precluded the possibility of subsequent bilateral agreements and aid packages between Kuwait and Egypt that continue to this day, including the Kuwaiti decision to provide Egypt with investment worth US$500 million following the Gulf War.[36] Unlike the 400,000 Palestinians in Kuwait and smaller numbers of other Arab expatriates who could not and did not go back,[37] Egyptians who left Kuwait were able to return in the years after the invasion. Many took advantage of this opportunity. Also, some among the 800,000 Egyptians working in Iraq who returned to Egypt because of the conflict subsequently travelled to Kuwait when the war ended, because returning to Iraq under Saddam Hussein was impossible.[38]

The 'Egyptianisation' of Arab migration

In 2000, a full ten years after the Iraqi invasion, the number of Egyptians in Kuwait was almost 200,000 and, according to the Egyptian Central Agency for Public Mobilization and Statistics (CAPMAS), higher than any other Arab expatriate community.[39] Three years later, estimates suggested that the numbers had risen to a peak of 260,000, as more Egyptians seized a boom in contractual opportunities in Kuwait and the wider Gulf region in the early and mid-2000s.[40] By 2011, according to Kuwaiti government statistics, 453,000 Egyptians were living in Kuwait, with around 36,000 believed to be working in the public sector, compared with 270,000 in the private sector, indicating that a further 147,000 were dependants, many of whom were employed or attended schools and universities in Kuwait.[41]

Increasing overall numbers since the mid-1990s suggest that Egyptians in Kuwait survived the de-Arabisation impact of the war, which polarised the region and caused the overall Arab expatriate population in Kuwait to decline dramatically from 80 per cent in 1975 to 30 per cent in 2003.[42] Egypt's alignment with Kuwait and a pre-established history of migration, in addition to increasing wealth disparity and the attraction of a vast and diverse Egyptian workforce to meet Kuwait's increased demand, undoubtedly contributed to this ability to compete with emerging labour markets from Asia, resulting in what can be described as an 'Egyptianisation' of the Arab expatriate population in Kuwait.

This omnipresence of Egyptians and the diversity of their occupations, both high- and low-skilled, was echoed by the variety of answers Kuwaitis gave during the interviews in response to the question 'What jobs are done by Egyptians in Kuwait?' They ranged from labourers, cleaners, guards, drivers and construction workers, to salespeople, teachers, engineers, businesspeople and physicians. Among those Egyptians interviewed, their words reflected a similar sense of prevalence and indispensability. According to Sarah, an Egyptian who was born and raised in Kuwait and was studying at university in Cairo: 'For every Kuwaiti working in the government, there is usually an Egyptian working in the same job and doing all the work, albeit for a far smaller salary and an inferior title.'[43] In the eyes of Gamal, who described himself as 'one thousand percent Egyptian' despite living in Kuwait for twenty-seven of his twenty-eight years:

> There is an Egyptian on every corner in Kuwait. There is an Egyptian worker in every bank, an Egyptian teacher in every school, an Egyptian engineer running every construction project, an Egyptian doctor in every hospital, an Egyptian guard in every building. We have a strong presence in Kuwait; we have a presence that they can't do without. Without us, they [Kuwaitis] are nothing.[44]

Sarah and Gamal's observations indicate a consciousness of their visible presence and belonging as Egyptians in Kuwait. Furthermore, their words reveal perceived powers in propagating knowledge and the social and economic transformation that is essential to Kuwaiti ideals of progress and development, as well as the necessity of their roles in processes of production and reproduction of space in Kuwait.⁴⁵

Navigating Kuwait

Adaptation to societal change

History and demographics support the notion of 'Egyptianisation' among the Arab foreign resident population and depict post-war Kuwait as a destination that is relatively conducive to Egyptian migration. But reflections of Egyptians and Kuwaitis in subsequent sections reveal a post-war environment that, while not overtly hostile to or dismissive of the need for an Egyptian presence, is often isolating, inhospitable and inflexible towards migrants and life circumstances that affect them at home and abroad. This, in turn, prompts Egyptians to cultivate compatible means of informal governance; in other words 'ways of getting by', to successfully navigate their lives in Kuwait.

Based on his observations and interactions in the workplace, Abdullah, a Kuwaiti businessman working in the construction sector, acknowledged the vast Egyptian population residing in Kuwait and explained the idea of underlying concessions between Egyptian expatriates and their hosts. Such allowances are tacitly accepted and intrinsic to everyday life for the sake of perceived mutual benefits that work within the constraints of the prevailing system, enabling it to function and perpetuate itself, while simultaneously advancing economic production.

> Without incentives, fair treatment and upward mobility, there is no outlet for them to succeed and do well. As Egyptians are smart—they are known by many to be smart—they work within the system to their advantage. You see, people will give it to you if the system will not. It was very much a Kuwaiti decision to allow this aspect of Egyptian corruption or *baksheesh* [a tip] to operate... Kuwaitis provide the environment in which Egyptians can practice *baksheesh*, and yet, ultimately, both benefit from the system... If Egyptians were not there, there would be nothing functioning in the likes of the municipalities.⁴⁶

At the same time, post-war suspicions, longstanding divisions and hierarchies centred around 'the other' are also apparent in observations among non-Kuwaitis and Kuwaitis on life in Kuwait. These reflections reveal the penetration and pervasion of state-sponsored policies and institutions designed to preclude integration of non-Kuwaitis, bolstered by intergenerational memories of invasion and occupation by outsiders.

The idea of 'the lights going out' is prevalent in Kuwaiti reflections among younger and older generations on life before and after the Iraqi invasion and occupation. Failaka Island, off the coast of Kuwait, is a pale imitation of what it was before the invasion, according to Fahad, a Kuwaiti banker who remembered going on holidays there as a child when it was a popular resort. Now, little remains there. During the invasion, he was in Egypt with his father at a wedding, and was forced to stay there for nine months before returning to Kuwait. 'Kuwait stopped—even after its liberation. Had it not been for the invasion, Kuwait would be like Dubai is now, and perhaps even better'. In other discussions on the subject, Kuwaitis conveyed lingering feelings of vulnerability, betrayal and resentment that was felt towards 'new enemies', referring to Arab regimes that sided with Saddam Hussein during the invasion, as well as the 'turning inwards' of Kuwaitis in relation to one another. During a conversation between two Kuwaiti women (both university students) about what they know from older relatives about the perceived impact of the war on Kuwaiti society, one described the changes before and after the invasion: 'Kuwait's previous sense of community has been lost; neighbours aren't close with each other, and everyone is seeking their own personal benefit as individuals. Competition has triumphed over community'.[47]

Discussions among Kuwaitis on the role of Egyptians within Kuwaiti society lent further insight into forms of exclusion and belonging and reveal a tacit acceptance and justification among Kuwaitis about why Egyptians and other non-Kuwaitis continue to have a place in Kuwait. During interviews with Kuwaitis on Egyptians and other Arab expatriates in Kuwait, among other issues, there was consensus that Egyptians were essential, but at times, unwanted 'imported labour'. In the words of one man reflecting on the perception of Egyptians before and after the invasion, they were seen as 'cogs in the wheel' of Kuwait's material recovery and post-war development. Similarly, conversations among Kuwaiti women alluded to reasons why Egyptians continued to travel to Kuwait and why Kuwait continued to accept them. In describing this idea, parallels can be drawn from international migration theories on the perpetuation of labour migration, as well as studies in other parts of the world, as one woman made sense of the seemingly rational exchange in granting temporary political and economic stability to a hardworking Egyptian.[48] She reinforced the idea of cogs built into Kuwait's rotating wheel of temporary labour migration:

> Our country offers them the political stability that their country does not have. Kuwait is safe. Also, the money they make here is always more than anything they

would make at home, even if it is not considered much in comparison to the salary of a Kuwaiti... They facilitate our lives here, apart from the traffic for a while, but that's no longer an issue... They do most of the work that we're not willing to do; the dirty work. Even when people complain about them taking our jobs, the reality is that a Kuwaiti citizen would not be willing to put in the same amount of effort and time that the non-Kuwaiti has to put in for that job he stole.[49]

During the discussion, the same woman acknowledged the theoretical importance of a shared language and culture. However, she revealed that in reality, this may not translate into deeper interaction outside formal airs and graces, or an unconditional acceptance of their presence in Kuwait:

> Generally, with Arabs, you could say that we share a bond. We're technically supposed to respect the Arabs, because we share a language and a religion and our countries are most likely allies. With Asians, we're so accustomed to them being inferior and coming from ignorant and poor countries, so we never see them as equals... I know Egyptians as guards and drivers. I say '*assalaam 'aleikom*' but we rarely interact on a deeper level than that.[50]

Another woman, also a university student, justified a distinction she saw between Egyptians and other Arab migrants, which, in the absence of personal experience, was likely reinforced by harmful stereotypes that appeared in the media on a daily basis, always mentioning the nationality or ethnicity of alleged criminals:[51]

> I think the Egyptians who work here are different from the rest of the Arabs. I noticed that the Lebanese and Syrians bring their wife and kids with them, but the Egyptians come alone, which makes them a little suspicious, particularly when they carry out crimes like rape and murder. I don't think single men should be allowed to come here. But the Egyptian teachers are good at private tutoring, which many Kuwaiti students need in middle school and high school.[52]

In a separate conversation, Abdulaziz, a Kuwaiti businessman in his thirties, when asked about the contribution of Egyptians in the workplace, joked about the introduction of bribery to the Kuwaiti municipalities and connected the presence of this practice to the Egyptians working there:

> It is a well-known fact that Egyptians, in general, administer the municipalities here, although Kuwaitis remain at the most senior levels. If you want to get permission to build something, the first person you will see is an Egyptian, and you will pay *baksheesh*. [Laughs] In Kuwait, we even imported corruption from Egypt.[53]

While the above excerpts acknowledge a valued place for Egyptians and other Arab expatriates in Kuwaiti society, they also contain references to societal problems that are visible in the media on a daily basis—traffic, crowded public services, crime and corruption. These problems are deflected onto migrants, and rarely attributed to problems that lie deeper within Kuwaiti attitudes, governance and legislation surrounding migration. Moreover, these modes of governance, while at times negotiable, include a minefield of stringent and discriminatory policies that Egyptians and other foreign residents must navigate, such as driver's licence restrictions, traffic campaigns targeting expatriates, and the introduction of a trial policy at a major public hospital that denied morning access to non-Kuwaiti patients seeking non-emergency care.[54]

Hierarchies within hierarchies

The atomisation of society and a multitude of boundaries across the Kuwaiti landscape was also expressed by Abdullah, the Kuwaiti developer mentioned previously, as he described the urban geography of Kuwait as '...made up of a series of red lines and borders, metaphorically speaking, reflected in its urban plan of de-centralized and self-sustaining suburbs.' The idea of 'the Other,' he said, 'is key to understanding life in Kuwait.' There are red lines between Kuwaitis and non-Kuwaitis, societal divisions within the Kuwaiti population embodied in the distinctions made between Hadar and Bedouin, and yet more lines between and within non-Kuwaiti expatriate 'communities'. Later in the discussion, Abdullah referred to a 'ladder' or hierarchy of expatriates that Kuwaitis 'operated', reifying Kuwaiti national identity, which non-Kuwaitis subsequently replicated in their navigation of the labour market in Kuwait.[55] He also reinforced the notion of Egyptians as indiscriminate 'masses', indicating that Egyptians have not escaped unharmed from the paradoxical phenomenon of increased dependency and simultaneous de-humanisation of expatriates in Kuwait—a trend that has become more pronounced since the exodus of Palestinians and other Arab foreign residents in the late twentieth century.

> While Egyptians have done a lot of things for Kuwait, they are considered lower on the ladder, perhaps for the reason that they are such a large and diverse population, but many of them are labourers, waiters, guards, drivers. Egyptians are just everywhere and occupy such a variety of jobs. They are not necessarily noticed or seen as contributing something tangible, something visible. They are not looked at with the same respect and gratitude as the Palestinians were before the invasion; they are just 'there', the masses, doing the work that needs to be done.[56]

Examples of what Rogers Brubaker and Frederick Cooper have described as 'categories of practice' in their analysis of identity as an analytical category are apparent in citizen and non-citizen boundaries and the reification of hierarchies and class divisions as a means of negotiating everyday life.[57] Within the non-Kuwaiti population, a replicated hierarchy was discerned and adhered to among Egyptians interviewed, who placed 'untouchable' Kuwaitis at the top, followed by other Gulf Cooperation Council (GCC) nationals, Westerners, and then Arabs, followed by Filipinos and then other Asian migrants (Indians, Bangladeshis and Sri Lankan nationals). Even within the 'Arabs' category divisions were perceived in terms of the labour market, with Lebanese at the top and Egyptians at the bottom, in what Mustafa, an Egyptian born and raised in Kuwait, who now worked as an administrative assistant in one of the Kuwaiti ministries, described as an 'unwritten hierarchy' that Egyptians must navigate to negotiate their existence among non-Kuwaitis in Kuwait:

> At the end of the day, it is up to the person to prove him or herself and negotiate through his education, charisma and experience. Generally speaking though, they [Kuwaitis] want Lebanese for sales and business roles, which suits the Lebanese as they would rather be free, operating in business rather than following orders like Egyptians generally do, particularly those working in the government. While an Egyptian man will be offered the lowest salary bracket because he is Egyptian, more often than not he will accept it. Meanwhile, a Lebanese man might be offered more because he is Lebanese, and even then, he is more likely to negotiate a hard bargain until he reaches higher up the salary bracket—even if inside he is dying for the job.[58]

For Ramy, forty-three, from Asyut in Upper Egypt, who worked as a janitor in a Kuwaiti bank, there was an additional hierarchy that transcended nationalities and was visible in interactions among Egyptians in Kuwait, as well between non-Kuwaitis and Kuwaitis. This implies the existence of multiple forms of governance, belonging and exclusion, including additional structures of class and social standing that have been imported from Egypt:

> I serve three Kuwaitis, two Indians, one Greek and five Egyptians on my floor with tea and coffee... Everyone is nice to me generally, but I think it is more out of pity than because I am a good person. Of course there is a large disparity between how they treat the Egyptian tea boy and how they treat an Egyptian manager. Of course there is me who doesn't have a high school diploma and Maher who is in charge of one of the large departments in the bank where I work... It is not really your nationality that makes people treat you improperly, it's your social standing. I am not saying I am mistreated at work, just that not all Egyptians are treated equally. Kuwaitis treat me as if I am someone who works for them, but Egyptians treat me as if they have a duty to care for me. They both treat me as a subordinate, it is just expressed in different ways.[59]

The perceived existence of such social structures, ordering and perpetuating an atomised society in Kuwait, within which one needs to navigate and negotiate social hierarchies, affirms the idea that to be an 'exception'—or a non-Kuwaiti in the case of Kuwait—is not a monolithic category. Rather, it is 'occupied by several groups, full of multiple meanings and continually generating its own exceptions'. More than that, these 'exceptions' or individuals, by virtue of their presence, are active participants in these processes of informal governance that are intrinsic to the functioning of Kuwait.[60]

Permanent temporariness

Lives in the balance

Having identified unwritten rules and tacit agreements that occur in the daily lives of those living in Kuwait, we move above and beyond these social structures to examine the notion of 'permanent temporariness' that is fundamental to Kuwait's migration policy, and consequently intrinsic to the temporal existence of Egyptians in Kuwait.

According to Kuwaiti residency law at the time of writing, foreign nationals, on the basis of their sponsored employment in Kuwait, may obtain a regular residence permit (*iqama*) for a period that does not exceed five years, as long as they hold a passport that is valid for the length of that period. Once the permit expires or if they lose their sponsorship, they must leave the country. In the case of the former, if requesting a new permit, this must be submitted one month before the current permit's expiry. If the request is denied then they must leave within one week of being notified of the denial if the permit has already expired.[61] As a result, what might be described as the 'luxury' of stability or certainty that accompanies legal citizenship and permanent residency is an impossibility for Egyptians and all other non-Kuwaitis in Kuwait. Hence, for as long as they remain in Kuwait, Egyptians find themselves 'permanently temporary', at the mercy of the Kuwaiti sponsorship system (*kafāla*).

Suspended in this state of constant uncertainty, and amid incessant coverage in Arabic- and English-language newspapers of quarterly raids and plans by the Ministry of Social Affairs and Labour to reduce the expatriate workforce by 100,000 per year, one persistent threat felt by Egyptians interviewed in Kuwait was being stopped by the police for a traffic or immigration violation, or losing sponsorship, any of which could result in immediate deportation.[62] A palpable fear of breaking rules or being subject to removal for no fault of their own was apparent among both higher- and lower-skilled workers, but particularly those at the bottom of all the aforementioned hierarchies in society. Low-skilled workers—often with the most to lose—described feeling inherently vulnerable, knew little of their rights, lacked faith in the importance the Kuwaiti authorities gave to these rights, and envisioned the alternative to their finite time in Kuwait as a life of poverty in Egypt. Nowras, a plumber in Kuwait aged twenty-seven, continued to pay 15 per cent of his monthly salary to the recruitment agency that brought him to Kuwait. He described leaving his dignity 'at the airport' and the exhausting precariousness of this life in Kuwait:

> Look, I am not a doctor or an engineer... I have to be careful everywhere I go and in everything I say—even though I never do anything illegal. I have to be careful because I am fragile, my situation is fragile, my social status is fragile... In the beginning, everywhere I went and all the time, people would hassle me and ask me to show them my *iqama*. It always took a long time before they were convinced that I was legally here. Also, because my *kafil* [sponsor] is not from a very popular family they would always question me about him. Take it from me... we are helpless. We are treated with an attitude: if you like it, you like it; if you do not like it, go back to your country. And they are right. Do you know why they are right? Because the law does not protect us. If the law was on our side I would not allow anybody, no matter who they were, to make me feel bitter. But it is out of my hands, and this is better than the alternative—begging on the streets of Egypt.[63]

Strategies in sponsorship

A complex picture of how Egyptians work the system and its logics of governance was also revealed through discussions with them on how they gained entry to Kuwait and how they have navigated the environment and negotiated the state of permanent temporariness in which they find themselves to their relative advantage. Gamal, mentioned above, arrived in Kuwait with his mother in 1986 after she accepted a teaching position at a Kuwaiti school. He is employed as a secretary, a job he secured with the help of connections (*wasta*) by way of his mother's former student, a Kuwaiti man who felt he owed his success in school to Gamal's mother and subsequently returned the favour by hiring Gamal to work for his father's business.

Manipulation of social channels as a means of procuring job opportunities and advancing economic gain was a tried and trusted method among Egyptians interviewed, and its apparent prevalence goes some way to explaining the enduring presence of Egyptians in Kuwait. 'Chain migration', in particular, using informal (and often illegal) avenues of facilitating additional migration and circumventing increasingly restrictive Kuwaiti migration policies, was among the strategies that Egyptians described using in interviews. Others included building personal relationships with sponsors or identifying symbioses by which to maximise economic gains during their time in Kuwait.[64]

Ramy, the janitor from Upper Egypt mentioned above, began his journey to Kuwait when a friend of a relative who sold permits for residency in Kuwait offered him 'the deal of a lifetime' to secure a permit for 10,000 Egyptian pounds (approximately US$1,420).[65] Like others interviewed, Ramy sold much of his land to pay for the permit, and after six months of waiting, he moved to Kuwait and found work through his sponsor. As he began to describe the process of moving, he laughed and said he preferred to call it 'humanitarian', rather than 'illegal', reflecting the wealth disparity that has prompted increasing numbers of Egyptians to fulfil similar duties for their households in travelling to Kuwait:

> I made a deal with the man and I gave him half of the money as a deposit until he secured the *iqama* [residency permit]. It took him around six months, I would call him around four or five times a week for six months, can you imagine? And all this just to ask if my *iqama* was ready or not. Every time I called he would tell me that it would be ready in the next two or three days. I would believe him because it was all I had to believe—I had nothing else but to believe him, no other option[66]

On arriving in Kuwait, Ramy stayed with someone he knew until he met with his *kafil*, who he describes as a 'kind-hearted person, unlike the stories that my friends (who also bought residency permits) told me about'. Fifteen years later, the relationship, as Ramy explained, had been enriched and evolved beyond the *kafala*, and while functioning in a context of exclusion and inequality, it continued to be mutually beneficial and sustainable for both parties, affording Ramy social and economic mobility during his time in Kuwait:

> Even after his name was removed from my *iqama* we remained in contact and he treated me like a brother rather than like a subordinate, which was the general expectation as I was told by my friends who had lived and worked in Kuwait. He was the one who helped me out with three of the five jobs that I have held throughout my stay here in Kuwait. On many occasions he invited me out for a nice meal at KFC and sometimes Pizza Hut. He always ensured that I would call him if I needed anything. At first I thought it was so he wouldn't get in trouble because of the illegal trade, but I later removed this prejudice from my mind. He is one of very few Kuwaitis who has been genuinely and selflessly nice to me. Today, I drive his children to school every morning before going to work. This is to say that he actually gave me one of his old cars for me to get around so I do not have to waste my money on bus memberships.[67]

For Bassam, a taxi driver in his twenties from Upper Egypt who has lived in Kuwait since 2010, his experience varied dramatically under different sponsors, revealing considerable barriers to mobility imposed by the system, but also the wherewithal and resilience among some Egyptians to circumvent such restrictions. Bassam, who was unable to secure a viable income for himself or his family in Upper Egypt, decided to come to Kuwait on the advice of his cousin who already lived there. After Bassam gave 20,000 Egyptian pounds (about US$2,840) to his cousin's connection in Kuwait who 'dealt' residency permits, his cousin arranged his travel and ultimately found him a job and accommodation within a taxi firm:

> After I handed over the money I prayed to God that everything would work out for me. *Al-hamd-ul-illah*, everything went smoother than I expected. That said, I left my first job here after three months. I was working for a very bad company. It gave me a bad impression of Kuwait. My previous *kafil* was a thief and he treated us like slaves. He physically and verbally abused us, would withhold our wages and wouldn't let us take holidays. I could not take it and I threatened to call the police on him. He was a crazy man and may God forgive him for what he did and for what he is probably still doing. He would abuse me by calling me names and telling me that I am stupid because I am Egyptian and he would do the same for all the other people with different nationalities. I thought all jobs would be like this and that I would just have to deal with it or leave... One day we got into a fight and I told him he was not better than me just because he was Kuwaiti... He eventually allowed me to leave after those three months.[68]

At the time of interview, Bassam was working as a taxi driver for a different firm, earning what he considered to be a reasonable income from commission, and had earned back his inheritance money and that of his mother's, which he had used to purchase his key to Kuwait. Bassam gave his current *kafil*, whom he describes as 'a very good man', paying 6 Kuwaiti dinars per day (about US$20) or 180 Kuwaiti dinars per month (about US$630). Anything Bassam earned above the 6 Kuwaiti dinars each day he kept for himself, and over time, he learnt how to maximise his profit through an expanding network of clients. He would 'befriend' customers and make deals with them, telling them that he would drive them the same route every day for a 'special price'. He gave an example of a Kuwaiti student he had been driving to university for more than eighteen months, and who sent Bassam new business in the form of his friends and relatives. Bassam was making around 450 Kuwaiti dinars per month (about US$1,573) and planned to save up a further 30,000 Egyptian pounds (about US$4,260) so that he could get married in Egypt. Based on his monthly earnings, he then planned to bring his wife to Kuwait until what he described as the current political and economic 'chaos' in Egypt dissipated, and he could return there with his family.[69]

'Egypt made me, Kuwait is sustaining me'

Returning to Egypt, generally after achieving financial milestones, was something that the majority of Egyptians yearned for at some point in the future, but which was tempered by fear and apprehension in summer 2013, as people watched new cycles of political and socio-economic instability unfold in Egypt. Indeed, Egyptians framed their existence in Kuwait in largely economic terms, indicating a symbiotic relationship that is grounded in a 'permanence of Egyptian temporary migration' to Kuwait and other GCC countries.[70]

During a discussion at an Egyptian coffeehouse in Farwaniya, Gamal, the twenty-eight-year-old secretary who has spent much of his life in Kuwait, talks more about his relationship with Egypt and Kuwait as a set of complementarities that he is able to manipulate to a certain extent. However, the parameters within which Egyptians from lower-income backgrounds are able to make these decisions often call into question the clear-cut distinctions between forced and voluntary migration upon which global policy responses to migration and development are based.[71]

> I have two homes in two separate countries. They complete each other. What I don't find in one place, I find in the other. I don't find compassion here in Kuwait, but I find it in Egypt. I don't find money and a stable life in Egypt, but I find it here in Kuwait... Do you know what happens to people who stay in Egypt like my cousin? They end up unemployed, failed and cheated and betrayed by the system. My cousin, who is a fine doctor, sits in a pharmacy below our house [in Egypt]. That's what he does instead of saving lives with the skills that he has learned... I make 400 Kuwaiti dinars a month (about US$1,399), that's more than my cousin makes; it is double what my cousin makes. You are laughing but this is a dark, dark comedy, believe me... At the end of the day, regardless of the hardships I occasionally face in this country, there is no other place that would take me in like Kuwait.[72]

The compulsion to leave behind the bleak economic situation in Egypt is reflected even more strongly by Ramy, who moved to Kuwait in 1998 after failing to make a viable income for himself and his family. For him and others interviewed, the decision to move to Kuwait was based on the weighed costs and benefits for their household, with the ultimate goal of achieving the financial stability through savings (*tahweesh*) before returning home. He was motivated by what he described as a 'general notion' among Egyptians that encourages travel to the Gulf to improve their quality of life, and was determined to provide more for his wife and children than his monthly wage of 500 Egyptian pounds (about US$70) as a tea boy in an Egyptian government facility.

THE EGYPTIAN 'INVASION' OF KUWAIT

Egypt compared to Kuwait is like the man who is dark-skinned, tall and handsome and has a kind and big heart but does not have much in his bank account, compared to the man who is not too pretty or easy on the eyes, very ill-tempered but a rich man, with money that will comfort you. Therefore, if you are looking for a husband for your daughter you will pick the rich man, because you don't want your daughter to live an uncomfortable life. This is why we choose to come to Kuwait, instead of staying in Egypt, because this way we can provide our children and our children's children with a better quality of life, not because we enjoy it, but because as parents it is our duty.[73]

In the words of Sharif, a thirty-year-old civil engineering graduate, 'Egypt made me, but Kuwait is sustaining me'. He described the limitations and complementarity of his relationships with Egypt and Kuwait through an analogy of marriage and separation. Five years previously, in 2008, Sharif travelled to Kuwait on the advice of a friend and bought an *iqama*. On arriving in Kuwait, he managed to secure a contract with a Kuwaiti engineering company that agreed to transfer his residency under the company name after he admitted his clandestine deal with a visa trader:

Well, I left Egypt for the same reasons all Egyptians leave Egypt… Why would someone in a marriage fall in love with somebody who is not part of the marriage? Well, because the other person is not fulfilling his/her emotional needs… You see, the day I decided to leave Egypt is the day I decided to get separated from Egypt. I got separated from Egypt because it is not fulfilling my needs as a citizen… Do not misunderstand me, Egypt is my first and most sincere love story of my life, but it is always healthy to take a break from what we love because what we love is not always what is good for us. I needed to solve my individual financial problems and be financially secure enough to at the least support a family and be able to get married. Egypt also needed to solve all of its political and economic troubles that I am no longer a part of because I have never been given the opportunity to be heard or to participate… Look, I love Kuwait because it is a blessing that God has granted me and it has been a very friendly host to me. However, this love is not enough to make me stay here forever. I doubt that the Kuwaitis would welcome me for that long anyway.[74]

Two months after the interview, Sharif injured himself in an accident in the workplace and was subsequently deported to Egypt. His departure serves as a stark reminder of the limited 'shelf life' of Egyptians perceived in Kuwait as imported and ultimately disposable labour in Kuwait. Furthermore, it represents the paradox of financial stability coupled with the uncertainty of time constraints placed on the lives of foreign residents in Kuwait, and ultimately the lack of rights protection afforded to Egyptians and other non-Kuwaitis, regardless of their nationality, ethnicity or skillset, which might otherwise assist them in negotiating restrictions in Kuwait.

The limits of staying power

Implicit and explicit in the above reflections of the Egyptians interviewed is that settling permanently in Kuwait is a virtual impossibility, due to institutions that govern their presence in Kuwait, such as sponsorship (*kafala*), but also written and unwritten restrictions on naturalisation and residency legislation. While on paper many Egyptians—as Arab Muslims who have lawfully resided for fifteen years consecutively in Kuwait and who have provided services needed in Kuwait—would appear to qualify for naturalisation, there is little evidence of this happening for Egyptians or other Arab residents.[75]

Statistics from the International Organization for Migration (IOM) in 2010 indicate that the average Egyptian resides in the Gulf for between five and fourteen years.[76] However, Egyptians encountered during the research, particularly highly skilled workers such as engineers and physicians, had spent more than twenty years in Kuwait, or were born in Kuwait to Egyptian parents. None of the second-generation Egyptians encountered admitted to wanting to stay in Kuwait, often describing it as 'boring'; some did not want to return to Egypt permanently, however, citing unfamiliarity with the country, but more importantly fears for their future given the recent unrest. Among first-generation Egyptians, the vast majority planned to return, either after a specific period of time or, in the case of those who had been in Kuwait for most of their working lives, after their retirement. While most wished to return in the near future, particularly lower-skilled workers who had left their families behind for a finite period, many viewed return with much trepidation, and hoped they would not be forced to make their final choice until the situation had improved in Egypt.

Limbo at home and abroad

For Mohammed, a physician, the invasion and subsequent liberation of Kuwait in 1990–91 was the 'migration opportunity' he was waiting for, and which benefitted him greatly. Whereas before the invasion he had struggled to find a job while on a short-stay visa in Kuwait, he described various ministries after the liberation 'fighting' over him—'Unlike today,' he joked—because the country 'needed all the help it could get to recover since it had plunged into the darkness overnight'.[77] He was also able to rescue and marry a Palestinian woman he had met and fallen in love with on a visit before the invasion, and subsequently brought her back to Kuwait with their two young children after she obtained Egyptian citizenship. His wife and grown-up children have since emigrated to Canada, unable to stay in Kuwait after Mohammed's retirement and unwilling to face inevitable return to Egypt—a country that is more foreign to them than Kuwait, and increasingly undesirable in their eyes.

Among those highly skilled workers interviewed, such as Mohammed, some had remained since their arrival around the time of the Gulf War due to demand in their professions. They also had the financial wherewithal and an increasing inclination to settle there, although they acknowledged it was a legal impossibility. Mohammed believed that retirement and leaving Kuwait constituted both a life goal and an ominous inevitability that was inherent in their daily lives as non-Kuwaitis in Kuwait. However, while they accepted and awaited the bittersweet reality of their ultimate departure, it was often hard to comprehend after so much time spent in Kuwait. Samer, born in Kuwait and working as a sales manager for a multi-national company, evoked similar feelings when describing his father's abrupt departure from Kuwait after more than thirty years:

> My father worked for thirty-two years as a credit manager for a Kuwaiti bank. They [my mother and father] liked the life in Kuwait—it was calm, they earned good money, they raised their children here and they had my aunt and her family living here. They didn't necessarily plan on going back to Egypt, hoping that there might be a way for them to stay on. When my father reached the retirement age [sixty], his sponsor agreed to renew the residency one year at a time. Once he reached sixty-three, one day the sponsor told him his time was over, and that he had no choice but to return to Egypt, and thanked him for his service. At this point, my father's view of Kuwait and his life here changed completely. He was very hurt that after thirty-two years of working for the bank and the relationships he had there that they could just say goodbye to him without any kind of appreciation or courtesy for his life... It's an unfair life, but it's in our faces...in the news, in our everyday interactions in Kuwait and we accept it. We have to accept it.[78]

Marianne, a second-generation Coptic Christian in her thirties, was also working as a physician. She hoped to move to the US with the idea of settling there with her husband, who is also Egyptian, their two children and her parents, who have yet to retire and are also in Kuwait. She is afraid if she does not find somewhere to settle soon, her two sons will be forced to complete military service in Egypt—'unthinkable', she says, considering the security situation there and the treatment of soldiers in barracks. She said, 'Everything is fleeting in Kuwait, it is a transitory existence, even relationships here on the whole. Even the furniture in my house, we either buy second-hand furniture or cheap furniture as we know we will leave here eventually'.[79] If she stays here for much longer, Marianne feels she will be living in limbo, with return to Egypt inevitable. Only if the situation were stable and they could find good jobs with good salaries would she feel able to consider the possibility of return. Aysem Şenyürekli and Cecilia Menjívar reported finding similar feelings of what they described as 'perpetual ambivalence' in their study on the hopes and fears around return migration among Turkish migrants residing in the US. There, too, a constant interplay of micro- and macro-level considerations that encouraged or discouraged return migration characterised decisions about whether or not to return to countries of origin. A degree of ambivalence is inherent in the process of migration as long as people's lives are established in two or more places. However, the extent to which migrants can actively formulate migration strategies when adapting to changing circumstances largely rests on the nature of governance in countries of origin and destination.[80]

Conclusion

Concern over developments in Egypt permeated statements about return among Egyptian expatriates in Kuwait. At the time of our field work in 2013, first- and second-generation Egyptians followed events in Egypt closely on satellite news and social media. Many admitted to stress and concern for friends and relatives in Cairo, as well as daily arguments in Kuwait with family and other fellow Egyptians over politics at home. But despite well-publicised deportations of Egyptians and recurring rumours of the suspension of family visit visas in the press, any detrimental effect on Egyptians in Kuwait of political instability in Egypt was only occasionally visible. Examples of incidents included the arrest and deportation of Egyptians, who were protesting in support of the Muslim Brotherhood, which were reported in Kuwaiti and Egyptian newspapers, or an appeal from the Egyptian ambassador to Kuwait, who pleaded for Egyptian nationals 'to exercise caution in their dealings', because Kuwait would 'take firm action and prevent gatherings and demonstrations that disturb security'.[81]

While reports of expulsions of Egyptians involved in protests have been limited since the start of the uprising in Egypt, the deportation of Egyptians and other expatriates without valid documentation appears to have continued as part of attempts to combat irregular migration.[82] Data on irregular migrants from a four-month amnesty in 2011 reveals that of those 24,433 Egyptian residency-permit violators, 2,664 (10.9 per cent) individuals regularised their status during the amnesty period, while 9,585 (39.2 per cent) left Kuwait and an estimated 12,184 (49.9 per cent) remained in an irregular status. Notably, of all the nationalities, the departure of Arab expatriates originating from countries experiencing instability at home was highest: the number of Egyptians who left during the 2011 amnesty was the highest numerically and second-highest proportionately, while the number of Syrians who left was the highest proportionately (53 per cent or 2,035 out of 3,788).[83] At this critical juncture for inter-regional migration, when the stakes have never been higher for these Arab expatriates to find ways to stay on, Kuwait would do well to more actively allay fears and diminish insecurities among the Egyptians, as well as other expatriates residing within its borders who are currently affected by widespread political and economic instability at home.

As our research shows, Egyptians have long been, and continue to be, an integral and visible part of life in Kuwait. Nevertheless, there are significant legal, political, social and economic restrictions on their right to belong, as well as their feelings of belonging, which is reflected by beliefs that Kuwaitis and Egyptians have about the role of Egyptians. The inequality, lack of integration and time limits enshrined in policy have led to a pervasive sense of permanent temporariness among the Egyptians themselves and their Kuwaiti hosts. Furthermore, our research posits that while this limbo status is longstanding, it has renewed importance today because of the continuing cycles of instability in Egypt that began January 2011, which have exacerbated preexisting insecurities among Egyptians in Kuwait.

In light of these findings, it is necessary to formulate active, yet pragmatic and viable responses that mitigate the human insecurities described above and also consider the functionality implicit in past and present participation of Egyptians and other expatriates in modes of social, economic and political production in Kuwait and beyond.

Potential responses to mitigate insecurities of those experiencing widespread instability in countries of origin might include: implementing a far-reaching amnesty programme for irregular workers to regularise their status; creating more opportunities for regular migration of lower-skilled workers; increased transparency and maintenance of open channels for family visit visas; and government-sponsored extensions of foreign residency permits for those who are unwilling or unable to return home due to widespread crisis there, but whose sponsors are no longer willing to employ them in Kuwait. Furthermore, in light of the current political climate in Egypt and the return of military-backed rule that is amenable to Kuwait, the creation of bilateral labour agreements and sustained investment in Egypt to promote the needed and desired economic exchange, job creation and voluntary return under conditions of certainty may also constitute viable alternatives to the status quo.

6

THE 'OTHER ARAB' AND GULF CITIZENS

MUTUAL ACCOMMODATION OF PALESTINIANS IN THE UAE IN HISTORICAL CONTEXT[1]

Manal A. Jamal

Much of the literature on migrants in the Gulf, especially in the United Arab Emirates (UAE), has focused on South and East Asian labourers.[2] A smaller body of academic scholarship has addressed the changing circumstances of the various Arab communities in that region,[3] especially Palestinian communities,[4] and particularly those in the United Arab Emirates (UAE).[5] What has been written on the Palestinian communities of the Gulf has overwhelmingly focused on Palestinians in Kuwait in light of their 1991 expulsion after Yasser Arafat supported Saddam Hussein's invasion of Kuwait.[6] Although preferred over other migrant communities for reasons of cultural affinity, the 'other Arabs' in the Gulf have also been perceived as a destabilising force. According to existing laws, Arab migrants have assumed preference in terms of their employment opportunities, and their prospects for attaining citizenship. For example, in the UAE, Article 9 of the labour law explicitly states:

ARAB MIGRANT COMMUNITIES IN THE GCC

Where national employees are not available, preference in employment shall be given to: 1) Arab employees belonging to an Arab country by nationality; 2) Employees of other nationalities.[7]

Despite popular perceptions and the legal privilege of 'other Arabs' in Gulf Cooperation Council (GCC) states, their presence has never constituted a straightforward relationship of accommodation and compatibility, which is to say relations have not always been harmonious.

Although the literature[8] suggests that a possible deterioration in this relationship transpired in the late 1970s and in the wake of the 1991 Gulf War,[9] an examination of British archival materials indicates that the presence of 'other Arabs', and Palestinians in particular, has often been perceived as a destabilising force, requiring careful reining in, and controlled inclusion since the late 1940s and especially during the late 1960s—not only by the Trucial States'[10] leaders, but even more so by British authorities.[11] According to many exchanges in archival correspondence, Palestinian communities were carefully watched from their earlier phases of migration to the UAE during the 1950s and 1960s.[12] Nonetheless, they remain welcome in the UAE, especially in their capacity as 'other Arabs', as long as they are non-political, and their relationship to Palestinian politics is limited to humanitarian support.

With this background in mind, this research project seeks to place the discussion in a more germane historical context. In particular, it explores the fate of Arabs of Palestinian origin in the UAE, establishing a more historically sensitive political chronology, culminating in events surrounding the First Gulf War and the Arab uprisings which began in 2011. The Palestinian community was selected because it comprises a substantial segment of total migrants in the UAE, and because of its precarious position as a historic burden of obligation and perceived threat to the UAE. Although the related dynamics of obligation and threat may be more pronounced, it is representative of 'other Arab' expatriate communities. The specific questions this project has sought to address are: in the context of the UAE, how the circumstances of Palestinians have changed since their arrival in the late 1940s and 1950s, and what factors have shaped these changes over time; how Palestinians, including younger generations, have negotiated and addressed their sometimes tenuous relations with the UAE; and what current dynamics portend for future relations between Emiratis and Palestinians.

This project relies on archival material and extensive primary interviews with residents of the UAE who are of Palestinian origin. Interviewees were carefully selected to represent the different emirates, as well as different socioeconomic backgrounds, and migrants from different Arab and Western countries.[13] Findings rely on thirty-four formal interviews with Palestinians based in the emirates of Dubai, Abu Dhabi, Ras al-Khaimeh, and Al-Ain, as well as a number of informal interviews that addressed a number of the issues raised in the questionnaire. The interviews were semi-structured and open-ended, and addressed the changing status of Palestinians in the Gulf. Research was conducted during two separate visits to the UAE: the first in July 2013 for two weeks, and the second for three weeks between December 2013 and January 2014.

Initially, the plan was to focus interviews on individuals who had lived in the UAE since the early 1970s, because they would have the experience to speak authoritatively on the changing circumstances of the Palestinian community during the 1970s and 1980s, and then comment on the subsequent impact of the First Gulf War and the Arab uprisings. These initial interviews, however, indicated that this sample was skewed, most likely because individuals still residing in the UAE were those who had done relatively well for themselves. These individuals were also more likely to have worked in different sectors from those employing to present-day Arab migrants, often lived in more insular communities, and were less likely than other Palestinian-origin migrants to have come from the West. To address this issue, the sample was diversified to include migrants who arrived in the 1980s, in the 1990s, and more recently. The final sample included migrants from the West Bank and Gaza Strip, Egypt, Jordan, Syria, the US and Canada, as well as a number of Palestinians born in the UAE—some whose families managed to obtain Emirati passports or citizenship, and others who were still on employment visas. The study also included interviews with officials at the Palestinian consulate in Dubai and the Palestinian Authority Embassy in Abu Dhabi. The interviews were conducted in Abu Dhabi, Dubai, Ras al-Khaimah, and Al-Ain. The research also involved attendance at a major Ramadan fundraising event for the Palestine Children's Relief Fund in Dubai in July of 2013, and visits to cafés and restaurants regularly frequented by Palestinians in the UAE. No formal interviews took place during these outings, but they were an opportunity to corroborate research findings through informal interviews and discussions. An interviewee from Abu Dhabi also organised an informal focus group discussion between 13 Palestinians in Abu Dhabi, during which participants talked about the changing circumstances in their community, their levels of integration, perceptions of belonging, and cultural activities in which they were involved, among other issues.[14]

The chapter begins with a discussion of the changing demographics of the Palestinian community, and the challenges of obtaining official data on the number of Palestinians in the UAE. The following section discusses why Palestinian migrants predominantly over-stayed their initial plans to reside in the country for two to three years, and how their circumstances compare to Palestinian migrant communities in other Arab countries. The research then addresses broader political developments and their impact on the treatment of the Palestinian community in the UAE. It then assesses generational differences in integration/socialisation, the sense of belonging in and to the UAE, and relations with Palestine. The concluding section addresses issues of citizenship and naturalisation as they relate to this community.

Two important observations have emerged from this research that have challenged existing assumptions about the status of non-national Arab migrants in the UAE and the GCC more generally. Firstly, an important generational divide challenges many of our preconceived notions about relations between locals and expatriates and Palestinians' sense of belonging in the UAE. Younger generations of Emiratis and expatriates view the UAE and their position in the world differently to older generations, and hence are more open to the changing circumstances and the possibilities of meeting, socialising and interacting with each other. The guardedness and cautiousness that characterised earlier generations is not salient in younger generations. Secondly, and perhaps more importantly, this research project reaffirms the primacy of socioeconomic privilege as it relates to citizenship. Although Emirati citizenship itself was not necessarily sought after, the attainment of legal citizenship in a stable country remained significant in the lives of Palestinians. Facilitated by globalisation, more privileged Palestinians in the UAE resolved the vulnerability of their statelessness in the UAE by maintaining their residency in the UAE (even if not permanently), and obtaining the legal citizenship of another country.

A number of scholars have argued that in many ways globalisation has rendered legal citizenship irrelevant. As Aihwa Ong has argued, because of globalisation, highly skilled individuals have attained citizenship rights in cross-national contexts, while less skilled individuals are further devalued and marginalised.[15] As is later explained in more detail, however, the more highly skilled middle-class and upper-middle-class Palestinians living in the UAE have been persistent about acquiring legal citizenship elsewhere. Almost across the board, they have managed to secure citizenship in other countries such as Canada and the US, and often in more than one country as a back-up plan. In most cases, they plan to stay in the UAE with their families indefinitely. Scholars such as Neha Vora have argued that migrant communities, such as the Indian merchant community, exercised forms of substantive citizenship, and by extension are 'integral to the production of national identity, not only as foils to the nation but also in their practices and narratives of belonging; therefore they are also politically and socially integrated to some extent in the UAE.'[16] Although this applies to the Palestinian middle class and upper middle class in the UAE, legal citizenship, even if not Emirati, remains crucial for their integration into Emirati society. This contrasts sharply with less privileged Palestinians who are at the mercy of changing UAE government policies.

It is important to note that these policies are not unique to the UAE, or the GCC region more generally, and do not depart significantly from developments elsewhere. As Zahra Babar explains in the introduction to this volume, migrants' rights are being challenged in other contexts, and the increasing prevalence of temporary work programmes, which in many ways are akin to the *kafala* (sponsorship) system, have also become more common in North America and Europe. Moreover, migrant policies that distinguish between groups and individuals based on skillsets are also not unique to GCC countries. What does distinguish the UAE, however, is the size of the local population relative to the overall population.

Overview

The arrival of the Palestinians in the UAE dates back to the late 1940s and 1950s, but similar to broader migration flows to the region, their numbers increased after the rise of oil economies in the wake of the 1973 oil boom and the need for expatriate labour and expertise.[17] Official correspondence during the late 1960s indicated that the British were particularly concerned about the potential of Palestinian influence in the UAE. A number of communications in 1969[18] discussed the possible threat that Palestinians posed in the Trucial States, including the number of Palestinians employed in each of the Abu Dhabi departments. By July of that year, British agents in the Trucial States heightened their local intelligence committee activities to more carefully monitor the Palestinian community. In a letter on 21 July 1969, Sir Edward Crawford, political resident in Bahrain, outlined the influence of Palestinians in the Northern Trucial States to A.J. Coles, a political agent in Dubai:[19]

> The enclosed memorandum is the result of some research we have done on this subject [Palestinian influence in Northern Trucial States]. It is rather long and I will therefore set out my main conclusions in brief:

a. In Dubai there is a good deal of pro-Palestinian activity of the fund-raising variety and the Municipality is particularly prominent in this. But Palestinians do not influence the Ruler on matters of importance and the situation is well under control;
b. Our information on Sharjah and Ras al Khaimah is not so good. But there is a sizeable community of Palestinians in Sharjah and while they do not represent a threat at the moment, a substantial deterioration in the Middle East situation could provide the opportunity for some of the young radicals in Sharjah to organize the Palestinians politically;
c. The situation in Ras al Khaimah is a cause for greater concern. There are a number of Palestinians in positions of influence and there is evidence that they use this influence effectively with the Ruler. Palestinians and other Northern Arabs are likely to try to use Ras al Khaimah increasingly as their point of entry into Northern Trucial States and the situation needs to be watched with special care.[20]

Of particular concern to British Trucial State officials was that the Ruler of Ras al Khaimah had issued a decree that provided for a levy of 1 per cent on the salaries of government servants, a small charge on all licence fees and customs dues, and a 2 per cent levy of all property and land deals, the proceeds going to Fatah's Fund.[21] All the construction companies, many of those active in commerce, and over 100 school teachers were of Palestinian and/or Jordanian origin. This set of exchanges concluded with a suggestion to continue to monitor the situation, especially in the states of Sharjah and Ras al Khaimah.

The tendency of Palestinians to be more politicised relative to other migrants heightened these concerns. From the outset, the community was also involved in organising cultural and social activities, including fundraising for less privileged Palestinians. Different rulers have supported these efforts; Shaikh Zayed, in particular, donated land for the building of the Palestinian Embassy and allowed the Palestine Liberation Organization (PLO) to run its own schools.

British fears about the 'other Arab' presence in the UAE extended to other communities and organisations. In particular, during the mid-1960s, the British took an unyielding position that the Trucial States would not join the Arab League, and they would not even allow for the establishment of an Arab League office in the Trucial States. They also insisted that no Arab League official would be allowed to enter the region, and if any officials slipped through 'illegally', they must be expelled. The British were keen to minimise Arab influence in the development of the UAE for fear that the more radical Arab states would challenge their control, and destabilise the overall politics. In effect, such policies ensured that the UAE would remain in the British sphere of influence and not shift closer to more radical Arab spheres. Additionally, special care was taken to monitor possible Arab subversives, especially Palestinians.[22]

On average, the share of Arab migrants in the GCC states decreased in the total population from 71 per cent in 1976 to 31 per cent by 1996.[23] During the earlier period of the late 1960s and early 1970s, it was more common for expatriate Arabs to work in government sectors, including in strategic sectors. In particular, a number of Palestinians assumed prominent positions in the UAE government, often serving as advisers to the rulers, such as Zaki Nusseibeh. Palestinians including Riad Kamal, the founder and CEO of Arab Tech, one of the foremost construction companies in the GCC region,[24] Khaldoun Tabari, the chief executive of Drake and Skull, and Mounir el-Khatib & Dr. Zuheir Alami, who founded Khatib & Alami and also came to dominate the construction sector.[25] Palestinians were also very prevalent in the education sector, and more have come to occupy management positions in the banking sector and the private sector more generally.

Although the UAE's monitoring of expatriate communities was not limited to the Palestinians or 'other Arabs', the Palestinian community was unique in terms of its statelessness and its more vulnerable and precarious position. Following the 1948 Arab-Israeli war, 700,000 Palestinians out of a total 1.3 million indigenous inhabitants fled or were expelled from the part of historic Palestine that became Israel; the majority became refugees in Jordan, Lebanon, and Syria and what came to be known as the West Bank and Gaza Strip.[26] Although stateless and without citizenship, with the exception of those in Jordan, Palestinians built vibrant communities in their diaspora.[27] The circumstances of the various Palestinian communities differ tremendously. For the most part, in GCC states, Palestinians have been treated as foreign guest workers and allowed to reside in the country if they are officially employed or married to a citizen of that country. They are legally forbidden from participating in political life, though allowed to organise cultural celebrations and fundraising events, and contribute substantial amounts to Palestinian relief efforts, and have fundraised for the PLO quite extensively in the past.[28] The 1991 mass expulsion of 400,000 Palestinians from Kuwait was a stark reminder of their statelessness and vulnerability and generated tremendous psychological anxiety and insecurity among diaspora Palestinians, especially in the GCC states. Despite the mistrust surrounding the presence of 'other Arabs' in the Trucial States and later in the UAE, they have remained essential to its social fabric; Emiratis have wavered between embracing their Arab brethren and quelling potential political influence.

Determining the official number of Palestinians in the UAE is as impossible today as it was during earlier periods[29]—for logistical reasons in determining who is a Palestinian, as well as a lack of transparency on the part of the government, and the lack of systematic, detailed record-keeping on the part of Palestinian authorities.[30] A 'common' 2010 figure often cited is that there are 150,000 Palestinians in the UAE.[31] Many, however, believe the figure is much higher because this estimate only includes those who are officially in the UAE using their Palestinian Authority-issued passports—or older, Israeli-issued identity cards—and the holders of travel documents issued in Syria and Egypt, which explicitly indicate that one is of Palestinian origin.[32] Other passports, and Jordanian passports in particular, do not indicate Palestinian origin, and it is well known that a sizeable percentage of Palestinians in the UAE carry Jordanian passports. Moreover, Palestinians from the West Bank and the Gaza Strip often carry Jordanian passports, and enter the UAE using these passports and not their Palestinian Authority-issued documents. Finally, a number of Palestinians born in the UAE eventually attained UAE citizenship, and are not officially documented as Palestinians. These individuals were granted citizenship by decree or royal favour for making important contributions to the UAE. More recently, there has been an influx of Palestinians from Western countries who carry foreign passports, and they are not officially recorded as Palestinians either. For the purpose of this research project, a broader conception of Palestinian is used: someone who identifies as such regardless of the citizenship he or she holds.

Overstaying the initial two-year plan

As stated earlier, almost everyone I interviewed had initially intended to stay in the UAE for two to three years—just long enough to save enough money to start a business elsewhere—but eventually over-stayed the planned visit. For the overwhelming majority, economic opportunities and the overall comfort and ease of life were the main incentives for deciding to settle in the UAE. It was expected that interviewees would present a more critical outlook on life for Palestinians in the UAE, especially those who had previously been more engaged in Palestinian politics. On the contrary, however, an overwhelming pragmatism shaped their perceptions of life in the UAE.

The economic opportunities, not only relative to opportunities in other Arab countries for skilled and highly skilled migrants, but also relative to many Western countries for highly skilled migrants, were the main reason that many migrants decided to make the UAE a 'temporary' permanent home.[33] Another reason is that many of the men who migrated as bachelors to the UAE married and had children, and returning to the West Bank or Gaza Strip subsequently became too difficult. Furthermore, all the interviewees highlighted the security of life in the UAE, and how this was an important incentive for deciding to stay. Especially among those who came from the West Bank and Gaza Strip, individuals often sent remittances back home, and hence the financial benefits of staying in the UAE were multiple. This sentiment was not only shared by those who had secured high-paying positions in the UAE public sector or in the private sector, but also among lower-paid migrants, such as those employed in the public education sector.[34] Those I interviewed who were employed in the sector earned 10,000 Emirati dirhams per month (about US$2,723).[35] Although this amount was much less than salaries earned by highly skilled workers in other sectors, it was considerably higher than the salaries earned by teachers in Jordan or other Arab countries. The UAE also allows two children of expatriate public-sector employees to attend public schools free of charge. This salary and associated benefits afforded Palestinians a decent standard of living in the UAE, and the opportunity to send remittances to their families.[36] Similarly, highly skilled workers employed in the private sector attained a standard of living that would be difficult to maintain elsewhere, especially in the Arab world beyond the GCC region. For many, the UAE was the preferred option compared to other GCC states because of its more liberal social environment.

A recurring point often raised in my interviews was that in the UAE there is some semblance of governance, or as some referred to it, 'rule of law', and that navigating the bureaucracy was straightforward. Interviewees often explained that the UAE often spared them red tape-related hassles that were quite common in other Arab countries:

> The discrimination against Palestinians is everywhere. Although I hold a Jordanian passport, I feel more protected here. The locals are more polite usually. Here everyone stands in line, for example... In Jordan, it is common for a 'real Jordanian' to cut in front of you. I wanted to pursue studies and work in nuclear energy in Jordan, but I was told that this would not be possible because I was of Palestinian origin. We are not treated as equal citizens in most places outside of Palestine. Passports or citizenship in some countries do not protect us.[37]

Interviewees from Egypt, for example, highlighted how difficult it was to get anything done through the Egyptian bureaucracy, and that one often had to bribe officials. This was not the case in the UAE, according to my interviewees.

For a number of Palestinian couples, especially those who are university educated, the UAE is one of the few places in the Arab world where both spouses can secure employment and work visas, and therefore live together. For example, one interviewee, Huda, was born in Palestine and raised in Egypt and previously held a refugee document issued in Egypt. After the signing of the Gaza–Jericho Agreements in 1994, she obtained a Gaza Palestinian Authority Passport, and consequently, turned in her refugee document. Her husband is a Palestinian from the West Bank and holds a West Bank Palestinian Authority passport and a Jordanian Passport (not citizenship).[38] As a result, her husband is unlikely to find employment in Egypt. Given the Israeli-imposed closure policies that forbid Palestinian travel between the West Bank and Gaza Strip,[39] technically Huda cannot live in the West Bank, and her husband cannot live in the Gaza Strip. Moreover, the likelihood that both will secure competitive jobs and working visas in Jordan are slim, if not non-existent.[40] The UAE was therefore an ideal option for them. Others also felt that the greater availability of jobs in the UAE permitted a degree of stability that would probably be difficult to find elsewhere.

Many of those interviewed felt that maintaining work visas that enabled residency was not necessarily very difficult and could be sustained indefinitely. This appeared to be a much more common sentiment among highly skilled migrants or those who worked in highly paid sectors. For the most part, individuals have sought various Western passports or citizenship as a back-up plan in case they lost their residency status in the UAE. In most cases, at least one family member could maintain employment and ensure residency for his/her spouse, unmarried daughters or parents. Although the 2008 Dubai financial crisis proved to be a testing period in this regard, many who lost their jobs worked around the bureaucratic hurdles to maintain their residency status.

Mohammed, for example, a Jordanian citizen, had an established position in a Dubai government body. Following the start of the financial crisis, there was little work in his office, and other expatriate colleagues were laid off. He knew that he too would eventually be laid off, not because he was a Palestinian, but because he was an expatriate, so he submitted his resignation.[41] To maintain his residency in Dubai, an Emirati friend and previous colleague listed him as a member of his company. Although Mohammed did not receive a salary, he could maintain a work visa for himself and a residency visa for his wife and children for about seven months until he found another full-time job. In the interim, he consulted for various private businesses owned by Gulf nationals. Similarly, when Huda lost her job, she was able to stay in the UAE because her husband did not lose his job.[42] For the most part, the financial crisis only affected residents of Dubai, and not those of other Emirates. However, even those who were laid off felt that it was because they were expatriates and not specifically because they were of Arab or Palestinian origin. Hassan, an Emirati Palestinian, argued that discrimination was personal and not systematic because individuals sometimes discriminated against others, but the system itself simply distinguished between national and expat. He further argued that it was necessary to keep in mind that Palestinians experience far worse discrimination in the West.[43] Moreover, most justified the government's rationale and felt that laying off expatriates was a legitimate course of action under the circumstances. By no means are these dynamics and perceptions representative of the experiences of all Palestinians in the UAE, but they are common among the upwardly mobile, upper-middle-class strata.

GCC states, and Abu Dhabi and Dubai in particular in the UAE, have become popular work destinations for Palestinians raised (often born) and educated in Western countries. Many of these individuals felt that the UAE offered them a unique opportunity to be in the Arab world, close to Palestine and other Arab countries, but still live in a more Western, socially open society. According to Wafa, born in the US and raised there and in Beirut, when she initially came to the UAE five years ago she had planned to stay for one or two years, mainly to stay close to Jordan, where her parents and family were living at the time. She also appreciated that she was close to other Arab countries, and that she had access to jobs and new opportunities.[44] Linda, an interviewee born and raised in Canada elaborated:

> I came here to work. It was the only place in the region where I could find a job and get paid well. I wanted to be in the Arab world. I was curious. In Lebanon or Palestine, I would not have the same opportunities, and this place is quite Western. I feel Dubai is a place for 'global Arabs'—we have studied in the West... We have been all over. I think of myself as 'third culture', that is, children who are raised in a culture outside of their parents' culture, and there are a lot of 'third culture' young Arabs in the UAE... We all hang out with each other.[45]

Linda's description captured the sentiment of many of the Palestinians born in the West or those who had spent a significant part of their lives there. For those who worked in film, art or advertising in particular, the UAE held exceptional promise. The younger generation at the earlier stages of their careers particularly felt that the UAE provided them with opportunities that surpassed those that would have been available to them in Canada or the US. Hani, a Palestinian born in Lebanon and raised in Canada, who has been in the UAE since 2004, explained, 'When I first came, I planned to stay for two years to gain experience... But then I became very comfortable, and I earned so much more than my friends in Canada. I also loved the weather.'[46] Along these same lines, Linda explained how her life is much more stable than the lives of many of her friends in Canada, who are still struggling to get their careers in order.[47]

Despite these advantages, many acknowledged there were drawbacks to staying and living in the UAE compared to living in the West. According to Wafa, 'You are limited in terms of being critical about anything... Everything is political, and you have no community to help you flourish.'[48] The spontaneous organisation of street culture is what Linda missed most from Canada. According to her, everything in the UAE was less spontaneous.[49] Hani was adamant that he would leave the UAE once he had children because he wants them to be brought up in a culture where there is less social and national stratification. According to him, 'I do not feel any one specific group is targeted. Everyone is being watched here, and not only Palestinians. Also, the drawback to living here is that we are made to feel that we are not part of the fabric of the country... We are only observers.'[50]

Impact of broader political developments and discrimination

Given near consensus in the literature that a preference for Asian workers became more prevalent from the late 1970s onwards, this research anticipated that issues of discrimination to mirror discussions raised in British archival protectorate exchanges. According to Andrzej Kapiszewski:

> At the beginning, the Arab workers were very welcome. Their linguistic and cultural compatibility with the local populations made them more attractive to nationals than other immigrants. The migrant Arabs set up the familiar Arab-type government administration and educational facilities, helped to develop health services, build the necessary infrastructure for these rapidly developing countries and run the oil industries.[51]

Kapiszewski elaborated, however, that the presence of Palestinians, which pushed the GCC states into an involvement in politics related to the Arab-Israeli conflict, was also considered a problem.[52] The interviewees, however, were much less critical than expected about discrimination in the workplace and the impact of broader political developments. For the most part, they argued that the key distinction in the workplace was between 'locals' (nationals) and expatriates, and that in fact Palestinians were often respected more than others. Given that Palestinians were previously well represented in the education sector, Palestinian teachers taught many Emiratis, so there was often an emotional affinity too.

Interviewees acknowledged that nationalisation policies were making it more difficult for Palestinians to gain employment in certain sectors, but that this was not specific to Palestinians but to expatriates more generally. Those who arrived in the 1970s felt that it was previously much easier to get jobs in the public sector. Moreover, if Palestinians were part of the management of a particular company, they were more likely to hire other Palestinians. According to Abu Tarek, a Palestinian from the West Bank who studied in Iraq and arrived in the UAE in 1975, 99 per cent of Abu Dhabi National Oil Company employees in the 1970s were Palestinian.[53] This type of national sector dominance has become far less likely. A number of interviewees, however, argued that a colonial mindset often shapes workplace relations. They felt that there was greater tension between Westerners and Arabs than between Emiratis and other Arabs. While previously, Emiratis privileged Westerners in the workplace, younger participants believed that these dynamics were not commonplace and/or were changing, and that in fact, younger Emiratis, along with Palestinians, were less tolerant of stereotypes that privileged Westerners. As Ali, an employee in the Abu Dhabi government, explained, 'I have not really felt discriminated against... There is the stereotype that we are stubborn, but they trust us to get the job done...Along with other Emiratis, we think it is funny how some Brits think they are superior'.[54] Many interviewees shared the sentiment that other Emiratis actually had great respect for them in the workplace, and that often they were entrusted with greater responsibilities because Palestinians have a reputation for being hardworking and reliable. One condition, however, overrode all others: employees had to remain apolitical, and were unable to challenge the Emirati political system or leadership. Even those interviewees who might be characterised as political activists in the countries they came from acknowledged this and abided unwaveringly.

With the same cautious reflection, most interviewees felt that although broader political developments had not affected them personally, they often felt greater surveillance during these periods. According to those who were in the UAE during the First Gulf War, they often 'heard' about people being dismissed from their positions. The expulsion of Palestinians from Kuwait in 1991 was a rude awakening and stark reminder of the vulnerable status of their 'permanence' in the UAE, or in the GCC more generally. As Abu Tarek explained, 'In 1991, I had been in the UAE for over seventeen years and people at work knew me and everyone trusted me. But a number of Jordanians, Palestinians and Yemenis lost their jobs during that period. We also felt under increased surveillance.'[55] The general sentiment was that everyone was fine as long as they were not politically engaged and were not critical of the UAE leadership. The UAE can provide lucrative opportunities if one understands his or her 'limits', as Abu Jamal explained.[56]

Despite these positive assessments about their positions and their standing in the workplace, almost all interviewees had heard that fewer and fewer Palestinians were being employed, and that many had been unable to attain working visas since 2009, especially since the start of the Arab uprisings. Hundreds of Palestinians from the Gaza Strip were subsequently expelled from the UAE in 2009 following Hamas' take-over of the Gaza Strip in 2008. A larger number of Palestinians were expelled after the assassination of Hamas leader Mahmoud Madbouh in Dubai in 2010 and the discovery that he had entered the UAE on false documents. Moreover, dozens of Shi'a Lebanese were also deported. These individuals simply received notices from immigration authorities that they must leave the country with their families. Authorities provided no explanations or opportunities for appeal.[57] Participants heard that along with Palestinians, Egyptians, Syrians, Tunisians, and Yemenis were also no longer being hired, and many had been laid off. Although in most cases, the interviewees were unable to substantiate these developments, it appeared that the Emirati government had implemented an 'undeclared' policy of reducing the number of employees from the countries influenced by the Arab uprisings or from the Palestinian territories. In most cases, there was no transparency about these developments. In the higher education sector, however, these policies were clearly outlined. As Shadia, a university professor who has lived in the UAE for over ten years, explained, 'We were "advised" not to teach anything related to the Arab Spring... In terms of new employees, there was a list of nationalities that we could no longer hire, and the list included Egyptians, Syrians and Tunisians... These nationalities change over time.'[58] Wafa, also a university professor, confirmed, 'Directives were sent out that we should not "do" anything Arab Spring-related... As for Palestine, there simply is no interest.'[59] In general, many sensed that there was more security and surveillance, less news coverage of the Arab world, and in general, media appeared to have become more of a tool for social manipulation than prior to the Arab uprisings.

THE 'OTHER ARAB' AND GULF CITIZENS

The generational divide

A clear generational divide emerged from the research findings over issues of integration and socialisation, trust, sense of belonging in the UAE, and relationships to Palestine. The younger generation, including those born in the UAE and those who had arrived since the early 2000s, were much more likely to socialise with Emiratis and in many ways felt more integrated. This generation also appeared to be more trusting of their context, and perceived it in relation to broader international or global developments. The older generation, including those who have been in the UAE since the 1970s, did not express feeling a sense of belonging in the UAE; this sentiment starkly contrasted with the attitudes of those who were born in the UAE, many of whom were surprised by the question and felt that the UAE was nothing but home to them.

Integration and socialisation

The older generation was reluctant to socially integrate. Even those who worked closely with Emiratis in a formal capacity did not socialise with locals. Emiratis reciprocated this sentiment and also did not socialise with expatriates, or even with the Palestinians who had been granted Emirati citizenship. For the older generation, namely those who arrived in the late 1960s or the 1970s, socialising remained limited to family, or in some cases the Palestinian community, and/or the broader Arab community, but did not include Gulf nationals. According to Abu Helmi, who moved to the UAE in 1973: 'We had no relations with other Emiratis... perhaps sometimes the relations were work related, but relations did not go beyond that. The fact of the matter is that they do not trust us, and we do not trust them.'[60] Especially among those who held Emirati citizenship there appeared to be increased social isolation, including from the Palestinian community. As Hassan,[61] an Emirati of Palestinian origin reflected, 'My parents were very secluded... I do not know why... Maybe because of my dad's position in the government he did not want to be involved... My dad is pretty apolitical so he is not very involved. This might be related to the disappointments of the 1960s and 1970s.'[62] Another Emirati Palestinian refused to meet because he did not want to engage in what he believed would be a 'political' interview. Other members of the community, however, were surprised and disclosed that although guarded, they were in fact very close to the Palestinian community. Similar to others of his generation, Hassan did not choose his friends based on nationality and had a number of Emirati friends.

Among the newer generations to arrive in the UAE, especially those who arrived in the 1990s and 2000s, there appeared to be more socialising, though not necessarily between families. In this newer generation, socialising is much more common, especially among males. Similarly, a lot of socialising and exchanges seemed to occur among Palestinians who identified as 'third culture' and younger Emiratis who have had more cross-cultural exposure. Given the greater prevalence of sex segregation among Emiratis in social settings, family visits also assume this pattern, in which women and children are more likely to socialise separately from men. Palestinian children born and raised in the UAE, especially those who attended public schools, continued to socialise and interact with their Emirati friends, even as they became older and/or after marriage. Although Palestinians without Emirati citizenship mostly attend private schools,[63] in general, there appears to be a move towards more socialising, interaction and integration, despite the more reserved ways of older generations.

Belonging and home

The generational divide was most evident in relation to participants' sense of belonging and the extent to which they considered the UAE home. For the older generation, their relationship to the UAE was more practical and pragmatic. It was about securing a livelihood and a standard of living in an otherwise precarious world. This relationship was not imbued with sentimentality—few from this generation regarded the UAE as home. Many of those who had arrived in the 1970s and 1980s had plans in place to leave the UAE once they retired. However, the new generation, especially the more highly skilled middle and upper middle classes, planned to stay in the UAE indefinitely. As for those born in the UAE, Emirati and expatriate alike, there was no question about their sense of belonging or whether or not the UAE was home.

The Palestinians who came to the UAE directly from the Palestinian territories during the 1970s and 1980s were perhaps most determined to return 'home' once they retired, or were unable to renew their post-retirement visas. Many among this generation had managed to build homes in the West Bank, and in some cases, had begun plans to start new businesses there once they returned. Unlike 'locals', however, once they retire from work, they are not entitled to any social security benefits, but only to a one-time compensation package of one month's salary for each year spent in the UAE. Given that, in most cases, their children and their families would remain in the UAE, they also hoped to spend part of each year in the UAE on a family or visitor's visa. Some groups, such as Palestinian refugees from Lebanon, however, were more restricted in their options. Abu Jamal, a refugee from Lebanon, for example, was nearing retirement age and was very apprehensive about returning to Lebanon, but was hopeful that he could stay in the UAE through family-sponsored visas arranged through his children.[64]

For the younger generation of highly skilled middle- or upper-class Palestinians, their sense of belonging was more about a 'cosmopolitanism' that they could not enjoy in other Arab countries. For many of these individuals, they saw the UAE as having a more connected, cosmopolitan position in the world compared to their parents or older generations. Especially among those who found themselves working in the inner circles of the government, the UAE provided opportunities that were often absent for Palestinians elsewhere. For many of these individuals, especially those who were working in Dubai's elite professional circles, they felt they were involved in something bigger than themselves. Similar to the older generation, who played key strategic roles in the governing bodies of the UAE, Dubai holds a special promise for some today. Mohammed, a Palestinian from Jordan, and Issam, from the West Bank, both worked in the inner circles of the Dubai government. According to Mohammed, the Dubai leadership included a number of expatriates in creating the 'Dubai dream'.[65] For Issam, the main distinction is that key government officials are masters of managing talent, and they respect knowledge and are not threatened by the talent of others, including the talent of Palestinians.[66] According to Issam, 'Dubai is the only place in the contemporary Arab world where you can dream something and make it happen... I was made to feel that I was part of the team that built Dubai.'[67] Previously, he had volunteered his services to officials in the Palestinian Authority, but they ignored his offer. Issam said that the Palestinian leadership ignored people's expertise, unless they were from the inner circles of Fatah, the governing body of the West Bank Palestinian Authority, and the leadership is usually only interested in donations.[68] To conclude that Palestinians have played key strategic roles only in the UAE, however, would be inaccurate. Palestinians have played important roles in the development of many GCC countries, as well as Jordan, for example. The UAE today, however, is distinct from other contexts in that involvement in its inner circle affords more extensive cosmopolitan access.

All those who were born in the UAE, both Emiratis and those from expatriate families, planned to stay in the UAE, or return if they were currently studying abroad, according to their parents. Hassan, for example, was born and raised in the UAE, but spent summers in Jordan visiting relatives. According to him, 'I felt more like an outsider in Jordan among Palestinians than I did here. I feel more assimilated here. This surprised me. You feel very safe here... there is much more sexual harassment against women and people can be much more vulgar in Jordan.'[69] Others expressed similar attitudes. Yasmin, a Christian Palestinian born and raised in the UAE, also felt that the UAE was home. As she explained, 'I feel I belong... my memories are here. My father, however, feels that he is obligated to pay back this country because of what he gained. Although he has been here for over thirty years, he only established a privately owned business once free zones became available. To this day, we do not own a house. My father feels that it does not make sense given the ninety-nine-year lease limits and visa requirements'.[70] Despite her father's constant reminders that they cannot take their stay in the UAE for granted, Yasmin feels this is her only home, and cannot imagine moving elsewhere.

Relationship to Palestine

Regardless of how cautious, engaged or involved various participants were, their self-identification as Palestinian was unwavering. Of all the Palestinians interviewed, only one Emirati of Palestinian origin (with a well-known Palestinian surname) refused to acknowledge his Palestinian origin. Three broad patterns emerged in the context of Palestinian identity. Those who arrived during the 1960s and 1970s were the most cautious, and often less likely to be involved in community events. Those who still had what were then Israeli-issued identity cards visited the West Bank annually or every other year with their families. Those who arrived in the 1980s and 1990s, especially from the West Bank, Gaza Strip, and Jordan, were more likely to be involved in organising humanitarian relief activities, and often were part of an organised Palestinian community. The younger generation, and those who arrived more recently, attended fundraising events and individual initiatives regularly, but were less likely to be part of an organised Palestinian community because their social networks were much broader. Almost all participants, including those from the older and more guarded generation, sent remittances to their families, especially those who still had families in the Palestinian territories. Hassan's father, for example, despite his cautiousness and lack of willingness to be involved with the Palestinian community, supported his entire extended family in the Gaza Strip, and sent *zakat* (alms) to numerous charities and orphanages, and others who needed it.

The Palestinians in the UAE did not organise themselves at national level, but rather limited their organisation to their respective emirates. The Palestinian Embassy in Abu Dhabi and the Palestinian Consulate in Dubai occasionally organise community events. In general, however, the community does not always trust them, given the level of corruption in the PLO and Palestinian Authority. According to most of my interviewees, various UAE leaders and government bodies gave their support at different periods, especially Sheikh Zayed, who prioritised the Palestinian cause over other Arab nationalist causes. The condition, however, was clear that support to Palestine or anything Palestine-related must remain apolitical and predominately humanitarian, ideally highlighting the support of the Emirati rulers.

Among the organised groups in the UAE, the Abu Dhabi Palestinian Business Council was heavily involved in fundraising activities to support different initiatives in the Palestinian territories, as well as Palestinian families in the UAE in need of assistance. It organises events and provides networking opportunities to ensure that the community stays connected. Annually, it pays for the tuition of over seventy-five Palestinian students in Abu Dhabi, whose families are unable to pay their private school tuition at the elementary, preparatory or secondary levels. It also fundraises to cover the tuition of students in need at Al-Quds University in the Palestinian territories. According to Kamal, a Palestinian businessman who is familiar with the work of the business council, members of the Palestinian community are very generous and willing to help Palestinians in the UAE, as well as in the Palestinian territories, but they do not trust the Palestinian Authority or the PLO. Much funding is often also channelled through official UAE institutions such as the Emirati Red Crescent or the Zayed Charitable and Humanitarian Foundation.[71]

Stateless multi-citizens and the class divide

With the exception of one family from Lebanon and one from Syria, and a few interviewees from Jordan, regardless of generation, most have worked or are working towards obtaining citizenship of a Western country, namely the US and Canada, and to a lesser extent and more recently New Zealand and Australia. Repeatedly, participants brought up the significance of a back-up plan in case another crisis like the 1991 invasion of Kuwait took place and Palestinians were expelled from the UAE. In some cases, families arranged to have their children born in the US and Canada during family vacations to ensure they obtained citizenship of that country. Parents also sent their children to study abroad and in the process arranged for them to obtain permanent US or Canadian residency in hopes of obtaining citizenship. Even when the children had no intention of remaining in the West, their parents felt it was their responsibility to ensure that their children had another passport in the case of an 'emergency.' Acquiring citizenship was often correlated with wealth or social class for those who did not carry refugee documents. In some cases, families had managed to secure citizenship in two or three countries. For the highly skilled middle or upper middle classes, Emirati citizenship was not an issue. According to an interviewee who had been born in the US and raised in the UAE, 'I would be required to given up my other citizenships. Perhaps I could give up my Jordanian citizenship, but why would I give up my Jerusalem ID or American passport for UAE citizenship?'[72] For others, however, especially those who carried refugee documents, the lack of citizenship was life-restricting; the prospects for studying aboard and acquiring the citizenship of another country were less likely because acquiring travel visas was difficult. Those who had sufficient resources could work around impediments and get citizenship of another country.

A growing trend among Palestinians in the UAE, especially those who carry refugee papers and have sufficient resources, is to obtain citizenship by investing in Saint Kitts and Nevis,[73] a two-island country in the West Indies. These islands rely on foreign direct investment from their Citizenship by Investment Program, which is outlined in their Citizenship Act of 1984.[74] Potential investors must go through various security checks before qualifying for citizenship. The minimum investment is US$400,000 for the main applicant, and the application fees are US$50,000 for the main applicant, US$25,000 for a spouse, US$25,000 for each child under eighteen, and US$50,000 for each child over eighteen. Investors can invest a minimum of US$400,000 in real estate or donate US$250,000 to the Sugar Industry Diversification Fund, which assists retired and displaced sugar workers. Applicants obtaining Economic Citizenship can resell their property as citizenship property five years after purchase. Yasmin's father, for example, invested US$400,000 in a tourist hotel for passports for himself, Yasmin, her mother and brother. Being Commonwealth passports they permit visa-free travel to over 120 countries. Yasmin's family is also in the process of obtaining Canadian citizenship, which would be more reliable in the event that they had to leave the UAE.[75] Another interviewee, a holder of a Lebanese refugee document and Jordanian citizenship, also managed to obtain Saint Kitts and Nevis citizenship.[76] His wife and children had secured Canadian citizenship, but because he had to stay in the UAE to work, he could not fulfil the Canadian residency requirements to obtain citizenship. Such possibilities, however, do not exist for those with lesser means, underscoring the primacy of class in determining citizenship outcomes.

It is important to bear in mind that in the particular case of Palestinian refugees, the UAE's denial of full citizenship rights is also not unique to this context, but rather a uniform policy adopted and applied in all Arab countries. Various Arab countries have adopted numerous resolutions ensuring that they provide Palestinians with residency, though not the political rights granted to their citizens—limited though they may be in some contexts. This was encapsulated in the Arab League's Casablanca Protocol of 1965. Various resolutions have also proposed that Palestinian refugee status be preserved to ensure that Israel does not evade its responsibility towards Palestinian refugees.[77]

Jordan is the only Arab country that granted citizenship to Palestinian refugees who were in the country following the 1948 and 1967 wars.[78] Egypt, Lebanon, Syria, Iraq, and more recently Yemen, issued the Palestinians special refugee documents that would serve as travel documents.[79] These documents do not confer permanent residency and need to be renewed every three months to three years depending on their exact category.[80] In common with other Arab states, labour laws in the UAE distinguish between 'nationals' and 'foreigners' in terms of equal opportunity, pay and benefits.[81] In Lebanon, Egypt and Iraq, Palestinians are subject to the same employment laws that apply to foreigners, with no regard for the country of their birth (even if born in the respective country), and the duration of their residency in that country.[82] As a result, unemployment among Palestinians in Lebanon is high, and in Jordan Palestinians with temporary Jordanian passports are not allowed to work in the public sector.[83] As Shiblak explained:

> With few exceptions, Palestinians in the Arab host countries are treated as foreigners and do not have access by right to government services such as education, health, and social benefits. Such access has been totally denied to Palestinians in Lebanon since 1948, in Egypt since 1980, and recently and to a lesser extent, in Jordan and Iraq.[84]

Pre-civil war Syria was distinct from a number of Arab countries because it granted Palestinians the same social and economic rights as its own citizens.

Conclusion

The presence of Palestinians in the UAE has never constituted a straightforward relationship of accommodation and compatibility. The idea of the 'political

Palestinian' constitutes the same threat to UAE officials today as it did to the British. The denial of UAE visas to Palestinians since 2009 reflects this mindset. Having said that, Palestinians who have proved their commitment to the UAE and have not challenged the status quo have garnered considerable respect. This discussion, however, needs to be framed more comparatively and incorporate the treatment of Palestinians in other contexts.

Although the distinction in perception and attitudes between older and newer generations of Palestinians is marked, especially among those who were born and raised in the UAE, the undercurrent of insecurity is real for all. The changes in attitudes of younger Emiratis and Palestinians, however, challenge perceptions about GCC states and the region more generally. Narrow discussions about pan-Arabism do not fully capture how this newer generation views itself in relation to the changing global position of the UAE—whether real or imagined. These changing dynamics are also likely to compel the UAE to reassess its relations with these migrant communities, especially the 'other Arabs.' The importance of class to this discussion cannot be overstated. Future research will require more careful examination of less privileged and underprivileged Arab communities in the UAE, especially those Palestinian communities that were under-represented in the research project.

7

YEMENI IRREGULAR MIGRANTS IN THE KINGDOM OF SAUDI ARABIA AND THE IMPLICATIONS OF LARGE SCALE RETURN

AN ANALYSIS OF YEMENI MIGRANTS RETURNING FROM SAUDI ARABIA

Harry Cook and *Michael Newson*[1]

Introduction

In June 2013, the International Organization for Migration (IOM) began monitoring and providing humanitarian assistance at the Al Tuwal border-crossing to Yemeni returnees from Saudi Arabia who were being deported as part of a government clampdown on irregular migration. Throughout these operations, which have continued, IOM officials carried out short surveys of some of the returnees. The results of these surveys provide a rare glimpse into the conditions and character of the Yemeni irregular migrant community in Saudi Arabia with regard to their activities in Saudi Arabia, as well as their relations with their communities of origin in Yemen.

This chapter begins with a short overview of the historical patterns of labour migration from Yemen to Saudi Arabia, covering the first major wave in the 1970s and 1980s, the mass returns of the early 1990s, and the subsequent (primarily irregular) migration flows of the 1990s and 2000s, up to the present-day returns of large numbers of irregular migrants beginning in early 2013. The chapter provides an analysis of the data IOM has collected on returnees at the Al Tuwal border to give some insight into the characteristics of this community and its relations with communities of origin in Yemen, before concluding with some considerations on the possible impacts of the Saudis' new labour mobility policies on communities in Yemen—which have, for decades, relied heavily on access to the Saudi labour market—and the future of Yemen–Saudi Arabia labour mobility.

Political instability in Yemen has taken a considerable turn for the worse. Power struggles and fighting between the Yemeni government and Houthi rebels throughout early 2015 finally resulted in the government of Saudi Arabia also getting involved, beginning a large-scale aerial bombing campaign on 25 March 2015. In the short term, these events are likely to severely disrupt labour mobility (both regular and irregular) between Yemen and Saudi Arabia—indeed outmigration from Yemen since 25 March has largely been to the Horn of Africa, with vulnerable Yemeni populations seeking safety there. In the longer term, however, the pattern of dependence on labour migration to Saudi Arabia outlined in this chapter is most likely to re-establish itself, with the push factors of poverty, political instability and poor job prospects in Yemen persisting, and the geographical, linguistic and cultural proximity of Saudi Arabia, the strong demand for low-skilled labour, and the ease of finding a job in Saudi Arabia continuing to attract Yemenis across the border, either through regular labour mobility programmes, or by irregular means.

Yemen–Saudi Arabia labour migration flows, 1970–90

The movement of Yemenis to Saudi Arabia for work has a long and important history that has left its mark on the social and economic development of both countries over the past several decades. While mobility between Saudi Arabia and Yemen has been ongoing for many decades, the first major movements of Yemeni labour migrants began in the early 1970s as resource-fuelled economic development in Saudi Arabia created massive demand for workers, while a stagnant economy and lack of employment opportunities domestically, in what were then North and South Yemen, incentivised Yemenis to take advantage of the opportunities available in Saudi Arabia. As James Allman and Allan Hill note, 'The [1975] Census showed that the lack of domestic economic opportunities... and the numerous opportunities in the oil-rich states of the Middle East, especially Saudi Arabia, had resulted in an out-migration of young males of prime ages of very large proportions'.[2]

Despite the importance of these flows in supporting the economic development of Yemen and Saudi Arabia, data and research on these movements are scarce. Providing an estimate of the flows and stock of Yemeni migrant workers in Saudi Arabia over this period is particularly challenging, given that North Yemenis enjoyed open access to the Saudi Arabia labour market until the First Gulf War in 1990, and that—despite restrictions placed on citizens of South Yemen, which required them to have a sponsor and work permit—movements of people from North and South Yemen to Saudi Arabia were relatively unrestricted, with little monitoring or formal mechanisms for managing flows.[3] As Thomas Stevenson notes, 'For all Yemenis, migration to Saudi Arabia was easy. They could obtain a visa at any port of entry, often without a passport; they did not require a sponsor for work or residence permits, and could own businesses'.[4] Thus, from the beginning of these large-scale movements, geographical proximity and a lack of administrative procedures allowed for a largely unmanaged and informal labour mobility process, similar to what may be observed in other regions with liberal mobility policies where large wealth and opportunity gaps exist. 'The first point is the amount of spontaneity involved in the migration process. With the ease of migrating for Yemenis (limited documentation, very small financial outlay, the support system of friends and relatives), the amount of planning has been minimized'.[5]

Estimates of the number of Yemenis working in neighbouring Gulf countries in the 1970s have been derived by several researchers using data primarily from the 1975 Census in North Yemen, administrative data from South Yemen, as well as employment statistics and census results from countries of destination. Based on the available data, most researchers have estimated a rapid increase in the Yemeni population in Saudi Arabia from between 290,000 and 350,000 Yemeni workers in neighbouring countries (with the vast majority in Saudi Arabia) in 1975, to approximately 541,000 in 1977. Additionally, government statistics from South Yemen indicate that 83,800 South Yemenis were registered as labour migrants in the Gulf in 1980. By 1990, the population of all Yemenis in Saudi Arabia was estimated to be between 800,000 and 1.2 million. While this migration took place from all regions of both North and South Yemen, it was more pronounced in North Yemen, particularly originating in the region of Ta'iz.[6]

The continual growth of the Yemeni population in Saudi Arabia from the early 1970s to 1990 is consistent with what we would expect given the strong economic pull factors of the growing Saudi economy, the limited opportunities available within Yemen's own labour market, as well as the administrative and logistical ease with which Yemenis could access the Saudi labour market. The estimates of Yemeni migrant stock in Saudi Arabia probably greatly underestimate the actual number of Yemenis who engaged in labour migration to Saudi Arabia over this period, with many Yemenis engaging in circular migration, travelling and working in Saudi Arabia for several years and then returning to Yemen. Labour mobility between Yemen and Saudi Arabia gained increasing importance in the daily lives of Yemenis over this period, with barely a family in Yemen not affected in some way by these movements.

Through their research on Yemeni returnees in the late 1980s and early 1990s, Stevenson and Nora Ann Colton provided insight into the demographics of returning labour migrants from Saudi Arabia just prior to and during a previous large-scale deportation of Yemenis in the First Gulf War:[7] the overarching feature of these studies is that the population was overwhelmingly male and relatively young, usually first engaged in migration in their twenties or thirties. Migrants were also highly likely to be married (96.9 per cent in Colton's sample of 353 people), with their wives and children remaining behind in Yemen. As Colton notes, her survey 'makes clear not only that these migrants were not the young singles leaving to accomplish a goal, but that they were married migrants disillusioned with agriculture and desiring to improve their standard of living'.[8]

Yemen in the 1970s and 1980s was an overwhelmingly rural and agrarian society: according to the 1975 census in North Yemen, 73.3 per cent of employment was in the agriculture and fishing sector and 64 per cent of the population lived in settlements of 250 people or less, with only 11 per cent living in settlements of over 2,000 people. The migration flows of the 1970s and 1980s—to Saudi Arabia, as well as within Yemen—marked the first major shift towards Yemen's urbanisation. Given the lack of selection criteria on the part of Saudi migration policy in relation to Yemen at the time, it is not surprising to see that the samples studied by Stevenson and Colton suggest the majority of migrants originated from rural backgrounds, with many having an occupational background in agriculture. Nevertheless, as Colton notes, the samples suggest a certain degree of 'self-selection' among Yemeni migrants to Saudi Arabia, with only 20 per cent identifying their occupation in Yemen prior to migration as farming. The sample generally reflects an occupational history in Yemen more aligned with occupational demand in Saudi Arabia than Yemen's broader employment picture. For example, 13.6 per cent of the sample identified themselves as construction workers before migration (compared to a national figure of 4.6 per cent) and 11.6 per cent as unskilled labourers, two occupations that were in high demand in Saudi Arabia as large-scale infrastructure projects developed. Colton's sample also suggests a migrant population to Saudi Arabia, which, though still largely unskilled with low educational achievement, nevertheless exhibits somewhat greater levels of education than the Yemeni population as a whole. Within Colton's sample, 35 per cent of informants had some formal education, whereas the results of the 1975 Census indicate 2.7 per cent from the population of North Yemen as a whole.

Given the low educational levels of Yemeni labour migrants and the nature of occupational demand within Saudi Arabia throughout the 1970s and 1980s, it is not surprising to see from the studies on this subject that the vast majority of Yemeni labour migrants worked in low-skilled and semi-skilled occupations. Of Colton's sample of returnees, only 15 per cent (listed as managers and clerical employees) may have been employed in occupations requiring higher skill levels. The research of J.S. Birks *et al.* also highlights the engagement of Yemeni migrants in Saudi Arabia in lower-skilled labour, primarily in the construction sector. However, in 1981 it notes the increasing competition from Asian workers, who showed greater ability to adapt to more capital-intensive and mechanised construction techniques that were increasingly being introduced in Saudi Arabia, due to somewhat higher educational levels.

These large-scale labour migration flows throughout the 1970s and 1980s had a tremendous impact on Yemen's social and economic development. The geographical proximity as well as the family links that existed between Yemenis in Saudi Arabia and their communities of origin meant that there were frequent return visits to Yemen by migrants, and they regularly sent home financial remittances to support family members. By 1987, financial remittances to Yemen were estimated at US$1.06 billion per annum, which represented a significant proportion of the country's GDP and its primary source of foreign currency.

At the same time, the large exodus of young, working-age men resulted in labour shortages in Yemen itself, particularly within rural communities that had historically depended on male labour to support agricultural crops. The results of these labour shortages were threefold: (1) agricultural production shifted towards less labour-intensive crops. Whereas in the early 1970s, cereals, coffee and cotton were common agricultural products in Yemen grown for domestic consumption as well as for export, by the end of the 1980s production of these staples had declined dramatically, being replaced largely by the production of qat,[9] which was less labour-intensive and more lucrative on the domestic market; (2) urbanisation favoured development of the service sector and capital-intensive manufacturing. Labour shortages in Yemen resulted in significant salary inflation, which discouraged the development of large, labour-intensive manufacturing projects, with urban migrants instead entering the service sector, with the development of manufacturing in Yemen, where it did take place, instead taking on a more capital-intensive model; (3) introduction of foreign labour in Yemen. While an increase in Yemeni women entering the labour market partly addressed the exodus of male workers, the continued labour shortage led to the first significant numbers of foreign workers, primarily from South and South-East Asia, entering the Yemeni labour market.[10]

Thus, the labour migration phenomenon of the 1970s and 1980s, while stimulating economic growth in Yemen and leading to measurable material improvements in the lives of migrants and their families, also resulted in a significant increase in Yemen's dependence on foreign markets, including the Saudi Arabia labour market, for employment opportunities and international agricultural markets for food staples. Throughout this period, Yemen became increasingly reliant on remittances from labour migrants in Saudi Arabia as a source of foreign currency and income to stimulate domestic consumption. At the same time, shortages in domestic labour brought about a shift away from labour-intensive crops, resulting in a decline in export crops such as coffee and cotton, as well as increasing reliance on imports of cereals and other agricultural products to meet domestic demand. Colton notes that the total area of cultivated land in North Yemen declined from 1.196 million hectares in 1974 to 836,000 in 1988, while grain imports increased from 220 million riyals in 1978 to 997 million riyals in 1987. Nader Fergany also studied the impact of migration on Yemen's development in the early 1980s, noting that 'The remittances [from Saudi Arabia] bought rather than produced what the country needed. Yemen's import list is now awesome in size and variety'.[11] At the same time during this period, Saudi Arabia became increasingly reliant on foreign labour to feed its labour market and infrastructure development, at first relying heavily on labour from Yemen and other neighbouring Arab countries and later on foreign workers from South and South-East Asia. However, although Saudi Arabia diversified the countries from which it was recruiting foreign workers, Yemen remained highly dependent on Saudi Arabia as its principle external labour market, leaving Yemenis highly vulnerable to downswings in the Saudi economy or changes in Saudi policy that affected migration flows.

Yemen–Saudi Arabia labour migration flows, 1990–2013

In 1990, Saudi Arabia instituted new regulations restricting Yemeni access to its labour market. In effect, the new regulations eliminated Yemen's privileged access to the Saudi labour market, instead imposing the same conditions on Yemenis as were required for workers of other nationalities, including requiring Yemeni workers to have a Saudi sponsor and a work permit to work legally in the country. The regulatory change was accompanied by a two-month grace period that allowed Yemeni workers time to regularise their status under the new rules. Nevertheless, the vast majority of Yemenis in Saudi Arabia were unable to regularise their status, leading to mass returns of migrants to Yemen.[12]

An estimated 800,000 Yemenis returned from Saudi Arabia between late 1990 and 1991.[13] These mass returns created considerable challenges for Yemen, whose government had to deal simultaneously with a loss of foreign capital as remittances dried up, as well as the need to absorb returnees into the Yemeni labour market. The return also placed considerable pressure on housing, because returnees were reluctant to return to their villages, having become accustomed to a more urban environment in Saudi Arabia, and instead sought accommodation and employment in Yemen's larger cities and towns. Stevenson's research indicates that over half of returnees had no housing that they could return to, either through family or available for rent, while the United Nations Development Programme estimated that poverty rates in Yemen increased from 15 to 35 per cent as a result of the mass return of Yemeni migrants from Saudi Arabia.[14]

While the most common reason provided by scholars and observers for the sudden shift in Saudi policy towards Yemeni workers is the government of Yemen's reluctance to condemn Iraq's invasion of Kuwait and its objection to Saudi Arabia's hosting of US troops, the reality is somewhat more complicated and instead points toward a much longer-term position than would result from a political spat. A number of factors contributed to Saudi Arabia's shift in policy towards labour migration from Yemen, which included: slowing growth of Saudi economic development due to lower oil prices in the 1980s; increases in domestic unemployment; a shift in migration patterns of Yemenis, who were increasingly bringing their families and taking up occupations in the service sector; increasing interest in the private sector in employing workers from Asian countries of origin; Saudi concern about the reunification of North and South Yemen; and political issues regarding Iraq's invasion of Kuwait.[15] As Colton notes, 'Saudi Arabia had been disengaging from the Yemeni labor market years before the Gulf crisis. In fact, most would agree that Saudi Arabia would not have taken such a bold step if it did not see the cost to its production as minimal'.[16] Thus, despite popular characterisations of Saudi Arabia's policy changes towards Yemeni labour migration as sudden and based on political disputes, it is clear that, as is the case in all major countries of destination, considerable reflection and longer-term objectives with regard to labour market development played an important role in shaping policy reforms.

The expectation among many observers of the situation in 1990–91 was that increased regulatory complications, along with increased competition from workers from Asian countries, would severely limit the mobility of workers between Yemen and Saudi Arabia in the ensuing years. However, as noted by Birks *et al.*, 'even if the labour-importing countries adopted a policy of discouraging or prohibiting Yemeni migrants, their administrative capability of enforcing such a decision would remain to be tested'.[17] Indeed, the lack of administrative capacity and/or political will within Saudi Arabia to effectively implement new regulations, as well as continued political instability and economic stagnation in Yemen, led to renewed large-scale movements of labour from Yemen to Saudi Arabia beginning as early as 1993. Given the increased administrative burdens for Yemenis to migrate and work in Saudi Arabia, as well as the relative ease in crossing the border and finding employment irregularly, it should come as no surprise that a large proportion of the renewed migratory flows from Yemen to Saudi Arabia took place through irregular channels. By 2007, a United Nations estimate put the number of Yemenis living in Saudi Arabia at 800,000, while more recent estimates had the numbers exceeding one million.[18] In 2013 alone, the Saudi Directorate General of Border Guards estimated 260,000 foreign nationals entered Saudi Arabia illegally across the Yemeni border, of whom approximately 70 per cent were Yemeni nationals.[19]

Introduction of the nitaqat *system and implementation of new regulations*

By 2011, because of rising rates of unemployment, as well as social and political instability in other parts of the region, the issue of labour market reform had reached the top of the political agenda for many GCC states. In the first half of 2013, the government of Saudi Arabia introduced changes to its foreign-worker system intended to reduce the size of the migrant workforce and favour employment of national workers in the medium term. At the same time, it stepped up efforts to enforce regulations surrounding foreign worker employment and remove irregular workers.

The government introduced the *nitaqat* (range, zone) system in late 2011. It adjusted the rules relating to the proportion of foreign workers allowed on an employer's payroll. Whereas the existing rules were unrealistic and largely ignored given the realities of the labour market, the new rules under the *nitaqat* system were more refined, taking into account differences in the need for foreign labour depending on occupations and employers' economic sectors, and adjusting the proportion of allowable foreign labour accordingly.

Beginning in April 2013, authorities embarked on a sustained effort to remove workers engaged in irregular employment, including those without proper work permits or who were otherwise violating the conditions of their permits. Their removal since the end of 2013 has been significant. Numbers vary according to sources, but reliable estimates suggest the removal of an estimated 1 million migrant workers between May 2013 and June 2014. The changes have affected Yemen the most; several sources estimated the total number of returnees to Yemen between April 2013 and mid-2014 to have been over 400,000.

The IOM established operations at the Al Tuwal border-crossing to monitor and provide assistance to Yemeni returnees. Al Tuwal has been the major gateway for returns from Saudi Arabia, accounting for an estimated 95 per cent of returnees. Since IOM's operations at Al Tuwal began in June 2013, the organisation has registered a relatively steady flow of returns, ranging between 17,000 and 58,000 people each month, with an overall average of 35,300 monthly returns between 1 June 2013 and 30 June 2014.[20] IOM also conducted short survey questionnaires among a sample of the returnees. Between October 2013 and June 2014, IOM completed a total of 34,800 such questionnaires. The results of these questionnaires form the basis for the remainder of this chapter. We aim to use the results to form a broad profile of the community of irregular Yemeni migrants in Saudi Arabia, as well as the linkages that exist between them and communities of origin in Yemen. We conclude by using the data to hypothesise on the potential impacts of Saudi policy changes on Yemeni communities of origin.

Explanation of the data

IOM's operations at the Al Tuwal border-crossing began in August 2013, to provide humanitarian support and coordination, as well as to monitor the flows of returnees. Between August 2013 and June 2014, IOM's operations at Al Tuwal provided 36,469 returnees with healthcare assistance, 31,568 with non-food items, and 232,993 with food.

Conditions are difficult at Al Tuwal and not conducive to information-gathering. Most returnees are eager to leave the border area and find transportation to the closest town as soon as possible. IOM's survey questionnaire at the border was thus limited to a few select questions to minimise disruption to returnees. Between October 2013 and June 2014, IOM officials conducted almost 35,000 interviews, representing about 10.7 per cent of the daily flow of returnees coming across the border.

We accessed and analysed the data with the support of IOM colleagues in Sana'a who were responsible for the collection and management of data from Al Tuwal. Among the interviews collected, a significant number included people who may have been forcibly returned twice or more after the most recent enforcement efforts began in April 2013. These interviews would have given an inaccurate picture of the community of irregular Yemeni workers in Saudi Arabia with regards to questions relating to length of stay in Saudi Arabia, employment, remittances, and so on. To control for this, and to use a sample we felt was more reflective of the conditions of irregular Yemenis in Saudi Arabia prior to April 2013, we removed from the interviewing sample those interviewees who indicated that they had been expelled twice or more and for whom the length of stay since their last expulsion was either less than one month or between one and twelve months. This left us with a sample size of 6,617 interviews to analyse. The vast majority (96.9 per cent) of respondents said that they had been deported because of a lack of appropriate documentation, thus clearly representing the target group of the most recent Saudi crackdown on irregular migration.

IOM's data collection team tried to ensure a broad sample free of bias. Nevertheless, as with all surveys, the sample was not truly random and depended on individuals cooperative and willing to be surveyed. The sample was also possibly biased towards returnees who were seeking either medical or food and non-food assistance on their return because, *prima facie*, one would expect these individuals to be more cooperative if they were seeking or receiving something from IOM in return. Therefore, before beginning any further analysis, we checked for any bias that this might cause in the sample. We did this by checking for correlations between cases where respondents had reported having some kind of vulnerability or having experienced some kind of abuse and answers that they had provided to other questions.[21]

Two significant correlations were of note. Firstly, those who reported suffering some kind of abuse were more likely to be short-stayers—those who reported having stayed in Saudi Arabia for less than one month; 47.3 per cent of the sub-sample reported having suffered some kind of abuse. More specifically, 46.8 per cent of short-stayers reported having suffered deprivation of food and water, compared to 32.4 per cent of those who reported having stayed in Saudi Arabia for between one and twelve months, 24.1 per cent between one and five years, and 20.8 per cent five or more years. Short-stayers were also more likely to have suffered physical, psychological or verbal abuse. Secondly, those who reported having some kind of vulnerability were more likely to be short-stayers—those who reported having stayed in Saudi Arabia for less than one month. Indeed, the majority of those who reported having some kind of vulnerability were short-stayers (53.2 per cent). More specifically, 43.8 per cent of short-stayers reported being sick, compared to 29.5 per cent of those staying between one and twelve months, 26 per cent one to five years, and 23 per cent more than five years.[22]

Furthermore, as data collection continued between October 2013 and May 2014, the number of short-stayers as a proportion of the sample increased (see Figure 7.1). This is to be expected within a random sample: new Yemeni migrants continued to enter Saudi Arabia and more of Saudi Arabia's original stock of Yemeni migrants were deported back to Yemen.

We adjusted our analysis to take into account the over-representation of short-stayers in the sample. Samples taken closer to the beginning of the policy changes should have been less affected by the issue of a rising number of short-stayers as a proportion of the whole in the wider population. These correspond to the sub-samples from October, November and December 2013; but by October deportations had already been taking place for six months, so the true proportion of short-stayers would need to be revised down somewhat. The issue of short-stayers being more likely to need assistance is harder to adjust for. However, we can estimate that the true population of short-stayers is likely to be less than 10 per cent of the total. As we know, in 2013 alone, the Saudi Directorate General of Border Guards estimated that 260,000 foreign nationals entered Saudi Arabia illegally across the Yemeni border, of whom approximately 70 per cent were Yemeni nationals.[23] This would mean around 15,080 new Yemeni entrants per month, including people deported multiple times.

Figure 7.1: Percentage of total respondents by length of stay reported in Saudi Arabia, over time

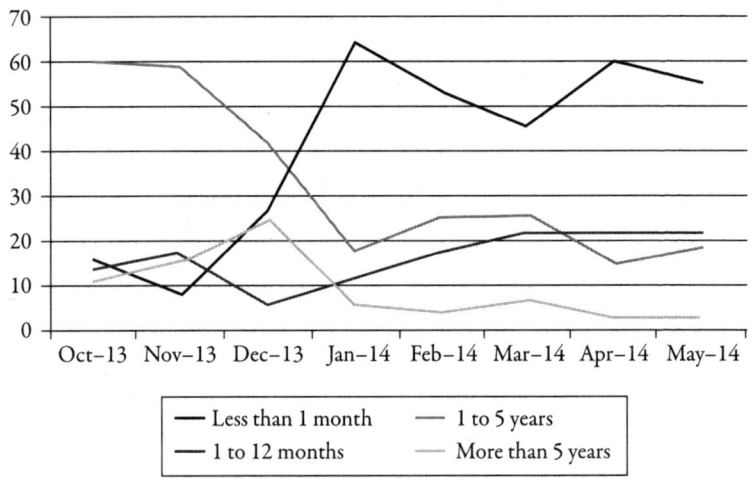

Profiling of sample

This section examines the basic characteristics of respondents in the sample, keeping in mind that our sample was only representative of the demographic affected by the policy changes (i.e. those Yemenis who had been residing in Saudi Arabia illegally). We offer some comparisons of characteristics of IOM's sample with those of Colton and Stevenson. In doing so, we must keep in mind that certain differences occur in the methodologies and the populations studied; in particular Colton's sample involved primarily voluntary returnees, and Stevenson's sample was of those deported in the early 1990s, which included all Yemenis living in Saudi Arabia, whereas those within IOM's sample involved only those Yemenis who were living in Saudi Arabia without proper documentation. With some caution and to the extent possible given the nature of the sampling, we analyse to what extent we can extrapolate these results to the wider Yemeni population that was or could be affected by the policy changes in Saudi Arabia.

Gender

In keeping with the results of surveys that Colton and Birks *et al.* conducted in the 1990s, the vast majority of respondents in the IOM sample were male

(93.9 per cent) and only 6.1 per cent female (margin of error <0.01 per cent based on sample size).[24] Furthermore, females were more likely than males to be short-stayers (59 per cent vs. 39 per cent respectively). Thus, females may have been slightly over-represented in our sample and their real population proportion is likely to have been lower. These findings were roughly in keeping with the overall estimates of returnees IOM monitors counted at the Al Tuwal border; of the 458,911 crossings observed between June 2013 and June 2014, approximately 5.3 per cent of returnees were estimated to be women and children.[25] We thus see that the large male dominance in this pattern of Yemen–Saudi Arabia migration that researchers witnessed in the 1970s, 1980s, and 1990s, seems to have remained consistent throughout the 2000s, up to the present day. We would, therefore, expect the wider population affected by Saudi policy changes to be overwhelmingly male.

Age

The average age of respondents in the sample was 27.5, with a median of twenty. As Figure 7.2 shows, the age range was quite wide but more than half of the respondents were aged between eighteen and twenty-six years old.[26] Again, this was in line with studies of Yemeni returnees from the early 1990s. Colton's survey had an average age of 42.8 with 51 per cent being in their twenties and thirties; however, Colton qualified this finding by stating that her survey was likely to have been biased towards older returnees because it took place in villages, with younger Yemenis more likely to stay in Saudi Arabia or return to larger urban areas in Yemen. Other studies, including Stevenson's, also remarked that Yemeni migrants to Saudi Arabia tended to be young, with the average age being in the mid-to-late twenties.

Family

The vast majority of respondents in the sample also stated that they did not have any relatives in Saudi Arabia (96.4 per cent), with only 3.6 per cent stating that they had children, parents, a spouse or some combination thereof remaining in Saudi Arabia. Again, this was largely in keeping with the surveys conducted in the 1990s, which found that the vast majority of respondents were married but with their family members remaining in Yemen rather than following them to Saudi Arabia.[27]

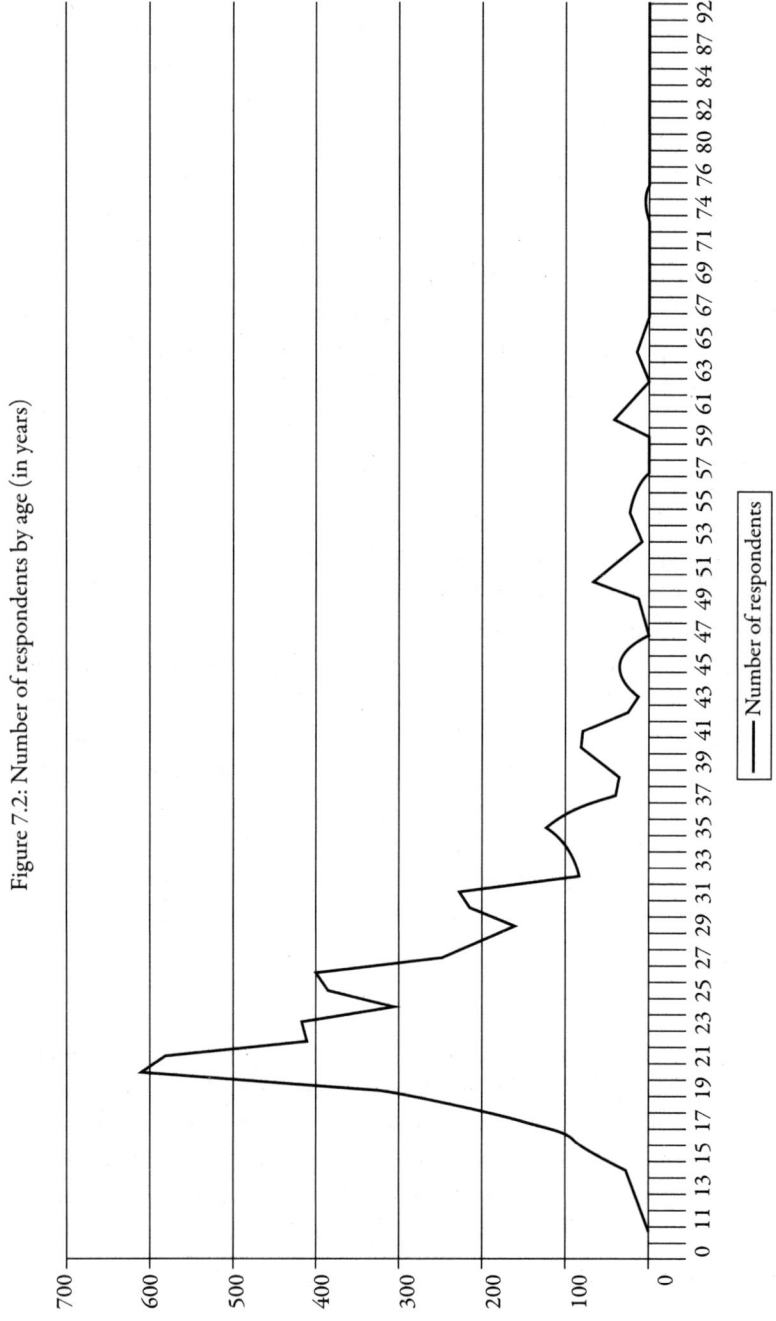

Figure 7.2: Number of respondents by age (in years)

Education

The level of education of the sample was relatively low with only 22.1 per cent of respondents having completed secondary/technical education or higher and 36.4 per cent having no education at all. Table 7.1 presents a breakdown by gender as the level of female education is significantly lower than that of males in Yemen.[28] Some 33.7 per cent of males in our sample reported having no education at all, whereas UNESCO data estimates an 83 per cent literacy rate for the population in Yemen (significantly higher than our sample). This is consistent with what we might expect for the sub-population being affected by the *nitaqat* policy changes given that those with a lower level of education are less likely to have entered through the regular process and with the appropriate paperwork for employment. Nevertheless, the education level is significantly higher than in the sample of returnees interviewed by Colton in the 1990s. Whereas Colton's sample included only 17.3 per cent of respondents with primary education or above, IOM's sample includes 53.4 per cent with this level of education. These changes, however, largely reflect the overall rising levels of education in Yemen. Nevertheless, despite the higher education level of IOM's sample compared to that of Colton, while Colton notes that her sample appears to be somewhat better educated than the Yemeni population as a whole (according to census data) at the time of the study, IOM's sample appears to demonstrate basic education levels below the current national average in Yemen. This may be reflective of the broader labour market opportunities for Yemenis in Saudi Arabia, which continue to appeal more to lower skilled workers with limited levels of education, or may simply be a characteristic of irregular Yemeni migrants in Saudi Arabia with a larger portion of more educated Yemenis holding legal working status.

Employment

By far the largest group of respondents stated that they had not been employed in Saudi Arabia (41 per cent). However, 90 per cent of those respondents also said that they had only been in Saudi Arabia for less than one month. When we exclude those cases, only 7 per cent of respondents said that they were not in employment during their stay in Saudi Arabia. Thus, with the usual caveats about the sampling, it is likely that approximately 93 per cent of Yemenis in the population within the purview of the policy changes, in longer-term expatriation in Saudi Arabia, were engaged in some kind of employment. If the sample includes some small bias towards those who were vulnerable or in need of assistance, having already excluded cases that reported staying in Saudi Arabia less than one month, we would not expect the sample proportion to be different from the broader population.

Table 7.1: Education level indicated by respondents

Level of education	Female	Male	Grand total	Percentage of females	Percentage of males	Percentage of total respondents
None	315	2,094	2,409	78.6	33.7	36.4
Read/write	49	697	746	12.2	11.2	11.3
Primary	23	1,978	2,001	5.7	31.8	30.2
Secondary	11	1,251	1,262	2.7	20.1	19.1
Technical	–	50	50	0.0	0.8	0.8
University	3	142	145	0.7	2.3	2.2
Master	–	4	4	0.0	0.1	0.1
Total	401	6,216	6,617	100.0	100.0	100.0

Source: IOM Sana'a.

Of those respondents who claimed to have employment, the construction and agricultural sectors were the main areas of employment. Some 42 per cent of respondents who claimed to have been employed had been in construction-related occupations,[29] and a further 20 per cent in occupations related to agriculture[30] (significant at p<0.01). Thus, in terms of occupational make-up, we see similar results to those derived from surveys in the 1990s, with Yemeni workers primarily concentrated in the construction and agriculture sectors. Indeed, compared to Colton's survey, we find a considerably greater concentration of Yemenis in the construction sector among IOM's sample. The sample appears to indicate that, not only had Yemeni labour migration not diversified much to countries beyond Saudi Arabia, but it also remained highly concentrated from a sectoral/occupational perspective, with Yemenis filling specific niche labour market needs in Saudi Arabia.

However, as Tables 7.2 and 7.3 show, quite a large proportion of Yemenis affected by *nitaqat* also worked in a number of other occupations that are classified as semi-skilled or vocational, including several in the service sector.

The occupations in the service sector where Yemenis from this sample appear to have engaged the most were those occupations where fluency in Arabic provided an advantage because the occupation requires a level of interaction with the Saudi population: 3.9 per cent were listed as vendors, 4.5 per cent worked in security, and 5.9 per cent were shopkeepers. Further studies would need to be conducted to determine where and the extent to which Arab language ability has acted as a competitive advantage in certain occupations for irregular Yemeni workers over labour migrants from Asian countries.

Table 7.2: Occupation of respondents

Type of work	Number of respondents	Percentage of respondents
Baker	27	0.4
Beggar	47	0.7
Blacksmith	126	1.9
Business owner	36	0.5
Butcher	7	0.1
Caretaker	9	0.1
Carpenter	214	3.2
Construction worker	1,050	15.9
Cook	70	1.1
Domestic worker	70	1.1
Dressmaker	26	0.4
Driver	125	1.9
Employee	30	0.5
Farmer	570	8.6
Fisherman	22	0.3
Labourer	158	2.4
Muezzin	3	0.0
No work	2,714	41
Other	20	0.3
Painter	179	2.7
Pharmacist	3	0.0
Plumber	41	0.6
Security guard	173	2.6
Shepherd	171	2.6
Shopkeeper	227	3.4
Smuggler	66	1.0
Technician	215	3.2
Trader	4	0.1
Vendor	149	2.3
Waiter	65	1.0
Total	6,617	100.0

Table 7.3: Occupation of employed respondents

Type of work	Number of respondents	Percentage of respondents
Baker	27	0.7
Blacksmith	126	3.3
Business owner	36	0.9
Butcher	7	0.2
Caretaker	9	0.2
Carpenter	214	5.5
Construction worker	1,050	27.2
Cook	70	1.8
Domestic worker	70	1.8
Dressmaker	26	0.7
Driver	125	3.2
Employee	30	0.8
Farmer	570	14.8
Fisherman	22	0.6
Labourer	158	4.1
Muezzin	3	0.1
Other	20	0.5
Painter	179	4.6
Pharmacist	3	0.1
Plumber	41	1.1
Security guard	173	4.5
Shepherd	171	4.4
Shopkeeper	227	5.9
Smuggler	66	1.7
Technician	215	5.6
Trader	4	0.1
Vendor	149	3.9
Waiter	65	1.7
Total	3,856	100.0

Chi square: 40, 419; p: <0.01.
Source: IOM Sana'a.

Region of work/residence in Saudi Arabia

Respondents were asked which region of Saudi Arabia was their most recent primary region of work or residence. Nearly 90 per cent of the sample reported Jizan (68.4 per cent) and Mecca (21 per cent). The rest of the sample was more evenly distributed among the other governorates. However, given that short-stayers were more likely to have reported Jizan as their most recent primary region of work or residence (86.6 per cent compared to only 6.3 per cent for Mecca), the bias in the sample towards short-stayers would suggest that the population of irregular Yemeni workers in Saudi Arabia residing in Jizan before the policy changes would have been likely to be somewhat lower, whereas the population in Mecca would have been higher than the proportions found in IOM's sample. Nevertheless, the sample clearly showed that Jizan was the primary destination for irregular migrants from Yemen. As a region in south-west Saudi Arabia bordering Yemen, this is not surprising, because irregular migration between neighbouring countries tends to be most concentrated within the border region itself (for example, the irregular flows of Mexican migration to the US are concentrated in the border states of California, Arizona, New Mexico, and Texas).[31]

Community of return

Respondents were asked which governorate in Yemen was their governorate of destination on their return. This is an important variable in our analysis because it allows us to infer which communities in Yemen *nitaqat* will most affect, and although it is not necessarily the case that respondents are returning home, it is likely that in the majority of cases the governorate of destination on their return is where they originally came from. With the caveat that this is an assumption, this variable may also allow us to see where the greatest impact may be felt by communities of origin.

Table 7.4 shows the breakdown of respondents by governorate of destination. The table also presents Yemen's 2004 census data on the population of each governorate. To estimate which governorates the *nitaqat* changes will affect the most, for each governorate we compared the proportion of Yemen's population living in a particular governorate with the proportion of respondents in our sample who have given that same governorate as their destination on returning to Yemen. We took the population proportions as our expected values and the sample proportions as our actual values for a chi-square[32] analysis. The final column presents differences between actual and expected values, with larger positive numbers indicating that a governorate would be disproportionately affected by the *nitaqat* changes.

As Table 7.4 shows, Al Hudaydah, Hajjah, and Al Mahwit received a disproportionately larger share of returnees, relative to the size of their populations. By contrast, Amanat Al Asimah, Ibb, Amran, and Hadramawt received a disproportionately smaller share. Thus, while it is clear that the phenomenon of irregular migration from Yemen to Saudi Arabia affects every region of Yemen, significant differences in the magnitude of the phenomenon from governorate to governorate mean that the three governorates of Al Hudaydah, Hajjah and—albeit to a lesser extent—Al Mahwit, clustered in north-west Yemen near the border, have been the most affected.

Table 7.4: Indicated communities of return of respondents

Destination governorate	No. of respondents	Percentage of respondents	Population of governorate according to 2004 Census	Percentage of population in governorate according to 2004 Census	Difference between actual and expected values
Abyan	36	0.6	433,819	2.2	−1.6
Aden	47	0.8	589,419	3	−2.2
Al Bayda	168	2.7	577,369	2.9	−0.2
Al Dhale'e	17	0.3	470,564	2.4	−2.1
Al Hudaydah	2,315	37.1	2,157,552	11	26.1
Al Jawf	10	0.2	443,797	2.3	−2.1
Al Mahrah	26	0.4	88,594	0.5	−0.03
Al Mahwit	365	5.8	494,557	2.5	3.3
Amanat Al Asimah	25	0.4	1,747,834	8.9	−8.5
Amran	83	1.3	877,786	4.5	−3.1
Dhamar	327	5.2	1,330,108	6.8	−1.5
Hadramawt	65	1	1,028,556	5.2	−4.2
Hajjah	1,169	18.7	1,479,568	7.5	11.2
Ibb	251	4	2,131,861	10.8	−6.8
Lahj	59	0.9	722,694	3.7	−2.7
Marib	26	0.4	238,522	1.2	−0.8
Raymah	187	3	394,448	2	1
Sa'ada	139	2.2	695,033	3.5	−1.3
Sana'a	101	1.6	919,215	4.7	−3.1
Shabwah	32	0.5	470,440	2.4	−1.9
Taizz	799	12.8	2,393,425	12.2	0.6
Total	6,247	100.0	19,685,161	100.0	–

Chi square: 115.3; p: <0.01.
Source: IOM Sana'a.

YEMENI IRREGULAR MIGRANTS

The governorates of former South Yemen posted values significantly below what would have been expected for their population sizes, ranging from −1.6 for Abyan to −4.2 for Hadramawt, with the exception of Al Mahrah, whose return rate was what would be expected relative to its population. Again, this appears to be in keeping with surveys and studies from the 1980s and 1990s, which indicated that Yemen–Saudi Arabia migration flows were primarily from North Yemen, with South Yemen experiencing significantly smaller flows, even relative to its smaller population.

Table 7.5: Duration of stay in Saudi Arabia by governorate of return

Governorate	*Duration of stay by governorate (percentage)*				
	Less than 1 month	1–12 months	1–5 years	More than 5 years	Total
Abyan	41.7	22.2	27.8	8.3	100
Aden	34	19.1	36.2	10.6	100
Al Bayda	32.7	17.3	40.5	9.5	100
Al Dhale'e	52.9	11.8	23.5	11.8	100
Al Hudaydah	38.6	15.7	33.7	12	100
Al Jawf	60	10	30	0	100
Al Mahrah	88.5	3.8	7.7	0	100
Al Mahwit	32.6	24.7	33.4	9.3	100
Amanat Al Asimah	40	16	36	8	100
Amran	41	20.5	32.5	6	100
Dhamar	40.1	20.2	34.9	4.9	100
Hadramawt	63.1	9.2	21.5	6.2	100
Hajjah	50.6	15.2	25.7	8.5	100
Ibb	39.4	21.9	31.5	7.2	100
Lahj	28.8	13.6	33.9	23.7	100
Marib	46.2	23.1	30.8	0	100
Raymah	41.7	16	35.3	7	100
Sa'ada	53.2	26.6	18.7	1.4	100
Sana'a	39.6	14.9	37.6	7.9	100
Shabwah	37.5	9.4	37.5	15.6	100
Taizz	30.5	17	44.1	8.4	100
(Left blank)	41.9	8.1	30.8	19.2	100

Source: IOM Sana'a.

We checked that these results were not due to sample bias towards short-stayers by cross-tabulating the destination governorate with length of stay in Saudi Arabia (see Table 7.5). Respondents destined for Al Mahwit and Al

Hudaydah may actually have been slightly under-represented in the sample, making the disproportionate impact greater, whereas Hajjah may have been slightly over-represented, making it weaker. It is likely that Hadramawt was over-represented, making the disproportionate lack of impact greater.

Intentions on return

Table 7.6 shows destination governorate by intended livelihood on return to Yemen. Overall, 37 per cent of the sample responded that they would seek to return to Saudi Arabia either immediately or in the future. The disproportionately most-affected governorates were slightly below this average, with 33.4 per cent of respondents heading for those governorates stating that they would return to Saudi Arabia in the future. The disproportionately least-affected governorates—with the exception of Amanat Al Asimah—were in fact above this average, perhaps making the impact on these governorates likely to be closer to average. Al Mahrah, in particular, appeared to be a destination for those wishing to return to Saudi Arabia (92 per cent).

Education by governorate

Table 7.7 shows destination governorate by respondents' level of education. The data is sorted in ascending order by the proportion of respondents who have no education. Respondents destined for Al Hudaydah and Hajjah were the most likely in the sample to have no education and the lowest education levels overall, with 87.3 and 85.9 per cent of returnees, respectively, having completed only primary education or lower, compared to 68 per cent for the remaining governorates.[33]

Although there is no clear cause for this discrepancy, Al Hudaydah and Hajjah were the largest populations in the sample—together representing 53 per cent of the sample—and thus represented a similarly large proportion of the Yemeni community in Saudi Arabia. The lower level of education for these groups, therefore, aligned with theories of international networking in labour migration channels, noting that large communities and network connections facilitate the mobility of new migrants from the same community. The geographical proximity as well as the large communities of migrants from Al Hudaydah and Hajjah already in Saudi Arabia may thereby have facilitated the mobility of less-educated migrants from psychological and logistical perspectives. Under the current policy of deportation of irregular Yemeni

Table 7.6: Expected livelihood strategy of respondents by governorate of return (percentage)

Destination governorate	Find work in Yemen	Remain in Yemen	Return to Saudi Arabia in future	Return to Saudi Arabia immediately	Study in Yemen	Unknown livelihoods	Total	Total percentage staying in Yemen	Total percentage returning to Saudi Arabia
Abyan	44.4	13.9	8.3	8.3	0.0	25.0	100	58.3	16.7
Aden	40.4	10.6	23.4	8.5	2.1	14.9	100	51.1	31.9
Al Bayda	38.7	8.3	34.5	9.5	0.0	8.9	100	47.0	44.0
Al Dhale'e	35.3	11.8	17.6	11.8	5.9	17.6	100	47.1	29.4
Al Hudaydah	41.5	10.5	25.2	8.3	1.3	13.2	100	52.0	33.4
Al Jawf	30.0	0.0	30.0	10.0	20.0	10.0	100	30.0	40.0
Al Mahrah	3.8	0.0	38.5	53.8	0.0	3.8	100	3.8	92.3
Al Mahwit	43.3	7.9	28.8	6.8	1.6	11.5	100	51.2	35.6
Amanat Al Asimah	36.0	0.0	48.0	8.0	0.0	8.0	100	36.0	56.0
Amran	60.2	7.2	15.7	7.2	1.2	8.4	100	67.5	22.9
Dhamar	41.3	15.3	20.2	8.3	1.8	13.1	100	56.6	28.4
Hadramawt	38.5	18.5	26.2	9.2	0.0	7.7	100	56.9	35.4
Hajjah	35.1	15.8	26.5	6.8	1.5	14.3	100	50.9	33.4
Ibb	44.6	12.4	19.9	12.4	1.2	9.6	100	57.0	32.3
Lahj	25.4	16.9	28.8	8.5	0.0	20.3	100	42.4	37.3
Marib	50.0	23.1	11.5	0.0	3.8	11.5	100	73.1	11.5
Raymah	40.6	14.4	19.8	9.6	2.1	13.4	100	55.1	29.4
Sa'ada	27.3	20.1	18.7	10.1	1.4	22.3	100	47.5	28.8
Sana'a	44.6	14.9	12.9	13.9	3.0	10.9	100	59.4	26.7
Shabwah	34.4	15.6	25.0	9.4	0.0	15.6	100	50.0	34.4
Taizz	44.2	12.0	24.3	7.8	1.0	10.8	100	56.2	32.0
Total	38.1	11.6	23.3	13.5	1.3	12.2	100	49.7	36.8

Source: IOM Sana'a.

ARAB MIGRANT COMMUNITIES IN THE GCC

Table 7.7: Education level of respondents by governorate of return

Governorate	None	Read/write	Primary	Secondary	Technical	University	Master's	Total respondents
Abyan	8.3	11.1	36.1	36.1	2.8	5.6	0	36
Aden	31.9	4.3	27.7	29.8	0	6.4	0	47
Al Bayda	17.9	14.9	38.1	26.2	0	3	0	168
Al Dhale'e	35.3	11.8	35.3	17.6	0	0	0	17
Al Hudaydah	45.7	12.7	28.9	11.8	0.3	0.6	0	2,315
Al Jawf	30	10	30	20	0	0	10	10
Al Mahrah	26.9	23.1	42.3	7.7	0	0	0	26
Al Mahwit	26.3	11.8	33.7	22.7	0.8	4.4	0.3	365
Amanat Al Asimah	16	12	44	16	4	8	0	25
Amran	31.3	3.6	38.6	20.5	1.2	4.8	0	83
Dhamar	30	10.7	32.7	22.6	0.3	3.7	0	327
Hadramawt	30.8	10.8	35.4	21.5	0	1.5	0	65
Hajjah	46.5	10.8	28.6	12.7	0.2	1.3	0	1,169
Ibb	21.5	10.8	34.3	28.3	2.4	2.4	0.4	251
Lahj	8.5	6.8	40.7	35.6	5.1	3.4	0	59
Marib	15.4	15.4	30.8	30.8	3.8	3.8	0	26
Raymah	26.7	9.1	30.5	27.8	1.1	4.8	0	187
Sa'ada	35.3	12.2	33.8	13.7	0	5	0	139
Sana'a	32.7	11.9	31.7	18.8	1	4	0	101
Shabwah	9.4	15.6	25	40.6	0	9.4	0	32
Taizz	21.4	8.8	28.9	34.2	2.3	4.4	0.1	799
(Left blank)	35.1	10.3	26.8	25.7	0.8	1.4	0	370
Total number	2,409	746	2,001	1,262	50	145	4	6,617

Source: IOM Sana'a.

migrants, the Saudi strategy has not only disrupted immediate job opportunities for Yemenis, but also served to dissolve the broader community connections that have facilitated the mobility of lower-skilled Yemenis from these provinces, thereby potentially having much longer-term disruptive effects on the historic flows of labour mobility from these governorates.

Remittances

As Table 7.8 shows, the majority (51.2 per cent) of the respondents in IOM's sample sent remittances to Yemen while they were in Saudi Arabia. Sending between 400 and 800 Saudi riyals (US$107–213) was the mode for the sub-sample of remittance senders, with 19.4 per cent of the total sample sending this amount.

Table 7.8: Amount of monthly remittances to Yemen

Remittances (Saudi riyals)	Number of respondents	Percentage of respondents
None	3,226	48.8
Less than 400	676	10.2
Between 400 and 800	1,282	19.4
Between 800 and 1,500	1,088	16.4
More than 1,500	345	5.2
Total	6,617	100.0

Exchange rate May 2014: 3.75 Saudi riyals = US$1.
Source: IOM Sana'a.

However, the proportion of remittance senders in the population in Yemen affected by the policy changes at the outset is likely to be far higher because 97.2 per cent of short-stayers also reported not sending remittances. Short-stayers were over-represented in our sample and, as per the reasoning in the section on the *Explanation of the data*, we estimated that the proportion of short-stayers in the initial population of Yemenis in Saudi Arabia who would be affected by the policy changes would be less than 10 per cent, whereas they accounted for 40 per cent of our sample. To adjust for this over-representation and better estimate the proportion of remittance senders in the population, we divided the total number of respondents who reported staying in Saudi Arabia for less than one month by four, then multiplied by

0.972, and added this to the total number of respondents who stayed for longer periods but did not send remittances. This came to an adjusted counterfactual of 1,295 respondents who did not send remittances. Table 7.9 shows a revised set of proportions, with a higher proportion of remittance senders, which should be closer to those of the actual population of irregular Yemeni migrants in Saudi Arabia.

Table 7.9: Amount of monthly remittances to Yemen by non-short-stayer respondents

Remittances (Saudi riyals)	Number of respondents	Percentage of respondents
None	1,295	27.6
Less than 400	676	14.4
Between 400 and 800	1,282	27.4
Between 800 and 1,500	1,088	23.2
More than 1,500	345	7.4
Total	4,686	100.0

Exchange rate May 2014: 3.75 Saudi riyals = US$1.
Source: IOM Sana'a.

The value of remittances sent was moderately positively correlated with a higher level of education (see Table 7.10).[34] Of those with a technical or university degree, 48 per cent and 41.4 per cent, respectively, sent 800 Saudi riyals or more, whereas only 11.9 per cent of those without a formal education, 16.5 per cent of those who could read and write, and 23.8 per cent of those with a primary-school education sent remittances above 800 Saudi riyals. Although these figures should not have come as a surprise, because those with higher levels of education can engage in better remunerated occupations, these are significant figures that should be taken into account as the government of Yemen contemplates future labour migration policy to Saudi Arabia. Looking at the added value in remittances received, particularly for those with a technical education, improved linkages between education/training and labour-market demand could greatly increase the financial value that communities in Yemen receive from emigration to Saudi Arabia.

The value of remittances also positively correlated with respondents' length of stay in Saudi Arabia: the longer respondents had stayed in Saudi Arabia, the greater the value of remittances they were likely to send. This was a strong and significant correlation, as Table 7.11 shows.

Table 7.10: Remittances value cross-tabulated with respondents' level of education

Education level	Education Level (percentage)/Remittance value (Saudi riyals)					
	None	Less than 400 SAR	400 to 800 SAR	800 to 1500 SAR	More than 1500 SAR	Total
None	61	11.2	15.8	9.5	2.4	100
Primary	43.8	10.7	21.5	18.1	5.7	100
Read/write	54.8	9.8	18.9	11.4	5.1	100
Secondary	32.4	8	23.2	28	8.4	100
Technical	24	6	22	36	12	100
University	32.4	8.3	17.9	26.9	14.5	100
Master	50	25	0	0	25	100
Total	48.8	10.2	19.4	16.4	5.2	100

Exchange rate May 2014: 3.75 Saudi riyals = US$1.
Source: IOM Sana'a.

The correlations we find between the value of remittances and education and duration of stay reflect the importance of a managed labour mobility policy in maximising the value of the migration process to the migrants, their families and Yemen more broadly. Higher levels of education, particularly in technical education for occupations in demand in Saudi Arabia, as well as a more stable, long-term residence situation in Saudi Arabia, result in significantly larger per-migrant remittance flows to Yemen.

Table 7.11: Remittance value correlated with duration of stay in Saudi Arabia

Education level	Remittance value (Saudi riyals)/Duration of stay (percentage)					
	None	Less than 400 SAR	400 to 800 SAR	800 to 1500 SAR	More than 1500 SAR	Grand Total
Less 1 Month	97.2	1.4	0.6	0.5	0.2	100
1–12 Months	31.8	19	25.6	18.5	5.1	100
1–5 Years	8.4	14.5	35.5	32.1	9.5	100
More than 5 years	14.2	17.1	31.6	25.8	11.3	100
Total	48.8	10.2	19.4	16.4	5.2	100

Chi square: 4480.38; p: <0.01; γ = 0.616.
Exchange rate May 2014: 3.75 Saudi riyals = US$1.
Source: IOM Sana'a.

Impact of nitaqat policy changes on Yemen

In 2013, high levels of poverty and food insecurity in Yemen, combined with localised conflict, continued to exacerbate chronic displacement and hunger. Local economies in Yemen were ill-equipped to provide sufficient livelihood opportunities for the large number of Yemeni migrants who began returning from Saudi Arabia from April 2013, creating great concern that this would place additional strain on already vulnerable communities in Yemen.

In 2014, according to the UN Office for the Coordination of Humanitarian Affairs (OCHA):

> Yemen continues to be a large scale humanitarian crisis, with more than half the population or 14.7 million people in need of some form of humanitarian assistance. The needs remain largely unchanged since 2013. They include 10.5 million food-insecure, of whom 4.5 million are severely food insecure. An estimated 1,080,000 children under five suffer from acute malnutrition, of whom 279,000 children who are severely acutely malnourished. In addition, about 13.1 million Yemenis, amounting to over half of the population, have no access to improved water sources or to adequate sanitation facilities, with rural areas the worst affected. A further 8.6 million people have insufficient access to health services.[35]

Additionally, the mixed migration flows out of the Horn of Africa continue to affect Yemen, and in many cases place additional strains on the domestic economy and labour market. This includes a steady, though probably reduced, inflow of refugees over and above the 243,000 refugees already registered in the country.[36] A total of 65,319 migrants arrived in Yemen in 2013, of whom around 20 per cent were Somali refugees and most of the remainder Ethiopian migrants.[37] This is somewhat lower than 2012 and 2011 (a decrease of 39 per cent and 36 per cent, respectively), partly because the *nitaqat* policy and enforcement changes have made the Yemen route to Saudi Arabia less viable for irregular migration. However, it still constitutes a significant inflow of people who are often highly vulnerable, and at the same time places additional strain on the Yemeni economy and labour market.

The mass return of at least 400,000 Yemenis with the possibility of an additional 400,000 still to come[38] is likely to place a substantial burden on a society that is already experiencing a humanitarian crisis. The following analysis attempts to gauge some of the main potential impacts of these changes on Yemen's economy and labour market.

Remittances

One of the largest, most immediate and tangible impacts of the policy changes for Yemen will be the loss of remittances that Yemenis in Saudi Arabia used to send. Sources indicate that at least 400,000 Yemenis were deported between April and December 2013.[39] Using our adjusted estimate of the proportion of remittance senders among the affected population, we have estimated a minimum loss of between 162,303,869 Saudi riyals (US$43,271,701) and 317,409,646 Saudi riyals (US$84,624,585 USD)[40] each month; this is equivalent to an annual loss of between US$519,260,412 and US$1,015,495,028. However, given that estimates have suggested the number of returnees to Yemen could double to 800,000 as Saudi Arabia's enforcement of its policies broadens, the impact on remittances could potentially become significantly worse, with a loss of annual remittance flows of US$1–2 billion, equivalent to between 2.9 and 5.7 per cent of the country's GDP or 19.4 and 40.8 per cent of its foreign exchange reserves.[41]

Labour market

In 2012, Yemen's male unemployment rate was approximately 13.4 per cent and as high as 28.1 per cent for males aged 18–24 years old, according to modelled International Labour Organization estimates. However, more recent data are hard to come by, and while macroeconomic stability has improved somewhat, with growth for 2013 estimated at 4 per cent,[42] it is unlikely that such improvements will have had any significant positive impact on unemployment figures. A sudden influx of at least 400,000 returnees to Yemen with limited spending power to stimulate consumption is thus likely to place a critical burden on the country's labour market, because this represents an increase of around 5.8 per cent in Yemen's labour force in the space of one year. Should the estimates of a total of 800,000 returnees be accurate, the proportion would increase to 11.6 per cent.[43]

Furthermore, extrapolating from IOM's sample, with an estimated 33.7 per cent of returnees having no formal education, 42 per cent having employment experience in construction, and 20 per cent in agriculture, the lack of education or skills diversity of returnees will make their absorption into the labour market even more challenging, requiring development of vocational training and re-skilling programmes to improve their prospects of employment.

Table 7.12: Differential regional impact of *nitaqat* policy changes

Destination governorate	Number of respondents	Percentage of respondents (actual values)	Yemeni population by governorate (expected values)	A: Difference between actual values and expected values	B: Total proportion reporting staying in Saudi Arabia for <1 month' minus sample average of 44.4 per cent	C: Total proportion staying in Yemen minus sample average of 49.7 per cent	D: Total proportion staying in Saudi Arabia minus sample average of 36.8 per cent	E: Governorate score for differential number of returnees (column A−B + 0.5xC−0.5xD)*	F: Total proportion reporting remitting <400 Saudi riyals' minus sample average of 5.1 per cent, multiplied by 0.1	G: Total proportion reporting remitting 400–800 Saudi riyals' minus sample average of 15.5 per cent, multiplied by 0.2	H: Total proportion reporting remitting 800–1,500 Saudi riyals minus sample average of 17.1 per cent, multiplied by 0.4	I: Total proportion reporting remitting > 1500 Saudi riyals minus sample average of 9 per cent, multiplied by 0.8	J: Governorate score for differential impact of remittances (column F + G + H + I + E)*
							(percentage)						
Abyan	36	0.6	2.2	−1.6	−2.7	8.6	−20.1	15.5	−0.2	0.8	−1.3	8.3	23.1
Aden	47	0.8	3.0	−2.2	−10.4	1.3	−4.9	11.3	0.1	−0.6	2.5	−0.4	12.9
Al Bayda	168	2.7	2.9	−0.2	−11.7	−2.7	7.2	6.5	0.3	0.5	1.0	6.1	14.4
Al Dhale'e	17	0.3	2.4	−2.1	8.5	−2.7	−7.4	−8.3	−0.5	0.4	−2.1	6.9	−3.6
Al Hudaydah	2315	37.1	11.0	26.1	−5.8	2.3	−3.4	34.8	0.9	1.4	−1.0	−4.6	31.4

YEMENI IRREGULAR MIGRANTS

Governorate											
Al Jawf	10	0.2	2.3	−2.1	15.6	−19.7	3.2	−29.1	−0.5	−3.1	1.2	0.8	−30.8
Al Mahrah	26	0.4	0.5	0.0	44.0	1.5	−1.2	−42.7	0.8	1.7	1.4	−3.1	−41.9
Al Mahwit	365	5.8	2.5	3.3	−11.8	−45.9	55.5	−35.5	−0.1	3.3	−0.4	−7.2	−40.0
Amanat Al Asimah	25	0.4	8.9	−8.5	−4.4	−13.7	19.2	−20.5	0.5	0.8	0.4	−1.4	−20.4
Amran	83	1.3	4.5	−3.1	−3.4	17.7	−13.9	16.2	−0.1	0.1	1.9	−0.4	17.6
Dhamar	327	5.2	6.8	−1.5	−4.4	6.9	−8.4	10.4	−0.4	0.0	−5.0	−3.5	1.5
Hadramawt	65	1.0	5.2	−4.2	18.7	7.2	−1.4	−18.5	0.5	−0.4	−2.8	−4.3	−25.5
Hajjah	1,169	18.7	7.5	11.2	6.1	1.2	−3.5	7.4	0.2	0.4	0.3	−2.8	5.6
Ibb	251	4.0	10.8	−6.8	−5.0	7.3	−4.5	4.1	0.0	1.3	2.7	3.6	11.6
Lahj	59	0.9	3.7	−2.7	−15.6	−7.3	0.5	9.0	−0.1	−2.3	−0.7	8.2	14.0
Marib	26	0.4	1.2	−0.8	1.7	23.4	−25.3	21.8	−0.1	0.5	1.1	−0.4	22.9
Raymah	187	3.0	2.0	1.0	−2.7	5.4	−7.4	10.1	0.1	−1.4	−1.6	−4.9	2.2
Sa'ada	139	2.2	3.5	−1.3	8.8	−2.2	−8.0	−7.2	−0.5	0.7	−0.1	−2.5	−9.7
Sana'a	101	1.6	4.7	−3.1	−4.8	9.7	−10.1	11.6	−0.5	−3.1	5.7	10.3	24.0
Shabwah	32	0.5	2.4	−1.9	−6.9	0.3	−2.4	6.4	0.1	1.5	3.8	−1.4	10.4
Taizz	799	12.8	12.2	0.6	−13.9	6.5	−4.8	20.1	−0.5	−2.3	−6.8	−7.2	3.2

* Higher positive numbers = greater impact.

Source: IOM Sana'a.

Differential regional impact

As noted previously, while labour migration to Saudi Arabia is a phenomenon that has affected all regions of Yemen, some have been significantly more affected than others and are therefore likely to suffer greater economic challenges because of the changes in Saudi policy. We have used the IOM data to try to discern where the impact of the policy changes will be most heavily felt. To do this, we have built on analysis developed in the preceding section to develop a scoring system for each governorate using a value derived by cross-tabulating the number of respondents reporting a particular governorate as their destination governorate with certain other variables, including the proportion of returnees who are short-stayers, the proportion anticipating staying in Yemen, and the estimated value of losses in remittances by region.[44]

Based on this analysis, we can discern that Al Hudaydah, with a score of 31.4, is likely to be the governorate that experiences the greatest impact by a considerable margin, with Abyan, Al Bayda, Amran, Lahj, Marib and Sana'a also experiencing disproportionately large impacts from the return of migrants. The consequences for the governorates of Al Hudaydah, Raymah and Hajjah may be particularly severe, given their already heightened humanitarian vulnerabilities as defined by several indicators.[45] The governorates of Al Mahrah and Al Mahwit, in particular, as well as Al Jawf, Amanat Al Asimah, and Hadramawt, are likely to be the least affected.

Conclusions

The results of the data IOM collected at the Al Tuwal border reflect the importance of the Saudi labour market to Yemen, and particularly to certain communities that depend on these flows, as well as the relative consistency in the character of these flows from the 1970s to the present. As the studies of Colton and Birks in the 1990s indicated, Yemeni migrants to Saudi Arabia in the 1970s and 1980s were primarily young males, with families remaining in Yemen. The flows were primarily from North Yemen and, although higher than the Yemeni average, education levels remained relatively low. The increased flows of labour mobility created, according to Colton, Birks and Fergany, a dependency not only on access to employment, but also on remittance flows to communities of origin, which had a profound impact on Yemen's development. As a result, the large-scale returns of Yemenis in the early 1990s had a devastating impact on Yemen's development, with certain regions with high return rates suffering considerable increases in unemployment, homelessness, and poverty.

The results from IOM's surveys to date tend to demonstrate a similar pattern: a largely young, male and low-skilled population with few having family remaining in Saudi Arabia. The vast majority of respondents indicate that they are returning to governorates within what was previously North Yemen, and particularly to the governorates of Al Hudaydah and Hajjah; again, this is consistent with studies from the 1980s and 1990s suggesting that the majority of labour mobility occurred from North Yemen, and particularly the western part of North Yemen. The occupational make-up of returnees in IOM's sample also remains quite consistent with those undertaken by Colton and Birks in the 1990s, with the largest portion of Yemeni returnees having worked in lower skilled occupations in the construction and agriculture sectors.

Taking the previous samples/studies and IOM's sample together—and bearing in mind the caveats of this exercise we have already referred to—we see a significant consistency in the development and nature of Yemen–Saudi Arabia labour mobility over the past several decades, with mobility and access to the Saudi Arabia labour market—either by regular or irregular means—being an important component of individuals' livelihood strategies and whole communities' economic development across generations, particularly in certain governorates. In many respects, the mobility patterns between Yemen and Saudi Arabia have reflected the type of mobility we see in many other parts of the world where a poorer country shares a large porous border with a more prosperous neighbour—the most obvious example being mobility patterns between the US and Mexico, which share similar characteristics in terms of demographics, geographical concentration, and community dependence on remittances. The changes in Saudi policy towards this mobility pattern, if continued, may thus put an end to a livelihood and development strategy that has shaped the lives of hundreds of thousands of Yemenis over the course of several decades, requiring these communities to find new means of supporting themselves. Continuing instability in Yemen, however, will limit such opportunities and heighten the risk of a protracted and deepening humanitarian crisis in Yemen.

The scale of remittances Yemenis in Saudi Arabia send home relative to the size of Yemen's economy, as well as the considerable proportion of returnees who state that they plan to return to Saudi Arabia either immediately or in the future, and the number of those who have been deported multiple times over the past twelve months (who were not included within this sample) highlights the importance of the Saudi labour market as a generator of income for communities in Yemen and an outlet to absorb excess labour supply in Yemen, as well as the risks Yemeni migrants are willing to take to continue to access the Saudi labour market. Given the obvious level of dependence of Yemeni communities on labour mobility, the development of regular, managed labour mobility programmes will have to be part of a broader solution to support the economic development of Yemen. Indeed, the results from IOM's sample suggest that a managed labour mobility programme, including greater security of status in Saudi Arabia and the development of skills that are in demand in the Saudi labour market, would be of considerable economic benefit to migrants, their dependants in Yemen, and the Yemeni economy more broadly. Saudi Arabia's interest in contributing to political and economic stability in its neighbouring countries will require policies not only of humanitarian assistance or military intervention in crises, but also policies that acknowledge the importance and maximise the value of labour mobility between Yemen and Saudi Arabia as a stabilising force, by expanding regular labour mobility opportunities between Yemen and Saudi Arabia.

APPENDIX

The first score provided in Column A was calculated by comparing the proportion of Yemen's population living in a particular governorate with the proportion of respondents in our sample giving that governorate as their destination. Column A presents differences between actual and expected values, with larger positive numbers indicating that a governorate would be disproportionately affected by the *nitaqat* changes.

The scoring system attempts to correct for our sample's bias towards short-stayers. Column D presents the difference between the percentage of short-stayers in the total sample and the percentage of short-stayers in the sub-sample who reported a particular governorate as their destination. Larger numbers indicate overrepresentation due to sample bias. Values in Column D will be deducted from those in column A.

Column C presents differences between the percentage of those in the total sample who stated that they intended to stay in Yemen after deportation and the percentages for the same variable in the sub-sample who reported a particular governorate as their destination. Larger numbers indicate a greater immediate, relative impact on the governorate and will be added to the score in Column A. The principle for Column C is similar to that of D, but focuses on respondents who stated that they would return to Saudi Arabia. Larger values indicate immediate, relative impact on the governorate and will be deducted from scores in Column A. However, the data only indicated respondents' intentions, which would not necessarily become reality. As discussed earlier in the paper, it was very possible that the many respondents who expressed their intention to return to Saudi Arabia would eventually be forced to return to Yemen if the *nitaqat* policy changes continued to be strictly enforced. Therefore, values in Columns C and D were discounted by half when put into the scoring system.

Column E calculates scores for each governorate based on their differential share of returnees, adjusted for the short-stayer bias and respondents' intentions regarding return or non-return, as discussed above (Column A–B + 0.5xC–0.5xD). Larger values represent a greater impact on a particular governorate. Based on this rudimentary scoring system, Al Hudaydah stands out as being by far the most affected governorate with a score of 34.8. Abyan (15.5), Amran (16.2), Marib (21.8) and Taizz (20.1) also stand out as having high scores.

The table then develops a separate, non-comparable score that builds on the first by factoring in the impact of cessation of remittances. This score makes the assumption that the majority of respondents who reported a particular governorate of destination were also sending remittances to that same governorate. This may not have been true in all cases, of course, but the score may nevertheless be instructive. Columns F, G, H and I show the value of remittances reportedly sent by respondents. Similarly to the first scoring system, they present the differences between the percentage of respondents in the total sample who reportedly sent remittances of a particular value and percentages for the same variable in the sub-sample who reported a particular governorate as their destination. Greater values of remittances are assigned greater weight; thus, the differences are multiplied by 0.1, those in G by 0.2, those in H by 0.8, and those in I by 0.8. The resulting values in Columns F, G, H, and I are then added to those in Column E and are displayed in Column J to provide another governorate score, which takes into account the impact of the loss of remittances. While the scores in Columns E and J are not designed to be comparable, those in J provide an indication of the differential impact of the policy changes on governorates, also attempting to factor in remittances.

8

AN EMERGING TREND IN ARAB MIGRATION

HIGHLY SKILLED ARAB FEMALES IN THE GCC COUNTRIES

Françoise De Bel-Air

Despite the common misconception that it is mostly men who migrate, half of the 195 million international migrants worldwide in the late 2000s were women, a proportion that was on the rise.[1] Policy and academic research on the Middle East has also increasingly focused on female migration from and to the region.[2] But the 'gender' angle on regional migration usually goes hand in hand with a focus on abuse and trafficking issues, for evident reasons, and has become the main target of international policymaking.

Abuses against female migrants in the Arab region—predominantly Asian female domestic workers, but also trafficked sex-workers from Morocco and, more recently, from conflict-ridden countries such as Iraq or Syria—are a reality. However, focusing on these elements of female migration not only undermines the agency of migrant women; it is also likely to hide other characteristics of migration involving women. Indeed, the scale and characteristics of female intra-regional mobility, mostly concerning the Gulf Cooperation Council (GCC) States, remain little known. The growing share of skilled and highly skilled, often unmarried, young Arab women is largely understudied. Shedding some light on this population, therefore, will not only emphasise a new phenomenon, but will also point at a new structural trend within Arab populations: the emergence of educated female professionals in societies characterised (in most Arab countries) by low female activity rates. Moreover, it challenges the dominant assumption that Arab migration to Gulf countries is a 'male-only' phenomenon, and that it merely involves women as married dependants.

This chapter aims to address the knowledge gap regarding highly skilled Arab female workers in the Gulf. Relying mostly on macro-demographic and survey data, it will provide empirical evidence describing this population in the Gulf countries, their integration into the labour force and their patterns of migration to the region. Highly skilled migration is defined as the migration of people with tertiary-level education, whether they achieved that level before or after migration. Migrants employed in the two upper-level occupational categories—'managers' and 'professionals/ specialists'—are also considered highly skilled.

Given a lack of data, however, this contribution can only be exploratory. After explaining existing gaps in the literature and demographic data, this chapter will sketch the macro-demographic picture of the highly skilled Arab women, within total, foreign and employed populations in Kuwait and in Bahrain. We will then attempt to emphasise some of the inner characteristics of this population using the results of a sample survey targeted at highly skilled Lebanese workers. Our underlying question will be the following: is there a gendered pattern of skilled Arab female migration to GCC countries, as opposed to, for example, a pattern driven by career-based choices? Survey data will also provide some insight on networks and recruitment channels Arab female migrants use to reach the Gulf. The last section of the chapter will examine the proximate determinants and structural factors pushing skilled Arab females out of their countries of origin, as well as those attracting them to the Gulf. The chapter then concludes that one element of Gulf states' exceptionalism, the generally low levels of Arab female economic activity (among citizens and migrants alike), is actually fading away.[3]

(Un-)documenting skilled Arab female workers: between political sensitivity of data and representation of Arab women

The migration of mostly unskilled, Asian women to the Gulf region—that of domestic workers, for example—has been extensively studied.[4] Yet

AN EMERGING TREND IN ARAB MIGRATION

Arab female migration to that region remains relatively understudied, for several reasons:

Sending states and the political sensitivity of data on emigration

Most Arab sending countries and especially Middle Eastern countries do not keep a record of their expatriates abroad, males and females alike, for a variety of reasons. This can be simply due to technical and administrative inefficiency. Also, past migration policies have affected perceptions of emigration: in Jordan, for example, the regime historically promoted an 'open door' to emigration, as a way to publicise the Arab identity of Hashemite Jordan. Lack of popular involvement, for which political consensus has to be gathered, also hampers the process of setting up expatriate registration systems: expatriate citizens often distrust their diplomatic representation abroad, or simply ignore it. Emigration is a selective process; when it concerns certain sectors of national societies more than others—Palestinians in Jordan; Christians in Syria, Lebanon and Palestine; educated citizens in the whole region—ignoring or concealing such movements avoids paving the way for future claims on behalf of these social groups. Indeed, keeping records on expatriates means acknowledging that they are a part of the citizenry: one 'counts' (i.e. is important) if one 'is counted' (i.e. enumerated).[5] Alternatively, denying the emigration phenomenon allows governments not to be held responsible for it. Highly skilled emigration is an especially sensitive issue in every sending country, because it is viewed as a sign of a regime's political failure to incorporate youth and intellectual elites into the citizenry. Regarding lone-female emigration, the Arab region's socially conservative societies regard it with suspicion, and it casts a negative light on sending states. In extreme cases, emigration may even bear a direct effect on countries' political stability: in Lebanon, for example, the issue of the number of expatriates and their sectarian distribution is at the heart of national politics, because the country's electoral system distributes functions according to confessional groups' relative size.[6]

Receiving states' demographic imbalance

On the receiving end, most GCC countries provide data on migrant communities, but it is not broken down by nationality or even by region of origin—except, to some extent, in Kuwait and in Bahrain. In the UAE and Qatar, where local populations are small demographic minorities, disclosing foreign residents' regional origin or nationality may lead to political claims from demographically dominant groups. Even in Saudi Arabia, where non-nationals (in official statistics) account for 'only' one-third of the total population, the same concern exists. Other more country-specific reasons can be added to this. In Saudi Arabia, for example, in the 1930s concessions for the exploitation of oil were given to private companies, which therefore took over the management of foreign labour flows. Visa trade also provided income to a portion of the citizens. Labour supply became increasingly disconnected from economic needs and irregular migration grew. Socio-political conditions led to loose, if any, migration management in an economy overwhelmingly dominated by private interests (with the exception of the energy sector), and Saudi Arabia's population data was scarce and relatively unreliable. As previously mentioned, in Arab countries a degree of suspicion around women who migrate on their own to the GCC pervades, because it jars local sensibilities and conservative values. Marriage of local males with foreign females is also an issue in these small societies,[7] and female citizens are not inclined to support the inward migration of single women. Therefore, female migration, especially skilled Arab migration, which unlike that of Asian domestic helpers happens out of the sphere of Gulf households, remains a sensitive issue.

The relevance of the gender issue for policymakers

More generally, data-producing non-governmental bodies, as well as sending countries' government agencies, record from expatriates the type of information that is most relevant to states' policies. For example, figures and economic profiles of migrants may be of interest to encourage expatriates to remit more or engage in investment projects in their country of origin. This kind of data, though, is not gender sensitive. In Jordan, for example, the Ministry of Labour has attempted for years to quantify Jordanian workers in the Gulf. The ministry's annual estimates do not take into account migrants' sex or the number of their dependants. As far as female migrants are concerned, until the mid-1990s most female Arab nationals, with the exception of Tunisians and Lebanese, displayed relatively low rates of celibacy and economic activity in their countries of origin. Policymakers and scholars, therefore, did not question the assumption that they would either stay behind while their husbands were working abroad, and possibly acquire some empowerment (providing they lived by themselves), or alternatively, migrate as their husbands' dependants. But as shown in the example of Morocco, where the development of human trafficking networks came under scrutiny during the 2000s, many Moroccan female company managers and professionals who had settled in Gulf countries called for bilateral government action against their being classed in the same category as victims of trafficking or immoral behaviour in their host countries.[8] Until that point, the Moroccan government had ignored these women, because they had mainly made their way to Gulf labour markets using their own employment networks, assets and skills.

Representations of highly skilled migration

Highly skilled migration most often appears as 'apolitical'. Previously seen as a 'brain drain', skilled migration, through the prism of dominant economic liberalism theories it is now viewed as a 'triple gain', for the receiving and sending countries as well as for the migrants themselves. Apart from expatriates' financial remittances, migration dynamics are meant to produce a 'brain chain' or even a 'brain gain' to support development in countries of origin.[9] Such a promotion of highly skilled migration goes hand in hand with a representation of these movements as 'natural' and 'a-cephalic';[10] in other words, driven by globalization's economic dynamics, as well as determined by migrants' individual agency and rational choices. Therefore, in the politicised context of Gulf migration studies that mainly focus on poor treatment of migrants, the highly skilled are less of a topic of interest. For all these reasons, data is lacking, which would allow measuring the scale of the phenomenon. Thus, describing Arab female migration too often relies on anecdotal evidence.

Highly skilled Arab female workers in the Gulf

A scarce literature

Fieldwork in the Gulf states and other Arab countries (mainly Jordan, as well as Lebanon and Syria) during the 2000s drew attention to the emergence of the phenomenon of the emigration to those states of young (between twenty and thirty-five years of age), mostly unmarried, skilled and highly skilled female professionals. The results of a Gallup poll, published in 'The Silatech Index: Voices of Young Arabs' in 2010, found that one in three young people across the Arab world wanted to migrate permanently to another country. A large proportion of young people from Jordan, Syria, Lebanon and Palestine who were surveyed chose the UAE as their preferred destination for permanent migration, followed by Saudi Arabia and the US. Young women from the region were in fact keener to emigrate to the UAE than young men.[11]

In the Gulf, these female emigrants are often employed in teaching and the health sector, tourism and hotel services, media, insurance and finance, and management and business.[12] Additionally, a new category of young female migrants has also emerged: young, rural, semi-skilled workers, trained in manufacturing. No statistical data from sending countries is available to confirm this field evidence. However, personal and informal accounts from young Arab women willing to leave other Arab countries for the Gulf, or already living there, suggest that they are indeed mostly unmarried and sometimes divorced.[13]

Scattered studies, focusing on Arab migration to GCC countries and on certain Arab nationalities' emigration patterns worldwide, provide very partial information on female migration to Gulf countries. Yet these accounts confirm the development of individual female emigration in general, especially from North African Arab countries, and the opening of such channels to the GCC countries. For example, Tunisia and GCC countries signed technical cooperation agreements in the 2000s, which led to modest, yet rising numbers of female migrants: 118 in 2000, 597 in 2008.[14] These women were said to be young and unmarried.[15] Morocco, which historically has sent migrants to Europe, has also experienced an increase in migration to the Gulf states. Beginning in the 1990s the progressive closure of Europe's external borders to non-European Union nationals spurred a need to redirect job seeker flows. Gulf markets opened to Moroccan oil-sector managers, engineers, hospitality sector specialists and airline company personnel, as well as to semi-skilled and unskilled workers. According to the Moroccan Consulate in the UAE, females made up the majority of these flows (70 per cent). Over the 2000s, irregular and unskilled labour seems to have taken over.[16] In Lebanon, the Observatoire Universitaire de la Réalité Socio-Economique (OURSE) at Saint-Joseph University (Beirut), conducted three surveys during the 2000s that focused on migration patterns and aspirations among Lebanese young people. The most recent survey, published in 2009, looked at 5,695 migrants, aged between eighteen and thirty-five, who migrated between 1992 and 2007 and had family members in Lebanon. It highlighted their growing attraction to the Arab states, namely the Gulf countries, over the period. On average, more than one-third of these expatriates settled in the GCC region, with similar proportions for males and females. The survey also emphasised that over the period studied, family reunification was losing importance as a spur for female migration (in general), as compared to job seeking abroad.[17]

AN EMERGING TREND IN ARAB MIGRATION

Highly skilled Arab female migrants in Kuwait and Bahrain

In receiving countries in the Gulf region, Kuwait and Bahrain are the only two states to provide a (limited) range of data broken down by sex and nationality group (Arab, Asian, etc.) However, neither country publishes data on population by regional origin broken down by educational level. To identify the highly skilled workers' category in the employed population, we therefore had to rely on nationality groups' occupational distributions,[18] taken from Public Authority for Civil Information (PACI) datasets[19] in Kuwait, and the 2010 population census in Bahrain, which offer a proxy estimate of this group.[20] In this section, we will not describe the highly skilled Arab females in Kuwait and Bahrain as a category per se; little besides the size of the community can be drawn from available published macro-demographic data. Rather, we will use available data to resituate this category in its wider socio-demographic context and examine how it intersects with other categories and features that characterise non-national populations (female labour, Arab origin, host country socio-economic set-up, country of origin, etc.) In so doing, we will gather elements to assess the existence of gender-specific dynamics underlying the migration of highly skilled Arab female professionals.

Table 8.1 shows that in 2010 in Bahrain and in 2012 in Kuwait, about one-third of foreign Arab female workers were highly skilled, which is a substantial proportion. However, compared to Arab females in working-age groups (15–64 years) as a whole, their share appears very small (8.4 and 5.6 per cent). This is due to the low levels of activity among Arab females in the two countries (respectively, 25 and 15.9 per cent of employed females in the total working-age population, only). These rates are even below the proportion of active Kuwaiti females (48 per cent of total), and much below that of active expatriate females as a whole in Kuwait (63.3 per cent).[21]

Every other element of the socio-demographic context of highly skilled Arab professionals differs between the two countries studied. Employed Arab females as a whole, for example, follow two kinds of occupational patterns. In Kuwait, the female workforce is mainly 'white collar': only 15 per cent of the female Arab workforce is employed in sales and services, and production. In Bahrain, by contrast, even though the kingdom hosts a similar share of highly skilled females to Kuwait, it also has a large proportion of unskilled women: 46 per cent are in the services and sales, and production sectors (i.e. at the bottom of the occupational ladder).[22]

Moreover, if compared to that of Arab males, the situation of highly skilled Arab females also differs between the two countries: in Kuwait, only

Table 8.1: Highly-skilled, employed and total (15–64 years) populations (Bahrain, 2010; Kuwait, 2012)

Occupation	Kuwait				Bahrain			
	Non-Kuwaiti Arabs		Total Non-Kuwaitis		Non-Bahraini Arabs		Total Non-Bahrainis	
	Males	Females	Males	Females	Males	Females	Males	Females
Legislators, senior officials and managers	34,327	2,998	58,693	5,451	4,263	614	25,021	3,056
Scientific, technical specialists	55,969	17,238	82,077	22,872	4,937	518	25,060	4,136
Total highly skilled workers	90,296	20,236	140,770	28,323	9,200	1,132	50,081	7,192
Total employed population	469,178	60,400	1,410,672	453,465	22,772	3,217	437,394	88,781
Total population (15–64 years)	549,905	241,770	1,499,975	716,747	25,473	20,282	628,816	331,918
% highly-skilled in employed population	19.2	33.5	10.0	6.2	40.4	35.2	11.4	8.1
% highly-skilled in total (15–64 years) population	16.4	8.4	9.4	4.0	36.1	5.6	8.0	2.2
% employed in total (15–64 years) population	85.3	25.0	94.0	63.3	89.4	15.9	69.6	26.7
sex ratio in employed population[23]	777		311		708		493	
sex ratio in total population	227		209		126		189	

Source: PACI (Kuwait) and CIO (Bahrain).

AN EMERGING TREND IN ARAB MIGRATION

Figure 8.1: Arab employed population by main occupation group and sex (Bahrain, 2010; Kuwait, 2012)

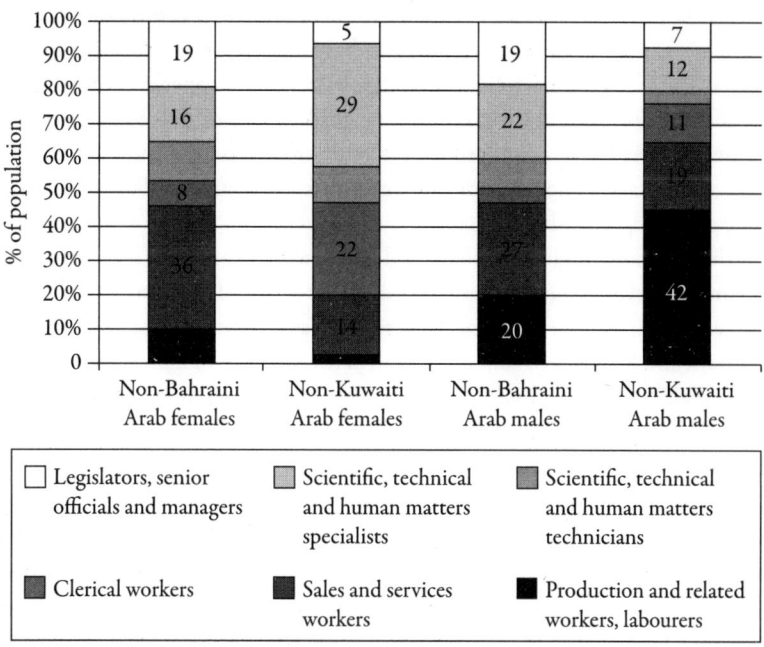

Source: PACI (Kuwait); CIO (Bahrain).

19 per cent of Arab men are highly skilled, whereas in Bahrain, by contrast, 41 per cent of Arab males are in this category: Arab males and females in Bahrain display a similar profile (Figure 8.1). But in stark contrast with the mostly white-collar Arab female labourers' profile in Kuwait, 61 per cent of men in the emirate are employed as blue-collar workers in the services and production categories.

Only using the two examples of Kuwait and Bahrain, it appears impossible to pinpoint either a gender-specific dynamic of employment, or any pattern common to Arab workers. The only features common to both countries are, paradoxically, the low rates of activity among expatriate Arab females, and the high share of the highly skilled among Arab female labourers, which both stand out in comparison to those from other regions (namely Asians), and contrasts with that of men in the case of Kuwait.

These two dynamics are in fact linked, and are rooted in one of the main elements of GCC countries' migration policies: migrant workers, Arabs and non-Arabs alike, are not allowed to settle permanently in the host region and the length of their stay is conditional on their labour contract. One of the many measures preventing long-duration stays in Gulf countries for most foreign workers is the restriction of family reunions: sponsorship of dependants in the host country is limited to expatriates in the upper-income bracket. In Kuwait, for example, a minimum monthly salary of 450 Kuwaiti dinars (around US$1,600) is required for a man to support his dependants, in addition to education, health, housing and other expenditures. Furthermore, a wife cannot sponsor her husband.

Therefore, the higher the share of dependants in a group of non-nationals, the more likely the men in that group are to be involved in relatively well-paid, skilled activities. The low rates of activity that characterise Arab women in Bahrain and Kuwait go hand in hand with the presence of many highly skilled Arab male expatriates residing in the two countries with their wives and teenage children.[24] Also of note is that highly skilled Arab female migrants appear to share the labour market with men.

Starting from this deductive argument, we will try to go one step further in understanding the dynamics of Arab workers' migration to the Gulf region, and assess the correlation between the nationality of workers and the proportion of highly skilled people among them. Given that no data is available on this issue, we will use the distribution of work permits by type and nationality of holder available for Kuwait in 2012.

Highly skilled workers in Kuwait: the nationality factor

Among residency permit holders[25] in Kuwait in 2012, Egyptians alone formed 63.7 per cent of all Arabs.[26] Regarding the distribution of work permits by type and holder's nationality, and in line with previous conclusions drawn from PACI data, it appears that the overwhelming majority of Arab female expatriates in the emirate were family dependants (wives and daughters, essentially): only 18.8 per cent of them were registered as workers.[27]

This figure is in marked contrast with that of non-Arab migrants: 75 per cent of Asian females, for example, were registered as active. Discrepancies can also be noticed in the Arab expatriate population: some nationalities—Lebanese and Egyptians—comprised up to 24 per cent of working females, and others—Syrians—much less (8.6 per cent).

Does this mean that Lebanese and Egyptian expatriates shared a similar socio-economic profile? Sex ratio figures by nationality tell another story. Egyptian male residents vastly outnumbered their female counterparts, with

Table 8.2: Non-Kuwaiti population by sex, migration status and country or region of citizenship of holder (December 2012)

Migration status	Workers				Family members		Total holders of residency permit		Sex ratio (males for 100 females)
Country of citizenship	Males	% workers in total	Females	% workers in total	Males	Females	Males	Females	
Syria	53,452	62.3	4,300	8.6	30,726	45,119	85,746	49,808	172
Lebanon	13,957	61.6	4,708	23.6	8,285	15,016	22,666	19,920	114
Jordan	15,893	55.4	4,609	17.5	12,220	21,532	28,691	26,390	109
Egypt	305,781	82.2	24,988	22.6	52,735	84,765	371,934	110,758	336
Other Arabs	13,144	60.9	4,001	20.1	7,917	15,428	21,586	19,865	109
Total Arab countries	402,227	75.8	42,606	18.8	111,883	181,860	530,623	226,741	234
Total Asia	871,289	91.8	352,151	75.5	53,517	107,677	949,235	466,284	204
Total Arabs & Asians	1,273,516	85.7	473,053	60.2	173,332	302,356	1,513,828	785,863	193

Source: Kuwait Ministry of Interior.

an overall sex ratio of 336 men per 100 women. Syrians' sex ratio was 172 men per 100 women, whereas Lebanese and Jordanians displayed more balanced sex distributions (114 and 108 men per 100 women, respectively). This means that a lot of Egyptian men were in Kuwait alone, which suggests that most of them performed low-skilled activities that prevented them from bringing their families to the country. By contrast, balanced sex ratios indicated that Lebanese and Jordanian men were most often employed in better-paid, white-collar activities that gave them the possibility of sponsoring dependants. As regards Arab employed women, it is then likely that their profiles similarly differed according to nationality: the proportion of skilled and highly skilled females was highest among Lebanese and Jordanian female expatriates.

The higher ratios of Jordanian and Lebanese female to male workers further suggest that a share of these women came to Kuwait on their own. Given their numbers (almost 25,000), Egyptian female professionals are unlikely to all be clustered in one major sector of activity or occupation level; some of them may be involved in unskilled, low-income activities similar to those performed by some Egyptian male expatriates. However, field evidence shows that Egyptian female professionals are often employed in middle-range, clerical jobs. Notably, other contributions to this volume confirm that Egyptian females in the Gulf are frequently employed in the education sector.[28]

In view of the scarce data available to account for Arab female expatriates' employment, a pattern based on skill level seems likely. However, the nationality-specific pattern of total and female employment in the Egyptian example, added to the diversity of national socio-economic contexts in the Arab world, overshadow any clear-cut gendered or Arab pattern of migration to GCC countries, taking Kuwait as an example. Therefore, the datasets we analyse now, which describe a population of highly skilled Lebanese workers in the GCC, should not be generalised as typical.

Personal characteristics of highly skilled Arab female professionals in the Gulf countries: a case study of Lebanese migrants

For reasons explained above, no existing data set permits a study of personal characteristics of highly skilled Arab female migrant professionals in the Gulf. We must therefore resort to field research. The data presented here is drawn from the results of an online questionnaire survey conducted in summer 2012, which tackled highly skilled Lebanese migrants abroad and their relation to their origin country.[29] Datasets for migrants residing in the GCC region at the time of the survey have been extracted and studied separately for this chapter.

AN EMERGING TREND IN ARAB MIGRATION

Before starting, we must delimit the scope and outreach of this study: as noted in the previous paragraph, Lebanese nationals' migration patterns may not necessarily apply to other Arab nationals. Also, the design of the survey sample (people having migrated after 1990), and the interviewees' recruitment patterns (through social networks) created the sub-sample of the Lebanese migrant population studied.

First we describe the general characteristics of the surveyed population, then introduce data focusing on migrants' education and employment patterns. The geographic concentration of respondents in Dubai (see Table 8.3) prevents us from comparing their profiles by country of residence: female respondents numbered only thirty-six, out of a total population of 144 migrants in GCC countries. Data disaggregated by place of residence would therefore have lacked consistency. Data for females will be systematically compared to that of males. Thereby, more material for discussing the existence of a gendered pattern of skilled migration to Gulf countries will be made available.

Table 8.3: Distribution of respondents to the survey residing in the Gulf States by country of current residence in the Gulf and sex (Summer 2012)

Country of residence	Percentage	
	Male	Female
Bahrain	0.9	0.0
Kuwait	12.0	5.6
Oman	1.9	5.6
Qatar	17.6	19.4
Saudi Arabia	25.0	16.7
United Arab Emirates (UAE)	42.6	52.8
Emirate of residence within UAE (% of all respondents)		
Abu Dhabi	9.3	5.6
Ajman	0	2.8
Dubai	30.6	41.7
Sharjah	1.9	0.0
Ras al-Khaimah	0.0	2.8
Total	100	100
	N=108	N=36

Source: CEDRE sample survey of Lebanese highly skilled migrants (see footnote 28). N = total sample size.

Demographic characteristics

A clear majority of respondents were located in the UAE, especially in Dubai, and to a much lesser extent in Qatar and Saudi Arabia. Females' geographic concentration was more acute than that of men: 72.2 per cent of female respondents had migrated to the Gulf directly after leaving Lebanon. The geographic turnover seems moderate among this population: on average, females had spent 6.4 years (men: 6.7 years) in their present country of residence. Some 70 per cent of females migrated from 2006, while most males (one-quarter) left Lebanon for the first time that same year. The 2006 war with Israel explains such a pattern, as does the relatively young age of these migrants (32 years for women and 34.4 for men, on average), who left after they had obtained their university degree from Lebanon.

As shown in Table 8.3, men outnumbered women by three to one in the surveyed population: this is relatively similar to the sex ratio characterising Lebanese migrants who held government, private-sector and business residency documents in Kuwait (hence, classified as workers in Table 8.1).

Figure 8.2 shows that almost half of female respondents (42 per cent) were classified as unmarried (single or divorced). By comparison, an earlier study of Lebanese who migrated between 1992 and 2007, covering Lebanese emigrants from all educational backgrounds and regions of des-

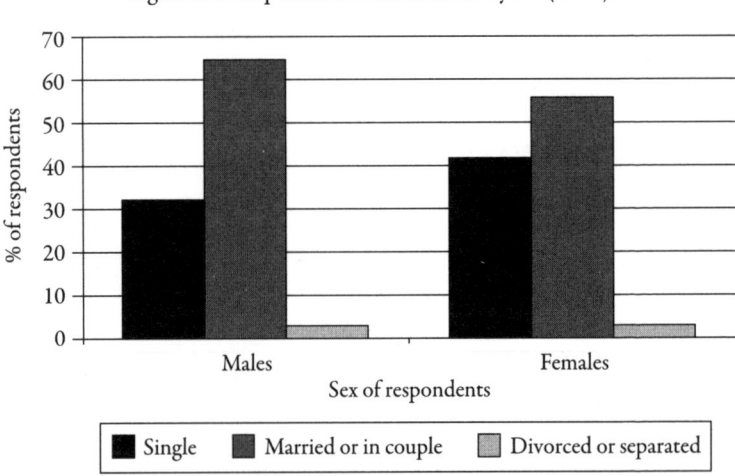

Figure 8.2: Respondents' marital status by sex (2012)

Source: CEDRE sample survey of Lebanese highly skilled migrants.

tination, estimated the respective proportions of married male and female emigrants to be 63.5 and 81 per cent.[30] This led the authors to conclude that females had simply followed their husbands abroad and emigrated as dependants. The sizeable proportion of non-married females in our surveyed population, however, goes against the dominant perception of females migrating as dependants.

Educational profile

Regarding their educational characteristics, some of the highly skilled Lebanese professionals in our sample first migrated to acquire degrees higher than those obtained in Lebanon, or degrees in a different field.[31] For females, as well as males, one-quarter of all degrees were received abroad. Half of these expatriates left Lebanon with a BA (or equivalent), and three-quarters with an MA (or equivalent); PhDs comprised 8 and 17 per cent of all degrees taken abroad, for men and women respectively. Males, slightly more than females, took degrees abroad that were business-oriented or sector-specific (e.g. MBA, qualification degrees or others).[32]

Table 8.4: Highest university degree obtained by respondents in Lebanon and abroad (Summer 2012)

	Males			Females		
	Lebanon	Abroad	All degrees	Lebanon	Abroad	All degrees
BA/BSc/Licence	52.8	5.3	40.4	58.3	0.0	43.8
Engineering degree/BE	12.0	0.0	8.9	5.6	0.0	4.2
MA/MSc/Master	17.6	26.3	19.9	25.0	41.7	29.2
MBA	12.0	42.1	19.9	5.6	25.0	10.4
Other postgraduate degrees	1.9	2.6	2.1	5.6	8.3	6.3
Other (qualification degrees)	1.9	15.8	5.5	0.0	8.3	2.1
PhD	1.9	7.9	3.4	0.0	16.7	4.2
Total	100.0	100.0	100.0	100.0	100.0	100.0

Source: CEDRE sample survey of Lebanese highly skilled migrants (see footnote 28).

Figure 8.3: Respondents' field of education by sex (2012)

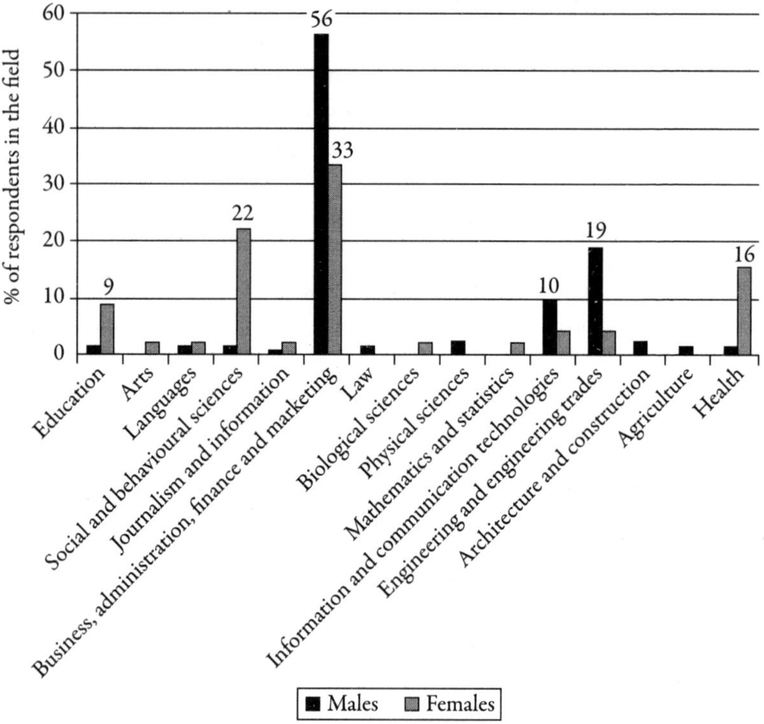

[Bar chart showing % of respondents in the field by field of education, split by Males and Females:
- Education: Males ~1, Females 9
- Arts: Females ~2
- Languages: ~2 (both)
- Social and behavioural sciences: Females 22
- Journalism and information: ~1
- Business, administration, finance and marketing: Males 56, Females 33
- Law: ~1
- Biological sciences: ~2
- Physical sciences: ~2
- Mathematics and statistics: ~2
- Information and communication technologies: Males 10, Females ~4
- Engineering and engineering trades: Males 19, Females ~4
- Architecture and construction: ~2
- Agriculture: ~1
- Health: Males ~1, Females 16]

Field of education (3 digits)   Classification: ISCED 2013 (narrow fields, 3 digits)

Source: CEDRE sample survey of Lebanese highly skilled migrants.

The distribution of respondents by field of study[33] (Figure 8.3) indeed emphasises the concentration of all respondents in the 'business, administration, finance and marketing' field of studies. However, this concentration is more acute for men than women, who also studied education, social sciences and health sciences in sizeable numbers.

Figure 8.4: Main economic occupation of respondents, by sex (2012)

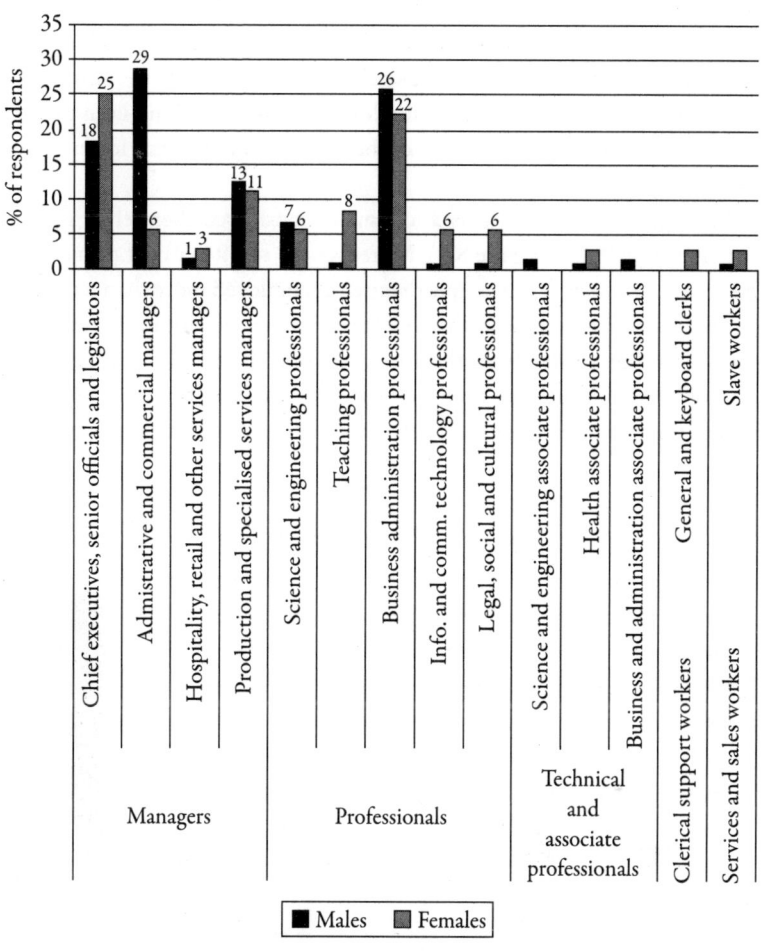

Source: CEDRE sample survey of Lebanese highly skilled migrants.

Socio-economic characteristics

Predictably, the overwhelming majority of interviewees were involved in managerial and professional occupations, mostly in the 'business and administration' field of both categories.³⁴ However, male managers slightly outnumbered female ones (61 and 44.4 per cent, respectively). Women also showed more diversity in their categories and fields of occupation (teaching and information technologies were exclusively female activities here). Also, more females than males were in skilled and low-skilled occupations, even though they earned similar degrees to those of their male counterparts. However, this was marginal.

Three-quarters of both males and females considered themselves 'permanent employees'³⁵ (see Figure 8.5). Moreover, up to 10 per cent of men and 5 per cent of women in the sample themselves employed more than ten workers. This is striking because in the Gulf foreigners are not meant to settle and limited-duration contracts are the norm. Not only did these people not feel a sense of precariousness in their country of residence, but they even felt invested there. This may be explained by the high levels of education and skills

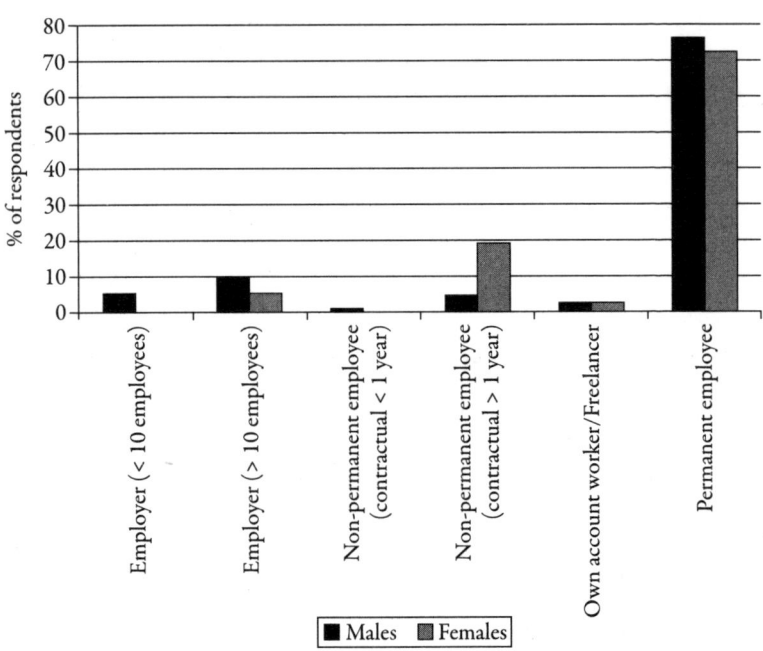

Figure 8.5: Respondents' professional status, by sex (2012)

Classification of professeional status: adapted from ICSE (ILO), 1993.

Source: CEDRE sample survey of Lebanese highly skilled migrants.

AN EMERGING TREND IN ARAB MIGRATION

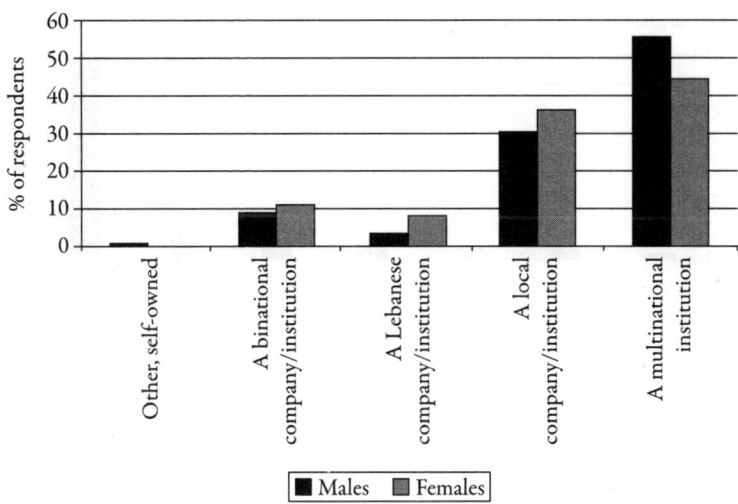

Figure 8.6: Ownership of the company employing respondents (2012)

Source: CEDRE sample survey of Lebanese highly skilled migrants.

in the males and females in the sample, as witnessed above. Additionally, with most of them residing in Dubai, the emirate's booming economy may have allowed companies there to provide prospective careers to highly skilled foreign professionals, males and females alike.

The survey results show diversity in the economic activity sectors employing the Lebanese respondents in our sample.[36] However, women were more often employed in 'Financial and insurance activities', 'Human health and social work activities' and 'Information and communication' (11 per cent each). 'Professional, scientific and technical activities', including management companies, a sector favoured by male managers and male and female 'professionals' as seen above in Figure 8.4, concentrated 17 per cent of the sample's females and 10 per cent of males. Males were more often involved in 'Information and communication activities' (18 per cent), as well as 'Construction' and 'Finances and insurances' (13 per cent). Concerning education fields and professional occupations, females and males differed only slightly in terms of their sectors of activity.

Similarly, as regards the type of ownership and the size of the companies[37] employing workers in the sample (Figures 8.6 and 8.7), the dominant trend was similar for both sexes: they were employed in multinationals or Gulf corpora-

Figure 8.7: Size of the company employing respondents (2012)

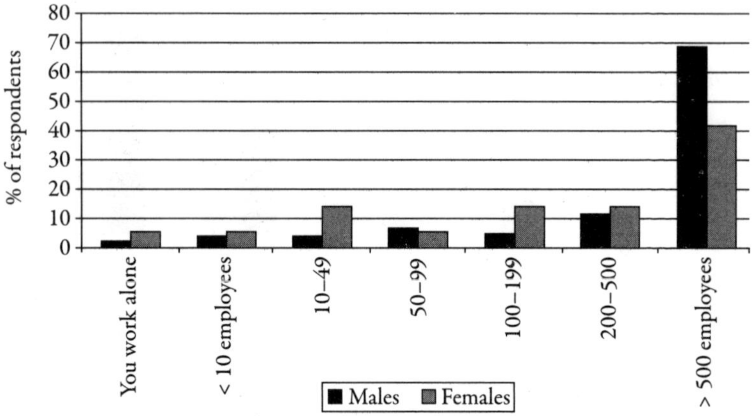

[Bar chart showing % of respondents by company size, split by Males and Females. Categories: You work alone, < 10 employees, 10–49, 50–99, 100–199, 200–500, > 500 employees. The > 500 employees category is dominant, with males around 68% and females around 42%.]

Source: CEDRE sample survey of Lebanese highly skilled migrants.

tions, most of them (40 to 70 per cent) of a very large size (500 workers or more). However, females' patterns were less accentuated than males'. For example, 60 per cent of them were distributed in all categories of company size. To conclude, in view of all the results presented so far, no clear gender-specific career patterns can be detected from the survey data. Female data may point to a slightly more diversified career path: females were less concentrated than males in fields of studies and in professions related to management and business. Many of them were in high-ranking managerial occupations, as well as in teaching professions, in information technologies, and in law-related occupations. Also, women were less often employed in very large multinational companies.

Arab skilled migration to the Gulf: networks and recruitment channels

Our sample provided some insight into the recruitment channels that first brought people to the Gulf. Men resorted significantly more than females to institutional placement methods such as placement agencies, and specialised press or websites. However, for both sexes, personal networks (friends and family) were the main support for recruitment in the GCC region. Even in the case of highly skilled professionals, such as our sample of Lebanese, who were most often employed in large international companies, personal connections played a major role in the recruitment process.

AN EMERGING TREND IN ARAB MIGRATION

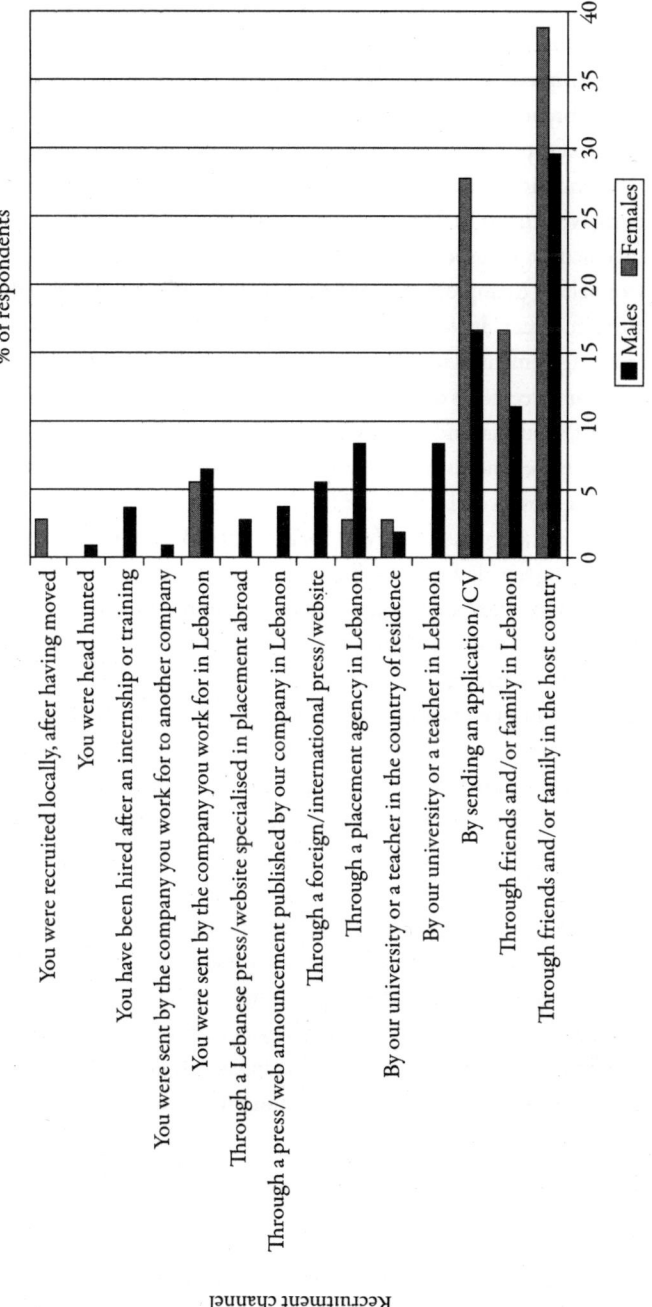

Figure 8.8: Respondents' first job in the Gulf: recruitment channels, by sex (2012)[38]

Source: CEDRE sample survey of Lebanese highly skilled migrants.

189

Our fieldwork in other countries across the Middle East[39] confirmed the recruitment patterns observed for this group of highly skilled Lebanese interviewees: recruitment methods included word of mouth from friends or relatives established abroad, as well as recruitment agencies collecting CVs or headhunting specific professionals, through specialised websites, newspapers or online advertisements. Positions in the public sector are sometimes offered by Gulf State governments to Arab professionals, under ad hoc bilateral agreements. Such agreements target specific professions (health professionals, teachers, security personnel, for example), and personal profiles, as well as specifying the duration of the contract. In Jordan, the health and education ministries signed cooperation agreements with their counterparts in Bahrain and the UAE in the 2000s. Similar agreements on bilateral technical cooperation were also signed in the 2000s with Tunisia, and were directed at single women in particular.

Indeed, some elements of a clear-cut gender-specific recruitment process could only be observed in the case of middle-range professionals, in semi-skilled or lower categories. *The New York Times* reported that a Gulf airline was hiring young female Egyptian flight attendants and that 'some Gulf-based employers now say they tailor recruitment procedures for young women with Arab family values in mind. They may hire groups of women from a particular town or region, for example, so the women can support one another once in the Gulf'.[40] This implies, however, that female employees are housed in specific locations such as company labour compounds, with secure dormitories, which prevents free contact between employees and the outside world.

In general, this appears to be a noticeable phenomenon in the Arab world: employers tailor labour conditions to conform with so-called social conservatism and 'Arab Muslim values' (gender segregation in the workplace, on public transport, etc.), and are designed to attract female employees who come from more conservative rural backgrounds or small cities, while resisting patriarchal opposition to female employment.[41] These procedures streamline women towards skilled and semi-skilled economic activities that Asian workers used to perform, such as in the manufacturing sector. But this apparently does not apply to highly skilled professions, which rely on personal and professional networks.

Structural determinants of skilled and highly skilled Arab female migration to the GCC

Migration to the GCC countries is first a matter of attraction ('pull') to that region where labour markets are in need of a constant supply of skilled labour, especially in Dubai and the UAE where most of our interviewees were employed. Males and females alike perceived Gulf markets as extremely open to skilled labourers, unlike Europe, for example. As far as the gender issue was concerned, gendered aspects of Gulf migration policies, such as the inability of a female labourer to support her husband as a dependant, did not apply to anybody in that population. Also, females in our sample who migrated alone to the Gulf denied having experienced gender-specific difficulties in the migratory process. For example, no extra requirements for obtaining sponsorship were mentioned.[42] This may be because our female interviewees had already succeeded in coming to the Gulf and could rely on personal networks, which may have facilitated the migration process. In addition, the desire to appear successful in one's professional endeavours may have encouraged some people to understate any obstacles encountered. Nevertheless, the question remains whether such constraints would be due to an expatriate's gender, her Arab origin, religious or national background, or to a combination of several of those and other factors. Only a large-scale survey involving a variety of nationalities and professional backgrounds could pinpoint a gender-based pattern of recruitment, which did not come to the fore from our limited sample.

We now examine some proximate determinants and possible 'push' factors underlying expatriates' experiences and decisions to migrate. Figure 8.9 shows the reasons the Lebanese respondents in our sample gave for why they left the country. At first glance, non-labour-related issues appear much less important for the interviewees, than labour-related ones.[43] Only 11 per cent of highly skilled females in our sample came to the Gulf following their husbands. In addition, that almost half of the females in the sample were unmarried clearly contradicts the assumption that female Arab professionals systematically migrate as dependants.

Proximate determinants to female highly skilled migration

Indeed, the demographic, educational and economic contexts have greatly evolved since the 1980s, when studies on Arab migration to the Gulf countries first exposed these dominant features of female migration.

In general, females now marry at a much later age in most Arab sending countries: the average age on first marriage is between twenty-five and twenty-seven years old, which is comparable to the situation in Europe. Moreover, while in the past female celibacy was almost non-existent, it has become a reality in the Gulf region: the group of women aged between thirty-five and

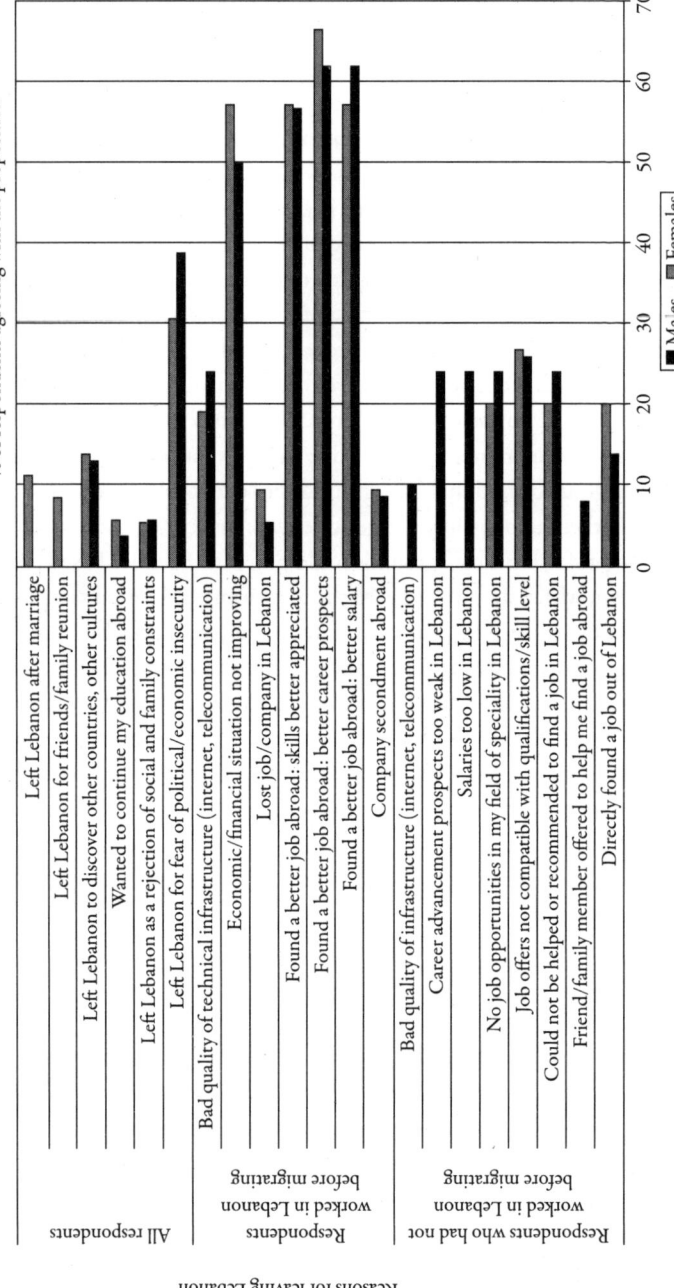

Figure 8.9: Reasons for leaving Lebanon, by sex (2012)

Source: CEDRE sample survey of Lebanese highly skilled migrants.

thirty-nine used to be almost exclusively composed of married, divorced or widowed women, but now contains sizeable proportions of unmarried females (12–16 per cent in Syria, Jordan, Iraq, and Palestine, and 20 per cent or more in Lebanon). In Jordan, 8.5 per cent of women aged between forty-five and forty-nine in the late 2000s remained unmarried. Early and universal marriage was for long a social norm in Middle Eastern countries; it was considered an essential factor in the reproduction of gender and age segregation patterns, which themselves sustained the reproduction and stability of the Arab family institution.[44] The emergence of celibacy may thus signify a progressive questioning of social norms.[45]

Additionally, generations born since the late 1960s have enjoyed progressive gender equality in education levels: in Jordan for example, the rate of enrolment in education between the ages of five years old and twenty-nine was 96 females per 100 males in 2004. In the same year, enrolment rates at university level from BA to PhD (i.e. of students born between 1975 and 1985) were even stronger for women than for men (102 women per 100 men), according to census data. Consequently, young women's aspirations have evolved accordingly: reproducing their mothers and grandmothers' socio-economic model of a life, geared towards marriage and children, male domination and economic dependence, was unappealing for most.

Structural factors leading to female migration

Despite such a change, females' economic participation remains low: only 20 per cent of females aged between thirty and thirty-four years old, for example, were active (i.e. employed or searching for employment) in Jordan in 2004. Limited progress has been made since then. Since the mid-1980s and the onset of the first structural adjustment policies conducted in all non-oil-producing Arab economies, states partly disengaged from the welfare-redistribution process and from the provision of public employment.[46] Previous models of educated, yet inactive, married females were thus no longer an option. These dynamics point to another factor likely to deter young graduates from local labour markets and spur increasing levels of emigration: that the region's labour markets remain closed to skilled and highly skilled young people.

Indeed, in the Middle East unemployment levels are generally highest among university graduates: in Jordan in 2011, the graduate unemployment rate was 16 per cent, compared to the (official) overall unemployment rate of 13 per cent. In Tunisia in 2010, 23 per cent of graduates were unemployed, compared to

13 per cent for the whole population; the situation worsened, reaching 32.6 per cent unemployment among graduates in 2013. In Morocco, the situation was the same in the 2000s: 25 per cent of graduates were jobless in 2005, compared to 5 per cent of the population who did not hold a degree.[47]

Such a paradoxical situation is because, since the mid-1980s, most countries in the region have enacted structural adjustment plans. These reforms drastically limited employment opportunities in the public sector. Such a dynamic was then further strengthened by the impact of globalisation on Arab economies. After the mid-1990s and throughout the 2000s, international treaties, bilateral and free trade agreements sped up privatisation processes and the restructuring of most economic sectors to improve productivity. However, these reforms also compelled employers to invest in labour-intensive, low-added-value economic sectors, relying on low-skilled workers—for example, industrial subcontracting, assembly and textile manufacturing. Meanwhile, average standards of living decreased everywhere in the region, as economic rationalisation hardened.

In the case of Lebanon, the perceptions expressed by interviewees in our sample showed a clear concern about low salaries, limited career prospects and stagnation of the socio-economic situation, as well as the limited size of the national labour market, which was unlikely to incorporate all citizens. Male and female respondents came to the GCC for different reasons, which interviews in Dubai in February 2013[48] confirmed. Interviewees denounced for instance the extent of corruption and clientelism plaguing the development of a functioning economy, the intersection of labour issues with political concerns—political and sectarian affiliations that affect recruitment of highly skilled professionals—as a major obstacle to incorporating Lebanese citizens' skills and experience in the country's labour market. This is very interesting, considering the dominant representation of Lebanese migration as essentially career-led and apolitical, and Lebanon's status as a globalised economy, strongly connected to Gulf markets. To sum up, the articulation of the issues of labour and migration is of a political nature. The migration of young professionals indeed points to the question of their political integration in their country of origin, and, consequently, to the question of citizenship in general. This is a concern for the highly skilled, too, even if they have globalised and transnational careers.

We expected that female respondents in our survey would cite a gender-based lack of empowerment as their reason for emigrating from Lebanon. Indeed, the young Arab unmarried professionals willing to migrate whom we had encountered in Amman in the 2000s[49] explained their decision as a means of empowering themselves: to achieve independence from their family and/or social environment, and to escape social alienation and persisting patriarchal patterns of social control, sometimes imposed on unmarried, yet highly educated and economically active females.[50] At the same time, they were hoping to overcome frustrating difficulties that undervalued their educational qualifications on the labour market. But it should be noted that migrating, in most cases, was not perceived as liberation, but rather as a personal and economic necessity.

However, among the Lebanese respondents only 5 per cent of the sample mentioned 'rejection of social and family constraints' as a reason for leaving Lebanon, with men and women on similar footing. This result possibly confirms the relevance of nationality—or more precisely, a country's dominant sociocultural background—in defining females' migration patterns and experience.

Conclusion

No clear-cut gendered pattern emerges from the data we gathered and analysed for this chapter. We are conscious that pinpointing gender-based dynamics goes far beyond simply comparing male and female dynamics and behaviours. However, we were limited in that respect by the nature of the data we used (demographic, macro-data), and even more so by the scarcity of available data and studies, from sending as well as from receiving countries, or from other academic and policymaking non-national bodies.

In contrast, the labour and career factors, which tended to bring together highly skilled migrants, male and female alike, appeared to strongly determine migration patterns. Additionally, the country of citizenship was pinpointed in the Kuwaiti and Bahraini macro-demographic data as another factor likely to affect migrants' experience.

Apart from nepotism affecting the Lebanese labour market, that the highly skilled Lebanese female migrants surveyed did not give any 'culture-based' reasons for migrating to the Gulf may be partly due to 'presentation of self' while abroad as different to other Arabs. However, the emergence of nationality as a factor, even if we keep in mind the social segmentation and stratification that characterise every Arab state, is hardly a surprise. Despite the prevalence of many common denominators among them, including cultural patterns, language, and to some extent religion, major discrepancies exist as well: Arab women come from twenty-two countries, with dissimilar levels of education, economic, legal and socio-political systems.

Such findings thus raise the issue of the categories used: the assumption of an 'Arab' migration pattern is undermined by the nationality factor. Those Gulf states that define specific conditions for immigrants appear very welcoming to highly skilled Lebanese, male and female, who do not seem affected by the abuses of foreign workers often reported in the region. Therefore, migrants' gender may be less of a discriminatory factor in the migration process than their level of skills and country of citizenship.

This also points to the rapidity of social change in the Gulf states, where voluntary policies of nationalisation of the labour force ('Saudi-isation', 'Omanisation', etc.) started to significantly enhance local females' economic participation, especially in white-collar positions. The fall of social and psychological barriers, which previously hindered women's entry into labour markets, may have opened avenues for skilled and highly skilled female professionals from other Arab countries. The social and economic separation between nationals and non-nationals, as well as between genders, which made Gulf States so exceptional, may begin to progressively fade away.

In any case, however, such partial results beg a wider-scale survey that involves highly skilled female migrants from several Arab countries and systematically compares their migratory patterns and experience. Moreover, a careful review of migration policy patterns that possibly affect every nationality and, transversally, females, would be extremely useful. In the meantime, one can only hope that the continuing process of demographic data production and dissemination in the Gulf region will expand and allow for a much deeper understanding of the socio-demographic dynamics that affect this region.

9

HIGHLY SKILLED LEBANESE TRANSNATIONAL MIGRANTS

A KUWAIT PERSPECTIVE

Garret Maher[1]

The lives of increasing numbers of individuals can no longer be understood by looking only at what goes on within national boundaries. Our analytical lens must necessarily broaden and deepen because migrants are often embedded in multi-layered, multi-sited transnational social fields, encompassing those who move and those who stay behind.[2]

Introduction

International migration streams have become increasingly important in supporting economic growth, particularly in countries where the local labour force is too small, or unwilling to work in specific types of employment. All of the Gulf Cooperation Council (GCC) countries share a strong reliance on foreign labour; Qatar, for example, has a non-national population of close to 90 per cent, the highest in the world.[3] Historically, Kuwait is no different:

when Kuwait achieved independence in 1961, at least half the population at that time consisted of non-Kuwaiti nationals,[4] and since the mid-1960s a large proportion of the population has always consisted of foreign nationals, averaging between 60 and 70 per cent of the total population.[5]

Although much has been written about these migrants, the focus has mainly been on low-skilled immigrants from South Asia and other Arab countries,[6] and research data relating to high-skilled transnational labour migrants of a specific nationality is limited. Despite the concerns of the Kuwaiti government that too many non-nationals are taking jobs in the country,[7] demand for highly skilled migrants throughout the region is large and ever increasing.[8] These migrants are defined as those in possession of a tertiary degree or extensive specialised work experience—such as architects, financial experts, engineers, technicians, scientists, health professionals and specialists in information technology (IT).[9]

Transnational migrants differ from traditional immigrants because they continually communicate with and regularly visit their country of origin, while simultaneously living, working and socialising in a second country. Traditional migrants, however, keep infrequent contact with their country of origin and often disassociate themselves from it indefinitely.[10]

This chapter's original contribution lies in its examination of aspects of transnational migration among high-skilled Lebanese migrants from a dual country perspective: that of the sending country, Lebanon, and of the receiving country, Kuwait. By using a dual, home and host country perspective, the chapter shows a more complete picture of specific aspects of transnational migration, in particular the motivations and drivers of migration—why migrants chose Kuwait as a destination, as opposed to other GCC countries. It then explores aspects of integration and socialisation to first identify from a research sample if the Lebanese in Kuwait are deemed to be integrated into Kuwaiti society, and to see if a transnational community has formed among other Lebanese in Kuwait. The chapter proceeds to explore temporal aspects of migration to discover how long the migrants plan on staying in Kuwait, and it then presents data on returned migrants and the reasons for their return to Lebanon. Finally, it explores remittances, which form a key feature of transnationalism, before offering several conclusions drawn from the research.

Lebanon is considered one of the world's most emigration-prone countries, with a multi-generational diaspora estimated at 15 million, a number that far exceeds the estimated population of Lebanon of 4.5 million people.[11] The GCC countries became particularly attractive for the Lebanese during the oil boom years of the 1970s, coupled with the civil war in Lebanon between 1975 and 1989, when an estimated half a million Lebanese migrated to the GCC region.[12] As early as 1975, Kuwait was the main destination for Lebanese migrants, with over 25,000 living there at that time.[13] Estimates suggest that between 1997 and 2007 about half of those who emigrated from Lebanon went to one of the Gulf states.[14]

Today Kuwait hosts a vibrant Lebanese community that numbers around 42,000 people, of whom it is estimated that over 60 per cent are considered highly skilled migrants.[15] Numerous push factors have led many to emigrate from Lebanon. Political instability, for instance, arguably linked with the ongoing Syrian crisis, which has seen more than 1 million Syrian refugees enter Lebanon, has put a strain on jobs and an already weak infrastructure.[16] Another structural push factor is successive Lebanese governments' economic policy, which has focused on development of tertiary sectors such as tourism and finance, thereby limiting growth and job creation in other sectors.[17] The geography of the region has also 'led it to become locked in an economic and political system that falls short of generating job opportunities and a decent standard of living for its citizens'.[18]

A transnational framework

Using a transnational framework, this chapter provides insight into the lives of Lebanese from home and host country perspectives. Before exploring the findings, it is necessary to specifically define transnationalism in the context of this chapter and how this theory relates to transnational Lebanese migrants. In the context of migration Nina Glick-Schiller *et al.* first coined the term 'transnationalism' when they defined transnationalism as 'the processes by which immigrants build social fields that link together their country of origin and their country of settlement'.[19] With the emergence of a new kind of migrating population, composed of those whose networks, activities and patterns of life encompass their host and home societies, came a new term to define this group: 'transnational migrants' who, in turn, practise transnationalism.[20] The use of the term 'transnational' to describe the processes and experiences of Lebanese immigrants is employed throughout this chapter, and in this context, the most appropriate definition suggests that transnationalism can be defined as representing the movements, linkages and exchanges of migrants across national borders. Such consistent movements, linkages and exchanges of transnational migrants can arguably create a 'third space' between Lebanon and Kuwait, and vice versa, particularly a new cultural or social space created by the migrant community in the host country.[21]

The chapter has drawn on transnational theory, which 'has successfully highlighted the significance of migrants' attachments to people and places transcending the confines of nation-states'.[22] It is probable that this research could not have been conducted without transnational theory, because without this strand of theory our understanding of migration, specifically highly skilled migration, could not be understood and explored to the extent that it has. Transnational theory has developed in response to the inadequacy of 'investigating population movements in terms of one-way movements that result in the gradual integration of migrants into the receiving country'.[23] Instead, a split design whereby research was conducted in Kuwait and Lebanon was selected, to enhance the study by exploring how exactly migrants are transnational. Such a design allowed for a more coherent representation of transnational processes.

Data and methodology

The data from this study was gathered from eighteen in-depth interviews with Lebanese migrants, eleven in Kuwait and seven in Lebanon, with a relatively even gender balance of eight females and ten males varied between the two countries. All of the interviewees were considered to be high-skilled and are broadly representative of the high-skilled Lebanese community in Kuwait based on their occupations; their stories characterise the broader migrant experience because they worked in a number of sectors including finance, IT, management, sales and education. Despite the limited sample size, the dual-site study approach provides a unique look at Lebanese migrants at home and abroad, and therefore the limitation of the sample size is compensated by this multi-site approach.

The interviews in Kuwait were initially organised through a number of Lebanese colleagues and personal contacts in Kuwait, and following this a snowballing method was used to get more contacts. Having used the snowballing technique in Kuwait, a number of contacts were already in place in Lebanon before the field trip to Beirut took place. This allowed for the time spent in Beirut to be fully utilised. All of the interviews were conducted in English. They included core themes to discover as much about the migrants as possible and the role that transnationalism and remittances played in their lives. Themes included: profiling (age, gender), their reasons for coming to Kuwait, their family status (single, married), their education, what employment they were engaged in, the rate of pay they earned, the type of accommodation they had, and if they remitted and how the remittances were used. This method provided an in-depth understanding of the migrant experience.[24]

The political and security situation in Lebanon caused some issues in getting data, and problems were also encountered in terms of punctuality and reliability. Given that the political situation in Lebanon has rapidly deteriorated in the past twenty-four months, in particular, and effects of the Syrian crisis have been severe, safety concerns were justifiable. Consequently, many international bodies and governments advised against any travel to Lebanon. Despite the political issues and warning against travel, the fieldwork in Beirut went ahead at the end of December 2013. During the research in Beirut, on 27 December 2013 a large bomb exploded, which killed eight people including former minister of finance Mohamad Chatah. This incident forced the cancellation of two interviews that were scheduled to take place that day, which could not be rescheduled due to time constraints. Other interviews had to be rescheduled on numerous occasions due to local political issues that made it unsafe to travel outside Beirut. Regrettably, many people who agreed to be interviewed at a certain place and time in Kuwait and Lebanon cancelled at the last minute or constantly postponed interviews, despite numerous promises to meet.

Migration: the choice of Kuwait

As discussed above, the history of Lebanese migration to Kuwait dates back many decades. A study from the early 1980s on immigrant labour in Kuwait showed that Lebanese nationals were in constant demand, and many of them worked—and continue to work—in executive, management and sales positions.[25] International research on recruitment of foreign workers is largely based on two strands: the recruitment of low-skilled, low-paid workers and the recruitment of high-skilled workers. Evidence from Kuwait shows that low-skilled migrants used migration networks of relations and friends as well as recruitment agents to find work.[26] Although migration networks play a key role in the movement of low-skilled labour migrants,[27] research on higher-status migrants, such as those who are highly skilled, suggests that they 'are less likely to need either the information or the sponsorship and material assistance which are common to chain migration networks'.[28] Arguably, higher-status migrant groups are characteristic of what Monica Boyd has identified as those within which 'personal networks fail to emerge'.[29]

Since the 1960s, the recruitment of migrant labour has been part of government policy in Kuwait. Minister of Social Affairs and Labour Thekra al-Rashidi caused much concern in March 2013 with the announcement of a plan to reduce the number of foreign expats by half, from 2 million to only 1 million by 2023, culling about 100,000 expats per year and targeting low-wage workers.[30] However, this decision does not affect high-skilled workers and university graduates are still eligible to apply for work permits.[31]

The benefits of migration to one of the GCC countries, for most, are the higher comparative wages and tax-free status offered.[32] For Lebanese nationals, the decision to migrate to Kuwait as opposed to one of the other GCC countries is obviously one of personal preference, considering that many cultural differences exist between Lebanon and Kuwait, including a ban on the sale of alcohol and pork in Kuwait. The decision to move to Kuwait is not one to be taken lightly.

Hassan, a male computer science graduate in his late twenties, employed at the National Bank of Kuwait (NBK), explained why he moved to Kuwait: 'mainly two things, first, after spending six years in Qatar I wanted a change, and second, the job that I got here was interesting and convinced me to come here, and it was a better paying job'.[33] Hassan had done some research before making his decision, such as speaking to his friends who were already in Kuwait, and despite lifestyle differences between Kuwait and Qatar, he felt 'the GCC is mainly the same, whether you are in Qatar, Kuwait or UAE... the weather, the culture, the people, the living standards, so it was not difficult for me to move to Kuwait'. In the case of Bashir, a married male health professional in his forties, he had also worked in Qatar for four years before moving to Kuwait: 'I came to Kuwait because it was a better package for me, better money, easier lifestyle, why not?'[34] All but one of the male respondents in Kuwait explained how they were attracted to Kuwait by the higher wages offered and what they perceived as the relatively easy lifestyle compared to that of Lebanon.

The findings for females were not entirely the same: although monetary gain was mentioned, their reasons for moving differed from those of males. Fay, a female academic in her early thirties who studied in Paris, France, explained her reasons for moving to Kuwait:

> Actually I was planning to stay in France, but my husband got a job in Kuwait, and we moved. Compared to Lebanon, life here is much easier, too many facilities [sic.], less stress. I came straight from Paris and had not lived in the GCC before; I was scared, but I was shocked that it was more open than I thought, I thought it was [culturally and politically] very close to Saudi Arabia.[35]

Nadia, a female financial professional also in her early thirties and an employee of NBK, explained:

> The first time I lived outside Lebanon we [Nadia and her husband] moved to Saudi Arabia, in Jeddah, after two years we moved to Kuwait. My husband's company in Saudi Arabia moved him here, but we definitely have a better lifestyle here, the salaries are much better...there is more freedom here, I can drive, I can work freely, it's much better.[36]

Evidence has shown that the reasons for choosing Kuwait as a migration destination show little variation. Throughout the sample, two main reasons for emigrating emerged: higher wages, and the relative freedom and ease of lifestyle. 'Freedom' in this context, which many interviewees referred to, can be defined as economic and political stability and freedom of movement, which is somewhat restricted in other GCC countries, and Saudi Arabia in particular. Another major feature is that the majority of migrants came to Kuwait directly from another GCC country, including Saudi Arabia, the UAE and Qatar, albeit with a short vacation in Lebanon before taking up their positions. That the majority came from another GCC country is important, because they acquired experience of life in the region before moving to Kuwait. Living in another GCC country before Kuwait also enabled many migrants to become aware of higher average wages in Kuwait compared to other GCC countries, as well as the restraints on lifestyle, which better prepared them for adaptation upon their arrival. Such movement between other GCC countries also fits into the theory of circular migration, which can represent the mobility of migrants by employment in multinational companies, as well as their transnational experiences in their home and host country (or countries) through regular exchanges, communication, investment and return trips.[37]

Here, it is also apparent that Gulf exceptionalism is perhaps a key driver for high-skilled migrants such as the Lebanese, as they traverse GCC countries in search of ever-increasing wages and political stability. The GCC countries, with the exception of Bahrain, 'seem relatively immune to popular mobilisations which challenged most of the other regimes in the region' and this stability is an incentive for Lebanese, and other Arab migrants, to be mobile citizens.[38] Although it can be argued that Gulf exceptionalism has many positives for high-skilled migrants, arbitrary monarchical decrees, including sudden changes in visa rules or granting power to authorities to deport an immigrant for a minor traffic offence, can have major impacts on all migrants.[39] Such haphazard decisions can affect the everyday lives of all migrants, but it is usually the more vulnerable, low-skilled migrants who suffer. However, as these societies continue to develop, such exceptionalism arguably has a limited future.

Jeffrey Grogger and Gordon Hanson have argued that better educated migrants are more likely to settle in destination countries with high rewards for skills, where skill-related earning differences are relatively large.[40] For example, a migrant housemaid or tea boy in Kuwait could expect to earn approximately US$300–500 per month, whereas most high-skilled migrants, such as a marketing manager, would earn—at the lower end of the scale—US$5,000 or more per month, all of which is tax free. Hillel Rapoport and Frederic Docquier have suggested that 'migration is primarily (but not only) driven by wage differentials'.[41] As mentioned above, the higher salaries for Lebanese migrants in Kuwait were an important factor in their decision to migrate, but data on wage rates among high-skilled migrants in Kuwait is limited in the literature. The findings suggest that migration is worthwhile, with seven out of the eleven interviewees in Kuwait earning within the top bracket. The average salaries among the interviewees in Kuwait are outlined in Table 9.1.

Table 9.1: Profile of Kuwait interviewees' monthly earnings

Kuwaiti dinars	Wage scale US$ equivalent[42]	No. of interviewees
<500	1,170	0
500–1,000	1,170–3,540	1
1,000–1,500	3,540–5,310	1
1,500–2,000	5,310–7,080	2
< 2,000	< 7,080	7

Nevertheless, despite the relative freedom, higher wages, and proximity to Lebanon, it is interesting to note that network connections failed to emerge in the interviews as a factor in migration decisions and employment, which correlates with other literature relating to high-skilled migration.[43] All of the interviewees, with one exception, found employment either through recruitment agents or direct contact with the company they wished to work for in Kuwait. One interviewee, Nadia, who found work through a friend of her husband, has a tertiary education and would arguably have gained similar employment through a direct application.

HIGHLY SKILLED LEBANESE TRANSNATIONAL MIGRANTS

Integration, social dynamics and cultural difference

Within a transnational context, the process of working in Kuwait, coupled with integration and cultural adaptation of migrants into the host community, is also of major significance. Transnationalism suggests that migrants maintain their culture by transferring cultural practices and sometimes creating a new cultural space in the host country, while also being involved in and sometimes accepted by the host country. Anna Bagnoli believes integration is defined as 'migrants being able to maintain their own cultural diversity whilst also being full participants in the host culture'.[44] The International Organization for Migration (IOM) generally defines integration as 'the process of mutual adaptation between host society and migrant'.[45] However, as Nasra Shah has highlighted, the process of naturalisation of long-term immigrants, and even the rights to citizenship of non-Kuwaitis born in the country, are extremely restrictive and far more difficult to obtain compared to the US or countries in Europe.[46] These restrictions include requiring non-nationals to have a comprehensive knowledge of Arabic, to be originally Muslim or to have converted to Islam at least five years before an application for citizenship, and to have resided in Kuwait for a minimum of fifteen years for Arabs, or twenty years for non-Arabs. Numerous arguments suggest that citizenship is a key component of long-term integration, because it enables migrants to participate more fully in the country in which they have become naturalised.[47] Although gaining citizenship is not absolutely necessary in terms of facilitating long-term integration, it arguably helps. The opportunity for long-term migrants to be fully integrated into Kuwaiti society is therefore limited.

When interviewees were asked if they were friends with any Kuwaiti people at work or in their social circles, the answers provided an interesting insight into their ability to integrate. Nadia explained: 'Well, it's a totally different culture, until now.[48] I don't have Kuwaiti friends, not at all, but at work I am on good terms with everyone... but it's a totally different culture'. Nadia was later asked if it was difficult to settle in Kuwait, to which she replied: 'For the first two months, because I didn't have anyone here [except my husband], no family members, no friends, I didn't have a driving license... but it got okay.'[49] Nadia's sentiments reflect those of the majority of interviewees. However, two of the males offered other insights. Hassan, who had also lived in Qatar, said:

> I was surprised; they were nicer than I was expecting. In Qatar I didn't interact with lots of Qataris, but here because of my job I work with them all, I find them more friendly, friendlier than the Qataris, but at the same time they are.... they have this show of.... we are Kuwaitis.[50]

Gino, a married man in his late thirties, who worked as a media manager and entrepreneur in the food and beverage industry, had a similar perception of Kuwait: 'I lived in Saudi before this for two years, so Kuwaiti [sic.] were good, plus I am doing a lot [of] business with them, I have a Kuwaiti business partner for my new food business and things are good with him.'[51] These excerpts suggest that despite some similarities in terms of language and religion (for some), the interviewees felt there was not enough in common to socialise or to try to integrate with Kuwaitis. Perhaps the attitudes of the Kuwaitis, as expressed by some, also played a part in whether they would ultimately engage with them or not. Undoubtedly this small sample cannot provide a full and clear picture of whether any high-skilled migrants in Kuwait can be integrated. Limiting the term 'integration' to mean engaging with nationals of the host country also somewhat restricts offering a full picture of integration. However, the literature suggests that limited interaction with the host society also limits integration.[52]

From a transnational perspective, however, the importance of maintaining ties with an immigrant's country of origin and with other Lebanese migrants in the host country is possibly of greater significance.[53] If few among the interviewees had social contact with Kuwaitis, who did they regularly interact with? Dina, a married woman in her mid-thirties, who has lived in Kuwait since 2011 and works as a human resources professional with a major franchise operator, revealed her pastimes and social relationships. 'All of my friends, the people I spend the most time with are Lebanese you know, because I am Lebanese, these are my people and we recognize each other. We don't all love each other but it is better to be with them than Kuwaitis.'[54] Fay explained:

> there is a Lebanese society here but I am not involved with it, a lot of my friends are Lebanese.... [but] for example if there is a party going on [at the] Lebanese Embassy I know about that, but I only go if it's an interesting event. I go to the Church here, the Maronite rite in the Cathedral.[55]

For others, engaging in recreational pastimes with other Lebanese is also important. Anthony, a single male in his late twenties who works as an advertising executive, explained: 'I like to do the gym you know, to stay fit, and I know lots of other [Lebanese] guys there. Kuwait is [different], the people are... different, so it's just easier to be with Lebanese than trying other people.'[56] For Hassan, playing football, which he did in Lebanon, has been an important part of his social life in Kuwait and has allowed him to continue a transnational practice, and arguably allows him to engage more with other Lebanese: 'I play football, mainly with Lebanese friends, also with colleagues from NBK... it's mainly Lebanese'. This sample of the findings[57] shows that on the surface, at least, Lebanese nationals seemed to socialise with one another regularly while residing outside their country of origin, and in a sense, can maintain transnational ties through these regular meetings, and through discussions of Lebanese news, politics, chat shows and who will win the latest Lebanese talent contest.[58] Consequently, this constant contact with other Lebanese nationals in Kuwait suggests that the majority of them can be labelled transnational migrants.

The study sought to understand if there was a sense of solidarity or community among the more than 40,000 Lebanese in Kuwait, and if they are indeed perceived to be members of a transnational community.[59] Hassan, who regularly socialises with other Lebanese, described his feelings: 'For me... they [Lebanese] don't try to enhance or to make the community better, everyone is doing this [working in Kuwait] for his own benefit; they don't help each other or provide support to other Lebanese... they are selfish'.[60] Elias, a married teacher in his late thirties who left Kuwait in 2011, echoed Hassan's sentiments: 'We knew lots of Lebanese, but they weren't our proper friends, really... when we came back that was how we felt, and now we are back, we know our friends and families, it is much better that way'.[61] Others echoed similar feelings: when pushed on why there was no real sense of community among the Lebanese in Kuwait, all of the respondents suggested that because Lebanon was so disparate in terms of religion and culture, that maybe because they were all from different parts of Lebanon, or even different areas in Beirut, that certain attitudes had migrated with them to Kuwait. However, despite the findings from this research having shown the lack of a sense of solidarity among Lebanese in Kuwait, there is a still a transnational Lebanese community. The migrants, by virtue of their contact with each other and discussion of life, politics, news, television programmes and entertainment in Lebanon, have created a transnational space in Kuwait.

Length of stay and return to Lebanon

Within the classification of high-skilled immigrants, it is important to highlight that all of the interviewees—those who had returned to Lebanon and those who still resided in Kuwait—were on temporary work visas that must be renewed every two years. This, of course, could ultimately determine the length of their stay and they were therefore defined as temporary migrants. High-skilled migrants have a propensity to migrate for short periods (between three and five years) and target earn. This is in comparison to lower-skilled, manual labourers who tend to stay in the migrant destination for much longer periods—perhaps ten years or more.[62] The research also sought to ascertain the long-term plans of the Lebanese migrants—how long they planned to remain in Kuwait—and also identify why some of those who returned to Lebanon had decided to leave. Fay discussed her intentions, after previously stating she would maybe stay in Kuwait for five to ten years:

> I don't see myself living my life in Lebanon; actually the political situation is not stable. Even if I have money the political situation will play the first role, my husband and I are planning to have our retirement... maybe in [the] south of France but sure not in Lebanon, I don't think we'll go permanently back to Lebanon. I think the political situation is becoming worse, especially for Christians.[63]

Hassan further elaborated on the sentiments expressed by Fay:

> I have no plans on how long we want to stay in Kuwait... maybe five years. You know mainly it's getting worse [in Lebanon] in terms of services, infrastructure, and education... mentality, so no [I don't plan to go back]. There is a lack of job opportunities, lack of good pay, and lack of basic services, water and electricity are expensive, a dream would be to go to the US, but I don't mind to stay here in the GCC, to Qatar or UAE.[64]

Rafi, a recently married events manager in her early thirties, had a different opinion:

> I would travel [to Lebanon] as soon as I can, but it [depends] on the situation in Lebanon, everyone loves to come back to Lebanon. The good thing about Kuwait is the security here, it's stable, politically, but in Lebanon it's not at all, that's why everyone is staying here. Here it's stable politically and economically comparing to Lebanon. I have a brother in the US and everyone wants to return, Lebanon is a beautiful country. Everyone loves to stay next to his family, his culture, you know. So I don't know [how long I'll stay].[65]

Nadia explained: 'We say five years; right now we are happy here because we are more settled, but once we get any good opportunity, definitely we will leave before the five years, we hope to stay there then forever, because we already have our home, our family, everything is done.'[66] For many high-skilled migrants, the desire to return home to their country of origin after an extended length of time working abroad is foremost in their mind. However, with the exception of Nadia, most of the interviewees felt that the political and economic situation in Lebanon had deteriorated badly and that it was better to stay in Kuwait, at least for the moment.

Yet despite the worsening political situation, those who had returned showed no signs of regret, although some did hint that they would possibly migrate again in the future. Norma, a married woman in her late thirties, who lived in Kuwait from 2009 until 2012 and worked in IT, explained her decision to return to Lebanon:

> Well, I just thought each year in Kuwait I was spending more and more money and my salary was the same, the price of everything was going up, food the most, but school fees too and with two children it was costing a lot of money. We did three years but then we wanted to come back here [to Beirut].[67]

Fay also spoke of how she knew people who returned: 'I know a couple of families who left Kuwait, they are feeling that life is becoming much more expensive here, so they prefer either to go back definitely to Lebanon or send their families [to Lebanon] and [the male would] stay here'.[68] Although food prices and, to a lesser extent, inflation have been increasing in Kuwait,[69] it can be argued that the cost of living in Lebanon has also increased.[70] Marco, a single man in his thirties who worked as an automobile sales executive in Kuwait and returned to Beirut in 2012, explained his decision to return: 'For me it was personal, Kuwait was good and I made some nice money from it, but I had some problems, I had to come home for my family'.[71] Again, despite the limited data it can be inferred that most of those who had returned to Lebanon did so for a variety of reasons, including family or personal reasons, as well as the perceived higher prices of some goods and services in Kuwait.

However, from a transnational perspective, regular trips back to the country of origin can also create a strong link between origin and receiving countries. The work of Murray Chapman and R. Mansell Prothero on circulation migration acknowledged that circulation links a migrant and their home through the flow of people, ideas, goods, remittances and even sociocultural influences.[72] Within a transnational context, Douglas Massey *et al.* have developed this definition, and suggested that, due to the extensive movement, 'communities of origin and destination increasingly come to comprise transnational circuits, social and geographic spaces that arise through the constant circulation of people, money, goods, and information'.[73]

The findings have shown that contact with Lebanon has been constant for all the interviewees. Regular contact via Skype, Viber and WhatsApp, and interaction through social networking sites such as Facebook and Twitter are hugely popular and have thereby created a sort of virtual migrant circuit. Continued contacts and social network development between migrants and non-migrants (such as those still in the home country) create a transnational social field or circuit between sending and receiving countries.[74] Perhaps of greater significance, though, are the physical return visits to Lebanon, because these enable migrants to maintain contact with people in their places of origin and disseminate updates from their local network.[75]

Fadi, a single man in his twenties who returned to Lebanon in 2010, did not divulge much about his reasons for returning, but described the process of return visits while living in Kuwait: 'I used to come back a lot because I missed it all... everything about it... [It] was my first time to live away from home. I travelled when I could but I'd say every two or three months for me'.[76] Nadia, who was married and still lived in Kuwait, had similar feelings: 'I go back every three months... almost, I go back for holidays, Christmas, Easter, summer... it's only two hours and fifteen minutes so Kuwait, as a location is perfect'.[77] Hassan's dialogue was also comparable: 'I would visit every three months at least three or four times a year, mainly on occasion during the holidays, Christmas and Eid and such things'.[78] Although the interviewees were not asked their religion, Hassan's answer reflected how multi-cultural and religiously diverse Lebanon is, in that he returned for both Christian and Muslim holidays.

Bashir, who still lived in Kuwait, said: 'I don't go that often, usually once a year during the summer here, to escape the hot [weather] for a few weeks. Maybe I would go more if I had the holidays but I work a lot'.[79] The proximity of Kuwait—less than two and a half hours away by plane—possibly enables more regular return trips than if they lived in Europe or the US, for example. Such regular trips by most of the migrants therefore proved that at least one aspect of physical transnationalism was present; however, to be truly transnational, further aspects of physical transnationalism were necessary, including remittances. The findings showed that such regular return trips have created circular migration, which represents the mobility of migrants in an increasingly globalised world. Through this circular, back and forth movement, a transnational space has been created between the home and host countries.

Remittances to Lebanon

A substantial body of literature addresses the role of remittances as a transnational practice.[80] Remittances are hugely important within transnational studies, as Ines Miyares *et al.* suggest: 'Remittances serve as a form of return migration in the transnational migration process'.[81] They are also considered to be the most visible indicator and measurement of ties that connect migrants to their home countries.[82] Remittances form an important component of transnational studies. They are a link between the country of origin and migrant destination, because 'migrants today intensively conduct activities and maintain substantial commitments that link them with significant others' in the country of origin.[83] However, within a transnational context numerous types of remittances and various motivations to remit exist.[84] Social remittances are a component of transnationalism because they represent the diffusion of culture and emergence of new types of identities in the area of origin once returned.[85] Within this study, two forms of remittances and their findings are explored: economic remittances, which refer to remittances in the form of money, as well as consumer goods and gifts; and also social remittances, which refer to the remittance of ideas and cultural practices.[86]

Historically speaking, evidence shows that remittances play an important role in Lebanese society, particularly from Arab oil-producing countries.[87] By the early 1980s, remittances accounted for about 40 per cent of national income in Lebanon.[88] Although this figure has subsequently fallen, contemporary remittances still account for around 15 per cent of annual GDP at over US$8 billion in 2010.[89] Possibly, the political economy in the area of origin also has an influence on remittance behaviour; for example, political and economic instability can devalue the currency in the area of origin, and this may restrict or delay remittances.

Do economic remittances still play a significant role for those involved in this study? Rafi explained: 'I send money every month to my savings there for when I go back, because I want to go soon and then buy a place in Batroun[90] when I go back, but wait and see what my new husband says.'[91] Anthony said: 'I send money to my personal savings account, let's say every three months, about 3,000 to 5,000 [Kuwaiti dinars] each time I do it. It will be mainly to buy a house... a home or like a land or something for myself'.[92] Fay expressed similar saving habits: 'we are saving to buy... not a house but we are not planning to go back to Lebanon so we are investing in land and other businesses... in Byblos [where my husband is from]'.[93] A common theme throughout the findings was that participants remitted to save, mainly for investment purposes or to buy a home for their eventual return.

Even those such as Fay, who have no intention of returning to Lebanon to live, still felt a need to invest in their country of origin. Bashir—the oldest interviewee, in his forties—had a different agenda: 'You know in Lebanon there is no government help for older ones [people], so I have to send for my parents, they have little money, so I send every month. I think many Lebanese have to do this'.[94] Maybe his answer differed from the others because his parents were possibly older, and as they aged he felt more of an obligation to care for them, whereas the younger interviewees, in their twenties and thirties, did not feel the need to remit to assist family members. It is expected that parents of high-skilled migrants would not need financial support, therefore Bashir's remittance behaviour is unique in this context. Ultimately, the majority of migrants do not wish to return, but at the same time they are investing in Lebanon for their future.

For those who had returned to Lebanon, when asked if they had saved money in Kuwait and what it was used for, their replies attested to individuals who were motivated by self-interest. Marco, a former sales executive, explained:

> When I got back last year [2012], I had done OK, I bought a car... then I thought about starting a business, but things like that is hard in Lebanon, too much papers and [red] tape, and signatures... in Kuwait you need the *wasta* [connections] and in Lebanon you need it too. So I said no, I will take a loan and buy a place, an apartment, and get a normal job, and that's what I did. It's OK for now, but someday I would like my own business.[95]

The remaining interviewees had similar stories; they saved and remitted while they were working in Kuwait and invested this on their return. Their investments varied: domestic appliances, a new car, investments in land and/or property. Viola, a single woman in her late twenties who had worked in a bank while in Kuwait, returned to Lebanon in 2010 and set up a business: 'When I got back I had been saving for a few years and where I'm from[96] I saw an opportunity and I [went] for it.... it's a small café.... [we] Lebanese we love our coffee shops and it has worked for me, busy time. I am not rich from it but it's OK'.[97]

There is much debate in the literature on the motivations for remitting, and from this debate two types of remittance behaviour emerge, altruistic and non-altruistic:

> Migrants who are motivated to remit by altruism derive satisfaction from increasing the welfare of their relatives and family. Migrants who are motivated to remit by self-interest focus... on sending money home in order to accumulate assets by investing in their home area ready for their own return in the future.[98]

Bearing in mind that the focus in this research is on high-skilled migrants, there is a major difference between their use of remittances and those of lower skilled migrants. For example, low-skilled migrants would be much more motivated to remit to family to repay debts associated with the cost of their migration, and then remit for family maintenance and possible reunification in the host country.[99] For low-skilled migrants, the sole purpose of finding temporary, short-term employment is to remit earnings to the family in the area of origin.[100] For high-skilled migrants, the motivations often differ. For example, migrants often remit to their parents to maintain favour in lines of inheritance, and in this sense, the desire to inherit family wealth is a common reasons for remitting.[101] Another key motivation for high-skilled migrants is investment in the migrant-sending area to secure status there, using reliable family members to invest the remittances in real estate or physical capital to ensure the family is maintained.[102]

Social remittances, which are defined as ideas and cultural values that transpire when migrants return, are also important, particularly from a transnational perspective. While the Lebanese speak the same language as Kuwaitis, many obvious cultural differences must be outlined before looking at the findings. Firstly, the interviewees came from a variety of religious backgrounds: Roman Catholic, Maronite Christian, Sunni Muslim and Shi'a Muslim. Secondly, they also spoke a minimum of three languages—Arabic, French and English—and some spoke a fourth language. Thirdly, Lebanon is culturally diverse, with both European and Arabic influences. Notwithstanding this cultural diversity, some of the interviewees mentioned cultural traits they picked up in Kuwait.

Nadia explained how she had been influenced: 'whenever someone comes over, usually in Lebanon when we want to say welcome, we say *ahla w sahla*, but now I say what the Kuwaitis say: *hala hala*, this is the only word I use'.[103] Hassan explained that he does not use any Kuwaiti Arabic words, but explained that: 'Maybe the laziness of Kuwaitis is one thing I have learned from here; life is slow and I get used to it, when I move again it will be hard to work a fast-paced life.'[104] Norma, who returned to Lebanon in 2012, brought back a cultural habit from Kuwait:

> The food, I never ate Indian food before I went to Kuwait; it is so popular over there I tried it. Now I like it very much and I eat it here [in Lebanon]; I like biryani and the tandoori. That's it though, nothing else I can think that came from Kuwait.[105]

These findings show that only a handful of interviewees remitted socially, using different Arabic words or adopting cultural traits; for the majority, no social remittance occurred, or at least they did not admit to any.

Conclusion

Over the past fifty to sixty years, Kuwait has been an important destination for Arab migrants, from within and without the GCC region. For highly skilled Lebanese, the findings of this study suggest that Kuwait remains an important destination, be it short-term, long-term, or as a stepping stone to or from another GCC country. Higher wages, easier lifestyle, security and political stability were all highlighted as reasons for migrating to Kuwait. The proximity of Kuwait, in terms of flying time and distance, shows that Kuwait is one of the most attractive migrant destinations for Lebanese within the GCC region, and this proximity has also led to the creation of a transnational migrant circuit, Lebanese migrants regularly returning home, on average, three to four times per year, and circulating money, goods and information.[106]

However, as the findings have shown, interactions and integration with Kuwaiti nationals are limited, and a number of factors influenced integration, including the presence of a large Lebanese migrant population. This enables new migrants to make friends much more easily among the Lebanese community in Kuwait and leads to less interaction with other nationalities. Similarly, most of the interviewees highlighted perceived cultural differences between Lebanese and Kuwaitis.

If integration is defined as 'the process by which immigrants become accepted into society, both as individuals and groups',[107] then conceivably, according to this definition, the Lebanese in Kuwait are in no way integrated into the local society. It must be outlined again that the Kuwaiti government also has its role to play and, unlike the US or countries in Europe, no official integration policy exists. The nature of visa renewals and length of stay also play an intrinsic role in determining future integration, and as the findings have shown, the Lebanese themselves do not know how long they plan to stay, which might be a factor in their lack of interaction or integration into Kuwaiti society.

Lebanon's economic and political fragility ultimately determines the future for all Lebanese migrants, despite investment in Kuwait: the prospect of return now or in the future seems a distant fantasy for most, for financial, emotional and social reasons. The literature suggests that migrants can create cultural space through their language, accent, dress, and the use of space, including the establishment of businesses and cultural expression.[108] The findings here suggest that a new transnational space in some form has been created, through activities such as playing football, and meeting with other Lebanese to discuss current affairs and entertainment.

Remittances are a key constituent of transnational migration because they embody a material expression of the continued link between migrants and their area of origin.[109] This study has shed some light on this aspect through its exploration of remittances and research in areas of origin in Lebanon, and also by providing a deeper understanding of the motivations for remitting.

Although somewhat limited in this short chapter, it has shown that for these high-skilled migrants, despite the differences between altruistic and non-altruistic remittances, both forms of motivation can be deemed transnational, because they are both aspects of remittance behaviour. The findings here show that the majority of Lebanese—those in Kuwait and those who have returned—remitted for reasons of self-interest, looking to invest or save for their own futures. However, only a minority remitted socially, transferring cultural traits from Kuwait to Lebanon. These findings offer a new insight into remittance behaviour, which conceivably indicates the changing nature of global society today.

10

SPORT LABOUR MIGRANT COMMUNITIES FROM THE MAGHREB IN THE GCC

Mahfoud Amara

Introduction

For the past twenty years, a significant influx of professional players, sport administrators, coaches and scientists, as well as physical education (PE) teachers and sports journalist, has arrived in states of the Gulf Cooperation Council (GCC). This pattern may increase in the next few years as a the region—and Qatar, the UAE and Bahrain, in particular—continues to grow as new global hub for the sport industry, particularly in the area of sport events, sport tourism and sport hospitality.[1] Sport is also employed in the branding and image-making of cities such as Dubai, Abu Dhabi, Manama and Doha. These cities are associated today with sport entertainment and are promoted as a must-see destination for sport tourists and fans of speedboat-racing, car-racing and golf, to name a few. Sport is shaping the urban landscape of cities in the GCC at multiple levels. New development projects have been and are being built, specifically around sport themes. As Nadine Scharfenort has described, sport is at the heart of neoliberal urbanisation policies of coastal cities in the Gulf region, which combine 'a confluence of strategies of consumerism, entertainment, and global tourism.'² One could argue that the GCC region is a visible product of 'glocalisation', offering its residents the experience of being at the centre of global consumption and post-modern Arab-Islamic culture. For Arab and Muslim labour migrants it fulfils the vision of living in an 'ideal city' (*al madina al-fadhil'a*); that is, the benefits of residing and working in wealthier, economically developed countries that offer the additional advantage of providing an Arab and Islamic environment.

The Gulf job market for those working in the sport sector is also growing rapidly because the region has become a magnet for the international sport industry. Arab migrants employed in the sport sector find themselves competing with a more international workforce, because a larger number of migrants from the West have come to work in the Gulf following the economic downturn in Europe and North America. Growing demand from Gulf citizens for jobs in the sport sector is also affecting job security for Arab migrants. Gradual labour nationalisation programmes in sport governing bodies and the private sector in the GCC region have encouraged an increasing entry of citizens into these occupations. This chapter investigates the impact of these global and local dynamics on Arab migrants, particularly those from the Maghreb region, who work in the GCC sport sector.

To make sense of the patterns and motives of sport migrants from the Maghreb and of Maghrebis from Europe to GCC countries, this chapter examines three main categories of sport migrants: those engaged in professional football, those who work in elite sport development, and those who work in sport television broadcasting. These categories encompass occupations in areas such as coaching and sport science, and include sport administrators, sport marketers, elite and professional athletes, broadcasters, match commentators and sport consultants.

Before elaborating on sport migrants working in these three sub-sectors of the sport industry, this chapter will touch on the literature about transnationalism in sport, the phenomenon of global sport migration, as well as the increasing commercialisation of sport as seen in the GCC region. As Rook Campbell has said: 'The region proves to be a rich illustration of the interconnectedness, hypermobility, network flows, and economic core characteristic of global sport and transnational labor markets'.³ As part of their overarching economic strategy to diversify their economies beyond hydrocarbons, the UAE, Bahrain and Qatar have all sought to invest in alternative sectors—and by hosting and sponsoring sport mega-events, sponsoring international sport clubs, and investing directly in clubs and sport products—the sport sector has emerged as a new locus of development. For decades, the historic occupational sectors of education, health, and engineering drew skilled migrants from non-oil Arab countries to the Gulf. The sport sector, a new domain that Arab migrants are populating, attracts Arab labour migrants with particular skills and expertise that include sport marketing, sport event management, elite sport development, professional sport and sport television broadcasting. Further study of this phenomenon is critical to broadening our understanding of intra-regional migration patterns as they evolve and change over time.

While most studies on sport labour migration have focused on professional sport in Europe, North America, and Australia, academic efforts to examine sport labour migration to emerging centres of the global sport industry such as the GCC have been limited. While the broader study of Gulf migration has gained increasing academic attention, the sport sector has been equally neglected. Sport has not been considered a critical economic sector in the Arab world, even though it is in fact an industry that generates profit and creates jobs. Historically, the promotion of sport by Arab states was conceived of as more of an ideological tool that states manipulated as a means of expressing nationalist sentiment, while simultaneously being used as an instrument of social control.[4] Qatar, the UAE and Bahrain have certainly been exceptions to this pattern, and by the 1990s were beginning to capitalise on the economic and commercial benefits of sport. Among other things, this chapter aims to address some of these social and political dynamics around regional sport development, and provides a focused case study of sport labour migrants to the GCC region from the Maghreb and Maghrebi community in Europe.

Global sport migration

Migration flows in sport can be understood as a legacy of colonial history, or a remnant of patterns of dependency between former colonies and colonisers. As Paul Darby has explained, the 'pattern of power relations in the soccer world bears considerable semblance to that which has underpinned broader inequalities between First and Third World nations.'[5] Sport migration is also a product of globalisation, characterised by increased interconnectedness between territories due to advances in transportation and communication. Richard Giulianotti and Roland Robertson describe this process of intersection between individuals, borders and territories around the globe, and have termed it 'transnationalism.' To explain this phenomenon in relation to sport, and football in particular, they argue:

Transnational processes in football have increased massively through intensified migration and advanced mediatisation. Most football clubs have greater interconnections with other nations, such as through the recruitment of migrant players and the attraction of foreign fans. In terms of electronic media, the World Cup has reached larger cumulative global television audiences, rising from 13.5 billion in 1986 to 33.4 billion in 1998. Crucial to that advance is connectivity, a twin process to that of transnationalism.[6]

Other impacts of transnationalism, or what Peter Mandaville has referred to as 'translocalism', have led to the phenomenal increase in global mobility across and within nation-state borders. For one, global growth in the movement of people and different categories of migrants has been extraordinary. Migrants today, for example, can be categorised as temporary guest workers, skilled expatriates and long-term economic migrants, as well as political exiles, refugees and asylum seekers. In contrast to the historic notion of migration as a permanent move between two states, these categories of migrants may experience migration as consisting of 'a contractual relationship, intermittent postings abroad, and sojourning, as opposed to permanent settlement and the exclusive adoption of citizenship of a destination country'.[7] This experience of migration holds particularly true in relation to current mobility patterns among professional athletes. A second factor that has increased mobility is the rise of global cities, which serve as migration hubs. Global cities are spaces rich in transnational significance, exemplified in places such as New York, London, Tokyo, and Dubai. Global cities are becoming a site for new 'trans-territorial economies, innovation in the special expression of capital mobility and processes of identity (re)formation and socio-cultural mélange'.[8] In a globalised economy, cities are capable of accumulating more wealth than nation states. A third factor is the emergence of 'migratory cities', which are created by historic labour patterns of migrants, evident today in much of the GCC region. According to Zahra Babar: 'The six GCC member states currently comprise the third largest regional hub of international migration... Recent estimates indicate that across the region about 40 percent of the population is non-national, and in several of the GCC countries the majority population is foreign.'[9]

The development of technology, communications, and travel and transport networks has also had a dynamic role to play in the movement of people all over the world, and no less so in the context of sport migration to the Gulf. Examining the significant number of foreign players whom football leagues have engaged in Europe, as Joseph Maguire has suggested, can help us to understand how the local and global intersect in migration processes. According to the system theory approach, Europe here represents the 'core' that 'dominate[s] and control[s] the exploitation of resources and production in professional football',[10] while Latin America, Africa, and to a lesser extent Asia, are the 'peripheries' and 'semi-peripheries' in the political economy of international football. The dynamics between core and peripheries depend on the type of sport and its economic performance, which influence the routes of sport labour migration. As Thomas Carter has outlined, they depend also on complex dynamic relations between migrants, institutions and places.[11]

In the sociology of sport literature, several typologies classify professional athletes and their motives.[12] One such typology is the 'mercenary', the professional athlete who is motivated mainly by a lucrative professional contract for short-term financial gain. The 'cosmopolitan', meanwhile, in addition to income, is motivated by the opportunity for a cosmopolitan experience in a different country and culture. It is not unusual nowadays to find professional players working in one country, with their families residing in another country, and speaking at least three languages—a transnational and cosmopolitan lifestyle. Then there is the 'settler', the professional player who remains in the host country for a long period of time. For example, Brazilian footballer Sonny Anderson played for almost nine years in France, albeit in several different cities and for different clubs. Having fulfilled conditions for residency and work permits, some of these settlers choose to adopt the nationality of their host country, or may be encouraged by their employer/club to opt for dual nationality, to overcome the restrictions imposed by the Union of European Football Associations (UEFA) on the number of foreign players per team. An example is the case of Brazilian striker Ronaldinho, who was granted Spanish citizenship while he was playing for FC Barcelona. 'Ambitious' sports migrants aim to improve their careers by moving to a better quality league and to play in top clubs. And finally, 'returnee' sport migrants move back to their country of origin after a short stint or perhaps even long-term settlement abroad.

The Arabian Peninsula, as recently at the early 1980s, was considered a very peripheral locus in the international world of sports. Today this is certainly no longer the case as the region has actively sought to play a greater role in international sport. Several of the GCC states have shown their desire to improve their sport performance standings—by seeking FIFA ranking and more Olympic medals—and to enhance their engagement in the business of sport, through sponsorship of and direct investment in top sport leagues and events. While previous studies on sport labour migration have focused on historic patterns and routes of migration, including North–North (from Eastern to Western Europe)[13] and South–North (from Africa[14] and South America to

Europe and the US), it can be argued that the GCC countries represent a new pattern. In the Gulf, we increasingly see North–South migration, as footballers from Europe (including from the Arab community in Europe) come to play in professional leagues in the GCC region,[15] and South–South migration, with the migration of South American, African and Arab athletes to the Gulf. This pattern is not only in relation to football players, but applicable to other categories of athletes. The Qatari national handball team, which reached the final of the 2015 Handball World Championship held in Qatar and became only the third non-European team to play for a medal in the history of the event, was made up of a multinational squad, with players who originally came from France, Montenegro, Bosnia, Spain, Egypt and Cuba, as well as Qatar.[16]

The commercialisation of sport in the GCC region

When examining the development of modern sport in the Gulf region, we cannot ignore the impact of globalisation on the one hand, the increasing interconnectedness between cultures and countries in the diffusion of modern sport worldwide; and on the other, localisation, or local attempts to adapt sporting practices to local cultures, to serve political and economic interests.[17] Thanks to significant revenues from oil and gas exports, countries in the Gulf region, particularly the UAE, Qatar, and to a lesser extent Bahrain, have embarked on a strategy of integrating their economies into the global sport industry. Sport is now at the core of the modern project of urbanisation in the region. 'Sport cities' and 'urban zones' built around sport themes, combined with the technology sector, retail and tourism, offer local populations, citizens and residents alike the possibility of being part of the global sporting experience. Examples of these regional initiatives include Dubai Sports City, Ferrari World in Abu Dhabi, Dubai Motor City in the UAE, and Aspire Zone in Qatar. According to Andrew Smith, these follow a pattern of 'more haphazard schemes used by Western cities where sports-city branding has been used to give coherence to existing sports resources bequeathed by large events'.[18] Smith continues: 'Dubai and Doha are inherently global cities, where Arab cultures have become fused with western and capitalist influences'.[19]

Moreover, as noted above, cities in the Gulf are becoming examples of global and migratory cities. The hosting of sporting events and increasing engagement of local authorities and businesses in sport is attracting a new migrant community of 'sport professionals', in addition to unskilled migrants needed to build sport facilities. This new migrant group includes professional athletes, sport scientists, coaches, event organisers, specialists in fitness and hospitality, and sport broadcasting technicians. With developed infrastructure, cosmopolitan populations comprising many nationalities, and expanding economic opportunities, Gulf cities such as Dubai, Doha, Abu Dhabi, Sharjah, and Manama aim to present an image of openness to 'modernisation' and a model for integrating with the norms of global (consumerist) sporting culture.

To maintain their competitive edge at regional, Asian, and international levels, most GCC countries—Saudi Arabia, with its larger population, to a lesser extent—have depended on foreign athletes, managers and coaches to run their domestic leagues and national teams. In the past it was the norm to attract famous players close to retirement to play in domestic football leagues, such as Gabriel Batistuta, Frank Leboeuf, Fernando Hierro, Frank de Boer, and Romário. This was for marketing or branding purposes, and to offer greater international visibility to domestic leagues. However, a new generation of athletes, including those from the Maghreb and of Maghrebi descent in Europe, are signing professional contracts in the UAE, Qatar and Saudi Arabia. To this end, the Qatari-based Aspire Academy launched an ambitious programme to scout for talented young athletes worldwide. These programmes, such as Aspire Football Dreams, were initially designed for humanitarian purposes, as stated on the Aspire webpage: 'the philosophy of Aspire is for every student-athlete to maximise his athletic talent and go on to play for his country's national team, which already more than 30 young talents achieved'.[20] Some Western media outlets, however, view these development projects differently, and depict them as Qatar's tool for lobbying and influencing international sport governing bodies.[21]

A selection of young athletes recruited from these programmes and others is being offered the opportunity to represent the GCC countries internationally; for example, in track and field sports, where the selection process for the national team of the country of origin, such as in Morocco, is highly competitive. Migrating to the GCC is potentially beneficial and can be seen as a form of 'entrepreneurial citizenship'. It promises a good salary, top-level training, an international career, and the chance to compete in the Olympics and World Championships. This trend may expand to other sports in the future, particularly other Olympic sports such as handball, basketball, swimming, archery, table tennis and martial arts, to name a few, where it is hard for countries with a small population—such as the GCC states—to gain a competitive advantage at continental and international levels without pursuing a naturalisation policy.

ARAB MIGRANT COMMUNITIES IN THE GCC

Having described the international context of labour sport migration and the 'sportification' of the Arabian Peninsula, or the manner by which sport becomes central to the development strategy and diversification of economies in the region, the next section is devoted to narratives about labour sport migration from the Maghreb in the sectors of professional sport (football), sport science or elite sport development, and sport television broadcasting.

Professional football in the GCC region

It can be argued that for some players the Gulf region is a 'safety net' that allows them to secure professional contracts with the hope of playing in high-profile continental competitions such as the Asian Football Confederation (AFC) Champions League. We may cite the example of French-Algerian players such as Nadir Belhadj (Al-Sadd), Karim Ziani (Al-Arabi), and Majid Bouguerra (formerly Doha). Sport leagues in the GCC, which are in the process of professionalisation, are attractive to sport migrants of Maghrebi origin in Europe, because it is possible to celebrate their hybrid identities—that is, a mixture of European and Arab/Berber cultures. Madjid Bougherra, the former captain of the Algerian National team and of Lekhwiya in Qatar, explained his decision to move from Glasgow Rangers in Scotland:

> After being at a club like Rangers you want to play for a team that can win trophies. It's difficult to play for a successful team one day and then play for a team fighting relegation the next. It didn't appeal to me so I started to think about different options... It's [Lekhwiya] a great place to live. There's good weather, it's quiet when you want to relax but there's also plenty to do. For my family it's perfect... Obviously there is money out here but I don't know what the fuss is about... There's a project here. They want to win the Champions League here, which is what it's all about over here.[22]

Table 10.1 includes a selection of professional players of Maghrebi origin playing in football leagues in the GCC. It is worth highlighting that although migrant footballers acknowledge that the level of competition in the GCC region is obviously lower than in Europe, the benefit of playing in a league in Qatar or the UAE, for example, depends on their position on the football pitch.[23] Managers are increasingly targeting young or experienced strikers (from Europe and Brazil). Therefore, one might argue that defenders may benefit more in terms of performance (in comparison to strikers) by having to defend against players such as Raúl González (Al-Sadd)[25] from Spain or Anderson Nenê (Al-Gharafa)[26] from Brazil. Some young Maghrebi players are even opting to

Table 10.1: Professional football players of Maghrebi origin playing in GCC clubs

Name	Place of birth	Country of origin	Date of birth	Club/Country
Boualem Khoukhi	Algeria	Algeria	7 September 1990	Al-Arabi/Qatar
Karim Ziani	France	Algeria	17 August 1982	Al-Arabi/Qatar
Hachem Bouzid	Tunisia	Algeria	27 January 1992	Al-Ahly/Qatar
Youssef Kaddioui	Morocco	Morocco	28 September 1984	Al-Kharitiyat/Qatar
Nadir Belhadj	France	Algeria	18 June 1982	Al-Sadd/Qatar
Saïd Boutahar	Netherlands	Morocco	12 August 1982	Al-Wakarah/Qatar
Madjid Bougherra	France	Algeria	7 October 1982	Lekhwiya/Qatar (Recently moved to Fujairah/UAE)
Karim Boudiaf	France	Algeria	16 September 1990	Lekhwiya/Qatar
Youssef Msakni	Tunisia	Tunisia	28 October 1990	Lekhwiya/Qatar
Otmane El Assas	Morocco	Morocco	30 January 1979	Umm Salal/Qatar
Abdelaziz Barrada	France	Morocco	19 June 1989	Al-Jazira/UAE
Kamel Chafni	France	Morocco	11 June 1982	Al Dhafra/UAE
Adil Hermach	France	Morocco	27 June 1986	Al-Wahda/UAE
Salaheddine Saidi	Morocco	Morocco	6 February 1987	Dubai/UAE
Issam Jemâa	Tunisia	Tunisia	28 January 1984	Kuwait SC/Kuwait
Chadi Hammami	Tunisia	Tunisia	14 June 1986	Kuwait SC/Kuwait
Ramzi Ben Younès	Tunisia	Tunisia	31 May 1978	Al-Naser/Kuwait
Yassine Naoum	Morocco	Morocco	22 August 1984	Al Sahel/Kuwait
Yemen Ben Zekri	Tunisia	Tunisia	6 October 1979	Al-Salmiya SC/Kuwait
Ammar Jemal	Tunisia	Tunisia	20 April 1987	Al-Fateh/KSA
Abdelghani Faouzi	Morocco	Morocco	13 July 1985	Irtihad/KSA
Mourad Delhoum	Algeria	Algeria	2 October 1985	Al-Nassr FC/KSA
Hassan Taïr	Morocco	Morocco	12 December 1982	Al-Shoalah/KSA
Farid Cheklam	Algeria	Algeria	21 September 1984	Najran FC/KSA

Source: collated from GCC football league and club websites, 2014.[24]

play for their host country; for example, Karim Boudiaf (Lekhwiya) and Boualem Khoukhi (Al-Arabi), who have been granted temporary passports to play for the Qatari National Football Team. It should be acknowledged, however, that the Qatari football experience has not been a positive one for all Maghrebi players. Former Morocco international Abdeslam Ouaddou, who joined Qatar Stars League in 2011, was one of the first to openly criticise employment conditions in Qatar:

> When you first arrive to Qatar it is beautiful, you see a country which is under construction, with tall skyscrapers... all very modern. The food is not bad and it is sunny. It is like you are in the middle of the desert and you are thirsty and you see a large oasis, you draw nearer and when you finally get there, it is empty. It is a mirage. You need to know that even if you sign for three or four years, you have no guarantee to reach the end of your contract... And in order to get out of the country your 'sponsor' must grant you an authorisation to leave.[27]

The controversial case of French-Algerian football player Zahir Belounis has shed light on the question of professional football contracts in Qatar and exposed the country to the criticism of international media and non-governmental organisations. Belounis, who played for El Jaish Sports Club, eventually returned to France in November 2013 after he and his family were prevented from leaving Qatar for two years. Given that football is at the centre of the branding strategy of GCC countries and a showcase for development and international prestige, the reform of sport employment legislation and improvement of working conditions are of paramount importance in gaining international credibility.

In applying typologies from the literature to sport labour migration, one can argue that the migration of professional players from the Maghreb and the Maghrebi community in Europe can be classified as follows:

- **Mercenaries**: those who are young or close to retirement and are looking for a lucrative short-term contract—or temporary passport—to play at a wealthy football club—or even a national team—in Qatar, the UAE or Saudi Arabia.
- **Nomadic cosmopolitans**: those who are attracted by a cosmopolitan lifestyle as well as Arab-Islamic culture. This seems to be appealing to Europeans of Maghrebi descent who find in the Gulf region a mixture of European culture, or at least access to consumer society, and Arab-Islamic culture. Moreover, playing in Saudi clubs, for example, gives Muslim professional players the opportunity to be close to Islamic holy cities to fulfil *Umrah* and *Hajj*[28].

- **Settlers:** those who choose to settle in the Gulf region to pursue careers as coaches or consultants for sport television channels. For example, former manager of the Qatari national football team Jamel Belmadi.[29] It should be noted that while settlement in the form of permanent residency or citizenship is more accessible in Europe, it is more difficult in the Gulf region because of restrictive legislation surrounding employment, residency and citizenship.

Elite sport development

GCC countries are pursuing elite sport development policies. They encourage the migration of talented athletes to the region, and also develop home-grown talent, as part of labour market nationalisation policies, to access coaching and decision-making positions in sport organisations. Elite sport in the GCC region operates in a different context to other countries, but pressure to perform is equally intense. A number of Gulf countries offer incentives for athletes from Africa, Eastern Europe and North Africa, such as naturalisation and granting temporary passports, along with better training conditions and higher standards of living. Sometimes this recruitment strategy puts migrant athletes under intense pressure to fulfil the expectations of their newly adopted country. Although doping cases have been few in number, they have occurred. An example of this is the case of Ramzi, a Bahraini runner originally from Morocco, who won the 1,500m at the Beijing Olympics, but subsequently tested positive for a prohibited substance. He was stripped of his gold medal and sentenced to a two-year ban by the International Association of Athletics Federations. The positive test and ban did not, however, have any consequences for his Bahraini nationality.[30] The hope was that he could participate in the 2012 Olympic Games, but in the end he did not qualify. However, in 2013 he was able to compete in the Asian Athletics Championships.

It is true that GCC countries, Qatar in particular, have increasingly invested in offering the best training facilities for top athletes, including in the domains of sport science and medicine. Aspetar Orthopaedic and Sports Medicine Hospital in Qatar has hosted professional football stars and other athletes from all over the world including Lacina Traoré (Everton), Mathis Bolly (Düsseldorf), Marouane Chamakh, Adlène Guedioura (Crystal Palace), and Habiba Ghribi from Tunisia, who was silver medallist in the 3,000m steeplechase at the London Olympics in 2012, to name just a few. Maghrebi migrants have played a role in the development of sport science and medicine.

For example, Dr Hakim Chalabi, the chief medical officer and executive director of the National Sports Medicine Program, is French of Algerian origin. According to estimates, around 200 physiologists, physiotherapists, sport medicine staff and administrators from the Maghreb work at Aspetar. The newly established Qatar anti-Doping Laboratory is also recruiting from the Maghreb. Many Tunisians who used to work at the anti-doping laboratory in Tunis, which the World Anti-Doping Agency suspended, migrated to work at the newly established Anti-Doping Laboratory Qatar (ADLQ).

Significant numbers of coaches from the Maghreb, or of Maghrebi origin, have also worked in the GCC region. Jamal Belmadi was appointed as the head coach of the national team in 2014 after he guided Qatar Stars League club Lekhwiya to league titles in 2011 and 2012.[31] There are also many coaches in Olympic sports such as track and field, handball, volleyball and judo. Djamel Bouras, who is French of Algerian origin, was gold medallist in judo in the 1996 Olympic Games in Atlanta and now lives between Qatar and France. After his victory at the 1996 Games, he reportedly dedicated his medal to 'all Muslims who suffer in the world.'[32] This provoked a number of comments in mainstream media in France. He was accused by extreme-right circles of being pro-Palestinian Hamas and pro-Lebanese Hezbollah. Unlike European countries, cities such as Doha and Dubai seem to be the places where it is possible for European migrants of Maghrebi origin to express their multi-faceted sense of belonging to a hybrid identity that incorporates European, Arab-Berber and Islamic cultures.

The level of migration of coaches and sport scientists from the Maghreb to the GCC region has caught the attention of media in Tunisia, Algeria and Morocco. Questions are now being raised about the reasons for their migration. Abdelkader Cheniouni, an Algerian sport journalist working in Qatar, said in an article he wrote for an Algerian newspaper:

> The ardent desire of our technicians to help their country [Algeria]... is sincere. However, this desire has to be conditioned by the gathering of good working conditions. This is the principal obstacle which opposes their readiness to serve the country which offered them a lot, but failed (or did not want) to capitalize on investment.[33]

Sport television broadcasting

As a consequence of the global diffusion of cultural industries, and benefiting from the opportunities global satellite and digital technologies have presented, Dubai, Doha and Abu Dhabi are emerging as the centres for Arab music, television and movie industries. Dubai Media City is a regional hub for multinational media organisations—including news agencies, publishing, online media, advertising, production, and broadcast facilities—and the Gulf countries now own a vast media empire and control most of the premier Arabic-language satellite television programmes. In sport, the number of Arab state-run and private free-to-air and pay-television sport channels has significantly increased in the past ten years. These channels offer diverse sport programmes, as well as national, regional and international sport competitions, ranging from traditional sports (camel and horse racing) to extreme sports (for example, the Offshore Powerboat Championships).

The GCC region, thanks to sport television channels such as beIN Sports (formerly Al Jazeera Sport), Abu Dhabi Sport, Dubai Sports, and Al-Kass, is evolving into a major hub of sports TV production and broadcasting, thereby attracting a large number of sports journalist, broadcasters, analysts and commentators, including from the Maghreb. Many left their countries in the late 1980s and 1990s to look for a better standard of living and security—in the case of Algerian journalists during the civil war in the 1990s—or simply to seek more freedom of expression—in the case of Tunisian journalists before the fall of Zine el-Abidine Ben Ali's regime.

The main motivation, however, may be professional, because sport channels in the Gulf have considerable financial support from the state to develop and expand their market. BeIN Sports, for example, currently dominates the broadcasting rights for major sport events and competitions for North Africa and the Middle East. It is expanding into Europe (France), North America (the US) and Asia (Indonesia).[34] As an indication of the level of investment that these channels receive, the former Al Jazeera Sport (now beIN Sports) was one of the first sports channels worldwide to broadcast matches from the 2010 FIFA World Cup in 3D. The Qatar-based channel has extended its broadcasting rights agreement with FIFA for the 2018 and 2022 FIFA World Cups in Russia and Qatar. The agreement covers cable, satellite, terrestrial, mobile, and broadband internet transmissions across twenty-three territories and countries in the Middle East and North Africa. The value of the deal was estimated to be in the region of US$1 billion (3.67bn riyals).[35]

Gulf sports channels recruit retired athletes from the Maghreb as consultants to analyse international competitions and to follow the performance of Arab athletes. These athletes include celebrities such as (the list is not exhaustive): Saïd Aouita and Hicham El Guerrouj (Morocco) for track and field; Salima Souakri (Algeria) for judo; and for football, Rabah Madjer and Rafik

Saifi (Algeria), Tarek Diab (former Tunisian minister of sport), Nabil Maâloul (Tunisia, and coach of Al-Jaish in Qatar), and Badou Ezzaki (Morocco). Moreover, to broaden their viewership, Gulf sports channels recruited journalists and match commentators from Egypt and the Maghreb. These two regions are the biggest markets for subscription-based channels in the Arab world. Football commentators, such as Issam al-Shawali (Tunisia)[36] and Hafid Derradji (Algeria) are seen as celebrities. They have contributed with their match commentaries to the 'glocalisation' or Arabisation of international football, particularly of high-profile matches such as *El Clásico* between Spanish rivals Real Madrid and FC Barcelona. Abaher El-Sakka has illustrated in his interviews with Palestinian fans of Real Madrid and Barcelona how al-Shawali has become very popular in Palestine and the rest of the Arab world:

> Because of the emotional register he utilizes and how sometimes he goes off topic to narrate the history of the Arab World and 'International Relations'. In addition to the 'pleasure of listening to classical Arabic', the comic and political narratives of the star commentator 'make you travel through football'... Hence in time of war, facing the occupation, the two clubs present a way-out that Palestinian political debate cannot offer.[37]

Despite the apparent discourse of Arab unity promoted by these sports channels internal politics in the region can have an impact on their market and brand. Tensions between GCC countries over the Muslim Brotherhood and the political crisis in Egypt—where the government accuses Qatar of supporting the Muslim Brotherhood, thus destabilising the GCC region, Egypt, and the rest of the Arab world—contribute to increase the presence/dominance of Maghrebi sports journalist on beIN Sports, replacing journalists from other GCC countries and Egypt who may leave the channel. In fact, according to Al Jazeera News, two Emirati commentators from the Doha-based beIN Sports channel were forced to resign by their government.[38] Reportedly, Saudi Arabia is joining forces with the UAE to financially support Abu Dhabi Sport, to put an end to the dominance of beIN Sports Arabia in the Middle East and North Africa.[39]

In addition, as a result of the Arab uprisings and growing suspicion over Al Jazeera's coverage of political turmoil in the Arab world, sports journalist from the Maghreb working in Qatar are accused in their countries of origin of promoting Qatar's political agenda. A case in point is Hafid Derradji, an Algerian sport journalist at beIN Sports Arabia, who is also a regular contributor to the Algerian press on different topics, particularly about Algerian politics, sport and media. He was one of the first to denounce Algerian state television's illegal broadcast of the Burkina Faso–Algeria 2014 World Cup qualifier game without permission from beIN Sports, the exclusive rights-holder for all qualification games for North Africa and the Middle East.[40] In response, Algerian francophone newspaper *Liberté* titled one of its articles 'Hafid Derradji, from Idol to... Pariah':

> Hafid Derradji received a red card from the majority of Algerian supporters. The Qatari Al Jazeera Sport commentator made a buzz, this time not in a positive sense. From one day to the next, the idol turned into a... pariah. This had been predicted. 'Algerian television made a serious and unprecedented act in broadcasting the match between Burkina Faso and Algeria. What Algerian television did was serious and illegal', he stated, adding a sort of veiled threat against Algerian state TV. 'This will not go without consequences'.[41]

Another Algerian newspaper, *Le Jeune Indépendant*, picked an even more controversial title to denounce the 'anti-nationalist' positions of Algerian journalists who worked for Qatar-based television channels: '"Arab Spring", Qatar, Al Jazeera, Hafid Derradji and "Lady" Benguenna: Algerian footprint to target Algeria'.[42]

Conclusion

The GCC is emerging as a new centre in the international network of sport migration and the business of sport, attracting coaches, athletes, and sport scientists from all over the world, including from the Maghreb. The GCC countries, particularly the UAE, Qatar, and to a lesser extent Saudi Arabia, are in need of skilled migrants to contribute to development of sport—elite and professional sport, and transfer of knowledge in sport sciences—and through sport—community sport, branding of the region through sport, and commercialisation of sport. While it is becoming more difficult to migrate to Europe and North America, sport labour migrants from the Maghreb, as with other Arab communities, are attracted to the GCC because it offers material facilities and the familiarity of Arab and Islamic cultures.

Competition is high between GCC countries to invest in the building of brand new sports facilities, organising sports events, and even building new cities around sport and leisure themes. GCC countries have also understood the importance of sport for 'soft power' and public diplomacy. Signing for a professional club in the region acts as a safety net for those who are close to retirement or cannot secure a lucrative contract in Europe. Signing a professional contract to play in a GCC country does not necessarily mean the end of international career and media exposure. Thanks to financial resources and developed training facilities, sport clubs from the region are qualifying for high-profile competitions at continental and international levels. Al-Sadd Football Club in Qatar, for example, won the Asian Champions League twice in 1989 and 2011, and was placed third in the 2011 FIFA Club World Cup behind FC Barcelona and Brazilian Santos. The experience of these players is not always positive, though, as with the contentious case of Zahir Belounis, due to loose legislation surrounding work contracts particularly in professional football.

For sport scientists from the Maghreb, or of Maghrebi origin, sport academies such as Aspire in Doha, or Aspetar and ADLQ, offer top of the range equipment for research and testing. Qatar, in particular, is becoming a top destination for sport clubs and athletes to prepare for international competitions or to organise training camps during the winter break in Europe.

The GCC region is becoming the new centre of media production and satellite broadcasting in the Arab world. It is attracting sports journalist, match commentators and technicians from the Maghreb who want to be part of the mega-project of sport television broadcasting in the region, particularly in Qatar and the UAE. Both countries, thanks to beIN Sports and Al-Kass in Qatar, and Abu Dhabi Sport and Dubai Sports in the UAE—joined by the Saudi-owned MBC Pro Sport—dominate broadcasting rights for major sport competitions and leagues, particularly European football leagues, for North Africa and the Middle East. BeIN Sports in particular is now expanding into Europe, North America and Asia. Important financial resources are being invested in sport broadcasting technology, equipment, studios and marketing.

Many well-known retired athletes, coaches, and sport stars from the Maghreb are now living between Doha, Dubai and their country of origin. Sport television channels in the GCC region and Arab viewers are benefiting from these former players and coaches' experience and expertise. Without these channels, many of them would arguably have been forgotten after retirement, as was generally the case with the previous generations of talented athletes and coaches. The best sports journalist and match commentators from the Maghreb are now working in the Gulf region. In addition to financial incentives, many from Algeria left during the 1990s because of political violence, and others from Tunisia during the Ben Ali era. Former Tunisian football star Tariq Diab, who worked as a football analyst for Al Jazeera Sport, went back to Tunisia after Ben Ali was ousted to become the new minister of sport under the Ennhada-led government of transition.

Although these channels have an ambition to brand themselves as channels for all Arabs, the rivalry in sport between countries in the Maghreb and Egypt shows how this notion of Arab unity and/or Arab solidarity is fragile. Additionally, the Arab uprisings are having an impact on the political dynamics of sport television broadcasting. Some sports journalist, such as Algerian Hafid Derradji, have been accused of serving Qatar's political agenda, and contributing to beIN Sports' (neo-liberal) dominance in the region.

To conclude, the aim of this chapter was to provide an overview of sport labour migration from the Maghreb to the GCC region. It did not consider the gender question, which is an important aspect. More empirical work needs to be undertaken to examine the patterns, motivations, and experiences of male and female Maghrebi sport migrants compared to those from the Mashraq, as well as to compare differences between sports. This would contribute to the study of global migration and, more specifically, global migration in sport.

11

ATTITUDES OF STUDENTS IN THE GCC REGION TOWARDS THE ARAB SPRING

A CASE STUDY OF STUDENTS IN THE UAE[1]

George Naufal, Ismail Genc and *Carlos Vargas-Silva*

Introduction

The Arab world has experienced an upsurge of anti-government protests and civil conflict since December 2010. This phenomenon has become known as the 'Arab Spring'. While the body of academic literature on the Arab Spring has grown at a fast pace, more research is needed to account for the complex and multiple dimensions of this phenomenon. Therefore, the purpose of this chapter is to present new empirical research on the Arab Spring and specifically to focus on the attitudes of residents of one country in the Middle East towards the Arab Spring.

Our analysis focuses on university students. The attitudes of university students are important because the Middle East and North Africa (MENA) region has experienced a substantial increase in the population aged between fifteen and twenty-four years of age.[2] Reports suggest that by far the majority of those involved in Arab Spring protests have been young people.[3] Furthermore, the Arab world has been particularly successful at increasing educational levels,[4] and these advances in schooling have occurred across most countries in the region and different social clusters, including females.[5] Higher levels of education are generally correlated with higher aspirations. Previous studies have suggested that one of the key reasons for the Arab Spring was that poor labour market prospects for educated young people could not accommodate the major expansion of education in the Arab world.[6]

The survey used in this chapter was conducted in the United Arab Emirates (UAE), which has been one of the world's main migrant destinations since the mid-1990s.[7] The GCC countries have transformed themselves into a prime destination for migrants from all over the world, and in 2013 the UAE hosted the fifth-largest international migrant population in the world.[8] While the Gulf region constitutes the third top destination for migrants, behind North America and Europe, the migration process is actually very different from historic migration destinations. What makes the Gulf region exceptional is not just its significant dependence on foreign workers, but the inherently temporary nature of the migration process. While migrants may spend decades in the Gulf, the large majority cannot acquire local citizenship or own real estate. In that sense, for many migrants the GCC countries are considered a step on the way to a more permanent destination.

Given that the UAE attracts migrants from many countries, this allows for comparisons regarding attitudes towards the Arab Spring among people from different regions of origin such as GCC, South Asian and Western countries. Students in the UAE are an ideal group for study because during the past two decades the UAE has become one of the leaders in the provision of higher education in the region. This analysis places particular emphasis on the correlation between attitudes towards the Arab Spring and three key aspects: religiousness, attachment to the GCC countries and country of origin.

Evidence from the Arab Barometer[9] in 2012 suggests that young Arabs in the region have lower levels of religiosity compared to the older generation.[10] Religiosity, or religiousness, is an important factor in this study because of the early successes of the Muslim Brotherhood in elections in Egypt, Libya and to a certain extent Tunisia. Furthermore, the rulers who were deposed by the Arab Spring were secular, hinting at a larger future role for religion. The previous empirical evidence predates the Arab Spring by several years.[11] Therefore, it is important to use more recent data, from 2013, to explore how religiosity relates to views about the Arab Spring given the theoretical expectations stated above. In addition, analysis that involves individuals from diverse regions of origin is important because it compares the views of those who have been directly affected by the Arab Spring in their home countries and the UAE with the views of those living in the UAE who have not directly been affected. Finally, we also examined respondents' attachment to GCC states, an emerging group of stable countries in an otherwise turbulent region.

Data and methodology

Sample

We conducted the fieldwork for this study over the period 10–17 November 2013 at AUS. The population sampled were all students enrolled in the Principles of Economics programme—including Microeconomics (ECO 201) and Macroeconomics (ECO 202)—at AUS during autumn 2013. Almost all students at AUS have to take at least one of the two courses to fulfil general education requirements for their respective degree programmes. Under those conditions, the sample collected was expected to be representative of the AUS student body. In autumn 2013, 29 sections of ECO 201 and ECO 202 were offered.[12] Out of those sections, questionnaires were given out in 22 randomly chosen sections (75 per cent of all sections were surveyed). Out of 700 copies of the questionnaire, we ended up with 536 complete questionnaires, representing 76 per cent of the total number given out. Participating faculty staff were told to briefly mention the research project and the importance of participating in the data collection, while stressing the right of students to refuse to answer any or all questions in the questionnaire.

The sample is equally divided by gender (Table 11.1). As expected, freshmen and sophomores made up almost 80 per cent of the sample: economic principles classes tend to be pre-requisites for other upper-level courses and therefore should generally be taken in the first two years at AUS. The mean of the reported grade point average is 2.7 and more than 70 per cent of the sample expected to achieve a B grade or higher in their course. The School of Business Administration accounted for half of the sample, while the College of Engineering comes second with around 32 per cent.

The timing of the data collection was important because ongoing regional events during those two weeks were likely to have affected student responses. During the data collection period no significant political or economic new events occurred. Egypt and Syria were still at the forefront of the news, with increasing levels of violence, while Lebanon, Libya and Yemen were also experiencing increased levels of instability. Perhaps the two most prominent events that occurred in 2013 were the deposition of Egypt's president, Mohamed Morsi (3 July 2013), and a chemical weapon attack in Syria (21 August 2013).[13] Both of these major events could to a certain extent have affected students' responses to questions related to the Arab Spring.

Table 11.1: Descriptive statistics of students

Gender	%	Age	
Male	50.7	Mean	19.1
Female	49.3	Min.	17
		Max.	25
		Median	19
Academic status			
Freshman	40.4		
Sophomore	36.3		
Other	23.3		
Grade point average		*Expected grade*	%
Mean	2.7	A	14.5
Min.	1.4	A–	13.4
Max.	4	B+	13.9
Median	2.7	B	28.3
		C or less	29.9
College	%		
School of Business Administration	51.1		
College of Engineering	32.2		
Other	16.7		

The questionnaire

The questionnaire consisted of a set of twenty-six questions divided into three main parts. The first part included students' characteristics and demographics. Among other questions, students were asked about the time they usually went to bed, how they ranked the types of books they enjoyed reading, and the number of children they wished to have, to build a proxy for religiousness. The majority of students were Muslim and practising Muslims were expected to wake up early for the morning prayer. A question about the time they usually went to bed preceded the question about the time they woke up to avoid a direct connection with religious activities. Students ranked preferences for different types of books (i.e. fiction, biography, religious, romance and scientific). Selecting religious books as their top choice should have correlated strongly with a higher level of interest in religious activities. Students could also report that they did not read a particular type of book. A question about preferences for different types of movies preceded the question about books. Several studies have shown that women who report greater religiousness (whether Muslim or not) tend to have higher birth rates than less religious women.[14] Finally, this first part the survey also asked about the level of attachment students felt towards the Gulf region by asking about their preferred location to raise their (in most cases future) children.

The second part of the questionnaire examined the migration history of the students and asked three questions: which country's passport they most frequently used to travel, their father's country of birth, and the year their father moved to the Gulf (for non-GCC students).

The third and final section of the survey dealt with attitudes towards the Arab Spring. The term 'Arab Spring' was not predefined in the survey. Students were asked to indicate on a scale between one (completely disagree) and ten (completely agree) what they thought about different statements about the Arab Spring. The list of statements describing the Arab Spring included:

- The beginning of democracy in the Middle East.
- An excuse to bring lawlessness and violence.
- A revolution against dictators and corruption.
- An opportunity to establish a stricter religious code.
- Another form of interference by the West.

Descriptive variables

Table 11.2 presents the descriptive statistics about the students' country of birth and other variables related to their migration history. Close to 42 per cent of the students in the sample were born in the UAE. UAE nationality is not granted by birth to those whose fathers are not UAE nationals. Therefore, it was not surprising that only around 14 per cent of the students used a UAE passport. This percentage correlated very strongly with the country of birth of the father (UAE: 13 per cent). In our analysis we have used country of birth as the main variable related to migration history, but as Table 11.2 shows, using a different variable is likely to affect the results. Other main countries of birth were Egypt, Saudi Arabia, India, Jordan, Pakistan and the US. For the purpose of our analysis, in the next section we aggregate countries of birth into four categories: GCC; those not in MENA or South Asia (Western); those in MENA, but not GCC (Non-GCC MENA); and those in South Asia (South Asia).[15]

Aggregating students into four main groups (GCC, Western, Non-GCC MENA and South Asia) attempted to capture the similar conditions and environments those students faced while living in the Gulf. With different backgrounds, students face different opportunities with respect to the job market in the Gulf and also with respect to mobility. For example, a student from the GCC will have more time to look for a job on graduating, whereas others will only have about a month to find a job (and subsequently a sponsor) after their student visa expires. Students who have a Western passport enjoy other options, which include the job market in the country of their Western passport. Arguably, non-GCC MENA students—for example, Arab students from Yemen, Egypt, Syria, Jordan, Lebanon and Palestine—are the least fortunate because they face major challenges in their country of origin (poor economic performance, events related to the Arab Spring) and also are constrained by the local job market in the Gulf (in terms of time and sponsorship).

Table 11.2: Country of birth and passport usage (%)

Country of birth	%	Country's passport used	%	Country of birth of father	%
UAE	41.6	UAE	13.6	UAE	13.4
Egypt	7.4	Jordan	12.3	Egypt	12.5
Saudi Arabia	6.9	Egypt	11.5	Palestine	9.1
India	5.2	India	8.5	India	8.9
Jordan	5	Pakistan	7.6	Pakistan	8
Pakistan	5	Syria	7.2	Syria	8.4
USA	4.8	USA	4.6	Lebanon	7.4

Responses by region					
Country of birth	%	Country's passport used	%	Country of birth of father	%
GCC	53.3	GCC	21	GCC	23.3
Western	8.7	Western	9.8	Western	1.4
Non-GCC MENA	19.2	Non-GCC MENA	44	Non-GCC MENA	40.8
South Asia	10.8	South Asia	17.9	South Asia	18.4

Note: Total sample: 536 students.

A CASE STUDY OF STUDENTS IN THE UAE

Table 11.3 presents the descriptive statistics for the variable regarding the preferred location to raise children. We created three groups of possible locations based on the country selected: GCC, Western and Other. We have used this variable as a measure of attachment to the GCC region. Close to 63 per cent of respondents said they would like to raise their children in a GCC country, with the UAE being the most popular location.

Table 11.3: Preferred location to raise children[16]

Region	%
Western countries	22.2
GCC countries	62.5
Other	15.3

Table 11.4 reports the results for the proxies of religious activities. Practising Muslims wake up early to perform the morning prayer. Around 10 per cent of the students wake up between 4 a.m. and 6 a.m. in the morning, and they are more likely to be practising Muslims than those who wake up later in the day. Almost one-quarter of the students selected religious books as their favourite type of book. Those who selected religious books as their favourite type of book are likely to be more religious than those who selected other types of books as their top choice (88.7 per cent of the 10.4 per cent waking at 4–6a.m.), and those who indicated that they did not read religious books at all (11.3 per cent).

The information in Table 11.4 is used to create four proxies for religiousness. Proxy 1 was a dummy variable that was equal to one if the student usually woke up between 4 and 6 a.m. Proxy 2 was a dummy variable that was equal to one if the student marked religious books as the highest preferred type of book. Proxy 3 was a dummy variable that was equal to one if Proxies 1 and 2 were both equal to one. Proxy 4 was a dummy variable that was equal to one if the student expressed an interest in having more than four children (a threshold was chosen because it represented the seventy-fifth percentile).

Table 11.5 presents the correlation matrix between the four religiousness proxies. Proxy 1 and Proxy 2 were positively correlated with a statistically significant correlation of almost 10 per cent. Proxy 3 and Proxies 1 and 2 were highly correlated. Proxy 4 was not correlated with any of the suggested variables. While we examined the results from all four proxies, we have only reported those from Proxy 1 because it is the only variable that captures an actual behaviour rather than a stated preference. The results are consistent across all four different measures of religiousness.

Table 11.4: Proxies for religiousness

Wake-up time (Proxy 1)	%
4–6 a.m.	10.4
After 6 a.m.	89.6

Type of book (Proxy 2; Proxy 1 and Proxy 2 form Proxy 3)

	Fiction	Biography	Religious	Romance	Scientific
Top choice (%)	27.0	11.3	23.5	19.5	13.6
Read, but not top choice (%)	11.3	12.6	10.6	15.1	15.3
Do not read	18.4	22.5	11.3	23.8	22.5

Children wanted (Proxy 4)

Mean	2.8
Min.	0
Max.	19
Median	3

Table 11.5: Correlation matrix among religiousness proxies[17]

	Proxy 1	Proxy 2	Proxy 3	Proxy 4
Proxy 1	1	–	–	–
Proxy 2	0.098**	1	–	–
Proxy 3	0.576***	0.355***	1	–
Proxy 4	0.011	–0.047	–0.031	1

Note: levels of significance indicated * = 1%, ** = 5%, *** = 10%.

Results

Country of origin

We have used country of birth as the main proxy for the broader concept of country of origin. Table 11.6 reports the mean responses for each group.

Those who were born in the West were more likely to see the Arab Spring as the beginning of democracy in the region and a revolt against dictators and corruption.[18] However, they also were more likely to see the Arab Spring as another form of Western interference. There was little difference between the responses of those who were born in a GCC country and those born in other MENA countries.

For reasons of space we have not presented a similar table to Table 11.6 for main passport used and region of father's birth. The results change when we focus on these variables as the indicators of country of origin. One key difference is that those whose fathers were born in Egypt were much more likely to see the Arab Spring as a revolution against dictators and corruption, and the beginning of democracy in the Middle East. This very positive view of the Arab Spring among Egyptian students occurred even in light of the high levels of conflict and uncertainty that the country was experiencing at the time of the survey.

Table 11.6: Mean and standard deviation of responses, by country of birth

Country of birth	Beginning of democracy	Lawlessness and violence	Revolt against dictators	Stricter religious code	Interference by West
GCC	5.4 (2.69)	4.3 (2.96)	6.3 (3.08)	4.8 (2.69)	5.4 (3.02)
Non-GCC MENA	5.6 (2.74)	4.6 (3.10)	6.7 (2.75)	4.6 (2.67)	5.5 (2.87)
South Asia	5.5 (2.86)	3.8 (2.75)	6.1 (3.36)	5.2 (2.82)	5.2 (3.34)
West	6.2 (2.48)	4.2 (3.02)	7.4 (2.56)	4.6 (2.54)	6.0 (2.69)

Note: Standard deviation appears in parenthesis.

In the Middle East, nationality often, if not always, dictates mobility and the range of opportunities that students, in particular Arab students, will encounter on graduating. At the bottom of the ladder, non-GCC MENA students are limited by constraints in the Gulf region (in terms of sponsorship and nationalisation policies set by the GCC countries) and by the lack of employment opportunities at home (due to political instability and poor economic performance). Students who are citizens of GCC countries do not face any of those constraints. Students with Western passports enjoy the ability to explore what the country of their citizenship can offer. One could argue that students from South Asian countries face similar constraints to the non-GCC MENA students. However, South Asian students do not face Arab Spring-like events back home and their passports offer much more mobility than that of Arab students subject to the region's many visa requirements.

Attachment to the GCC

In this section, we have examined the students' attachment to the GCC countries according to their stated preferences of geographical location to raise children. The survey explicitly asked students where they would like their children to live (conditional on their wanting to have children). The results were bimodal, with the leading preferred destinations being Western and GCC countries (with a clear majority for the UAE). However, the responses were very similar across both groups, suggesting that attachment to the GCC region was not a major factor defining attitudes towards the Arab Spring.

Religiousness

With the rise of the Muslim Brotherhood in Tunisia and subsequently in Egypt, concerns over abandoning Arab secular states in favour of more religious political systems have taken centre stage in public discussion about the Arab Spring. In an attempt to better understand the relationship between religion and attitudes towards the Arab Spring, we have explored the relationship between the proxies for religiousness described above and attitudes towards the Arab Spring.

Table 11.7 presents the results of this exercise. Several key results are important to highlight. For example, those with religiousness Proxy 3 (wake up early and prefer religious books) were significantly less likely to see the Arab Spring as a revolution against dictators and corruption, and also less likely to see it as another form of Western interference. However, with that exception there were no major differences in the results across degrees of religiousness.

Table 11.7: Mean and standard deviation of responses by religiousness

Proxy of religiousness	Beginning democracy	Lawlessness and violence	Revolt against dictators	Stricter religious code	Interference by West
Proxy 1	5.8 (2.86)	4.1 (3.17)	5.6 (3.27)	4.8 (2.61)	5.1 (3.19)
Non-religious	5.5 (2.69)	4.3 (2.97)	6.5 (2.93)	4.80 (2.72)	5.5 (3.01)
Proxy 2	5.5 (2.87)	4.5 (3.07)	6.0 (3.19)	4.9 (2.71)	5.2 (3.06)
Non-religious	5.5 (2.66)	4.2 (2.97)	6.6 (3.19)	4.8 (2.70)	5.5 (3.02)

Proxy 3	6.1 (3.35)	4.1 (3.16)	4.6 (3.43)	5.0 (2.74)	3.4 (2.96)
Non-religious	5.5. (2.68)	4.3 (2.99)	6.5 (2.94)	4.5 (2.70)	5.5 (2.96)
Proxy 4	5.8 (2.77)	4.0 (3.12)	6.6 (3.07)	5.0 (2.75)	5.3 (2.96)
Non-religious	5.5 (2.71)	4.3 (2.98)	6.4 (2.97)	4.8 (2.70)	5.4 (3.04)

Note: Standard deviation appears in parenthesis.

Summary and conclusion

Our findings regarding the students' views on the Arab Spring can be summarised as follows:

1. Most students agreed with the statements that the Arab Spring was a revolt against dictatorships and corruption, and the beginning of democracy in the Middle East. In this sense, the general view of the Arab Spring was positive. This was particularly the case among students of Egyptian descent, who were very optimistic about the Arab Spring. This was perhaps surprising given the high levels of violence in Egypt close to the period of the survey.
2. Attachment to the GCC countries did not seem to have a major impact on attitudes towards the Arab Spring. This was also something of a surprise because those with a greater attachment to the GCC countries have more at stake in the outcome of the Arab Spring.
3. Those with higher levels of religiousness were significantly less likely to see the Arab Spring as a revolution against dictators and corruption, and also less likely to see it as another form of Western interference.

When interpreting the results, one must consider the composition of the sample population. Students at AUS come from relatively wealthy backgrounds, and study in a co-educational environment—a relatively new opportunity in the Gulf region. Students in our sample represent a small share of young people in the region, enrolled at a private US-type tertiary educational institution. In that sense, the conformity of the results is not surprising. Most AUS graduates face better labour-market opportunities than the average Middle Eastern youth. For all of these reasons, one cannot extrapolate the results here to the general youth population in the Middle East.

APPENDIX

SURVEY OF STUDENTS' ATTITUDES IN THE GCC TOWARDS THE ARAB SPRING (NOVEMBER 2013)

For all categories, the GCC countries were: Bahrain, Kuwait, Oman, Qatar, Saudi Arabia and the UAE.

Western countries given as the country of birth included: Canada, Germany, France, Ireland, Norway, Sweden, UK and US; non-GCC MENA countries included: Algeria, Egypt, Iraq, Jordan, Lebanon, Libya, Morocco, Palestine, Sudan, Syria and Yemen; South Asian countries of birth included Bangladesh, India and Pakistan.

Respondents gave Western countries of passport use including Canada, France, Germany, Japan, Norway, Sweden, UK and US. Non-GCC MENA countries included: Egypt, Iraq, Jordan, Lebanon, Libya, Morocco, Palestine, Sudan, Syria and Yemen. South Asian countries included Bangladesh, India and Pakistan.

For the father's place of birth, Western countries given included: Austria, France, Sweden, UK and US; non-GCC MENA countries included: Algeria, Egypt, Iraq, Jordan, Lebanon, Libya, Morocco, Palestine, Sudan, Syria, Tunisia and Yemen; and South Asian countries included: Bangladesh, India and Pakistan.

Demographics/Students' characteristics:

1. Gender: Male Female
2. Age: 17 18 19 20 21 22 23 24 Older than 24
3. Which country were you born in? _____
4. Academic status: Freshman Sophomore Junior Senior

5. GPA at AUS: _____
   Note: If this is your first semester at AUS then respond with N/A
6. Expected letter grade in this course: _____
7. College: SBM CEN CAS CAAD
8. What is the highest degree that your father has received?
   No degree Primary Middle school High school University degree Masters/PhD
9. Which sector does your father work in?
   Public (government) Private
10. What is your family's income per year?
    [< 200,000 AED] [200,000 to 400,000 AED] [400,000 to 600,000 AED] [600,000 to 800,000 AED] [> 800,000 AED]
11. How many siblings do you have? _____
12. How many children would you like to have? _____
13. If you plan to have kids, in which country would you like your children to live in the future? _____
14. How often do you visit your home country?
    Note: if you are a UAE citizen then respond with: I live in my home country
    At least 1 a year Every other year Rarely Never
15. What time do you usually go to bed?
    [8 pm—10 pm] [10 pm—12 am] [After 12 am]
16. What time do you usually wake up?
    [4 am—6 am] [6 am—8 am] [8 am—10 am] [After 10 am]
17. Please rank these movie types in order of preference (if you don't watch a type of movie, please write N/A under that one. For others please rank 1 to 5 with 1 as the highest preference and 5 as the weakest).
    Fiction   Action   Documentary   Comedy   Romance
    _____   _____   _____   _____   _____
18. Please rank these book types in order of preference (if you don't read a type of book, please write N/A under that one. For others please rank 1 to 5 with 1 as the highest preference and 5 as the weakest).
    Fiction   Biography   Religious texts   Romance novels   Scientific magazines
    _____   _____   _____   _____   _____

APPENDIX

Migration History:

19. Which country's passport do you frequently use to travel? _____
20. In which country was your father born? _____
21. Which year did your father move to the Gulf? _____
    Note: If you are a GCC citizen then respond to this question with: since birth
    If your father is not living in the Gulf then respond with: n/a

Attitudes towards the Arab Spring:

22. Using a ranking system from 1 to 10 (where 1 you completely disagree and 10 you completely agree) define these consequences of the Arab Spring?
    a. The beginning of democracy in the Middle East
       1 2 3 4 5 6 7 8 9 10
    b. An excuse to bring lawlessness, violence and pillage
       1 2 3 4 5 6 7 8 9 10
    c. A revolution against dictators and corruption
       1 2 3 4 5 6 7 8 9 10
    d. An opportunity to establish a stricter religious code
       1 2 3 4 5 6 7 8 9 10
    e. Another form of interference by the West
       1 2 3 4 5 6 7 8 9 10
23. Do you view the Arab Spring as positive or negative? 1 to 10 (where 1 is completely negative and 10 is completely positive)
    1 2 3 4 5 6 7 8 9 10
24. Have you or your family been affected in any of the following ways by the Arab Spring?
    1. Yes
       i. Injuries in the family
       ii. Deaths
       iii. Loss of assets
    2. No
25. How do you expect the Middle East will be in 5 years from now, compared to the current state?
    Worse   Same   Better

26. Out of the following listed challenges that the Middle East is facing, rank them using a ranking system from 1 to 10 (where 1 is not important and 10 is very important)

Unemployment
1 2 3 4 5 6 7 8 9 10
Environment
1 2 3 4 5 6 7 8 9 10
Conflict
1 2 3 4 5 6 7 8 9 10
Religious extremism
1 2 3 4 5 6 7 8 9 10
Water supply
1 2 3 4 5 6 7 8 9 10
Retirement benefits
1 2 3 4 5 6 7 8 9 10
Cost of living
1 2 3 4 5 6 7 8 9 10
Migration of talented and educated people out of the Middle East
1 2 3 4 5 6 7 8 9 10

NOTES

1. INTRODUCTION

1. See, among others: Gardner, Andrew, *City of Strangers: Gulf Migration and the Indian Community in Bahrain*, Ithaca: Cornell University Press, 2010; Kamrava, Mehran and Zahra Babar (eds), *Migrant Labor in the Persian Gulf*, New York: Columbia University Press, 2012; Vohra, Neha, *Impossible Citizens: Dubai's Indian Diaspora*, Durham: Duke University Press, 2013; Khalaf, Abdulhadi, Omar AlShehabi and Adam Hanieh (eds), *Transit States: Labour, Migration, and Citizenship in the Gulf*, London: Pluto Press, 2015.
2. Sources: Kingdom of Bahrain—Central Informatics Organization, http://www.cio.gov.bh/cio_eng/Stats_SubDetailed.aspx?subcatid=604; Annual Abstract 2013, State of Kuwait—Central Statistical Bureau, 56, http://www.csb.gov.kw/Socan_Statistic_EN.aspx?ID=18; Population Statistics Bulletin, Sultanate of Oman—National Centre for Statistics & Information, 14; http://www.ncsi.gov.om/NCSI_website/PublicationAttachment/pouplation%2013-8-%202014.pdf; Annual Abstract 2014, State of Qatar—Ministry of Development Planning and Statistics, http://www.qsa.gov.qa/eng/GeneralStatistics.htm#Annual_Abstract_2014; Demographic Research Bulletin 1428, Saudi Arabia—Central Department of Statistics & Information, http://www.cdsi.gov.sa/english/index.php?option=com_docman&task=cat_view&gid=43&Itemid=113; Population by Emirates 1975–2005, United Arab Emirates—National Bureau of Statistics, http://www.uaestatistics.gov.ae/EnglishHome/ReportDetailsEnglish/tabid/121/Default.aspx?ItemId=1869&PTID=104&MenuId=1
3. Winckler, Onn, *Arab Political Demography: Population Growth, Labour Migration and Natalist Policies*, Eastbourne: Sussex Academic Press, 2009, p. 1.
4. Ibid.
5. Haque, Mohommad Shahidul and Robert Pitea, 'Arab Youth and Labour Mobility', in *Intra-Regional Labour Mobility in the Arab World*, International Organization for Migration (IOM), Egypt: 2010, p. 49.

6. Data extracted from: Roper, Steven D. and Lilian A. Barria, 'Understanding Variations in Gulf Migration and Labor Practices', *Middle East Law and Governance* 6, no. 1 (2014): p. 40.
7. Data extracted from: Kapiszewski, Andrzej, 'Arab versus Asian Migrant Workers in the GCC Countries', *Working Paper*, United Nations Expert Group Meeting on International Migration and Development in the Arab Region, Beirut: 2006, p. 10. While demographic data is considered to be politically sensitive in many states, the GCC states tend to be particularly cautious about publishing data on their populations. In some GCC countries even the total number of nationals or the citizen population is not made public. Obtaining data that is disaggregated by gender, ethnicity, and nationality of foreign population remains extremely challenging for a variety of reasons. Significant gaps exist in the data regarding the Arab migrant population in the region, and what is available is scattered, scant and inconsistent between the six states, making it difficult to provide substantive comparative analyses. Tables 2 and 3 use official data and semi-official data, as well as estimates that other scholars have referred to in their work. While far from complete or comprehensive, these tables provide at least some sense of the Arab migrant populations present in the region from the mid-1990s to the most current year available. In addition to the data available from GCC state statistical offices, for data on Gulf demography also see: Baldwin-Edwards, Martin, 'Labor immigration and labor markets in the GCC countries: national patterns and trends', *Kuwait Programme on Development, Governance, and Globalisation in the Gulf States Paper*, No. 15, London: Mar. 2011; Kapiszewski, 'Migrant Workers'; and Tattolo, Giovanna, 'Arab Labor Migration to the GCC States', *Working Paper*, Jean Monnet Observatory on trans-Mediterranean Relations.
8. See: *Intra-Regional Labour Mobility in the Arab World*, IOM, Egypt: 2010, p. 4; and Thiollet, Hélène, 'Migration as Diplomacy: Labor Migrants, Refugees, and Arab Regional Politics in the Oil-Rich Countries,' *International Labor and Working-Class History* 79 (Spring 2011): p. 3.
9. Nassar, Heba, 'Intra-regional Labour Mobility in the Arab World: An Overview', in *Intra-Regional Labour Mobility in the Arab World*, IOM, Egypt: 2010, pp. 11–40.
10. Nassar, 'Overview', p. 18; and Tattolo, 'Arab Labor', p. 5.
11. Tattolo, 'Arab Labor', p. 5.
12. *Intra-Regional Labour*, pp. 18–19.
13. Ibid., p. 4.
14. Ibid.
15. Ibid., p. 16.
16. Nassar, 'Intra-regional', p. 17.
17. Winckler, *Demography*, p. 159.
18. Richards, Alan and John Waterbury, *A Political Economy of the Middle East*, 3rd ed., Colorado: Westview Press, 2008, pp. 113–33.

19. Ibid., pp. 137–41.
20. Winckler, *Demography*, p. 110.
21. Kapiszewski, 'Migrant Workers', p. 6.
22. Winckler, *Demography*, pp. 113–114.
23. Ibid., p. 113.
24. Ibid.
25. Ibid.
26. *Intra-Regional Labour*, p. 21.
27. Thiollet, 'Diplomacy', p. 12.
28. Kapiszewski, 'Migrant Workers', pp. 4–21.
29. Winckler, *Demography*, p. 91.
30. Ibid.
31. Ibid., p. 102.
32. Ibid., p. 120.
33. Ibid., p. 121.
34. Ibid., p. 115.
35. El-Sayad Hassan, Khaled, 'Intra-regional Migration as a Tool to Absorb Arab Unemployment,' in *Intra-Regional Labour Mobility in the Arab World*, IOM, Egypt: 2010, p. 72.
36. Nassar, 'Overview', pp. 32–3.
37. Ibid., p. 32.
38. Ibid.
39. Castles, Stephen and Mark J. Miller, *The Age of Migration: International Population Movements in the Modern World*, 4th ed., London: Palgrave Macmillan, 2009, p. 25.
40. Thiollet, 'Diplomacy', p. 6.
41. Castles and Miller, *Age*, pp. 164–6.
42. Ibid., p. 8.
43. Winckler, *Demography*, p. 117; Tattolo, 'Arab Labor,' p. 4.
44. Tattolo, 'Arab Labor', p. 11.
45. Ibid., p. 4.
46. See, for example, the collection of articles in Kamrava and Babar (eds), *Migrant Labor*; Vora, *Impossible*; Gardner, *Strangers*.
47. Castles and Miller, *Age*, pp. 186–7.
48. Gardner, Andrew, Sylvia Pessoa, Abdoulaye Diop, Kaltham Al-Ghanim, Kien Le Trung and Laura Harkness, 'A Portrait of Low-Income Migrants in Contemporary Qatar', *Journal of Arabian Studies* 3, no. 1 (June 2013): p. 11.
49. Cerna, Lucie, 'Policies and Practices of Highly Skilled Migration in Times of Financial Crisis', *International Migration Papers No. 99*, Geneva: International Labour Office, 2010: pp. 1–5.
50. Castles and Miller, *Age*, p. 188.

51. Gardner *et al.*, 'Portrait', pp. 11–13.
52. Winckler, Onn, 'How Many Qatari Nationals Are There?', *Middle East Quarterly*, (Spring 2015): p. 6.
53. The *mu'azzib* is a term which refers to a visa sponsor in Kuwait. (For further discussion on this concept, see Chapter 4 of this volume).
54. See, for example: Ann M. Lesh, 'Palestinians in Kuwait', *Journal of Palestine Studies* 20, no. 4 (Summer 1991): pp. 42–54; and Kamrava, Mehran, *The Modern Middle East: A Political History since the First World War*, 3rd ed., Berkley, CA: University of California Press, 2013, pp. 324–5.
55. See, for example: Gamburd, Michele, *The Kitchen Spoon's Handle: Transnationalism and Sri Lanka's Housemaids*, Ithaca, NY: Cornell University Press, 2000; Shah, Nasra, 'Gender and Labour Migration to the Gulf Countries', *Feminist Review* 77 (2004): pp. 183–5; and Fernandez, Bina, 'Household Help? Ethiopian Women Domestic Workers' Labor Migration to the Gulf Countries', *Asian and Pacific Migration Journal* 20, nos. 3–4 (2011): pp. 433–53.
56. For more on this, see: Poros, Marisa, *Modern Migration: Gujarati Indian Networks in New York and London*, Stanford University Press, 2011; and Sharpe, Pamela, *Women, Gender and Labour Migration: Historical and Cultural Perspectives*, Routledge: 2002.
57. Sharpe, *Perspectives*, p. 86.

2. WORKING FOR THE NEIGHBOURS: ARAB MIGRANTS IN QATAR

1. Girgis, Maurice, 'The GCC Factor in Future Arab Labor Migration', *Fourth Mediterranean Development Forum*, Jordan: 2002, p. 42.
2. Girgis, 'GCC Factor', pp. 14–15.
3. See, for example: Baldwin Edwards, Martin, 'Labor Immigration and Labor Markets in the GCC Countries: National Patterns and Trends', *Research Paper 15*, London School of Economics Programme on Development, Governance, and Globalisation in the Gulf States, London: 2011; Kamrava, Mehran and Zahra Babar, 'Situating Labor Migration in the Persian Gulf', *Migrant Labor in the Persian Gulf*, Hurst/Columbia University Press, London/New York: 2012, pp. 8–9.
4. Winckler, Onn, *Arab Political Demography: Population Growth, Labour Migration and Natalist Policies*, Eastbourne: Sussex Academic Press, 2009, pp. 150–3.
5. Randeree, Kasim, 'Workforce Nationalization in the Gulf Cooperation Council States', *CIRS Occasional Paper*, Center for International and Regional Studies—Georgetown University School of Foreign Service in Qatar, Doha: 2012, pp. 8–20.
6. For more on the *nitaqat* and its impact on Saudi Arabia's foreign workers, refer to Chapter Seven of this volume by Harry Cook and Michael Newson.
7. Ibid.
8. Winckler, *Demography*, p. 157.
9. Girgis, 'GCC Factor', p. 10.

10. Ibid., p. 14.
11. Ibid., p. 42.
12. Shah, Nasra, 'Arab Migration Patterns in the Gulf", *Arab Migration in a Globalized World*, International Organization for Migration (IOM), Geneva: 2004, p. 101.
13. Fortstenlechner, Ingo and Emilie Jane Rutlege, 'The GCC's "Demographic Imbalance": Perceptions, Realities and Policy Options', *Middle East Policy*, No. 4, Washington, DC: 2011, p. 30.
14. Ibid., p. 31.
15. El-Sayad Hassan, Khaled, 'Intra-regional Migration as a tool to absorb Arab unemployment', in *Intra-Regional Labour Mobility in the Arab World*, IOM, Egypt: 2010, p. 71.
16. Ibid.
17. Ibid.
18. Fortstenlechner and Rutlege, '"Imbalance"', p. 30.
19. Ibid.
20. Dito, Mohammed, 'Labor Migration in the GCC Countries: Some Reflections on a Chronic Dilemma', *Viewpoints: Migration and the Gulf*, The Middle East Institute, Washington, DC: 2010, p. 72.
21. Kamrava, Mehran, *Qatar: Small State, Big Politics*, Ithaca: Cornell University, 2013.
22. *Bulletin: Labor Force Statistics 2012*, Qatar Statistics Authority, Qatar: Apr. 2012, p. 55.
23. *Bulletin*, p. 18.
24. In June 2013, two previous public-sector entities, the Qatar Statistics Authority and the General Secretariat of Development Planning, were dismantled and reformed as the Ministry of Development Planning and Statistics.
25. 'Table No. 6 "Economically Active Population by Nationality, Sex, and Age Group"', in *Qatar Statistics Authority Quarterly Labor Force Survey Web Report 2nd Quarter, Qatar: Aug. 2013*, http://www.qsa.gov.qa/Eng/Last_Archive/2013/Archive.htm
26. Ibid.
27. *Qatar National Vision 2030*, General Secretariat of Development Planning, State of Qatar, 2008.
28. *Integrating Foreign Workers Issues into Qatar Strategies and Policies*, The Permanent Population Committee, Qatar, 2011, pp. 33–5.
29. For more information on the *kafala*, see Kamrava, Mehran and Zahra Babar, *Migrant Labor*, Hurst/Columbia University Press, London/New York: 2012.
30. Arab Labor Organization, http://www.alolabor.org/final/index.php?lang=ar
31. Tattolo, Giovanna, 'Arab Labor Migration to the GCC States', p. 5.
32. Ibid.
33. Copies of Labour Agreements provided to author by Qatari Ministry of Labour. Labour Agreement with Morocco signed on 17/05/1981, Tunisia 30/11/1981, Somalia 30/03/1981, and Sudan 22/10/1981.

34. Article 5, *An Additional Protocol to the Convention regulating the use of Moroccan workers in Qatar between the Government of the State of Qatar and the Government of the Kingdom of Morocco*, n.d.
35. Correspondence between author and the Qatari Ministry of Labour, July–Aug. 2013.
36. This figure differs by a couple of hundred thousand people from the figure provided by the Qatar Statistics Authority's Labour Force Survey estimate of 1,347,060.
37. Statistical data on Arab migrants in labour force provided to author by Qatar's Ministry of Labour, 21 July 2013.
38. Babar, Zahra, 'Free Mobility within the Gulf Cooperation Council', *CIRS Occasional Paper Series*, Georgetown University School of Foreign Service in Qatar: 2011, pp. 4–5.
39. Ibid., p. 5.
40. Correspondence between author and the Qatari Ministry of Labour, Sept. 2013.
41. Table created by author based on data provided by the Qatari Ministry of Labour in Aug. 2013.
42. What this data omits is the presence of sponsored wives who may be working in Qatar while remaining on their spouses' sponsorship. Female dependants of sponsored workers are permitted to obtain employment without change of sponsorship, and their participation in the labour force thus goes uncounted and remains invisible.
43. Data provided to author by Qatari Ministry of Labour, Sept. 2013.
44. Andrew Gardner, Sylvia Pessoa, Abdoulaye Diop, Kaltham Al-Ghanim, Kien Le Trung and Laura Harkness, 'A Portrait of Low-Income Migrants in Contemporary Qatar', *Journal of Arabian Studies*, 3.1 (June 2013), p. 6.
45. Breakdown of the Arab expatriate workforce in Qatar compiled by author based on data provided by the Qatari Ministry of Labour, Aug. 2013.
46. Ibid.
47. Ibid.
48. Ibid.
49. Gardner *et al.*, p. 4.
50. Actual breakdowns by sector: Education: total jobs 30,409, of which foreigners occupy 19,757 and Arabs 4,469; Finance and insurance: total jobs 11,458, of which foreigners occupy 8,656 and Arabs 8,272; Professional, scientific, technical fields: total jobs 25,533, of which foreigners occupy 25,232 and Arabs 21,036. Source: Qatar Statistics Authority Labor Force Survey, 2013.
51. Gardner, Pessoa, Diop, Al-Ghanim, Le Trung and Harkness, "A Portrait of Low-Income Migrants in Contemporary Qatar", pp.11–14.
52. Ibid.

3. ARAB MIGRANT TEACHERS IN THE UNITED ARAB EMIRATES AND QATAR: CHALLENGES AND OPPORTUNITIES

1. Ridge, Natasha, 'Education and the Reverse Gender Divide in the Gulf States: Embracing the Global, Ignoring the Local', 2014, p. 17.
2. Ibid., p. 56.
3. Ibid., p. 120.
4. Ibid., pp. 17–49.
5. UAE Ministry of Education, 'Open Data: 2010–2011', https://www.moe.gov.ae/English/Pages/opendata.aspx, last accessed 20 Jan 2014.
6. Social and Economic Survey Research Institute (SESRI), personal communication, 2014.
7. Penson, Jonathan and Akemi Yonemura (eds), *Next Steps in Managing Teacher Migration: Papers of the Sixth Commonwealth Research Symposium on Teacher Mobility, Recruitment, and Migration*, London: UNESCO and Commonwealth Secretariat, 2012, p. v (Foreword).
8. Arnold, Fred and Nasra M. Shah (eds), *Asian Labor Migration: Pipeline to the Middle East*, London: Westpoint, 1986; Khalaf, Sulayman and Saad Alkobaisi, 'Migrants' Strategies of Coping and Patterns of Accommodation in the Oil-rich Gulf Societies: Evidence from the UAE', *British Journal of Middle Eastern Studies* 26 (1999): 2, p. 296.
9. Winckler, Onn, 'Labor Migration to the GCC States: Patterns, Scale, and Policies', Middle East Institute, 2010, www.voltairenet.org/IMG/pdf/Migration_and_the_Gulf.pdf, last accessed 11 Dec. 2013, p. 9.
10. Ibid., p. 10.
11. Ibid., p. 12.
12. Kapiszewski, Andrzej, 'Arab Versus Asian Migrant Workers in the GCC Countries', United Nations Expert Group Meeting on International Migration and Development in the Arab Region, 2006, http://www.un.org/esa/population/meetings/EGM_Ittmig_Arab/P02_Kapiszewski.pdf, last accessed 15 Dec. 2013, p. 10.
13. Naufal, George, 'The Economics of Migration in the Gulf Cooperation Council Countries', paper presented at the Center for International and Regional Studies (CIRS), Monthly Dialogue, Doha, Qatar, 9 Sep. 2013.
14. Chalcraft, John, 'Monarchy, Migration and Hegemony in the Arabian Peninsula', LSE Global Governance, 2010, http://eprints.lse.ac.uk/32556/1/Monarchy,_migration_and_hegemony_ per cent 28working_paper%29.pdf last accessed 27 Nov. 2013, p. 6.
15. Ibid., p. 17.
16. Rahman, Anisur, 'Migration and Human Rights in the Gulf', The Middle East Institute, 2010, http://www.voltairenet.org/IMG/pdf/Migration_and_the_Gulf.pdf last accessed 15 Dec. 2013, p. 17.

17. Kapiszewski, 'Migrant Workers', p. 8.
18. Al-Alkim, Hassan Hamdan, *The Foreign Policy of the United Arab Emirates*, London: Saqi, 1989; Kapiszewski, ibid.
19. Winckler, Onn, *Population Growth, Migration and Socio-Demographic Policies in Qatar*, Tel Aviv: The Moshe Dayan Center for Middle Eastern and African Studies, 2000; Kapiszewski, ibid.
20. Kapiszewski, ibid.
21. Chalcraft, 'Monarchy', p. 15.
22. Ibid., p. 17.
23. Kapiszewski, 'Migrant Workers', p. 5.
24. Chalcraft, 'Monarchy', p. 10.
25. Ibid., p. 13.
26. Chalcraft, 'Monarchy', p. 19.
27. Rahman, 'Human Rights', p. 17; Engman, Michael, 'Half a Century of Exporting Educational Services: Assessing Egypt's Role in Educating the Arab World', Sciences Po, 2009, http://www.ecipe.org/media/publication_pdfs/Engman_HalfCenturyofExportingeducational_services_Egypt102009.pdf, last accessed 18 Dec. 2013.
28. Shah, Nasra M., 'Restrictive Labour Immigration Policies in the Oil-rich Gulf: Effectiveness and Implications for Sending Asian Countries', United Nations Expert Group Meeting on Social and Economic Implications of Changing Population Age Structure, 2006, https://www.un.org/esa/population/migration/turin/Symposium_Turin_files/P03_Shah.pdf, last accessed 5 Jan. 2014, p. 18.
29. Rahman, 'Human Rights', p. 17.
30. Rahman, 'Human Rights', p. 17; Thiollet, Hélène, 'Migration as Diplomacy: Labor Migrants, Refugees, and Arab Regional Politics in the Oil-Rich Countries', OXPO, 2011, oxpo.politics.ox.ac.uk/publications/working_papers/wp_10–11/OXPO_10_11c_Thiollet.pdf, last accessed 28 Nov. 2013, p. 13.
31. Naufal, 'The Economics of Migration in the Gulf Cooperation Council Countries', CIRS Monthly Dialogue lecture, 9 September 2013.
32. Kapiszewski, 'Migrant Workers', p. 9.
33. Ibid.
34. See Chapter 2 of this volume.
35. Ravenstein, E.G., 'The Laws of Migration', *Journal of the Statistical Society* 48 (1885): 52, pp. 167–235.
36. Sharma, Rashmi, 'Teachers on the Move: International Migration of School Teachers from India', *Journal of Studies in International Education* 20 (2012), pp. 262–83.
37. Voigt-Graf, Carmen, 'Fijian teachers on the move', *Asia Pacific Viewpoint* 44 (Aug. 2003): 2, pp. 163–75.
38. Manik, Sandhana, 'To Greener Pastures: Transnational Teacher Migration from South Africa', *Perspectives in Education* 25 (June 2007): 2, pp. 55–65.

39. Ibid.
40. Rashmi Sharma, 'Teachers on the Move, pp. 262–83.
41. Ridge, 'Education and the Reverse Gender Divide', p. 32.
42. Engman, 'Exporting Educational Services', pp. 3–41.
43. Ridge, 'Reverse Gender Divide', p. 47.
44. UAE Ministry of Education, 'Open Data', https://www.moe.gov.ae/Arabic/Pages/opendata.aspx, last accessed 25 Mar. 2014.
45. Statistics Authority, 'Qatar in Figures Index Page: Education Tab', 2002, http://www.qsa.gov.qa/eng/publication/qif/2002/qifindex.htm
46. Statistics Authority, 'Qatar in Figures', Dec. 2011, http://www.qsa.gov.qa/eng/GeneralStatistics.htm, pp. 22–4.
47. Ravenstein, 'The Laws of Migration', pp. 167–235; Engman, 'Exporting Educational Services', pp. 3–41.
48. Sönmez, Sevil, Yorghos Apostopoulos, Diane Tran, and Shantyana Rentrop, 'Human Rights and Health Disparities for Migrant Workers in the UAE', *Health and Human Rights* 13 (2011): 2, p. 3.
49. Khalaf and Alkobaisi, 'Migrants' Strategies', p. 278.
50. Ridge, Natasha, 'Teacher Quality, Gender and Nationality in the United Arab Emirates: A Crisis for Boys', Mohammed Bin Rashid School of Government, 2010, http://www.dsg.ae/portals/0/Working%20Paper%2010–06%20English.pdf, last accessed 6 Jan. 2014.
51. Thiollet, 'Migration as Diplomacy', p. 3.
52. Zohry, Ayman, 'Assessment of International Migration in the Arab Region', paper presented at Regional Conference on Population and Development in the Arab States, Cairo, 2013.
53. Naufal, 'Economics of Migration'.
54. Engman, 'Exporting Educational Services', p. 3.
55. Ibid., p. 4.
56. Ibid., p. 3.
57. Ibid.
58. Engman, 'Exporting Educational Services', p. 6.
59. Graz, Liesel, *The Turbulent Gulf: People, Politics, and Power*, London: I.B. Tauris, 1992, pp. 220–1; Kapiszewski, 'Migrant Workers', p. 7.
60. 'Secondary Schools Are Not Doing Their Job', *Gulf News*, 4 Oct. 2010, http://gulfnews.com/opinions/editorials/secondary-schools-are-not-doing-their-job-1.691118, last accessed 18 Jan. 2014.
61. Abi-Mershed, Osama, ed., *Trajectories of Education in the Arab World: Legacies and Challenges*, Abingdon: Routledge, 2009, p. 231.
62. Sulayman Khalaf and Saad Alkobaisi, 'Migrants' Strategies of Coping and Patterns of Accommodation in the Oil-rich Gulf Societies: Evidence from the UAE', *British Journal of Middle Eastern Studies* 26 (1999): 2, p. 296.

63. Jones, Calvert, 'Bedouins into Bourgeois? Social Engineering for a Market Economy in the United Arab Emirates', manuscript submitted for publication, Yale University Press, 2013.
64. Khalaf and Alkobaisi, 'Strategies of Coping', pp. 271–98; Farah, Samar, 'Private Tutoring Trends in the UAE', Dubai School of Government, June 2011, pp. 1–7.
65. Engman, 'Exporting Educational Services', p. 26.
66. Sabry, Sara, 'Teachers in the UAE warned against offering paid private lessons', *Gulf News*, 1 Sep. 2012, http://gulfnews.com/news/gulf/uae/education/teachers-in-uae-warned-against-offering-paid-private-lessons-1.1068666, last accessed 28 Jan. 2014.
67. Farah, 'Tutoring Trends', pp. 1–7; Hajras, Mohammad, 'Private lessons are a disease everyone suffers from', Al Khaleej, 19 Apr. 2011, http://www.alkhaleej.ae/portal/516e46d0-c7f0-48e9-98a0-03ed804a7b09.aspx
68. Sabry, 'Teachers in the UAE'.
69. Farah, 'Tutoring Trends in the UAE', pp. 3–4.
70. Ridge, 'Reverse Gender Divide', p. 122.
71. Ibid.
72. Ridge, Natasha, Samar Farah and Soha Shami, 'Patterns and perceptions in male secondary school dropouts in the United Arab Emirates (Working Paper No. 3)', Sheikh Saud bin Saqr Al Qasimi Foundation for Policy Research. 2013, www.alqasimifoundation.com/en/Publications/Publications/PublicationsDetail.aspx?UrlId=5b7010ff-6e67-48e7-9723-25e0c26e6799, p. 13.
73. Ridge, 'Reverse Gender Divide', p. 100.
74. Education Zone in Ras Al Khaimah, personal conversation with author, 2013.
75. Ridge, 'Reverse Gender Divide', p. 31.
76. Ibid., p. 109.
77. Farah, 'Tutoring Trends', pp. 3–4.
78. Supreme Education Council (SEC), *Schools and Schooling in Qatar 2009–2010*, Doha: Evaluation Institute, 2011.
79. Toumi, Habib, 'Report: Around One Third of Teachers in Qatar Lack Proper Qualifications', *Gulf News*, 5 Sep. 2011, http://gulfnews.com/report-around-one-third-of-teachers-in-qatar-lack-proper-qualifications-1.861612, last accessed 18 Jan. 2014.
80. Ibid.
81. Ibid.
82. See Chapter 2 of this volume.
83. Convenience sampling is a non-random process that involves selecting the most accessible participants. Additional information can be found in: Morse, Janice M., 'Sampling in grounded theory', *The Sage Handbook of Grounded Theory*, edited by Antony Bryant and Kathy Charmaz, London, England: SAGE Publications Ltd., 2007. doi: http://dx.doi.org/10.4135/9781848607941.n11., pp. 229–44.

84. American Federation of Teachers' Educational Foundation, 'International Teacher Mobility Survey', 2013, https://afl.salsalabs.com/o/4013/c/839/images/International%20Teacher%20Mobility%20Survey_238.pdf, last accessed 28 Nov. 2013.
85. NVivo is a software programme that allows text-based data to be classified, sorted and analysed. The researchers used this software to run word frequency queries, word tree diagrams and thematic analyses of transcriptions. For more information about NVivo see: http://www.qsrinternational.com/products_nvivo.aspx
86. 'PPP conversion factor (GDP) to market exchange rate ratio', last modified 2014, data.worldbank.org/indicator/PA.NUS.PPPC.RF
87. In Qatar, most government schools are now called 'independent schools', funded by the government and monitored by the SEC. There are also cases of public-private partnership schools where the term 'semi-independent' is used. In the UAE, government schools also include Madares Al Ghad (Schools of Tomorrow) and model schools. The Ministry of Education started K-12 Madares Al Ghad in 2007 as government schools, with an emphasis on the English language. UAE model schools are supervised by regional education zones and emphasise the use of technology in the classroom.
88. Classroom management has consistently been ranked globally as a concern for teachers, along with mixed student abilities. However, Ridge found in the UAE that male Arab migrant teachers have weaker classroom management skills, because they are less student-centred and less pedagogically competent than their national female counterparts. For additional information see: Kratochwill, Tom, 'Classroom management: Teachers' modules', *American Psychological Association, History of research on classroom management* in C.M. Evertson and C.S. Weinstein (eds), *Handbook of classroom management: Research, practice, and contemporary issues* (2009), http://www.apa.org/education/k12/classroom-mgmt.aspx, pp. 17–43; Ridge, Natasha, 'Teacher quality, gender and nationality in the United Arab Emirates: A crisis for boys (Working Paper No. 10–06)', Dubai School of Government, 2010, pp. 1–34.
89. The following words were removed from the word cloud because they were repeated frequently throughout the transcriptions, but broadly represent school-related themes for all teachers and are not specific to the UAE and Qatar (with the exception of the words UAE, Qatar, and Doha which were repeated frequently because they are the sites for the study): school, teachers, students, teaching, UAE, Qatar, work, classes, Doha.
90. According to respondents in the UAE and Qatar, the Ministry of Education or the SEC require teachers to complete a portfolio as part of their annual teacher evaluation. All respondents have indicated that the time dedicated to building these portfolios is extensive and, at times, counterproductive.
91. David Chapman *et al.*, 'Academic Staff in the UAE: Unsettled Journey', unpublished journal article, *Higher Education Policy*, 2013, pp. 9–10.

92. Zohry, 'Assessment', pp. 3–5.
93. Sharma, Rashmi, 'Teachers on the Move: International Migration of School Teachers from India', *Journal of Studies in International Education* 20 (2012): 10, p. 275.
94. Shah, Muhammad J., et al., 'Job satisfaction and motivation of teachers of public educational institutions', *International Journal of Business and Social Science* 3 (2012): 8, pp. 278–89.
95. Chetan, Dave, Natasha Ridge, and Soha Shami, 'Teacher Effectiveness in English Language Instruction', unpublished data, 2014.
96. Ibid.
97. Ridge, 'Privileged and penalized', p. 175.
98. Tromans, Carla, Leonie Daws, Brigid Limerick and Jill Brannock, 'Winning the Lottery? Beginning teachers on temporary engagement', *Teachers and Teaching: Theory and Practice*, 7:1, (2001), pp. 25–42.
99. Sharma, 'Teachers on the Move', pp. 13–14; Eurostat, 'Push and Pull Factors of International Migration', pp. 74–5; Khalaf and Alkobaisi, 'Strategies of Coping', pp. 273–5.

4. THE MODEL IMMIGRANT: SECOND GENERATION HADRAMIS IN KUWAIT AND THE LEGACY OF A 'GOOD REPUTATION'

1. Grateful acknowledgement goes to the Center for International and Regional Studies (CIRS), Georgetown University School of Foreign Service in Qatar, for funding the fieldwork research at all phases. Special thanks go to all members of the CIRS and to Dr Mehran Kamrava, Zahra Babar and Nerida Child Dimasi for their support, and also to the members of the CIRS working groups for their important comments and questions about the research.
2. See Al-Shamsi, Maitha, *Al-hijrah al-wafidah ila duwal majlis al-taʿawun al-khaliji*, Markaz al-imarat li al-dirasat wa al-buhuth al-istiratijiyyah, 2010; Farjani, Nadir, *Al-hijrah ila al-naft: abʿad al-hijrah li al-ʿamal fi al-buldan al-naftiyyah wa atharuha ʿala al-tanmiyah fi al-watan al-ʿarabi*, Markaz dirasat al-wihdah al-ʿarabiyyah, 1983; al-Najjar, Baqir, *Hulum al-hijrah: al-hijrah wa al-ʿamalah al-muhajirah fi al-khalij al-ʿarabi*, Markaz dirasat al-wihdah al-ʿarabiyyah, 2001; al-Musa, Abd al-Rasul and Keith McLachlan, *Immigrant Labor in Kuwait*, Croom Helm, 1985; Appleyard, Reginald, *Emigration Dynamics in Developing Countries: The Arab Region*, Ashgate, 1998; Shah, Nasra, 'Structural Changes in the Receiving Country and Future Labor Migration—The Case of Kuwait', *International Migration Review* 29, no. 4 (1995): pp. 1,000–22; McMurray, David, 'Recent Trends in Middle Eastern Migration', *Middle East Report* 211 (Summer 1999): pp. 16–19; Evans, Lynn and Ivy Papps, 'Migration Dynamics in the GCC Countries' in *Emigration Dynamics in Developing Countries: The Arab Region*, Reginald Appleyard (ed.) Ashgate, 1998, pp. 202–34; 'al-Gardawi, 'Abd al-Raouf, *siyasat al-ʿamalah al-wafida*

bi-duwal majlis al-taʿawun al-khaliji, Center for Gulf and Arabian Peninsula Studies, 2010.

3. See Hoerder, Dirk, 'Segmented Macro Systems and Networking Individuals: The Balancing Functions of Migration Processes' in *Migration, Migration History, History: Old Paradigms and New Perspectives*, Jan Lucassen and Leo Lucassen (eds), Peter Lang, 1997, pp. 73–84; Faist, Thomas, 'The Crucial Meso-Level', in *International Migration, Immobility and Development: Multidisciplinary Perspectives*, Thomas Hammar *et al.* (eds), Oxford: Berg, 1997, pp. 187–217.

4. Hadramis are defined as people coming from the Hadramawt region in South Yemen. Characteristically, Hadramawt is known for its active history of out-migration. The vast majority of Hadrami immigrants in Kuwait originated from agrarian villages of the coast of Hadramawt region. Being a Hadrami has a strong geo-cultural connotation, which differentiates them from all other Yemenis including their closest neighbours, the Mahris.

5. *Muʿazzib* is a term that refers to either a *kafil* (legal sponsor) or someone who has helped in granting the Hadrami a visa to Kuwait (discussed in detail below).

6. Perhaps with the exception of Anh Nga Longva's *Walls Built on Sand*, which was not a full ethnographic undertaking, but an 'observation (not participation) from a distance' in immigrants' daily lives: Longva, Anh Nga, *Walls Built on Sand: Migration, Exclusion, and Society in Kuwait*, Boulder, CO: Westview Press, 1997, p. 15. Similarly, Attiya Ahmad's *Beyond Labor* in which the author uses an Asian female immigrant's story as an ethnographic representation of Kuwait's migration of dozens of 'bachelor workers': Ahmad, Attiya, 'Beyond Labor: Foreign Residents in the Persian Gulf', in *Migrant Labor in the Persian Gulf*, Mehran Kamrava and Zahra Babar (eds), Hurst, 2012, pp. 21–40. Both works are related to Asian rather than Arab migration to Kuwait. They made references to ordinary locals, but no specific case was offered that represented the perspective of the receiving society on migration. However, for ethnographies of Asian immigrants in the Gulf see Gardner, Andrew, 'Gulf Migration and the Family', *Journal of Arabian Studies* 1, no. 1 (2011): pp. 3–25; Vora, Neha, *Impossible Citizens: Dubai's Indian Diaspora*, Durham, NC: Duke University Press, 2013; Osella, Caroline, and Fillipo Osella, 'Migration, Networks and Connectedness Across the Indian Ocean', in *Migrant*, Kamrava and Babar, pp. 105–36.

7. See Ghabra, Shafeeq, *Palestinians in Kuwait: The Family and the Politics of Survival*, Boulder, CO: Westview Press, 1987; Arzuni, Khalil, *Al-hijrah al-lubnaniyyah ila al-Kuwayt 1915–1990*, Beirut: Maktabat al-Faqif, 1994; Ramadan, Ahmed, 'Egyptian Migration', in *Migration: Immigration and Emigration in International Perspective*, Leonore Adler and Uwe Gielen (eds), Westport: Praeger, 2003, pp. 311–27; Farjani, *Al-hijrah ila al-naft*, devoted no more than four pages to the migration of southern Yemenis in all of the Arabian Peninsula states (pp. 91–5).

8. On the categorisation process see Alajmi, Abdullah, 'House-to-House Migration:

The Hadrami Experience in Kuwait', *Journal of Arabian Studies* 2, no. 1 (2012): pp. 1–17; Russell, Sharon Stanton, 'Politics and Ideology in Migration Policy Formulation: The Case of Kuwait', *International Migration Review* 23, no. 1 (1984): pp. 24–47.
9. Two major destinations for Hadrami immigrants were and still are Saudi Arabia and the UAE, but unfortunately no systematic studies exist about Hadrami migration to these countries.
10. See Jacobsen, Frode, *Hadrami Arabs in Present-Day Indonesia: An Indonesia-oriented Group with an Arab Signature* (Routledge, 2009); Manger, Leif, *The Hadrami Diaspora: Community-building on the Indian Ocean Rim*, Berghahn, 2010; Mohammad Ba Matraf, *Al-hijrah al-Yamaniyya*, Wizarat shu'un al-mughtaribin and al-afaq, 2001; Salih al-Hamid, *Tarikh Hadramawt*, Maktabat al-irshad, 1968; Bujra, Abdalla, *The Politics of Stratification: A Study of Political Change in a South Arabian Town*, Oxford University Press, 1971; Le Guennec-Coppens, Françoise, 'Social and Cultural Integration: A Case Study of the East African Hadramis', *Africa* 59 (1989): pp. 185–95; Mobini-Kesheh, Natalie, *The Hadrami Awakening: Community and Identity in the Netherlands East Indies, 1900–1942*, Cornell University Press, 1999; Linda Boxberger, *On the Edge of Empire: Hadramawt, Emigration, and the Indian Ocean, 1880s-1930s*, State University of New York Press, 2002; Ewald, Janet and William Gervase Clarence-Smith, 'The Economic Role of the Hadrami Diaspora in the Red Sea and Gulf of Aden, 1820s to 1930s', in *Hadhrami Traders, Scholars, and Statesmen in the Indian Ocean, 1750s-1960s*, Ulrike Freitag and William Gervase Clarence-Smith (eds), Brill, 1997, pp. 281–96; al-Shumayri, Abd al-Wali, *Min a'lam al-ightirab al-Yamani*, Wizarat shu'un al-Mughtaribin, 2002, collected autobiographies of more than 40 Hadrami immigrants, all of whom were *Sayyids*, merchants, or religious scholars who travelled overseas in the nineteenth and early twentieth centuries.
11. See Ewald and Clarence-Smith, 'Economic Role', p. 296; Le Guennec-Coppens, Françoise, 'Changing Patterns of Hadhrami Migration and Social Integration in East Africa', in *Hadhrami Traders*, Freitag and Clarence-Smith, p. 171.
12. (est. $N = 4,000$): this number represents a sample population from the first generation (individuals above forty-five years old) and second-generation (from eighteen to forty-five years old).
13. A gathering or living place for males only, where newcomers from Hadramawt are received, provided with temporary settlement and then directed to jobs.
14. Kuwait's 1957 and 1965 censuses offered good estimates of different Arab populations and regional identities.
15. See Vargas-Silva, Carlos, *Handbook of Research Methods in Migration*, Edward Elgar Publishing, 2012; Apitzsch, Ursula and Irini Sioutti, *Biographical Analysis as an Interdisciplinary Research Perspective in the Field of Migration Studies*, Research Integration, 2007; Iosifides, Theodoros and Deborah Sporton,

'Biographical Methods in Migration Research', *Migration Letters* 6, no. 2 (2009): pp. 101–8; Lawson, Victoria, 'Arguments within Geographies of Movement: The Theoretical Potential Migrants' Stories', *Progress in Human Geography* 24, no. 2 (2000): pp. 173–89; Brettell, Caroline, *We Have Already Cried Many Tears: The Stories of Three Portuguese Migrant Women*, Waveland Press, 1995; Gmelch, George, *Double Passage: The Lives of Caribbean Migrants Abroad and Back Home*, University of Michigan Press, 1992; Constable, Nicole, *Maid to Order in Hong Kong: Stories of Filipina Workers*, Cornell University Press, 1997.
16. See section on the *mu'azzib*, which discusses its meaning in more details.
17. Young people refers to males only, as I had no access to women in this research; hence also the lack of reference to mothers.
18. The development of this image will be illustrated later on.
19. Interview with Fayiz, October and November 2013, Nuzha, Kuwait.
20. Al-Hawwati, 'Al-takayyuf al-ijtima'i li al-'a' idin min al-Kuwayt 1990', *buhuth nadwat al-mughtaribin al-yamaniyyin* (2001): pp. 30–1. No reliable information exists about the number of Hadrami immigrants before or after the Gulf War. Al-Hawwati estimated that 20,000 Yemeni families returned from Kuwait following the 1991 war but does not specify how many Hadrami families may be included in that figure. In all, however, Yemeni official censuses have estimated the returnees from Kuwait to Hadramawt's villages and towns at around 25,000. Today, Yemeni officials in Kuwait estimate that the whole Yemeni community is approximately 7,000–8,000, the vast majority of whom are Hadramis. This figure appears reasonable when compared to Hadramis' own estimates of their numbers in Kuwait, which round up to 7,000.
21. Interview with Fayiz, October and November, 2013, Nuzha, Kuwait.
22. Fuligni, Andrew, *Family Obligations Among Children in Immigrant Families*, Migration Policy Institute, 2006.
23. Interview with Yaslam, July 2013, Shuwaykh, Kuwait.
24. A Kuwaiti word for 'men's gathering place'; usually located at the entrance of the house.
25. In 1967 the socialist government imposed restrictions on out-migration that lasted for several years. In the 1970s, however, Hadramis began travelling again, mainly to neighbouring Gulf states. See Bujra, *Stratification*; Alajmi, 'House-to-House Migration'; Lackner, Helen, *P.D.R. Yemen: Outpost of Socialist Development in Arabia*, Ithaca, 1985.
26. The numbers of Hadrami immigrants on each boat sailing to Kuwait were reasonable estimates made by a number of twelve Hadramis; I gathered their life histories in another research. Because of the illegal nature of Hadrami transportation and entrance to Kuwaiti ports no records were kept or revealed. Hence, informants agreed that on a single boat there could have been from 100 to 150 individuals, particularly at the peak of Hadrami migration to Kuwait in the 1950s and 1960s.

For more on these senior Hadramis life histories and the movement between Kuwait and Hadramawt see Alajmi, Abdullah, *In the House, Around the House: An Ethnography of Hadar Hadrami Migration to Kuwait*, London School of Economics, 2007.

27. See Lienhardt, Peter, *Disorientations: A Society in Flux: Kuwait in the 1950s*, Ithaca, 1993; Russell, 'Politics and Ideology', p. 45.
28. Interview with Ashur, September–December 2006, Khaitan, Kuwait.
29. An off-shore station for shipping goods and people from and to Kuwait, once owned and operated by local merchant families. Now replaced by modern ports, the remnants of the *niq'ah* were reconstructed as symbols of old and pure Kuwaiti success in the face of the harshness of the pre-oil era.
30. Seccombe, Ian, 'Labor Migration to the Arabian Gulf: Evolution and Characteristics 1920–1950', *Bulletin of the British Society for Middle Eastern Studies* 10, no. 1 (1983): pp. 3–20.
31. See Dickson, H.R.P. et al., *The Arab of the Desert*, Harper Collins, 1951, on African slavery in Kuwait; also Longva's *Wall Built on Sands* gives a brief account on the symbolic value of slaves in Kuwaiti *Hadar* houses in Kuwait's pre-oil era, particularly for the patriarchal outlook of the family, pp. 69, 75.
32. Official Kuwaiti television still broadcasts a famous musical about the 1950s, in which a woman says to her fiancé, 'I want a car, complemented by a *siby*... and I want you to let me know how much money you make'. Interestingly, this musical is seen by Kuwaitis as representing an era of ease, openness and growth, and they express a longing for that time. To many Kuwaitis, the house with a car and a servant came to be equated with family well-being and satisfaction, achievement, and responsibility for the individual household.
33. The ordinary Kuwaiti who said, 'I can't live with them and I can't live without them' was just articulating that paradoxical process of inclusion designed for exclusion.
34. *Kafil* is the local and legal term for sponsor.
35. See Al-Naqib, Khaldun, *Al-mujtama' wa al-dawlah fi al-khalij al-'arabi wa al-jazirah al'arabiyyah: min manthur mukhtalif*, Markaz dirasat al-wihdah al-'arabiyyah, 1987.
36. Interview with Umar's father, December 2013, Khaldiyya, Kuwait.
37. Interview with Umar, October 2013, Khaldiya, Kuwait.
38. See Sun-He Park, Lisa, 'Continuing Significance of the Model Minority Myth: The Second Generation', *Social Justice* 35, no. 2 (2008): pp. 134–44; Yoon, In-Jin, *On My Own: Korean Business and Race Relations in America*, University of Chicago Press, 1997.
39. Interview with Umar, October 2013, Khaldiya, Kuwait.
40. Ibid.
41. See Wessendorf, Susanne, *Second Generation Transnationalism and Roots Migration*,

Ashgate, 2013; Bryceson Fahy, and Ulla Vuorela, *The Transnational Family: New European Frontiers and Global Networks*, Berg Publishers, 2002.

42. See Hoerder, Dirk, 'Transnational—Transregional—Translocal: Transcultural', in *Research Methods*, Vargas-Silva, pp. 69–91; Sana, Mariano and Douglas Massey, 'Household Composition, Family Migration, and Community Context: Migrant Remittances in Four Countries', *Social Science Quarterly* 86, no. 2 (2005): pp. 509–28.
43. Interview with Salim, September 2013, Jilib al-shuyukh and Sharq, Kuwait.
44. Kuwaiti foreign residence by law requires a minimum salary of 400 Kuwaiti dinars for an immigrant to bring his spouse and children under eighteen years old to the country. Given that Hadramis do not allow their wives to work outside the home in Kuwait, bringing their wives and children to Kuwait increases working immigrants' expenses.
45. See Conway, Dennis and Robert Potter, *Return Migration of the Next Generation: 21st Century Transnational Mobility*, Ashgate, 2009; Christou, Anastasia, *Narratives of Places, Culture and Identity: Second-Generation Greek-Americans Return 'Home'*, Amsterdam University Press, 2006.
46. Anthropologist David Mosse showed how for young immigrants' migration may not in fact improve income or security (may indeed undermine it by perpetuating debt and dependency)', p. 60. Mosse, David *et al.*, 'Brokered Livelihoods: Debt, Labor Migration and Development in Tribal Western India', *The Journal of Development Studies* 38, no. 5 (2002): pp. 59–88.
47. For an estimated exchange rate with US dollars, see the beginning of this paper.
48. Debt is an endless process among generations. It is not pursued further here because it is not within the scope of the research and is essentially related to the important role of other family members (i.e. women) whom it was not possible to interview in this community. On Hadrami debt see Hadrami historian Al-Mallahi, *Al-hadarim fi Mombassa wa dar al-salam 1930–1960*, unpublished manuscript, 2000; also Boxberger, *On the Edge of Empire*, 97–120.
49. Interview with Salim, September 2013, Jilib al-shuyukh, Kuwait.
50. This is a husband's gift of presents and money to the bride on the first morning after the wedding.
51. See Hockey, Jenny, and Allison James, *Social Identities Across the Life Course*, Palgrave Macmillan, 2003; Green, Paul, 'Generation, Family, and Migration: Young Brazilian Factory Workers in Japan', *Ethnography* 11, no. 4 (2010): pp. 515–32.
52. Al-Kaf, Saqqaf, *Hadramawt 'ibra arba'ata 'ashara qarnan*, Maktabat usamah, 1990; Ulrike Freitag, 'The Diaspora Since the Age of Independence', in *Hadhrami Traders*, Freitag and Clarence-Smith, pp. 315–29.
53. This phase of Hadrami migration in Kuwait was beyond the scope of the research. However, Yemeni official censuses have estimated the number of returnees from Kuwait to Hadramawt's villages and towns to be around 25,000 (Source: Central

Statistical Organization, Yemeni Ministry of Planning and Development: 'The final results of the returnees after 2–8–1990', Sana'a, 1991). More than two-thirds of returnees to Hadramawt during the Gulf War came from Kuwait; see Van Hear, Nicholas, 'The Socio-Economic Impact of the Involuntary Mass Return to Yemen in 1990', *Journal of Refugee Studies* 7, no. 1 (1994): pp. 18–38. The Yemeni government's pro-Iraq position during Iraq's occupation of Kuwait hardened Kuwaiti immigration policies towards Yemenis in general. The effect of the 1991 war on Hadramis in Kuwait was disastrous, particularly on both those who had spent most of their lives as immigrants in Kuwait and Kuwaiti-born Hadramis. The Hadramis of Kuwait experienced the harsh process of re-migrating back to Hadramawt during the Gulf War, the majority empty-handed and unprepared for different or new types of work there.
54. Interview with Mubarak, November 2013, Hawalli, Kuwait.
55. Personal discussion.
56. Islamic donations such as *zakat* and *sadaqat* played a vital role, and still do, in maintaining the basic material lives of ex-immigrants. Other cases of total dependence reveal how the livelihoods of a whole household relied on the monetary aid received annually from a *mu'azzib*. The research recorded more than forty-five households in one village of coastal Hadramawt that regularly received such endorsements from Kuwait.
57. Interview with Mubarak, November 2013, Hawalli, Kuwait.
58. See Assiri, Abd al-Rida, *Kuwait's Foreign Policy: City-State in World Politics*, Westview Press, 1990; Jill Crystal, *Oil and Politics in the Gulf: Rulers and Merchants in Kuwait and Qatar*, Cambridge University Press, 1995.
59. This is a common, and sometimes derogatory phrase among Hadramis in Kuwait, many of whom believe that Palestinians and Lebanese are better liked by Kuwaiti businesses than Yemeni or Hadrami.
60. Interview with Mubarak, November 2013, Hawalli, Kuwait.
61. See Foner, Nancy and Joanna Dreby, 'Relations Between the Generations in Immigrant Families', *Annual Review of Sociology* 37 (2011): pp. 545–64; Alba, Richard and Mary Waters (eds), *The Next Generation: Immigrant Youth in a Comparative Perspective*, NYU Press, 2011.

5. THE EGYPTIAN 'INVASION' OF KUWAIT: NAVIGATING POSSIBILITIES AMONG THE IMPOSSIBLE

1. The authors extend their sincere thanks to the staff and faculty of the Center for International and Regional Studies, Georgetown University School of Foreign Service in Qatar, for making this research project possible. We are also grateful to participants of the two Arab Migrant Communities in the GCC Working Group sessions for their valuable insights and experience on the subject. Finally, our immense gratitude and appreciation go to our research assistants and all those individuals in Kuwait, who took the time to share their insights.

NOTES pp. [85–89]

2. Saʿad al-ʿAjami, 'al-khaitān: al-qāhira fī-l-kuwait' ('Kheitan: Cairo in Kuwait'), *Alriyadh Newspaper*, 12 Aug. 2007, http://www.alriyadh.com/2007/08/12/article272088.html, last accessed 15 Nov. 2013.
3. The *bidoon* in Kuwait are a stateless community, the vast majority of whom belong to Arab tribes that had settled in the desert prior to the country's independence. The word *bidoon* refers to *bidoon jinsiyya*, literally meaning 'without nationality' or 'without citizenship'.
4. 'MPC Migration Profile', Migration Policy Centre (MPC), June 2013, http://www.migrationpolicycentre.eu/docs/migration_profiles/Egypt.pdf, last accessed 16 Apr. 2014.
5. These figures from the Kuwaiti Ministry of the Interior do not necessarily represent accurate numbers of irregular migrants. Mansour al-Shammary, 'al-jālīya al-hindiyya al-akbar fī-l-kuwait talaiha al-masriyya' ('Indian community is the largest in Kuwait, followed by the Egyptian [community]'), *Alrai*, 23 May 2013, http://www.alraimedia.com/Article.aspx?id=437885, last accessed 15 Nov. 2013.
6. 'al-idāra al-markaziyya li-l-iḥṣāw'... (3065850) milīūn nasama 'adad sukān al-kuwait fī 2011' ('Central Administration for Statistics... 306,580 persons, the population of Kuwait in 2011'), *Kuwait News Agency (KUNA)*, 18 Mar. 2013, http://www.kuna.net.kw/ArticleDetails.aspx?id=2227920&language=ar, last accessed 15 Nov. 2013.
7. Vora, Neha, *Impossible Citizens*, Durham, NC: Duke University Press, 2013.
8. Ahmad, Attiya, 'Beyond Labor', in *Migrant Labor in the Persian Gulf*, Mehran Kamrava and Zahra Babar (eds), New York: Columbia University Press, 2012, p. 22.
9. See Rodríguez, Nestor and Jacqueline Maria Hagan, 'Fractured Families and Communities: Effects of Immigration Reform in Texas, Mexico and El Salvador', *Latino Studies* 2, no. 3 (2004): pp. 328–51; Flahaux, Marie-Laurence, 'The Influence of Migration Policies in Europe on Return Migration to Senegal', *University of Oxford International Migration Institute*, Working Paper No. 93 (July 2014); Cassarino, Jean-Pierre, 'Theorising Return Migration: The Conceptual Approach to Return Migrants Revisited', *International Journal on Multicultural Societies* 6, no. 2 (2004): pp. 253–79.
10. While efforts were made to ensure a diverse range of participants, a slight bias towards higher-skilled Egyptians can be discerned. Given the small sample size, we do not consider it representative of the Egyptian population in Kuwait. All of the names used in this chapter are pseudonyms. Most interviews were conducted in Arabic, while a smaller number were conducted in English.
11. The education distribution within this sample size correlates with a 2010 International Organization for Migration (IOM) study of the Egyptian diaspora, which revealed that more than a quarter of Egyptians have a 'less than university' degree. See IOM, 'A Study on the Dynamics of the Egyptian Diaspora: Strengthening Development Linkages', IOM Cairo (2010): p. 29.

12. Data released by the Egyptian Ministry of Manpower and Emigration in 2002 revealed that 41.0 per cent of Egyptians working in Arab countries were classified as scientists and technicians, 2.4 per cent were managers, 1.5 per cent were clerical workers, 12.7 per cent worked in sales and services, 8.6 per cent in agriculture, and 8.6 per cent in production. See Zohry, Ayman and Barbara Harrell-Bond, 'Contemporary Egyptian Migration: An Overview of Voluntary and Forced Migration', American University of Cairo (Dec. 2003): p. 35, http://www.migrationdrc.org/publications/working_papers/WP-C3.pdf, last accessed 5 May 2014.
13. Muhammad al-Bahr, 'al-safir al-ḥamad yuhdī al-majmaʻ al-ʻilmi al-maṣrī wathīqa nādira li-tārīkh ʻalāqāt al-buldān' ('Ambassador al-Hamad presents the Egyptian Scientific Academy with a rare document [revealing] the history of relations between the two countries'), *Kuwait State News Agency (KUNA)*, 5 July 2013, http://www.kuna.net.kw/ArticleDetails.aspx?id=2320749&language=ar, last accessed 27 Nov. 2013.
14. Casey, Michael S., *The History of Kuwait*, Westport, CT: Greenwood Press, 2007, p. 63.
15. Khalaf, Sulayman and Hassan Hammoud, 'The Emergence of the Oil Welfare State: The Case of Kuwait', *Dialectical Anthropology* 12, no. 3 (1987): p. 354.
16. Freeth, Zahra, *Kuwait Was My Home*, London: George Allen & Unwin, 1956, p. 44.
17. Sell, Ralph R., 'Egyptian International Labor Migration and Social Processes: Toward Regional Integration', *International Migration Review* 22, no. 3 (1988): p. 92.
18. Shah, Nasra M., 'Migration to Kuwait: Trends, Patterns and Policies', Paper prepared for a conference at the American University in Cairo, 23–25 Oct. 2007, http://www.aucegypt.edu/GAPP/cmrs/Documents/Nasra_Shah.pdf, last accessed 28 Jan. 2014.
19. Russell, Sharon Stanton, 'Politics and Ideology in Migration Policy Formation: The Case of Kuwait', *International Migration Review* 23, no. 1 (Spring 1989): p. 32.
20. al-Taher, Issam, *al-kuwait... al-ḥaqiqa (Kuwait: The Reality)*, Amman: Dar Al-Shorok, 1996, p. 206.
21. Barnett, Michael N. and Jack S. Levy, 'Domestic Sources of Alliances and Alignments: The Case of Egypt. 1962–73', *International Organization* 3 (1991): p. 383.
22. Hillal Dessouki, Ali E., 'The Shift in Egypt's Migration Policy: 1952–1978', *Middle Eastern Studies* 18, no. 1 (Jan. 1982).
23. IOM, 'A Study on the Dynamics of the Egyptian Diaspora': p. 16.
24. Russell, 'Politics and Ideology': p. 36.
25. Ismael, Jacqueline S., 'The Conditions of Egyptian Labor in the Gulf: A Profile on Kuwait', *Arab Studies Quarterly*, (1986): p. 390.

26. Sell, 'Egyptian International Labor Migration and Social Processes', p. 94.
27. al-Moosa, Abdulrasool and Keith MacLachlan, *Immigrant Labour in Kuwait*, Dover, NH: Croom Helm, 1985, p. 54.
28. Longva, Anh Nga, *Walls Built on Sand: Migration, Exclusion and Society in Kuwait*, Boulder, CO: Westview Press, 1997, p. 31.
29. 'Kuwaitisation' was made explicit for the first time in the 1985–90 Five-Year Plan, which prioritised population balance over economic growth, but resurrected the notion of preference for Arab over Asian migrants within the basic labour law. See Russell, Sharon Stanton and Muhammad Ali al-Ramadhan, 'Kuwait's Policy since the Gulf Crisis', *International Journal of Middle East Studies* 26, no. 4 (1994): pp. 569–87.
30. Sell, 'Egyptian International Labor Migration': p. 91.
31. Russell and al-Ramadhan, 'Kuwait's Policy': p. 576.
32. Ibid., p. 580.
33. Ibid., p. 576.
34. Kapiszewski, Andrzej, 'Arab versus Asian Migrant Workers in the GCC Countries', United Nations Expert Meeting on International Migration and Development in the Arab Region, Beirut, 15–17 May, 2006, p. 9.
35. Russell, Sharon Stanton, 'International Migration and Political Turmoil in the Middle East', *Population and Development Review* 18, no. 4 (1992): pp. 722–3.
36. Ahmed, Ahmed A., 'Public Commercial Investments in Arab Countries', *Middle Eastern Studies*, no. 2 (1995): p. 305.
37. Lesch, Ann M., 'Palestinians in Kuwait', *Journal for Palestine Studies* 20, no. 4 (Summer 1991): pp. 42–54.
38. IOM, 'Dynamics', p. 17.
39. Ibid., p. 18.
40. Ibid., p. 20; Kapiszewski, 'Migrant Workers', p. 9.
41. The popular areas of employment reflecting the diversity of the Egyptian labour force have included: local and national government administration, education, medicine, construction and maintenance, in particular. See, for example, al-Jasser, Hamad, '2/3 Kuwait Population Foreign, Half from Indian Subcontinent', *Dar al-Hayat Newspaper*, 30 Mar. 2012, http://www.al-monitor.com/pulse/business/2012/04/two-thirds-of-the-kuwaiti-popula.html, last accessed 7 Dec. 2014.
42. Kapiszewski, 'Migrant Workers', p. 9.
43. Interview with Sarah; September 2013; Kuwait.
44. Interview with Gamal; September 2013; Kuwait.
45. Lefebvre, Henri, *The Production of Space*, trans. Donald Nicholson-Smith, Malden, MA: Blackwell Publishing, 1991.
46. Interview with Abdullah; September 2013; Kuwait.
47. Discussion between Noura and Fatima; August 2013; Kuwait.
48. For examples, see Massey, Douglas, *et al.*, 'Theories of International Migration: A

Review and Appraisal', *Population and Development Review* 19, no. 3 (Sept. 1993): pp. 431–66; Massey, Douglas, 'The New Immigration and Ethnicity in the United States', *Population and Development Review* 21, no. 3 (Sept. 1995): pp. 631–52; Krissman, Fred, 'Sin Coyote Ni Patrón: Why the 'Migrant Network" Fails to Explain International Migration', *International Migration Review* 39, no. 1 (Mar. 2005): pp. 4–44; Bernardi, Fabrizio, *et al.*, 'The Recent Fast Upsurge of Immigrants in Spain and their Employment Patterns and Occupational Attainment', *International Migration* 49, no. 1 (Feb. 2011): pp. 148–87.

49. Discussion between Noura and Fatima; August 2013; Kuwait.
50. Ibid.
51. 'Maṣrī akhraj ithbātuh fasaqatat 'al-farawla' faharab wa-ta'thar suqūtan wa-uhīl ila al-mukāfaha', 'Egyptian expat arrested after pills fell from his pocket during an ID inspection', *Al-Anba' Newspaper*, 16 July 2013, http://egykwt.com/node/88802, last accessed 28 July 2013); 'Sordid saga ends as defiant 'Hawally monster' hanged—Fellow Egyptian arsonist also executed for murders', *Kuwait Times*, http://news.kuwaittimes.net/sordid-saga-ends-as-defiant-hawally-monster-hanged-fellow-egyptian-arsonist-also-executed-for-murders/, last accessed 18 June 2013.
52. Discussion between Noura and Reem; August 2013; Kuwait.
53. Interview with Abdulaziz; August 2013; Kuwait.
54. Harper, Justin, 'Kuwait bans expats from hospital and driving', *The Daily Telegraph*, 9 July 2013, http://www.telegraph.co.uk/news/health/expat-health/10160479/Kuwait-bans-expats-from-hospital-and-driving.html, last accessed 7 Apr. 2015. It is also worth mentioning that existing health policies restrict access for non-Kuwaitis to certain medicines in public hospitals.
55. Longva, *Walls Built on Sand*, pp. 229–30.
56. Interview with Abdullah; September 2013; Kuwait.
57. Rogers Brubaker and Frederick Cooper, 'Beyond "identity"', *Theory and Society*, 29 (2000): p. 4.
58. Interview with Mustafa; September 2013; Kuwait.
59. Interview with Ramy; September 2013; Kuwait.
60. Vora, *Impossible Citizens*, p. 20.
61. Article 12, Amiri Decree 17 of 1959. See Zahra, Maysa, 'Kuwait's Legal Framework of Migration', Gulf Research Center/Migration Policy Centre, GLMM-EN-No. 3/2013, http://gulfmigration.eu/media/pubs/exno/GLMM_EN_2013_03.pdf, last accessed 25 Jan. 2013.
62. 'Current Situation of Expats in Kuwait Similar to Scary Movie', *Arab Times*, 9 June 2013, http://www.arabtimesonline.com/NewsDetails/tabid/96/smid/414/ArticleID/197097/reftab/96/t/Current-situation-of-expats-in-Kuwait-similar-to-scary-movie/Default.aspx, last accessed 10 June 2013; '213 Expats Deported for Violating Traffic Rules: Al-Ali', *Arab Times*, 29 Apr. 2013, http://www.arab-

timesonline.com/NewsDetails/tabid/96/smid/414/ArticleID/195681/reftab/96/Default.aspx, last accessed 30 Apr. 2013; 'al-safāra al-maṣriyya bi-l-kuwait taṭālib al-maṣriyyin li-ltizām bi-qūwānīn al-murūr wa-l-iqāma' ('Egyptian embassy demands commitment to traffic and residency laws'), *Masrawy.com*, 9 June 2013, http://tinyurl.com/kvlhbqg, last accessed 10 June 2013.

63. Interview with Nowras; September 2013; Kuwait.
64. Shah, Nasra M., and Indu Menon, 'Chain Migration Through the Social Network: Experience of Labor Migrants in Kuwait', *International Migration*, no. 2 (1999).
65. Based on interviews, the average price for a residency permit was believed to be 30,000 Egyptian pounds (about US$4,260).
66. Interview with Ramy; September 2013; Kuwait.
67. Interview with Ramy; September 2013; Kuwait.
68. Interview with Bassam; September 2013; Kuwait.
69. Kuwait's family reunification policy is conditional on the salary of the worker. For workers in the government sector, the salary must amount to 450 Kuwaiti dinars (US$1,573). For those working in the private sector, the salary must amount to 650 Kuwaiti dinars (US$2,273) or more. For an overview of Kuwaiti legislation, see: Zahra, 'Legal Framework'.
70. Zohry and Harrell-Bond, 'Contemporary Egyptian Migration', p. 32.
71. Van Hear, Nicholas, Rebecca Brubaker and Thais Bessa, 'Managing Mobility for Human Development: The Growing Salience of Mixed Migration', UNDP Human Development Research Paper 2009, New York, http://hdr.undp.org/en/content/managing-mobility-human-development, last accessed 5 May 2014.
72. Interview with Gamal; September 2013; Kuwait.
73. Interview with Ramy; September 2013; Kuwait.
74. Interview with Sharif; September 2013; Kuwait.
75. See Zahra, 'Legal Framework'.
76. IOM, 'Dynamics', p. 31.
77. Interview with Mohammed; September 2013; Kuwait.
78. Interview with Samer; September 2013; Kuwait.
79. Interview with Marianne; September 2013; Kuwait.
80. Şenyürekli, Aysem R. and Cecilia Menjívar, 'Turkish Immigrants' Hopes and Fears around Return Migration', *International Migration*, 50, no. 1 (Jan. 2012): pp. 4–19.
81. 'al-safāra al-maṣriyya tadaʿu abnāʾ al-jalīa li-iltizām bi-lqūwānīn wa-l-niẓām al-kuwaitiyya' ('The Egyptian embassy calls upon the Egyptian community to abide by the Kuwaiti laws and system'), *Al-Anba Newspaper*, 28 June 2013, http://www.alanba.com.kw/ar/arabic-international-news/egypt-news/392147/28-06-2013, last accessed 30 June 2013.
82. '600 Set for Deportation', *Arab Times*, 27 Jan. 2013, http://www.arabtimesonline.com/NewsDetails/tabid/96/smid/414/ArticleID/203239/reftab/36/Default.aspx, last accessed 30 Jan. 2014.

83. Shah, Nasra, 'Recent Amnesty Programmes for Irregular Migrants in Kuwait and Saudi Arabia: Successes and Failures', 2014: p. 7.

6. THE 'OTHER ARAB' AND GULF CITIZENS: MUTUAL ACCOMMODATION OF PALESTINIANS IN THE UAE IN HISTORICAL CONTEXT

1. Funding from Georgetown University SFS-Qatar's Center for International and Regional Studies (CIRS). The CIRS Arab Migrants in the GCC Research Initiative made this project possible. First, I would like to thank all my interviewees in the UAE, and the generous feedback and support of the CIRS Working Group on Arab Migrants in the GCC, especially the careful reading and feedback from Zahra Babar and Mehran Kamrava. My heartfelt thanks also go to Hayfa Abdul Jabar, Nezar Andary, Hanan Awad, Matthew Buehler, Nadia Rahman, as well as Natasha Ridge, Soha Shami and Marwah Al Hassan from the Al Qasimi Foundation, who helped me arrange interviews and provided me with valuable feedback on this project.
2. See, for example, contributions in the edited volume Kamrava, Mehran and Zahra Babar (eds), *Migrant Labour in the Persian Gulf*, London: Hurst & Co. Ltd, 2012, such as Gardner, Andrew, 'Why Do They Keep Coming? Labor Migrants in Gulf States', pp. 41–58. Other works include Choucri, Nazli, 'Asians in the Arab World: Labor Migration and Public Policy', *Middle Eastern Studies* 22, no. 2 (Apr. 1986): pp. 252–73; Shah, Nasra M., 'The Role of Social Networks among South Asian Male Migrants to Kuwait', *Emigration Dynamics in Developing Countries Volume II: South Asia*, Reginald Appleyard (ed.), Aldershot: Ashgate Publishers Ltd, 1998.
3. Stevenson, Thomas B., 'Yemeni Workers Come Home: Reabsorbing One Million Migrants.' *Middle East Report* 23, no. 2 (Mar.–Apr. 1993): pp. 15–20; Shah, Nasra, 'Arab Labor Migration: A Review of Trends and Issues', *International Migration* vol. 32, no. 1 (Jan. 1994): pp. 3–29; Shah, Nasra, 'Arab Migration Patterns in the Gulf', *Arab Migration in a Globalized World*, International Organization for Migration and League of Arab States, Geneva: International Organization for Migration, May 2004, pp. 91–113; Kapiszewski, Andrzej, 'Arab Labor Migration to the GCC States', in ibid., pp. 115–33; Choucri, Nazli, 'New Perspectives on Political Economy of Migration in the Middle East', in Appleyard (ed.), *Emigration Dynamics*; and Fergany, Nader, 'Aspects of Labor Migration and Unemployment in the Arab Region', Almishkat Center for Research, Egypt, 2001, www.worldbank.org/mdf/mdf4/papers/fergany.pdf
4. For exceptions, see Brand, Laurie A., *Palestinians in the Arab World: Institution Building and the Search for State*, New York: Columbia University Press, 1988; Rouleau, Eric, 'The Palestinian Diaspora in the Gulf.' *MERIP Reports* Vol. 15, No. 4 (May 1985): pp. 13–15; Smith, Pamela Ann, 'The Palestinian Diaspora, 1948–1985', *Journal of Palestine Studies* Vol. 15, No. 3 (Spring, 1986): pp. 90–108; Shami, Seteney S., 'Emigration dynamics in Jordan, Palestine and Lebanon', in Appleyard (ed.), *Emigration Dynamics*.

5. For brief discussions, see, for example: Smith, 'The Palestinian Diaspora', pp. 90–108; Said Zahlan, Rosemarie, *Palestine and the Gulf States: The Presence at the Table*, New York: Routledge, 2009; and Almezaini, Khalid S., *The UAE and Foreign Policy: Foreign Aid, Identities and Interests*, New York: Routledge, 2012.
6. See, for example, Ghabra, Shafeeq N., *Palestinians in Kuwait: The Family and the Politics of Survival*, Boulder, CO: Westview Press, 1987; Lesch, Ann, 'Palestinians in Kuwait', *Journal of Palestine Studies* 20, no. 4 (1991): pp. 42–54; Abed, George T., 'Palestinians and the Gulf Crisis', Journal of Palestine Studies 20, no. 2 (Winter, 1991): pp. 29–42; Le Troquer, Yann and Rozenn Hommery al-Oudat, 'From Kuwait to Jordan: The Palestinians' Third Exodus', *Journal of Palestine Studies* 28, no. 3 (Spring 1999): pp. 37–51; Al-Nakib, Mai, 'Outside the Nation Machine: the Case of Kuwait', *Strategies* 13, No. 2 (2000): pp. 201–20; and for a seminal piece on the subject matter, Al-Nakib, Mai, "The People are Missing": Palestinians in Kuwait', *Deleuze Studies* 8, no. 1 (2014): pp. 23–44.
7. For more on the legal privileging of Arab workers in GCC states, see Kapiszewski, Andrzej, *Arab Versus Asian Migrant Workers in the GCC Countries*, United Nations Expert Group Meeting on International Migration and Development in the Arab Region, Population Division, Department of Economic and Social Affairs United Nations Secretariat Beirut, 15–17 May 2006, p. 8.
8. For example, Kapiszewski in *Migrant Workers* (p. 6) argued that Gulf authorities became worried about non-local Arabs bringing and spreading radical social and political ideas. According to Shah in 'Arab Migration Patterns' (p. 100), however, among the reasons Asian workers replaced Arab ones were better compliance and obedience to employers, and host country policies to diversify the backgrounds of their migrant workers.
9. Although the non-Gulf countries of Egypt, Morocco and Syria were part of the allied coalition that invaded Iraq, their populations strongly opposed the war and their governments' involvement. Moreover, along with the PLO, Algeria, Libya, Sudan, Tunisia and Yemen sided with Iraq, or at least did not oppose the invasion, arousing the ire of Kuwait.
10. The Trucial States were those territories that had signed treaties with the British government establishing an informal protectorate between these sheikhdoms and the British government. These territories consisted of Abu Dhabi, Dubai, Sharjah, Ras al-Khaimah, Umm al-Qaiwain, Ajman and Fujairah, and, from 1931, Bahrain.
11. See for example, Reeve, A. (Political Agent in Abu Dhabi) letter to Sir Stewart Crawford (Political Resident in Bahrain), 'Palestinians in Abu Dhabi', 12 June 1969, in *Records of the Emirates 1966–1971*, A.L.P. Burdett (ed.), vol. 4: 1969, Farnham Common: Archive Editions, 2002; Crawford, Sir Stewart (Political Resident in Bahrain) letter to A. Reeve (Political Agent in Abu Dhabi), 'Palestinians in Abu Dhabi', 30 June 1969, in Burdett (ed.), *Records of the Emirates*; Crawford, Sir Stewart (Political Resident in Bahrain) letter to A.J. Coles (Political Agent in

Dubai), 'Palestinian Influence in Northern Trucial States', 21 July 1969, in Burdett (ed.), *Records of the Emirates*.

12. Crawford, 'Palestinian Influence'.
13. Out of a total of thirty-four interviewees, four took place in Ras al-Khaimah, two in Al-Ain, thirteen in Dubai and fifteen in Abu Dhabi. Twenty-one interviewees were male and thirteen were female. Five were born and raised in the UAE, and three held Emirati citizenship or passports.
14. Despite attempts to ensure that the sample was representative, it did not adequately capture the lives and sentiments of lower-middle-class Palestinians and those who had not succeeded in the UAE. This research, therefore, presented a far more positive assessment of the community's circumstances. Ideally, it would have also included interviews with Palestinians who had lost their jobs and left the UAE because they were unable to secure visa renewals, but this was not logistically possible.
15. Ong, Aihwa, *Neoliberalism as Exception: Mutations in Citizenship and Sovereignty*, Durham and London: Duke University Press, 1996, p. 7.
16. Vora, Neha, 'From Golden Frontier to Global City: Shifting Forms of Belonging, "Freedom", and Governance among Indian Businessmen in Dubai', *American Anthropologist* vol. 113, no. 2: pp. 306–18.
17. See for example, Kapiszewski, 'Arab Labor Migration', p. 119.
18. These communications included outgoing dispatches, meeting minutes, dispatches from British representatives abroad, and domestic correspondence with foreign representatives in the given country, and/or with other branches of the British government.
19. A political officer or agent was an official of the imperial civil administration appointed by the British government to serve as an adviser to a ruler of a protectorate.
20. Crawford, 'Palestinian Influence'.
21. Crawford, 'Palestinian Influence', p. 414. Fatah is one of the largest political organisations of the Palestine Liberation Organization.
22. Jamal, Manal A., The "Tiering" of Citizenship and Residency and the "Hierarchization" of Migrant Communities: the United Arab Emirates in Historical Context', *International Migration Review* (2015), 49: 601–632. doi: 10.1111/imre.12132.
23. Shah, 'Arab Migration Patterns', p. 97.
24. Riad Kamal is also a member of the board of trustees of the Welfare Association, a prominent Palestinian philanthropic association based in Geneva, Switzerland.
25. Palestinians in this sector arrived in the late 1960s and early 1970s and were initial founders of these companies.
26. For a detailed discussion about the Palestinian diaspora and domestic Arab politics, see Brand, *Palestinians in the Arab World*.

27. See, for example, Farsoun, Samih K. and Christina E. Zacharia, *Palestine and the Palestinians*, Boulder, CO: Westview Press, 1997.
28. Ibid., p. 155.
29. According to official UAE statistics this figure was 36,504 in 1981. The PLO, however, estimated that the figure was closer to 70,000. For more on these figures, see Smith, 'The Palestinian Diaspora, 1948–1985'.
30. The Palestinian Embassy refused to provide this data without permission from the Palestinian Authority President's Office in Ramallah. Attempts to access this information from UAE institutions raised extensive questioning and it was recommended not to pry into obtaining such sensitive data.
31. Meeting with official in the Palestinian Authority Embassy in the UAE, 21 July 2013.
32. Palestinians from the Gaza Strip who left before the 1967 Arab-Israeli war, as well as Palestinians who are residents of Egypt as refugees or otherwise, often hold Egyptian-issued travel documents.
33. For more on this logic of explaining why migrants come and stay, see Gardner, 'Why Do They Keep Coming?', pp. 41–58.
34. Nationalisation policies mean that female Emirati teachers have almost uniformly replaced female teachers from elsewhere in the Arab world in girls' schools. In boys' schools, Emiratis only constitute 30 per cent of total teachers, and the majority of male teachers are from Jordan (often of Palestinian origin), Egypt and Syria.
35. For comparison, a UAE national earns AED 30,000 (US$8,168) per month for the same job.
36. Interviews with Jamal and Ata, Ras al-Khaimah, 5 Jan. 2014. Both sent remittances to their families in Jordan.
37. Interview with Jamal.
38. Jordanian passports do not confer citizenship or residency rights. Citizenship in Jordan is determined by the possession of a national identification number. Palestinian Jordanian passport holders without an identification number are entitled to a five-year renewable passport, work permit and access to education through payment.
39. For more on the Israeli military closure of the Gaza Strip, refer to Relief Web's summary: http://reliefweb.int/report/occupied-palestinian-territory/what-closure-gaza, last accessed 30 Dec. 2016.
40. Interview with Huda, Dubai, 28 Dec. 2013.
41. Interview with Mohammed, Dubai, 31 Dec. 2013.
42. Interview with Huda.
43. Interview with Hassan, Abu Dhabi, 23 July 2013.
44. Interview with Wafa, Abu Dhabi, 7 Jan. 2014.
45. Interview with Linda, Dubai, 1 Jan. 2014.
46. Interview with Hani, Dubai, 31 Dec. 2013.

47. Interview with Linda, Dubai, 1 Jan. 2014.
48. Interview with Wafa.
49. Interview with Linda.
50. Interview with Hani.
51. Kapiszewski, 'Arab Labor Migration', p. 119.
52. For more on this discussion, refer to Kapiszewski, *Migrant Workers*, p. 119.
53. Interview with Abu Tarek, Abu Dhabi, 18 July 2013.
54. Interview with Ali, Al Ain, 27 Dec. 2013.
55. Interview with Abu Tarek.
56. Interview with Abu Jamal, Abu Dhabi, 27 July 2013.
57. For more on this for example, see Human Rights Watch, 'Letter to Minister of Interior in the UAE regarding Arbitrary Deportation of Lebanese and Palestinian Residents', 19 July 2010, https://www.hrw.org/news/2010/07/19/letter-minister-interior-uae-regarding-arbitrary-deportations-lebanese-and, last accessed 30 Dec. 2016.
58. Interview with Shadia, 1 Jan. 2014.
59. Interview with Wafa, Abu Dhabi, 7 Jan. 2014.
60. Interview with Abu Helmi, Al Ain, 27 Dec. 2013.
61. Interview with Hassan. Like other Emirati Palestinians of his generation who were born and raised in the UAE, Hassan appeared quite comfortable moving between his Palestinian and Emirati selves. In more formal settings, including work, he wore Emirati dress and spoke with an Emirati dialect. At home and in more relaxed settings, he wore more Western dress and spoke with the Palestinian dialect he grew up speaking at home.
62. Interview with Hassan.
63. Similar to other expatriate communities, Palestinian children must attend private schools, unless one of their parents is employed in the public sector; then they can enrol two of their children in public schools.
64. Interview with Abu Jamal, Abu Dhabi, on 27 July 2013.
65. Interview with Mohammed.
66. Interview with Issam, Dubai, 1 Jan. 2014.
67. Ibid.
68. Ibid.
69. Interview with Hassan.
70. Interview with Yasmin, Dubai, 3 Jan. 2014.
71. Interview with Kamal, Abu Dhabi, 7 Jan. 2014.
72. Interview with Faisal, Dubai, 8 Jan. 2014.
73. These islands are also known as the Federation of Saint Christopher and Nevis.
75. Interview with Yasmin.
76. Interview in Abu Dhabi, 6 Jan. 2014.
77. For more on this discussion, see Abbas Shiblak, 'Residency Status and Civil Rights

of Palestinian Refugees in Arab Countries', *Journal of Palestine Studies* 25, no. 3 (Spring 1996): pp. 36–45.
78. Jordan did not grant citizenship to 1967 Palestinians refugees from Gaza.
79. For more on this discussion see Shiblak, 'Residency Status', p. 39.
80. Ibid., p. 40.
81. Ibid., p. 43.
82. Ibid., p. 42.
83. After King Hussein's 'administrative disengagement' from the West Bank in 1988, the passports of Palestinian residents of the West Bank were made 'temporary' and would only serve as travel documents and not proof of citizenship as they previously had done. For more on this, refer to ibid., p. 41.
84. Ibid., 43.

7. YEMENI IRREGULAR MIGRANTS IN THE KINGDOM OF SAUDI ARABIA AND THE IMPLICATIONS OF LARGE SCALE RETURN: AN ANALYSIS OF YEMENI MIGRANTS RETURNING FROM SAUDI ARABIA

1. The authors gratefully acknowledge the support provided by Dax Roque in gathering background information, as well as IOM colleagues based in Yemen, particularly Teresa Zakaria for sharing the data collected through her team's operations and for her advice on the analysis. The authors would also particularly like to thank Johan Gonzalez for his support in managing and providing advice on the data.
2. Allman, James and Allan Hill, 'Fertility, Mortality, Migration and Family Planning in the Yemen Arab Republic', *Population Studies* 32, no. 1 (Mar. 1978): pp. 159–71.
3. Colton, Nora Ann, 'The Dominant Role of Migration in the Development of the Republic of Yemen', *Critique: Critical Middle Eastern Studies* 4, no. 6 (1995): pp. 57–79.
4. Stevenson, Thomas, 'Yemeni Workers Come Home: Reabsorbing One Million Migrants', *Middle East Report* 181 (Mar–Apr 1993): pp. 15–20.
5. Colton, Nora Ann, 'Homeward Bound: Yemeni Return Migration', *International Migration Review* 27, no. 4 (Winter 1993): pp. 870–82.
6. Ibid.
7. Colton's own survey of returnees was conducted in the winter and spring of 1989 in the region of al-Hujariyya (North Yemen) and involved interviews (in a group and individually) of 353 returnees who had gone back to Yemen voluntarily. As Colton notes, these returnees were part of a trickle of return migrants that began picking up pace in the 1980s with the slowdown of the oil industry. Stevenson's research involved interviews and focus groups with Yemeni returnees and affected host communities in the provinces of Aden, al Bayda, Hajja, al-Hodeida, Ibb, Sana'a, and Ta'iz throughout July and Aug. 1992.
8. Colton, 'Homeward Bound', pp. 870–82.

9. Qat is a plant native to Yemen and the Horn of Africa. A large portion of the Yemeni population chew qat leaves, which act as a mild stimulant.
10. Birks, J.S., A. Sinclair and J.A. Socknat, 'Aspects of Labour Migration from North Yemen', *Middle East Studies* 17, no. 1 (Jan 1981): pp. 49–63.
11. Fergany, Nader, 'The Impact of Emigration on National Development in the Arab Region: The Case of the Yemen Arab Republic', *International Migration Review* 16, no. 4 (Winter 1982): pp. 757–80.
12. See Colton, 'Homeward Bound', pp. 870–82; Stevenson, 'Yemeni Workers Come Home', pp. 15–20.
13. Colton, 'Homeward Bound', pp. 870–882.
14. Stevenson, 'Yemeni Workers Come Home', pp. 15–20.
15. Ibid.
16. Colton, 'The Dominant Role of Migration', pp. 57–79.
17. Birks *et al.*, 'Aspects of Labour Migration from North Yemen', pp. 49–63.
18. Regional Mixed Migration Secretariat, 'The Letter of the Law: Regular and Irregular Migration in Saudi Arabia in a Context of Rapid Change', *Mixed Migration Research Series* 4 (Apr. 2014).
19. *Yemen Post*, 17 Feb. 2014.
20. These figures include returnees who may have been deported multiple times over this time period.
21. This is the best proxy available for us to check whether those who sought either medical or food and non-food assistance were more likely to have had substantially different responses to survey questions than the wider population.
22. According to IOM data collectors, 'sick' in these cases usually meant quite extreme deprivation of food and water.
23. *Yemen Post*, 17 Feb. 2014.
24. Although the sample is not perfectly random, as discussed in the preceding section, we would not expect the sampling method to create a bias with regard to gender.
25. These figures include those who may have been deported multiple times within this period, therefore it is not an accurate reflection of the total number of returnees over this period.
26. Although the sample is not perfectly random, as discussed in the preceding section, we would not expect the sampling method to create a bias with regard to gender.
27. Females were more likely to say that they had relatives in Saudi Arabia, with 87.3 per cent saying that they had no children compared to 96.9 per cent of males; 5.2 per cent of females said that they had children, 3.2 per cent that they had parents, and 1.75 per cent that they had a spouse in Saudi Arabia. Although the questionnaire could not ascertain whether or not these family members were dependants, these figures could have indicated acute protection concerns if minors

were becoming separated from their mothers as a result of the policy changes. This is clearly an important issue and ascertaining the extent of the problem and appropriate policy responses, if any, would require further investigation which is beyond the scope of this paper.

28. *Adult and Youth Literacy, 1990–2015: Analysis of data for 41 selected countries*, UNESCO Institute of Statistics (Quebec: UNESCO, 2012), p. 9.
29. Occupations including plumber, carpenter, blacksmith, painter, and general construction labourer.
30. Occupations including fisherman, shepherd, and farmer.
31. Migration Policy Institute, http://www.migrationpolicy.org/article/mexican-immigrants-united-states#Distribution%20by%20State%20and%20Key%20 Cities, last accessed 30 Dec. 2016.
32. A chi-square test is a statistical test used to determine independence and goodness of fit. Testing independence determines whether two or more observations across two populations are dependent on one another.
33. To check that these associations were not due to certain governorates being a destination for those entering and being deported multiple times, we cross-tabulated governorate of destination with length of stay in Saudi Arabia and then also with respondents' intention on return. There did not appear to be an association.
34. Among respondents ($\gamma = 0.277$, chi-square p: <0.01), given the sample size, this is significant to the 0.01 level.
35. OCHA, *Yemen Humanitarian Response Plan—2014*, 12 Feb. 2014.
36. Ibid.
37. Regional Mixed Migration Secretariat, 'Migrant Smuggling in the Horn of Africa and Yemen', *Mixed Migration Research Series* 1 (June 2013).
38. According to numerous estimates on the size of the irregular Yemeni population in Saudi Arabia.
39. USAID, 'Yemen—Complex Emergency', *Fact Sheet* no. 1 (Dec. 2013).
40. Assuming respondents sent a minimum of 1 Saudi riyal and a maximum of 2,400 Saudi riyals per month.
41. According to World Bank data putting Yemeni reserves at USD 5,344,296,890 in 2013: http://data.worldbank.org/indicator/FI.RES.TOTL.CD, last accessed 30 Dec. 2016.
42. International Monetary Fund, *Arab Countries in Transition: An Update on Economic Outlook and Key Challenges*, Washington DC, 9 Apr. 2014.
43. Even if, as our sample indicated, approximately 37 per cent of deportees attempted to enter Saudi Arabia again, many would have been delaying their inevitable return to Yemen if the *nitaqat* policy changes continued to be strictly enforced.
44. For a full explanation of the scoring system, see Appendix.
45. OCHA, *Yemen Humanitarian Response Plan—2014*.

8. AN EMERGING TREND IN ARAB MIGRATION: HIGHLY SKILLED ARAB FEMALES IN THE GCC COUNTRIES

1. Morrison, Andrew R., Maurice Schiff and Mirja Sjöblom (eds), *The International Migration of Women*, Washington DC: World Bank and Palgrave Macmillan, 2008.
2. Mostly stemming from international and non-governmental organisations. For example: International Organization for Migration (IOM), *Arab Migration in a Globalized World*, Geneva: IOM, 2004; IOM, *Female Migrants: Bridging the Gaps Throughout the Life Cycle*, Geneva: IOM, 2006; UNDP and Arab Fund for Economic and Social Development, The Arab Human Development Report 2005, 'Towards the Rise of Women in the Arab World', New York: UNDP, Regional Bureau for Arab States, 2006; ESCWA, 'Gender and Migration', ESCWA Centre for Women Newsletter 1, no. 3 (Jan. 2007); UNFPA, 'A Passage to Hope: Women and International Migration: State of the World's Population 2006', New York: UNFPA, 2006; Et-Tayeb, Aicha, 'The Participation of Female Migrants in the Socio-Economic Development Scene in Two Maghreb Countries: Social Reading of Status and Roles', *A Study on the Dynamics of Arab Expatriate Communities: Promoting Positive Contributions to Socioeconomic Development and Political Transitions in their Homelands*, IOM (ed.), Cairo: IOM and League of the Arab States, 2012: pp. 21–40.
3. For a demographic approach to Gulf states' exceptionalism and its evolution, see Fargues, P. and F. De Bel-Air, 'Migration to the Gulf States: the Political Economy of Exceptionalism', in *Global Migration: Old Assumptions, New Dynamics*, D. Acosta Arcarazo and A. Wiesbrock (eds), Santa Barbara, CA: Praeger, 2015, pp. 139–166.
4. Among others: Eelens, F., T. Schampers and J.D. Speckmann (eds), *Labour Migration to the Middle East: From Sri Lanka to the Gulf*, London: Kegan Paul International, 1992; ILO, *Gender and Migration in Arab States: The Case of Domestic Workers*, Beirut: ILO, 2004; Human Rights Watch, *'As If I Am Not Human': Abuses against Asian Domestic Workers in Saudi Arabia*, New York: HRW, 2008; Longva, Anh Nga, *Walls Built on Sand: Migration, Exclusion and Society in Kuwait*, Boulder, CO: Westview Press, 1997; Moors, Annelies and Marina de Regt, 'Migrant domestic workers in the Middle East', *Illegal Migration and Gender in a Global and Historical Perspective*, Schrover, M. *et al.*, Amsterdam: Amsterdam University Press, IMISCOE Research, 2008, pp. 151–71.
5. Adapted from Zarkovic Bookman, Milica, *The Demographic Struggle for Power: the Political Economy of Demographic Engineering in the Modern World*, London, Portland: Frank Cass and Co., 1997, p. 71.
6. Maktabi, Rana, 'The Lebanese Census of 1932 Revisited. Who Are the Lebanese?' *British Journal for Middle Eastern Studies* 26, no. 2 (1999): pp. 219–41.
7. On the debate over marriage with foreign females, see, for example: Kridia, Marwa, 'Marrying foreign women in the Emirates: a widespread phenomenon with worrying consequences', *Elaph*, 27 Aug. 2010, http://www.elaph.com/Web/

news/2010/8/591205.html; Osman, Mohamed and Fazeena Saleem, 'Many Qataris frown on marrying foreigners', *The Peninsula*, 19 Apr. 2014, http://thepeninsulaqatar.com/news/qatar/280351/many-qataris-frown-on-marrying-foreigners, last accessed 15 September 2014.

8. CCME, 'Femmes marocaines dans le Golfe: Entre clichés et réalités', 21 December 2009, last accessed 15 Apr. 2014, http://www.ccme.org.ma/fr/maj/3807; Boumnade, Ilham, 'Au-delà des clichés', *L'Economiste*, 26 November 2013, last accessed 15 Apr. 2014, http://www.leconomiste.com/article/913301-marocaines-du-golfe-au-del-des-clich-s

9. De Haas, Hein, 'Migration and Development. A Theoretical Perspective', IMI Working Paper 9, Oxford: International Migration Institute, 2008; de Haas, Hein, 'Turning the Tide? Why "Development Instead of Migration" Policies are Bound to Fail', IMI Working Paper 2, Oxford: International Migration Institute, 2006.

10. Levatino, Antonina, 'Highly-skilled Migration and the Global Economy of Knowledge', paper presented at the workshop Disciplining Global Movements. Migration Management and its Discontents, Osnabruck University, 3 November 2010.

11. Davids, Gavin, 'Young Arab Women More Likely to Migrate to UAE—Survey', *Arabian Business.com*, 28 November 2010, http://www.arabianbusiness.com/young-arab-women-more-likely-migrate-uae-survey-364426.html, last accessed 15 Apr. 2014.

12. Kridia, Marwa, 'Disappointment Overshadows the Life of Unmarried Female Expatriates', *Elaph*, 29 November 2010, accessed 15 Apr. 2014, http://www.elaph.com/Web/news/2010/11/614499.html?entry=articlemostvisitedtoday

13. De Bel-Air, Françoise, 'Gender Politics and Migration Policies in Jordan', *CARIM ASN 2011/03*, Florence: Robert Schuman Centre for Advanced Studies and European University Institute, 2011.

14. Boubakri, Hassan, 'Femmes et migrations en Tunisie', *CARIM ASN 2011/17*, Florence: Robert Schuman Centre for Advanced Studies, European University Institute, 2011, p. 9.

15. Et-Tayeb, Aicha, 'The Participation of Female Migrants', p. 28.

16. Khachani, Mohammad, 'La migration marocaine dans les pays du Golfe', *CARIM ASN 2009/34*, Florence: Robert Schuman Centre for Advanced Studies and European University Institute, 2009.

17. Kasparian, Choghig, *L'émigration des jeunes Libanais et leurs projets d'avenir*, Beirut: Presses de l'Université Saint-Joseph, 2009, pp. 16, 25.

18. Occupations are categorised according to (slightly adapted) ISCO 88 international classification of occupations—major (1-digit) group titles.

19. The source of data used here is the Public Authority for Civil Information (PACI), the body in charge of issuing Civil Identification Cards to every resident (all ages, all nationalities including nationals) in Kuwait. Since the mid-1990s, PACI pop-

ulation figures have proved more accurate than census figures published by the Central Statistics Bureau; Shah, Nasra, *Population of Kuwait: Structure and Dynamics*, Kuwait: Kuwait University Academic Publication Council, 2010, Chapter 1.
20. Indeed, it offers a minimum estimate. Most highly skilled occupations can only be filled by highly educated workers, whereas tertiary-educated workers can be employed in occupations demanding lower skill levels (de-skilling process).
21. In both countries, Asian expatriates comprise the bulk of non-national populations: in Bahrain in 2010 Asians made up 84.4 per cent of the non-nationals; in Kuwait in 2012, they accounted for 55 per cent, while Arabs made up 41 per cent of all foreign residents. Their characteristics thus exerted a major influence on global figures for non-nationals.
22. It should be noted that Arab women in Bahrain are very few, as emphasised in Table 8.1 (only 3,217 of them being employed).
23. This is the male-to-female sex ratio calculated by dividing the total number of males by the number of females, then multiplying this figure by 100. A value above 100 means that there are more males than females in the population.
24. Our population of reference is 15–64 years.
25. A category that comprises neither the citizens of other GCC states residing in Kuwait, nor the *bidoon* (stateless Arabs).
26. http://gulfmigration.eu/population-by-nationality-group-2012/ (last accessed 30 Dec. 2016); in late 2013 in Saudi Arabia, Egyptians were also the most numerous among Arab nationals, with an estimated 1 million or more resident in the Kingdom (press releases by Saudi government officials, see: http://gulfmigration.eu/estimates-of-non-nationals-by-country-of-citizenship-saudi-arabia-november-3–2013/).
27. The migration status (worker, family dependant, etc.) is inferred from the distribution of expatriates by type of residence permit held as of 31 Dec. 2012, according to Kuwaiti residency law. Workers hold permits for government labour (no. 17), non-government labour (no. 18), business (no. 19) or domestic help (no. 20). Family members hold the dependants' permit (no. 22). Other residents may hold a temporary three-month permit (no. 14), self-residence (no. 24) or student permit (no. 23), which are not included in the table but are included in the total figures for permit holders. The figures exclude *bidoon* residents, non-Kuwaiti GCC citizens and those in irregular situations.
28. See contributions by Garrett Maher (Chapter Nine), Abbie Taylor, Susan Martin and Nada Soudy (Chapter Five), and Natasha Ridge, Soha Shami, and Susan Kippels (Chapter Three) in this volume.
29. The survey was undertaken as part of a project that CEDRE (French-Lebanese Scientific and Educational Cooperation) funded entitled 'Highly-skilled migration, professional circulations and relations to the country of origin: the case of

Lebanon', conducted by the French Institute for the Near East (IFPO), Beirut, MIGRINTER/Poitiers University, France, and the Sociology Department of Saint-Joseph University, Beirut, in 2011–13. I worked on a project with Rita Yazigi, Department of Sociology, Saint-Joseph University. Our common research focused on highly skilled Lebanese migrants and their relationship to Lebanon, their reasons for leaving and the types of remittances they sent home. The project specifically targeted Lebanese highly skilled migrants who left Lebanon for the first time in 1990 or later, having earned their first tertiary degree in Lebanon before leaving and who were employed abroad at the time of the survey. Our sample of interviewees was recruited randomly from social network affiliates, mainly from Facebook and LinkedIn. A sample of 1,500 interviewees worldwide was identified for a preliminary study, out of which 1,000 agreed formally to take part in a second, in-depth survey. After a phase of elaboration (using LimeSurvey software) and testing, our questionnaire study was then distributed to this batch (Summer 2012). Respondents contacted by mail had to fill in the questionnaire online. Out of 1,000 candidates contacted, 382 questionnaires could be used when the session closed in Oct. 2012—many respondents had changed contact details, lost jobs, returned to Lebanon, etc. Only parts of the material gathered has been processed and used. For this chapter, I extracted those respondents living in the GCC states (108 men and 36 women), and separately used the aspects of their contributions relevant to the present project. My thanks to Rita Yazigi for allowing me to use the material we gathered together. The sample survey is referred to hereafter as "CEDRE sample survey of Lebanese highly skilled migrants."

30. Choghig Kasparian, *L'émigration des jeunes*.
31. Some degrees must still be earned abroad, because they may require candidates to undertake extensive work experience, such as MBAs, for example. We considered all of them as having been completed, for the purposes of processing of data.
32. Most 'other degrees' are management degrees in specific economic sectors (tourism, health, accountancy, teaching, etc.)
33. The classification used is ISCED (2013 revision), elaborated by UNESCO.
34. 'Administrative and commercial managers' and 'Business and administration professionals'.
35. The classification of respondents' professional status is adapted from the International Classification of Status in Employment (ICSE), ILO, 1993.
36. Economic activities are categorised according to ISIC (Rev. 3) international classification of industries.
37. Only one respondent said she was working for the state.
38. The project specifically targeted highly skilled Lebanese migrants who left Lebanon for the first time in 1990 or later. The recruitment channels used here refer to the first time the interviewees left Lebanon. The bulk of our sample had left in 2006 or later and had spent most of their time in the current location in the Gulf (see "demographic characteristics" of sample).

39. On Jordan, for example, see De Bel-Air, Françoise, 'Jordan, a land of no return? Highly-skilled migration, before and after the Arab Spring' in *Migration in the Middle-East and North Africa: Skilled Migrants, Development and Globalization*, Philippe Fargues and Alessandra Venturini (eds), London: I.B. Tauris, 2015.
40. Zoepf, Katherine, 'Generation Faithful: In Booming Gulf, Some Arab Women Find Freedom in the Skies', *The New York Times*, 21 Dec. 2008.
41. For a view from Jordan, see Kawar, Mary, *Gender, Employment and the Life Course: The Case of Working Daughters in Amman*, Amman: Konrad Adenauer Stiftung and Community Centres Association, coll. Jordan Studies Series, 2000.
42. To our knowledge, there do not seem to be gender-specific requirements for Arab females willing to migrate to the Gulf on their own, other than the sponsorship of a Gulf national or company, which applies to every foreign labourer or sojourner.
43. Total exceeds 100 per cent, because several answers could be given.
44. Fargues, Philippe, 'Changing Hierarchies of Gender and Generation in the Arab World' in *Family, Gender and Population in the Middle-East—Policies in Context*, Carla Obermeyer (ed.), Cairo: The American University of Cairo Press, 1995, pp. 179–98.
45. De Bel-Air, Françoise, 'Mariage tardif et célibat au Moyen-Orient: quels enjeux?', in *Métamorphoses du mariage au Proche-Orient*, Barbara Drieskens (ed.), Beirut: IFPO, 2008.
46. The exception is Lebanon, where no structural adjustment programmes were enacted, despite the country's large debt, due to lack of economic planning and political instability.
47. Respectively: Jordan's Department of Statistics, Tunisia's Institut National de la Statistique and Morocco's Haut-Commissariat au Plan.
48. Interview with a sub-sample of the survey's GCC respondents—those living in Dubai—in Feb. 2013 (23 interviews: 5 women and 18 men).
49. Informal personal communications from young Iraqi, Jordanian, Palestinian and Syrian graduate job seekers and professionals, Amman, 2005–07.
50. Some middle-class families in fact accept young females' independent life projects, despite social reproduction norms.

9. HIGHLY SKILLED LEBANESE TRANSNATIONAL MIGRANTS: A KUWAIT PERSPECTIVE

1. This research could not have taken place without the generous support, both financial and academic, of Georgetown University's Center for International and Regional Studies in Qatar. I also wish to gratefully acknowledge the support of my research assistant, for all her work in transcribing interviews.
2. Levitt, Peggy and Nina Glick Schiller, 'Conceptualizing Simultaneity: A Transnational Social Field Perspective on Society', *International Migration Review* 38, no. 3 (2004): p. 1,003.

3. Human Rights Watch, World Report (2013), http://www.hrw.org/world-report/2013/country-chapters/qatar, last accessed (30 Dec. 2016).
4. Shah, Nasra, 'Migration to Kuwait: Trends, Patterns and Policies', paper prepared for the Migration and Refugee Movements in the Middle East and North Africa Conference (2007), p. 4.
5. Kuwait Statistical Review (2013), http://www.csb.gov.kw/Socan_Statistic_EN.aspx?ID=19, last accessed 30 Dec. 2016.
6. See, among others, Shah, Nasra and Sulayman al Qudsi, 'The Changing Characteristics of Migrant Workers in Kuwait', *International Migration Review* 25, no. 1 (1989).
7. Shah, Nasra, 'Kuwait's Revised Labor Laws: Implications for National and Foreign Workers', *Asian and Pacific Migration Journal* 20, no. 3–4 (2011): p. 340.
8. See, for example, Chiswick, Barry (ed.), *High-Skilled Immigration in a Global Labor Market*, Washington DC: Rowman and Littlefield, 2010.
9. Vertovec, Steven, 'Transnational Networks and Skilled Labour Migration', paper given at the 'Ladenburger Diskurs "Migration" Gottlieb Daimler—und Karl Benz Stiftung', Ladenburg, 14–15 Feb. 2002, p. 4.
10. Landolt, Patricia, 'Salvadoran Economic Transnationalism: Embedded Strategies for Household Maintenance, Immigrant Incorporation, and Entrepreneurial Expansion', *Global Networks* 1, no. 3 (2001): p. 217.
11. Hourani, Albert and Nadim Shehadi (eds.), *The Lebanese in the World: A Century of Emigration*, London: I.B. Tauris, 1991, p. 6.
12. Migration Policy Centre, *Lebanon: The Demographic-Economic Framework of Migration*, Robert Schuman Centre for Advanced Studies, 2013.
13. Labaki, Boutros, 'Lebanese Emigration During the War: 1975–1989', in *The Lebanese in the World*, Hourani and Shehadi (eds), p. 605.
14. Migration Policy Centre, *Lebanon*.
15. Al Monitor, http://www.al-monitor.com/pulse/fa/contents/articles/business/2012/04/two-thirds-of-the-kuwaiti-popula.html, last accessed 24 Nov. 2013.
16. United Nations Refugee Agency, http://www.unhcr.org/533c1d5b9.html, last accessed 14 Apr. 2014.
17. Tabar, Paul, 'Lebanon: A Country of Emigration and Immigration', paper presented to Forced Migration and Refugee Studies (FMRS) at the American University in Cairo (2010).
18. Ibid.
19. Glick-Schiller, Nina, Linda Basch and Cristina Szanton-Blanc, 'Transnationalism: A New Analytic Framework for Understanding Migration', in *Towards a Transnational Perspective on Migration: Race, Class, Ethnicity, and Nationalism Reconsidered*, N. Glick-Schiller, L. Basch, and C. Szanton-Blanc (eds), New York: The New York Academy of Sciences, 1992, p. 1.
20. Ibid.

21. Gutiérrez, David G., 'Migration, Emergent Ethnicity, and the "Third Space": The Shifting Politics of Nationalism in Greater Mexico', *Journal of American History* (1999: Special Edition: Rethinking History and the Nation State: Mexico and the United States): p. 481.
22. Olwig, Karen, '"Transnational" Socio-Cultural Systems and Ethnographic Research: Views from an Extended Field Site', *International Migration Review* 37, no. 3 (2003): p. 787.
23. Ibid.
24. Hoggart, Keith, Loretta Lees and Anna Davies, *Researching Human Geography*, London: Arnold, 2001, p. 21.
25. Al-Moosa, Abdulrasool and Keith McLachlan, *Immigrant Labour in Kuwait*, Kent: Croom Helm, 1985, p. 17.
26. Shah, Nasra, 'Relative Success of Male Workers in the Host Country, Kuwait: Does the Channel of Migration Matter?', *International Migration Review* 34 (2000): p. 60.
27. Chamberlain, Mary, 'The Family as Model and Metaphor in Caribbean Migration to Britain', *Journal of Ethnic and Migration Studies* 25, no. 2 (1999): p. 251.
28. Johnston, Ron, Andrew Trlin, Anne Henderson and Nicola North, 'Sustaining and Creating Migration Chains Among Skilled Immigrant Groups: Chinese, Indians and South Africans in New Zealand', *Journal of Ethnic and Migration Studies* 32, no. 7 (2006): p. 1,228.
29. Boyd, Monica, 'Family and Personal Networks in International Migration: Recent Developments and New Agendas', *International Migration Review* 23 (1989): p. 655.
30. Al-Saadi, Yazan, 'Kuwait's Foreign Labor: Here Today, Gone Tomorrow', http://english.al-akhbar.com/node/16439, last accessed 7 Feb. 2014.
31. Trenwith, Courtney, 'Kuwait Reveals Exemptions to Work Visa Ban', *Arabian Business*, http://www.arabianbusiness.com/kuwait-reveals-exemptions-work-visa-ban-495628.html, last accessed 7 Feb. 2014.
32. Gardner, Andrew, 'Why do they keep coming? Migrant labor in the Persian Gulf states', in *Migrant Labor in the Persian Gulf*, Mehran Kamrava and Zahra Babar (eds), London: Hurst and Company, 2012, p. 41.
33. Pseudonyms have been used throughout the chapter for all interviewees.
34. Interview, October 2013, Salmiya, Kuwait.
35. Interview, October 2013, Mishref, Kuwait.
36. Interview, January 2014, Salmiya, Kuwait.
37. Massey, Douglas S., Luin Goldring and Jorge Durand, 'Continuities in Transnational Migration: An Analysis of Nineteen Mexican Communities', *The American Journal of Sociology* 99, no. 6 (1994): p. 1,495.
38. Lynch, Marc, 'Will the GCC Stay on Top?', *Foreign Policy*, http://foreignpolicy.com/2011/12/15/will-the-gcc-stay-on-top/, last accessed 4 May 2015.
39. 'Kuwait is deporting people for Minor Traffic Violations', *Business Insider*, http://

www.businessinsider.com/kuwait-deporting-people-traffic-offenses-2013-5?IR=T, last accessed 5 May 2015.
40. Grogger, Jeffrey and Gordon Hanson, 'Income Maximization and the Selection and Sorting of International Migrants', *Journal of Development Economics* 95 no. 1 (2011): p. 42.
41. Rapoport, Hillel and Frederic Docquier, *The Economics of Migrants' Remittances*, Discussion Paper Series, Institute for the Study of Labor, no. 1531 (2005), p. 9.
42. Approximate exchange rate, Dec. 2013.
43. Boyd, 'Family and Personal Networks', p. 655.
44. Bagnoli, Anna, 'Between Outcast and Outsider; Constructing the Identity of the Foreigner', *European Societies* 9, no. 1 (2007): p. 34.
45. International Organization for Migration, 'Migrant Integration', http://www.iom.int/cms/en/sites/iom/home/what-we-do/migrant-integration.html, last accessed 19 Jan. 2014.
46. Shah, Nasra, 'Second Generation Non-nationals in Kuwait: Achievements, Aspirations and Plans', Kuwait: Kuwait Programme on Development, Governance, and Globalisation in the Gulf States, 2013.
47. Sumption, Madeleine and Sarah Flamm, *The Economic Value of Citizenship for Immigrants in the United States*, Migration Policy Institute, 2012, p. 4.
48. Nadia moved to Kuwait in Dec. 2011.
49. Interview, January 2014, Salmiya, Kuwait.
50. Interview, October 2013, Salmiya, Kuwait.
51. Interview, January 2014, Salmiya, Kuwait.
52. Portes, Alejandro, Luis E. Guarnizo and Patricia Landolt, 'The Study of Transnationalism: Pitfalls and Promises of an Emergent Research Field', *Ethnic and Racial Studies* 22, no. 2 (1999): p. 227.
53. Levitt, Peggy, Josh De Wind and Steven Vertovec, 'International Perspectives on Transnational Migration: An Introduction', *International Migration Review* 37, no. 3 (2003): p. 566.
54. Interview, October 2013, Mishref, Kuwait.
55. Ibid.
56. Interview, October 2013, Salmiya, Kuwait.
57. The majority of interviewees had similar responses.
58. Based on personal observations on social occasions with Lebanese friends.
59. Sana, Mariano, 'Buying Membership in the Transnational Community: Migrant Remittances, Social Status, and Assimilation', *Population Research and Policy Review* 24, no. 3 (2005): p. 232.
60. Interview, October 2013, Salmiya, Kuwait.
61. Interview, December 2013, Beirut, Lebanon.
62. Iredale, Robyn, 'The Migration of Professionals: Theories and Typologies', *International Migration* 39, no. 5 (2001): p. 11.

63. Interview, October 2013, Mishref, Kuwait.
64. Interview, October 2013, Salmiya, Kuwait.
65. Interview, November 2013, Salmiya, Kuwait.
66. Interview, January 2014, Salmiya, Kuwait.
67. Interview, December 2013, Beirut, Lebanon.
68. Interview, October 2013, Mishref, Kuwait.
69. 'Kuwait inflation cools but food prices a worry', *Trade Arabia*, http://www.tradearabia.com/news/REAL_225403.html, last accessed 23 Jan. 2014.
70. 'Beirut becoming less affordable for expats', *Daily Star* (Lebanon), http://www.dailystar.com.lb/Business/Lebanon/2012/Jun-15/176892-beirut-becoming-less-affordable-for-expats.ashx, last accessed 23 Jan. 2014.
71. Interview, December 2013, Beirut, Lebanon.
72. Chapman, Murray and R. Mansell Prothero, 'Themes on Circulation in the Third World', *International Migration Review* 17 (1983): p. 611.
73. Massey *et al*., 'Continuities in Transnational Migration': p. 1,500.
74. Sarah Mahler, 'Theoretical and Empirical Contributions Toward a Research Agenda for Transnationalism', in *Transnationalism from Below*, Michael Smith and Luis Guarnizo, New Brunswick: Transaction Publishers, 1998, p. 69.
75. Guarnizo, Luis, Alejandro Portes and William Haller, 'Assimilation and Transnationalism: Determinants of Transnational Political Action among Contemporary Migrants', *American Journal of Sociology* 108, no. 6 (2003): p. 1,222.
76. Interview, December 2013, Beirut, Lebanon.
77. Interview, January 2014, Salmiya, Kuwait.
78. Interview, October 2013, Salmiya, Kuwait.
79. Ibid.
80. Ibid., p. 1,218.
81. Miyares, Ines, Richard Wright, Alison Mountz, Adrian J. Bailey and Jennifer Jonak, 'The Interrupted Circle: Truncated Transnationalism and the Salvadoran Experience', *Journal of Latin American Geography* 2, no. 1 (2003): p. 75.
82. Levitt, Peggy and Nina Nyberg-Sørensen, 'The Transnational Turn in Migration Studies', *Global Migration Perspectives*, http://www.gcim.org/gmp/Global%20Migration%20Perspectives%20No%206.pdf, last accessed 17 Jan. 2014.
83. Vertovec, Steven, 'Migrant Transnationalism and Modes of Transformation', *International Migration Review* 38, no. 3 (2004): p. 970.
84. See, for example, Maher, Garret, 'A Transnational Migrant Circuit: Remittances from Ireland to Brazil', *Irish Geography* 43, no. 2 (2010): pp. 177–99.
85. Faist, Thomas, 'Transnationalization in International Migration: Implications for the Study of Citizenship and Culture', *Ethnic and Racial Studies* 23, no. 2 (2000): p. 201.
86. Maher, 'A Transnational Migrant Circuit': p. 180.

87. Hourani, Guita, 'Lebanese Migration to the Gulf', *Middle East Institute Viewpoints* (2010): p. 4.
88. Labaki, Boutros, 'The Role of Transnational Communities in Fostering Development in Countries of Origin: The Case of Lebanon', United Nations Expert Group Meeting on *International Migration and Development in the Arab Region: Challenges and Opportunities* (2006), p. 4.
89. Most recent figures from: The World Bank, *Migration and Remittances Factbook*, (2011), p. 30.
90. Coastal area in Northern Lebanon.
91. Interview, November 2013, Salmiya, Kuwait.
92. Ibid.
93. Interview, October 2013, Mishref, Kuwait.
94. Interview, October 2013, Salmiya, Kuwait.
95. Interview, December 2013, Beirut, Lebanon.
96. Jounieh—coastal city 20 km north of Beirut.
97. Interview, December 2013, Jounieh, Lebanon.
98. Page, Ben, 'Remittances', in *International Encyclopedia of Human Geography*, Nigel Thrift and Robert Kitchin (eds), Oxford, Elsevier, 2009, p. 334.
99. Maher, 'A Transnational Migrant Circuit', p. 187.
100. Ibid.
101. Lucas, Robert and Oded Stark, 'Motivations to Remit: Evidence from Botswana', *Journal of Political Economy* 93 (1985): p. 904.
102. Taylor, J. Edward, 'The New Economics of Labour Migration and the Role of Remittances in the Migration Process', *International Migration* 37, no. 1 (1999): p. 73.
103. Interview, January 2014, Salmiya, Kuwait.
104. Interview, October 2013, Salmiya, Kuwait.
105. Interview, December 2013, Beirut, Lebanon.
106. Massey *et al.*, 'Continuities in Transnational Migration': p. 1,494.
107. Boucher, Gerry, 'Ireland's Lack of a Coherent Integration Policy', *Translocations* 3 (2008), http://www.imrstr.dcu.ie/currentissue/Vol_3_Issue_1_Gerry_Boucher.pdf, last accessed 20 Jan. 2014.
108. Sorrels, Kathryn, 'Placing Culture and Cultural Space in the Global Context', presented at the National Communication Association 93rd Annual Convention (diss., Chicago, 14 Nov. 2007).
109. Sana, Mariano and Douglas S. Massey, 'Household Composition, Family Migration, and Community Context: Migrant Remittances in Four Countries', *Social Science Quarterly* 86, no. 2 (2005): p. 510.

10. SPORT LABOUR MIGRANT COMMUNITIES FROM THE MAGHREB IN THE GCC

1. See Amara, Mahfoud, *Sport, Politics and Society in the Arab World*, London: Palgrave Macmillan, 2012; Amara, Mahfoud and Eleni Theodoraki, 'Transnational Network Formation through Sports Related Regional Development Projects in the Arabian Peninsula', *International Journal of Sport Policy* 2, no. 2 (2010): pp. 135–58; Campbell, Rook, 'Staging Globalization for National Projects: Global Sport Markets and Elite Athletic Transnational Labor in Qatar', *International Review for the Sociology of Sport* 46, no. 1 (2010): pp. 45–60; Amara, Mahfoud, '2006 Qatar Asian Games: A "Modernization" Project from Above?' *Sport in Society* 8, no. 3 (2005): pp. 493–514.
2. Scharfenort, Nadine, 'Urban Development and Social Change in Qatar: The Qatar National Vision 2030 and the 2022 FIFA World Cup', *Journal of Arabian Studies: Arabia, the Gulf, and the Red Sea* 2, no. 2 (2012): p. 211.
3. Campbell, 'Staging Globalization', p. 48.
4. Amara, Mahfoud, 'Sport and Political Leaders in the Arab World', *Histoire@ Politique: politique, culture, société* 23, (2014), www.histoire-politique.fr, last accessed 1 November 2014; Ian, Henry, Mahfoud Amara and Mansour Al Tauqi, 'Arab Sport nationalism and the Pan-Arab Games', *International Review for the Sociology of Sport* 38, no. 3 (2003): pp. 295–310.
5. Darby, Paul, *Africa, Football and FIFA: Politics, Colonialism and Resistance*, Sport in the Global Society Series, London: Frank Cass, 2002, p. 6.
6. Giulianotti, Richard and Roland Robertson, 'Recovering the social: globalization, football and transnationalism', *Global Networks* 7, no. 2 (2007): p. 171.
7. Mandaville, Peter, *Transnational Muslim Politics*, London: Routledge, 2003, p. 15.
8. Ibid., p. 18.
9. Babar, Zahra, 'Migration Policy and Governance in the GCC: A Regional Perspective', *Labor Mobility: An Enabler for Sustainable Development*, Emirates Center for Strategic Studies and Research, 2013, p. 122.
10. Maguire, Joseph, 'Sport Labor Migration Research Revisited', *Journal of Sport and Social Issues* 28, no. 4 (2004): p. 478.
11. See Carter, Thomas F., 'Re-placing Sport Migrants: Moving beyond the institutional structures informing international sport migration', *International Review for the Sociology of Sport* 48, no. 1 (2013): pp. 66–82; Falcous, Mark, and Joseph Maguire, 'Globetrotters and Local Heroes? Labor Migration, Basketball, and Local Identities', *Sociology of Sport Journal* 22 (2005): pp. 137–57; Takahashi, Yoshio, and John Horne, 'Moving with the Bat and the Ball: preliminary reflections on the migration of Japanese baseball labor', *International Review for the Sociology of Sport* 41, no. 1 (2006): pp. 79–88.
12. See Maguire, Joseph, *Global Sport: Identities, Societies, Civilisations*, Cambridge, MA: Polity, 1999; Magee, Jonathan and John Sugden, 'The World at their Feet:

Professional Football and International Labor Migration', *Journal of Sport and Social Issues* 26, no. 4 (2002): pp. 421–37.

13. See Bromberger, Christian, 'Foreign Footballers, Cultural Dreams, and Community Identity in some North-Western Mediterranean Cities', in *The Global Sports Arena: Athletic Talent Migration in an Interdependent World*, John Bale and Joseph Maguire (eds), London: Frank Cass, 1994, pp. 171–82; Lanfranchi, Pierre and Matthew Taylor, *Moving with the Ball: the Migration of Professional Footballers*, London: Palgrave Macmillan, 2001; Magee and Sugden, 'The World at their Feet', pp. 421–37.

14. Darby, Paul, 'Ethnographie des académies de football au Ghana', *Afrique Contemporaine: L'Afrique, la mondialisation, et le ballon rond* 233, no. 1 (2010): pp. 77–87.

15. Cricket offers a similar pattern of migration today with the business growth of cricket in the Indian sub-continent, which indeed explains why the International Cricket Council moved to Dubai Sport City.

16. *Deutsche Welle*, 'Qatar's foreign legion primed for handball date with Germany', 27 Jan. 2015, http://www.dw.de/qatars-foreign-legion-primed-for-handball-date-with-germany/a-18219900, last accessed 1 Mar. 2015.

17. Amara, *Sport, Politics and Society in the Arab World*, p. 94.

18. Smith, Andrew, 'The Development of 'Sports-City' Zones and their Potential Value as Tourism Resources for Urban Areas', *European Planning Studies* 18, no. 3 (2010): p. 365.

19. Ibid., p. 405.

20. Aspire, 'Aspire Football Dreams', http://www.aspire.qa/Sports/AspireFootball Dreams/Pages/AspireFootballDreams.aspx., last accessed 5 Jan. 2015.

21. ESPN.com, 'Behind Qatar's football success', 23 Dec. 2010, http://espn.go.com/sports/soccer/news/_/id/5933045/how-qatar-became-player-world-soccer, last accessed 10 Jan. 2011.

22. *The Scotsman*, 'Madjid Bougherra: "I'd play at Rangers for free"', 13 Jan. 2014, http://www.scotsman.com/sport/football/spfl-lower-divisions/madjid-bougherra-i-d-play-at-rangers-for-free-1-3265774, last accessed 1 Nov. 2014.

23. Interview with *La Gazette du Fennec*, 23 Feb. 2013, http://www.youtube.com/watch?v=LMJdeNffDlY, last accessed 30 Dec. 2016.

24. Saudi Arabian Football Federation (www.thesaff.com.sa); UAE Arabian Gulf League (http://web.agleague.ae/ar); Qatar Football Association (http://www.qfa.com.qa/).

25. The club paid £38 million for his transfer, according to estimates. He earned £191,000 a week, tax-free and could have potentially earned bonuses of up to £244,000 a year. Source: Goal.com, 'The Goal Rich List 2013', 20 Feb. 2013, http://www.goal.com/en-us/slideshow/2467/38/title/the-goal-rich-list-2013, last accessed 30 Dec. 2016.

26. A former Paris Saint-Germain player who signed for Al-Gharafa on an eighteen-month contract. Doha News, 'Former PSG Player Nene Arrives in Qatar to Finalize $14.7 Million Move to Al Gharafa', 15 Jan. 2014, http://dohanews.co/former-psg-player-nene-arrives-in-qatar-to-finalize/, last accessed 1 Feb. 2014.
27. Translated from French: *Le Monde*, 'Abdeslam Ouaddou: Le Qatar m'a traité comme un esclave', 22 Apr. 2013, http://www.lemonde.fr/sport/article/2013/04/22/le-qatar-m-a-traite-comme-un-esclave_3164114_3242.html#, last accessed 25 Apr. 2013.
28. *Umrah* is considered a small or minor pilgrimage, while *Hajj* is a major pilgrimage among Muslims. The *Umrah* is a pilgrimage that can be made any time of the year while Hajj is to be performed in the twelfth and final month in the Islamic Lunar Calendar, marking the end of the year.
29. After a professional career playing in France, England, Spain, and Qatar, as well as internationally for the Algerian national team, in 2010 Belmadi started his career as a coach with Lekhwiya in Qatar. He led the team to the title for two consecutive seasons (2010–12). He was appointed as head coach of the Qatari national team in 2014.
30. ESPN, 'Rashid Ramzi still might compete', 25 Oct. 2011, http://espn.go.com/olympics/trackandfield/story/_/id/7149151/disgraced-bahrain-runner-rashid-ramzi-compete-2012-london-olympics, last accessed 15 January 2013.
31. BBC Sport, 'Algerian Djamel Belmadi Appointed Qatar Coach', 17 Mar. 2014, http://www.bbc.co.uk/sport/0/football/26612328, last accessed 20 Mar. 2014.
32. *Libération*, 'Djamel Bouras, 26 ans, champion olympique de judo, accusé de dopage, clame son innocence', 17 Apr. 1998, http://www.liberation.fr/portrait/1998/04/17/djamel-bouras-26-ans-champion-olympique-de-judo-accuse-de-dopage-clame-son-innocence-verdict-demain-_233364, last accessed 12 Dec. 2015.
33. Translated from French: *Le Soir d'Algérie*, 'Ils sont des dizaines à exercer dans des clubs et des sélections de ce pays du golfe', 25 May 2009, http://www.djazairess.com/fr/lesoirdalgerie/83655, last accessed 30 May 2009.
34. Amara, Mahfoud, 'The Political Economy of Sport Broadcasting in the Arab World', in *Sport, Public Broadcasting, and Cultural Citizenship*, Jay Scherer and David Rowe (eds), London: Routledge, 2013.
35. See FIFA.com, 'Al Jazeera Sport buys broadcast rights to 2018 and 2022 FIFA World Cups™', 26 Jan. 2011, https://www.fifa.com/aboutfifa/organisation/news/newsid=1371497/, last accessed 1 Feb. 2012; *The National Business*, 'Al Jazeera wins Middle East TV rights to World Cups', 26 Jan. 2011, http://www.thenational.ae/business/media/al-jazeera-wins-middle-east-tv-rights-to-world-cups, last accessed 1 Feb. 2012.
36. Video of Issam Al-Shawali commentating during the final minutes of the play-off between Algeria and Egypt in Sudan to qualify for the 2010 FIFA World Cup, Al Jazeera Sport, http://www.youtube.com/watch?v=2AVwdo7_rTQ, last accessed 30 Dec. 2016.

37. El-Sakka, Abaher, 'Supporters à distance: les fans du Barça et du Real en Palestine', in *Jeunesses Arabes, du Maroc au Yémen: loisirs, cultures et politiques*, Laurent Bonnefoy and Myriam Catusse (eds), Paris: La Découverte, 2013: pp. 105–13.
38. Al Jazeera News, 'UAE journalists in Qatar pressured to quit', 9 Mar. 2014, http://www.aljazeera.com/news/middleeast/2014/03/saudi-uae-journalists-qatar-urged-quit-20143915551210408.html, last accessed 12 Mar. 2014.
39. The Saudi-owned Middle East Broadcasting Center (MBC) Group launched its own sport channel, MBC Pro Sports.
40. *Le Journal International*, 'Algeria: the Soccer Scandal', 19 Oct. 2013, http://www.lejournalinternational.fr/Algeria-the-soccer-scandal_a1376.html last accessed 12 Mar. 2014.
41. Translated from French: *Liberté*, 'Hafid Derradji, d'idole à... paria!', 14 Oct. 2013, http://www.liberte-algerie.com/actualite/hafid-derradji-d-idole-a-paria-ses-commentaires-ont-fait-reagir-la-toile-dz-208669, last accessed 2 Mar. 2014.
42. Translated from French: 'Lady' Benguenna is Algerian senior Al Jazeera news anchor and presenter Khadija Benguenna, ranked by Forbes among 100 most influential women in the Arab world. *Jeune Independent*, '"Printemps arabe", le Qatar, Al Jazeera, Hafid Derradji et "Lady" Benguenna L'empreinte algérienne pour frapper l'Algérie', 18 Oct. 2013, http://www.presse-dz.com/revue-de-presse/lempreinte-algerienne-pour-frapper-lalgerie, last accessed 2 March 2014.

11. ATTITUDES OF STUDENTS IN THE GCC REGION TOWARDS THE ARAB SPRING

1. The authors would like to thank the Center for International and Regional Studies at Georgetown University's School of Foreign Service, Qatar, for the funding of this project. Special thanks go to Mehran Kamrava, Zahra Babar and all participants in Arab Migrant Community Working Group workshops in Doha. The authors also thank Sara Abdallah for excellent research assistance.
2. The growth in the population of young people aged 15–24 in the MENA region was 88 per cent in 2010, double that of 44 per cent in 1980; Roudi, Farzaneh, 'Youth Population & Unemployment in the Middle East & North Africa', Population Reference Bureau, 2011.
3. Khondker, Habibul Haque, 'Role of the New Media in the Arab Spring', *Globalizations* 8, no. 5 (2011): pp. 675–79.
4. Malik, Adeel and Bassem Awadallah, 'The Economics of the Arab Spring', *World Development* 45, (2013): pp. 296–313.
5. Kuhn, Randall, 'On the Role of Human Development in the Arab Spring', *Population and Development Review* 38, no. 4 (2012): pp. 649–83.
6. Campante, Filipe and Davin Chor, 'Why was the Arab World Poised for Revolution? Schooling, Economic Opportunities, and the Arab Spring', *The Journal of Economic*

    Perspectives 26, no. 2 (2012): pp. 167–87. Randall, *On the Role of Human Development in the Arab Spring*.

7. See Appendix for the full text of the survey.
8. Malit, Froilan and Ali Al Youha, 'Labor Migration in the United Arab Emirates: Challenges and Responses', Migration Policy Institute, September 2013, http://www.migrationpolicy.org/article/labor-migration-united-arab-emirates-challenges-and-responses, last accessed 30 Jan. 2014.
9. The Arab Barometer was established in 2005 as a way of collecting data in several Arab countries across different annual migration waves.
10. Michael Hoffman and Amaney Jamal, 'The Youth and the Arab Spring: Cohort Differences and Similarities', *Middle East Law and Governance* 4, no. 1 (2012): pp. 168–88.
11. Ibid.
12. ECO 201 is not a pre-requisite for ECO 202, or vice versa. Students can take either one first. Also, very rarely do students take both during the same semester.
13. On 3 July 2013 the Egyptian army removed Mohamed Morsi from power following several days of protests. On 21 August surface-to-surface missiles carrying the chemical agent sarin struck several of the Ghouta suburbs, such as Markaz Rif Dimashq district in Damascus. For more information see Wedeman, Ben, Reza Sayah and Matt Smith, 'Coup topples Egypt's Morsy; deposed president under "house arrest"', CNN, 4 July 2013, http://edition.cnn.com/2013/07/03/world/meast/egypt-protests/index.html?hpt=hp_t1, last accessed 16 Apr. 2014; and United Nations, 'United Nations Mission to Investigate Allegations of the Use of Chemical Weapons in the Syrian Arab Republic: Report on the Alleged Use of Chemical Weapons in the Ghouta Area of Damascus on 21 August 2013', http://www.un.org/disarmament/content/slideshow/Secretary_General_Report_of_CW_Investigation.pdf, last accessed 16 Apr. 2014.
14. Westoff, Charles and Tomas Frejka, 'Religiousness and Fertility among European Muslims', *Population and Development Review* 33, no. 4 (2007): pp. 785–809.
15. See Table 11.2 notes for further details.
16. Western countries included: Australia, Canada, France, Holland, Japan, Norway, Spain, Sweden, Switzerland, UK and US.
17. Proxy 1 is a student waking up between 4 and 6 am. Proxy 2 is a student ranking religious books as the highest preferred type of books. Proxy 3 is Proxies 1 and 2 together. Proxy 4 is a student expressing an interest in having more than four children in the future.
18. For reasons of space, we omitted several of the tables and figures which provide more information on these findings. The results are available from the authors on request.

INDEX

Abu Dhabi, United Arab Emirates
   Ferrari World, 222
   National Oil Company, 123
   Palestinian migrants, 113, 115, 129
   Sport TV, 229, 230, 232
   sports industry, 217, 223, 228
Abyan, Yemen, 153, 164, 168
adventure seekers, 61
affirmative action, *see* nationalisation programmes
Ahmad, Attiya, 87
al-Ain, United Arab Emirates, 113
Alami, Zuheir, 117
alcohol, 202
Alexandria, Egypt, 88
Algeria, 224, 228, 229, 230
Alkobaisi, Saad, 46
Allman, James, 135
Amanat Al Asimah, Yemen, 152, 154, 164
American Federation of Teachers, 50
American University of Sharjah (AUS), 237–45
Amran, Yemen, 152, 164, 168
Anderson, Sonny, 221
Anti-Doping Laboratory Qatar (ADLQ), 228, 232
Aouita, Saïd, 229

Arab Agreement for Mobility of Arab Labour No. 2 (1967), 4
Arab Barometer, 236
Arab Declaration of Principles on the Movement of Manpower (1984), 41–2
Arab Economic Unity Agreement (1964), 4
Arab Labor Organization, 26, 41
Arab League, 116
   Casablanca Protocol (1965), 131
   Mobility Agreement (1975), 20, 41
Arab nationalism, 42, 90, 92, 129
Arab Spring (2010–11), 17, 45, 61, 235–45
   Bahrain, 203
   and education, 124, 236
   Kuwait, 87
   Lebanon, 237
   Qatar, 230, 231
   Syria, 237
   Tunisia, 229, 232, 236, 244
   United Arab Emirates, 17, 112–13, 124, 236–45
   Yemen, 237
Arab Tech, 117
Arab–Israeli conflict, 122
   Arab–Israeli War (1948), 117, 131

INDEX

Six Day War (1967), 42, 91, 131
Suez Crisis (1956), 42
al-Arabi SC, 224, 226
Arafat, Yasser, 111
Asian Athletics Championships, 227
Asian Football Confederation (AFC), 224
Asian migrants
  abuse of, 169
  assimilation, 8
  citizenship, 8, 23
  cultural degradation, fear of, 8, 23, 41
  dependants, 31
  domestic workers, 22, 169, 170, 172
  family unification, 22
  and Gulf War (1990-91), 43
  Kuwait, 4, 23, 72, 86, 97, 99, 198
  manufacturing, 190
  Qatar, 4, 27
  Saudi Arabia, 3-4, 138, 139
  United Arab Emirates, 4, 42, 43, 87, 111, 115, 122
  unskilled workers, 11, 22, 23, 37, 170, 172
  and wage differentials, 5, 6, 7, 8, 22
  women, 15, 23, 169, 170, 177, 178
  Yemen, 138
Asian migration, 3-4, 5, 6, 7, 8, 9
Aspetar Orthopaedic and Sports Medicine Hospital, Qatar, 227-8, 232
Aspire, 222, 223, 232
Asyut, Egypt, 88, 99
Australia, 14, 129

Bahrain
  Arab Spring (2011), 203
  Asian migrants, 3-4
  British Protectorate (1880-1971), 115
  demographics, 171

female migrants, 170, 175-8, 181, 195
Jordanian migrants, 190
Lebanese migrants, 181
Maghrebi migrants, 223, 227
nationalisation programme, 21
Qatar, migration to, 30
skilled workers, 170, 175-8, 181, 195
sports industry, 217-19, 222, 223, 227
unemployment, 20
baksheesh, 95, 97
balance of power, 24
Baluchistan, 72
Bangladesh, 99
Barcelona, FC, 221, 230
Batistuta, Gabriel, 223
Batroun, Lebanon, 211
al-Bayda, Yemen, 164
Bedouin, 98
Beijing Olympics (2008), 227
beIN Sports, 229, 230-31, 233
Belhadj, Nadir, 224
Belmadi, Jamal, 228
Belounis, Zahir, 224, 232
Ben Ali, Zine el-Abidine, 229, 232
Benguenna, Khadija, 231
Berbers, 224
'Beyond Labour' (Ahmad), 87
Bidoon, 3, 86
Birks, J.S., 137, 140, 144, 164, 165
de Boer, Frank, 223
Bolly, Mathis, 227
Bosnia, 222
Boudiaf, Karim, 226
Bouguerra, Majid, 224
Bouras, Djamel, 228
Boyd, Monica, 201
brain drain, 44, 173
Brazil, 221, 224, 232

INDEX

Brubaker, Rogers, 98
Burkina Faso, 231
Byblos, Lebanon, 211

Cairo, Egypt, 88
camel racing, 229
Camp David Accords (1978), 93
Campbell, Rook, 218
Canada, 14, 107, 113, 114, 121–2, 129–30
Carter, Thomas, 221
Casablanca Protocol (1965), 131
categories of practice, 98
chain migration, 101, 201
Chalabi, Hakim, 228
Chamakh, Marouane, 227
Chapman, David, 61
Chapman, Murray, 209
Chatah, Mohamad, 201
chemical weapons, 238
Cheniouni, Abdelkader, 228
chi-square analysis, 151
Christianity
    Egypt, 86, 107
    Lebanon, 171, 208, 210, 213
    Palestine, 171
    Syria, 171
circular migration, 136, 203, 209
citizenship, 8, 12, 13, 14, 23, 24
    Australia, 14, 129
    Canada, 14, 114, 129, 130
    and cheap labour, 8, 23, 24
    Jordan, 117, 120, 130, 131
    Kuwait, 13, 66, 69, 72, 100, 205
    New Zealand, 129
    Palestinians, 14, 113, 114, 117, 118, 119, 120, 125, 129–31
    Saint Kitts and Nevis, 130
    United Arab Emirates, 14, 113, 114–16, 118, 125, 130
    United States, 14, 114, 129

Clásico, El, 230
coffeehouses, 85, 92, 104
Coles, A.J., 116
Colton, Nora Ann, 136–7, 144–5, 147–8, 164–5
Commonwealth, 40, 130
Cooper, Frederick, 98
Coptic Christianity, 86, 107
corruption, 17, 44, 95, 97, 243
cosmopolitanism, 127, 221, 226
Crawford, Edward, 115
crime, 97
Crystal Palace F.C., 227
Cuba, 222

Dakhliya, Egypt, 89
Dave, Chetan, 62
demographics, 2, 6, 8, 11, 23, 171–2
dependants, 31, 52, 178
Derradji, Hafid, 230–31, 233
development aid, 6, 39, 89
Diab, Tarek, 230, 232
Dito, Mohammed, 24
Djibouti, 27
Docquier, Frederic, 204
Doha, Qatar, 51, 217, 222, 223, 228
domestic workers, 15, 32
    Asian, 22, 169, 170, 172
    Hadrami, 13, 66, 70, 72, 84
doping, 227, 232
Drake and Skull, 117
Dubai, United Arab Emirates, 96
    female migrants, 181, 182, 187, 191, 194
    financial crisis (2008), 120–21
    Hadrami migrants, 81
    Indian migrants, 87
    Lebanese migrants, 181, 182, 187, 191, 194
    Madbouh assassination (2010), 124
    Media City, 229

INDEX

Motor City, 222
Palestinian migrants, 113, 115–16, 120–21, 124, 127, 129
Sports City, 222
sports industry, 217, 223, 228
Sports TV, 229, 232
Düsseldorf, Fortuna, 227

education; teacher migration, 4–6, 12, 39–63, 90
and Arab Spring, 124, 236
challenges, 54–5
commitment, 56–7
Egypt, 12, 32, 40, 45–6, 48, 49, 52, 56, 90, 97, 101
Fiji, 43–4
India, 44, 61
insecurity, 46, 59–60
international tests, 47, 63
Jordan, 32, 40, 48, 49, 52, 116
Kuwait, 72, 78, 90, 101, 204
Lebanon, 32, 49, 181–4, 204, 207
motivations for migration, 43–5, 52–3, 57–9
Palestine, 32, 45, 48, 116, 119, 120, 123, 126
perceptions of teachers, 50–61
permanent residency, 60–61
private tutoring, 47, 48, 97
process of migration, 53
Qatar, 12, 26, 32, 39–63
recognition, 60–61
social integration, 54
South Africa, 44
Sudan, 32, 49
Syria, 32, 40, 48, 49
Trucial States (1820–1971), 116
United Arab Emirates, 12, 39–63, 48, 49, 119, 123, 124, 126
United Kingdom, 44
women, 181–4, 193

Yemen, 137, 147, 148, 154, 156, 158, 159, 161, 164
Egypt
Arab nationalism, 42, 90, 92
Arab–Israeli War (1967), 91
baksheesh, 95, 97
and balance of power, 24
Camp David Accords (1978), 93
Central Agency for Public Mobilization and Statistics (CAPMAS), 93
Christianity, 86, 107
coffeehouses, 85, 92, 104
coup d'état (2013), 89, 238
education, 12, 32, 45–6, 48, 49, 49, 52, 56, 90, 97, 101
emigration policy, 5, 92
Gulf War (1990–91), 42, 93
Infitah (1973–81), 92
Iraq, migration to, 93
Kuwait, migration to, 13, 73, 85–109, 178, 180
Ministry of Education, 45
Ministry of State for Emigration Affairs, 92
Muslim Brotherhood, 108, 230, 236, 244
Palestinian migrants, 106, 118, 119, 120, 131
Qatar, migration to, 27, 28–9, 31–4, 41; teachers, 45–6, 48–9, 52, 56
refugees, 9, 117
remittance flows, 7, 45
Revolution (2011), 17, 109, 230, 236, 237
Saudi Arabia, migration to, 93
Scientific Academy, 89
skilled workers, 12, 31–5, 94, 178
socialism, 42
sports industry, 222, 230
Syrian migrants, 9

INDEX

teacher migration, 45–6, 48, 49, 52, 56, 90, 97, 101
United Arab Emirates, migration to, 41, 42, 45–6, 48, 52, 124, 239
unskilled workers, 32, 34, 37, 180
women, 178, 190
Eid, 75, 210
Ennahda, 232
entrepreneurial citizenship, 223
Ethiopia, 160
Everton F.C., 227
exceptionalism, 9, 11, 17, 87, 170, 203
Ezzaki, Badou, 230

Facebook, 209
Failaka Island, Kuwait, 96
family unification, 22, 174, 178
    Hadramis in Kuwait, 77–80
    Lebanese migrants, 183
    Palestinians in UAE, 120, 127
    Yemenis in Saudi Arabia, 139
Farwaniya, Kuwait, 104
Fatah, 127
Fergany, Nader, 138, 164
Ferrari World, Abu Dhabi, 222
FIFA (Fédération Internationale de Football Association), 220, 221, 229, 231, 232
Fiji, 43–4
financial crisis (2008), 120–21
football, 206–7, 214, 220–33
France, 202, 221, 222, 224, 226, 228, 229
freedom of expression, 229

Gallup, 173
Gardner, Andrew, 34
Gaza Strip, 113, 117, 119, 120, 128
    Gaza–Jericho Agreements (1994), 120
    Gaza War (2008–9), 124

generational divide, 14
    Hadramis in Kuwait, 68–71, 75–7, 80–84
    Palestinians in UAE, 114, 125–8
Geneva Refugee Convention (1951), 8–9
al-Gharafa SC, 224
Gharbiya, Egypt, 89
Ghribi, Habiba, 227
Girgis, Maurice, 22
Giulianotti, Richard, 219–20
Giza, Egypt, 88
Glick-Schiller, Nina, 199
global cities, 220, 222
globalisation, 9, 10, 114, 173, 194, 219, 222
glocalisation, 218, 230
González, Raúl, 224
Greece, 99
Grogger, Jeffrey, 204
Guedioura, Adlène, 227
el-Guerrouj, Hicham, 229
Gulf exceptionalism, 9, 11, 17, 87, 170, 203
Gulf nationalism, 23
Gulf News, 46
Gulf War (1990–91), 7–8, 42–3, 96
    Egyptians, 42, 92–3, 106, 107
    Hadramis, 69, 81, 83
    Jordanians, 8, 42, 124
    Palestinians, 8, 13–14, 42–3, 106, 111, 117, 123–4, 129
    Saudi Arabia, 8, 135, 136, 139, 140
    Syrians, 8
    United Arab Emirates, 112, 113, 123–4
    Yemenis, 8, 42, 69, 81, 83, 124, 135, 136, 139, 140
Hadramawt, Yemen, 12, 69, 70, 71, 75, 78, 82, 152, 153, 164
Hadramis, 12–13, 65–84

301

INDEX

attitude survey, 67
citizenship, 66, 69
demographics, 67
education, 78
family, 77–80
generations, 68–71, 75–7, 80–84
good reputation, 66, 68, 69, 84
Gulf War (1990–91), 69, 81, 83
hierarchy, 68, 71
'house-to-house' migration, 72
human trafficking, 71
income, 78–9, 79
in Indonesia, 67
'izbahs, 67, 71, 77–9
kafala, 66, 71, 74–7
kafil, 74–5, 83
in Malaysia, 67
marriage, 78–80, 103
as model minority, 66, 68, 84
mu'azzibs, 13, 66, 68–71, 73–7, 79, 80, 82, 84
and nostalgia, 73
rabah, 68, 69, 81
remittance flows, 69, 71, 78–9, 82–3
in Saudi Arabia, 81, 84, 152
sibyan, 72, 76–7
social capital, 66
standard view of, 67
success of, 67, 68
talabat, 78–9
in Tanzania, 67
'uggal, 68, 69, 71, 75, 83
in United Arab Emirates, 81
Hajj, 226
Hajjah, Yemen, 151–2, 154, 164, 165
Hamas, 124, 228
al-Hami, Hadramawt, 71
handball, 222
Hanson, Gordon, 204
Hassan, Khaled El Sayad, 23
Hawally, Kuwait, 85–6

healthcare, 89, 98
Hezbollah, 228
Hierro, Fernando, 223
Hill, Allan, 135
Horn of Africa, 134, 160
horse racing, 229
al-Hudaydah, Yemen, 151–2, 154, 164, 165, 168
human rights, 10
human trafficking, 15, 71, 169
humanitarian crises
  Horn of Africa, 160
  Palestine, 112, 128
  Syria, 9, 199, 201, 237
  Yemen, 133, 141–2, 160, 165

Ibb, Yemen, 152
IBM, 50
ideal city, 218
India
  education, 44, 61
  Kuwait, migration to, 85, 86, 99, 213
  United Arab Emirates, migration to, 87, 115, 239
Indonesia, 67, 229
inequality, 2
Infitah (1973–81), 92
insecurity, 13, 46, 59–60, 70, 109, 117, 132
integration, 2, 10, 22
  Asian migrants, 8, 37
  Egyptians in Kuwait, 93, 95, 109
  Lebanese in Kuwait, 16, 198, 200, 205–7, 214
  Palestinians in UAE, 14, 113–15, 125–6
  teachers, 41, 50, 51, 54
International Association of Athletics Federations, 227
International Institute for Capacity Building in Africa, 40

INDEX

International Labour Organization (ILO), 92, 161
International Organization for Migration (IOM), 14, 106, 133, 134, 141–66, 205
International Teacher Mobility Survey, 50
Iosifides, Theodoros, 68
iqama, see residence permits
Iran, 90
Iraq
  and balance of power, 24
  Egyptian migrants, 93
  Gulf War (1990–91), *see* Gulf War
  human trafficking, 169
  Kuwait, migration to, 89
  Palestinian migrants, 123, 131
  Syrian refugees, 9
  women, 193
Israel
  Arab–Israeli War (1948), 117, 131
  Camp David Accords (1978), 93
  Gaza–Jericho Agreements (1994), 120
  Gaza War (2008–9), 124
  identity cards, 118, 128
  Lebanon War (2006), 182
  and refugees, 131
  Six Day War (1967), 42, 91, 131
  Suez Crisis (1956), 42
Jabriya, Kuwait, 86
el-Jaish Sports Club, 224, 230
al-Jawf, Yemen, 164
al-Jazeera, 229, 230, 231, 232
Jeune Indépendant, Le, 231
Jilib al-Shuyukh, Kuwait, 77, 86
Jizan, Saudi Arabia, 150–51
Jordan, 3, 5, 6, 7
  Arab–Israeli War (1967), 91
  Bahrain, migration to, 190
  citizenship, 117, 120, 130, 131

  education, 32, 40, 48, 49, 52, 116, 119
  emigration policy, 171
  Gulf War (1990–91), 8, 42, 124
  Kuwait, migration to, 85, 90, 91, 92, 180
  Ministry of Labour, 172
  Palestinian migrants, 117–21, 128–31, 171
  Qatar, migration to, 27, 29, 30, 32, 41, 49, 52
  refugees, 9, 117
  skilled workers, 32–5
  Syrian migrants, 9
  teacher migration, 48, 49, 52, 116, 119
  unemployment, 193
  United Arab Emirates, migration to, 41, 48, 52, 129, 190, 239, 240
  women, 173, 180, 193, 195
kafala, 9, 10, 23, 26, 28
  Kuwait, 66, 71, 74–7, 91, 100–103, 106
  Saudi Arabia, 139
  United Arab Emirates, 115
kafil, 74–5, 83, 101, 102, 103
Kamal, Riad, 117
Kapiszewski, Andrzej, 122
al-Kass, 229, 232
KFC, 102
'Khaitan: Cairo in Kuwait', 85
Khalaf, Sulayman, 46
el-Khatib, Mounir, 117
Khoukhi, Boualem, 226
knowledge economy, 25–6
Kuwait, 85–109, 197–215
  Alien Residence Law (1959), 90
  anti-government demonstrations (1967), 42
  Arab Spring (2011), 87
  Arab–Israeli War protests (1967), 42

303

INDEX

Asian migrants, 3–4, 23, 72, 86, 97, 99, 198
Baluch migrants, 72
Bangladeshi migrants, 99
Bedouin, 98
Bidoon, 3, 86
citizenship, 13, 66, 69, 72, 100, 205
corruption, 95, 97
crime, 98
demographics, 171
development strategy, 89–91
education, 72, 78, 90, 101, 204
Egyptian migrants, 13, 73, 85–109, 178, 180
Failaka Island, 96
family unification, 77–80
female migrants, 170, 175–82, 195
Filipino migrants, 99
Greek migrants, 99
Gulf War (1990–91), *see* Gulf War
Hadar, 75, 98
Hadrami migrants, 12–13, 65–84
Hawally, 85–6
healthcare, 89, 98
hierarchies, 98–100
Indian migrants, 85, 86, 99, 213
Iranian migrants, 90
Iraqi migrants, 89
Jabriya, 86
Jilib al-Shuyukh, 77, 86
Jordanian migrants, 85, 90, 91, 92, 180
kafala, 66, 71, 74–7, 91, 100–103, 106
kafil, 74–5, 83, 101, 102, 103
Labour Law (1964), 90
Lebanese migrants, 16, 73, 83, 85, 90, 97, 99, 178, 180–82, 197–215
Ministry of Interior, 68, 75, 86
Ministry of Social Affairs and Labour, 100

nationalisation programme, 21, 202
Nationality Law (1959), 72, 90
Omani migrants, 72
otherness, 87, 98
Palestinian migrants, 8, 13–14, 83, 89–92, 98, 106, 111, 117, 123
protests, 42, 108
Qatar, migration to, 30
remittance flows, 210–13, 214
residence permits, 91, 100–103, 105
Salmiya, 85–6
Salwa, 86
sibyan, 72, 76–7
skilled workers, 23, 107, 170, 175–80, *176–7, 179*, 195, 197–215
Sri Lankan migrants, 99
Suez Crisis protests (1956), 42
Syrian migrants, 85, 89, 97, 178, 180
traffic, 85, 97–8
unemployment, 20
United Arab Republic protests (1959), 42
unskilled workers, 23, 100–101, 201
wasta, 75, 101, 212

Lahj, Yemen, 164
Lebanon, 197–215
  Arab Spring (2011), 237
  Bahrain, migration to, 181
  Chatah assassination (2013), 201
  Christianity, 171, 208, 210, 213
  Civil War (1975–90), 16, 199
  education, 32, 49, 181–4, 204
  Hezbollah, 228
  Israel–Hezbollah War (2006), 182
  Kuwait, migration to, 16, 73, 83, 85, 90, 99, 178, 180–2, 197–215
  Oman, migration to, 181
  Palestinian migrants, 117, 121, 127, 129, 130, 131
  Qatar, migration to, 27, 30, 32–5, 49, 181–2, 202, 203, 205

INDEX

remittance flows, 7, 210–13, 214
Saudi Arabia, migration to, 181, 182, 203, 206
Shi'a Islam, 124
skilled workers, 16, 32–5, 170, 178, 180–8, 190–91, 193–6, 197–215
Syrian migrants, 9
teacher migration, 49, 207
United Arab Emirates, migration to, 124, 127, 129, 181–2, 187, 203, 240
women, 170, 172–4, 178, 180–8, 190, 191, 193–6, 202–3
Leboeuf, Frank, 223
Lekhwiya SC, 224, 226, 228
Liberté, 231
Libya, 91, 236, 237
London, England, 220
2012 Olympics, 227
Longva, Anh Nga, 74

Maâloul, Nabil, 230
Madbouh, Mahmoud, 124
Madjer, Rabah, 229
Maghreb, 17, 218, 223–33
Maguire, Joseph, 220
al-Mahrah, Yemen, 153, 154, 164
al-Mahwit, Yemen, 151–2, 153, 164
Malaysia, 67
Manama, Bahrain, 217, 223
Mandaville, Peter, 220
Manik, Sandhana, 44
Mansoura, Egypt, 89
manufacturing, 32, 34, 36, 138, 174, 190
Marib, Yemen, 164, 168
marriage, 170, 172–4
 Egyptians in Kuwait, 103
 Hadramis in Kuwait, 78–80, 80
 Lebanon, 182–3, 191, 193, 194–5, 201

Maghreb, 174
Palestinians, 117, 119, 120, 126
Yemenis in Saudi Arabia, 136, 145
Massey, Douglas, 209
Mauritania, 27
MBC Pro Sport, 232
Mecca, Saudi Arabia, 150–51, 226
media, 229–33
Menjívar, Cecilia, 108
mercenaries, 221, 226
Mexico, 151, 165
middle class, 6
 Egypt, 90
 Kuwait, 72, 85
 Palestinians in UAE, 114, 115, 126, 127, 130
migratory cities, 220
Ministry of Education Egypt, 45
Ministry of Interior, Kuwait, 68, 75, 86
Ministry of Labour
 Jordan, 172
 Qatar, 12, 28, 30, 31, 34
 Saudi Arabia, 21
Ministry of Social Affairs and Labour, Kuwait, 100
Ministry of State for Emigration Affairs, Egypt, 92
Montenegro, 222
Morocco
 human trafficking, 169, 172–3
 Qatar, migration to, 27–8
 remittance flows, 7
 sports industry, 223, 227, 228, 229, 230
 unemployment, 194
 United Arab Emirates, migration to, 42, 174
 women, 169, 172–3, 174
Morsi, Mohammed, 89, 238
mu'azzibs, 13, 66, 68–71, 73–7, 79, 80, 82, 84

305

INDEX

Muslim Brotherhood, 108, 230, 236, 244

Nasser, Gamal Abdel, 90, 91
National Bank of Kuwait (NBK), 202, 203, 207
national security, 22, 27, 92
nationalisation programmes, 21, 42, 92, 196, 202, 218
nationalism, 23, 42, 90, 92, 129
naturalisation, 12, 14, 23, 106, 114, 205, 223
Nenê, Anderson, 224
neoliberalism, 7, 23
New York, United States, 220
New York Times, 190
New Zealand, 129
Nhavoto, Arnaldo, 40
nitaqat system, 15, 21, 140–41, 147–8, 151, 160–64, 167, 196
nomadic cosmopolitans, 221, 226
North Yemen (1962–90), 134, 135, 140, 153, 164, 165
Nusseibeh, Zaki, 117
NVivo, 51

Observatoire Universitaire de la Réalité Socio-Economique (OURSE), 174
Offshore Powerboat Championships, 229
oil, 2, 5, 10, 16, 39, 122, 135, 174, 222
   1970s boom, 41, 91, 115, 198–9
   1980s market collapse, 6, 42
   Kuwait, 91
   Moroccan migrants, 174
   Saudi Arabia, 135, 139, 172
   United Arab Emirates, 123
Olympic Games, 221, 223, 227, 228
Oman
   Kuwait, migration to, 72
   nationalisation programme, 21, 196

Qatar, migration to, 30
   unemployment, 20
Ong, Aihwa, 114
Operation Desert Storm (1991), 93
otherness, 87, 98
Ouaddou, Abdeslam, 226

Pakistan, 239
Palestine, 3, 12, 13–14, 111–32
   Arab nationalism, 42, 129
   Arab–Israeli War, First (1948), 117, 131
   Arab–Israeli War, Third (1967), 91, 131
   Australia, migration to, 14, 129
   Canada, migration to, 14, 107, 113, 114, 121–2, 129–30
   Children's Relief Fund, 113
   Christianity, 171
   citizenship, 14, 113, 114, 117, 118, 119, 120, 125, 129–31
   education, 32, 45, 48, 116, 119, 120, 123, 126
   Egypt, migration to, 106, 118, 119, 120, 131
   family unification, 120, 127
   Fatah, 127
   Gaza War (2008–9), 124
   Gaza–Jericho Agreements (1994), 120
   generational divide, 114, 125–8
   Gulf War (1990–91), 8, 13–14, 42, 106, 111, 117, 123–4, 129
   Hamas, 124, 228
   humanitarian support, 112, 128
   Iraq migration to, 123, 131
   Israeli identity cards, 118, 128
   Jordan, migration to, 117–21, 128–31, 171
   Kuwait, migration to, 8, 13–14, 83, 89–92, 98, 111, 117, 123–4

INDEX

Lebanon, migration to, 117, 121, 127, 129, 130, 131
New Zealand, migration to, 129
passports, 113, 118, 119, 120, 129, 131
Qatar, migration to, 27, *29*, 30, 32, 41
refugees, 117, 130–31, 120, 127, 130–31
remittance flows, 45
skilled workers, 14, *32–4*, 35
socialism, 42
sports industry, 230
Syria, migration to, 117, 118, 129, 131
teacher migration, 45, 48, 116, 119, 123
third culture, 121, 126
Trucial States, migration to, 112, 115–17
United Arab Emirates, migration to, 13–14, 41, 48, 111–32, 240
United States, migration to, 14, 113, 114, 129–30
women, 173, 193
Yemen, migration to, 131
Palestine Liberation Organization (PLO), 8, 111, 116, 117, 129
Palestinian Authority, 113, 118, 120, 127, 129
pan-Arabism, 4, 20, 22, 90, 132
Paris, France, 202
passports
   confiscation of, 45
   Jordan, 118, 119, 131
   Kuwait, 100
   Palestinians, 113, 118, 119, 120, 129, 131
   United Arab Emirates, 113
permanent temporariness, 13, 87, 100–101, 104

Philippines, 99
Pizza Hut, 102
pork, 202
private tutoring, 47, 48
production of space, 87, 95
Programme for International Student Assessment (PISA), 47, 63
protests, 42, 108
Prothero, R. Mansell, 209
Public Authority for Civil Information (PACI), 175, 178

Qatar, 19–37, 197
   Anti-Doping Laboratory Qatar (ADLQ), 228, 232
   Asian migrants, 3–4, 27, 31, 37, 43
   Aspetar Orthopaedic and Sports Medicine Hospital, 227–8, 232
   Aspire, 222, 223, 232
   Bahraini migrants, 30
   beIN Sports, 229, 230–31, 233
   demographics, 171
   dependants, 30, 31
   Djiboutian migrants, 27
   education sector, 12, 26, 39–63, 48, 49
   Egyptian migrants, *see under* Egypt
   Emirati migrants, 30
   handball team, 222
   al-Jazeera, 229, 230, 231, 232
   Jordanian migrants, 27, 29, 30, 32–5, 41, 49, 52
   kafala, 26, 28
   al-Kass, 229, 232
   knowledge economy, 25–6
   Kuwaiti migrants, 30
   Labour Law, 19
   Lebanese migrants, 27, 30, 32–5, 49, 181–2, 202, 203, 205
   Maghrebi migrants, 17, 223–33
   Mauritanian migrants, 27

INDEX

Ministry of Labour, 12, 28, 30, 31, 34
Moroccan migrants, 27–8
National Football Team, 226
national security, 27
National Sports Medicine Program, 228
National Vision 2030, 26
nationalisation programme, 21, 26
Omani migrants, 30
Palestinian migrants, 27, 29, 30, 32–5, 41, 49
Saudi migrants, 30
skilled workers, 25, 26, 31–4
Somali migrants, 27
sports industry, 17, 217–19, 222–33
Stars League, 226, 228
Statistics Authority, 30
Sudanese migrants, 27, 28–9, 31–5, 41, 49
Syrian migrants, 27, 28–9, 32–5, 49, 52
Tunisian migrants, 27
unemployment, 20–21
unskilled workers, 19, 25, 32, 34
World Cup, 229
Yemeni migrants, 27, 41
QSR International, 51
al-Quds University, 129

Ramadan, 113
Ramzi, Rashid, 227
Rangers F.C., 224
Rapoport, Hillel, 204
Ras al-Khaimeh, United Arab Emirates, 51, 113, 116
al-Rashidi, Thekra, 202
Ravenstein, Ernst Georg, 43
Raymah, Yemen, 164
Real Madrid C.F., 230
Red Crescent, 129
refugees, 4
  Palestinian, 117, 130–31, 120, 127, 130–31
  Somali, 160
  Syrian, 9, 199
remittance flows, 7, 45, 210–11
  Egypt, 7, 45
  Hadramis, 69, 71, 78–9, 82–3
  Kuwait, 210–13
  Lebanon, 7, 210–13, 214
  Morocco, 7
  Palestine, 45
  Saudi Arabia, 7, 14–15, 137, 157–61, 165–6, 168
  social remittance, 211, 213
  Syria, 45
  Yemen, 14–15, 45, 69, 71, 78–9, 82–3, 137, 157–61, 165–6, 168
residence permits, 91, 100–103, 105
Ridge, Natasha, 62
Robertson, Roland, 219–20
Romário, 223
Ronaldinho, 221
Russell, Sharon Stanton, 90
Russia, 229

Sadat, Anwar, 91, 92
al-Sadd SC, 224, 232
Saifi, Rafik, 229–30
Saint Kitts and Nevis, 130
Saint Mark's Coptic Orthodox Church, Hawally, 86
Saint-Joseph University, Beirut, 174
el-Sakka, Abaher, 230
Salmiya, Kuwait, 85–6
Salwa, Kuwait, 86
Sana'a, Yemen, 142, 164
Santos FC, 232
Saudi Arabia, 133–66, 202
  Arab–Israeli War (1967), 91
  Asian migrants, 3–4, 138, 139

INDEX

demographics, 172
Directorate General of Border Guards, 140, 143
Egyptian migrants, 93
female migrants, 173, 196
Gulf War (1990–91), 8, 135, 136, 139, 140
Hadrami migrants, 81, 84
Lebanese migrants, 181, 182, 203, 206
MBC Pro Sport, 232
Ministry of Labour, 21
nitaqat system, 15, 21, 140–41, 147–8, 151, 160–64, 167, 196
Qatar, migration to, 30
remittance flows, 7, 14–15, 137, 157–61, 165–6, 168
sports industry, 223, 226, 230, 232
unemployment, 20–21, 140
United Arab Emirates, migration to, 239
Yemeni Civil War (2015–), 134
Yemeni migrants, 8, 14–15, 81, 84, 133–66
Scharfenort, Nadine, 217
Scotland, 224
Second World War (1939–45), 41, 45
Şenyürekli, Aysem 108
settlers, 221, 227
sex industry, 15, 169
sexual harassment, 128
Shah, Nasra, 205
Shami, Soha, 62
Sharjah, United Arab Emirates, 116
Sharmah, Rashmi, 44
Sharqiya, Egypt, 89
al-Shawali, Issam, 230
Shi'a Islam, 124
al-Shihr, Hadramawt, 71
Silatech Index, 173
Six Day War (1967), 42, 91, 131

al-Siyasah, 91
skilled workers, 5, 10, 11–12, 16, 22
  Bahrain, 170, 175–8, 181, 195
  and citizenship, 12
  education sector, *see under* education
  Egyptian, 12, 31–5, 94, 178
  Kuwait, 23, 107, 170, 175–80, 195, 197–215
  Lebanese, 16, 32–5, 170, 178, 180–8, 190–91, 197–215
  Palestinians, 14, 118, 119, 126, 127, 130
  Qatar, 12, 25, 26, 31–2
  Syrian, 32–5, 178
  United Arab Emirates, 12, 14, 118, 119, 126, 127, 130
  women, 15, 23, 169–96
Skype, 209
smallpox, 89
Smith, Andrew, 222
Smith, Ransford, 40
snowballing, 89, 200
social remittance, 211, 213
socialism, 4, 22, 42
Sohag, Egypt, 88
Somalia, 27, 160
Souakri, Salima, 229
South Africa, 44
South Yemen (1967–90), 134, 135, 140, 153
space, production of, 87, 95
Spain, 222, 224, 230
sponsorship, see *kafala*
Sporton, Deborah, 68
sports industry, 17, 217–33
Sri Lanka, 99
Stevenson, Thomas, 135, 136, 139, 144, 145
strikes, 42
structural adjustment plans, 194
structural unemployment, 6

INDEX

Sudan, 3
  education, 32
  Qatar, migration to, 27, 28–9, 29, 31, 41, 49
  skilled workers, 31–5
  teacher migration, 49
  United Arab Emirates, migration to, 41
Suez Crisis (1956), 42
Syria, 3, 5, 6, 7
  and balance of power, 24
  chemical weapons, 238
  Christianity, 171
  Civil War (2011–), 9, 199, 201, 237
  education, 32, 40, 45, 48, 49, 52
  Gulf War (1990–91), 8
  human trafficking, 169
  Kuwait, migration to, 85, 89, 97, 178, 180
  Palestinian migrants, 117, 118, 129, 131
  Qatar, migration to, 27, 28–9, 32, 41, 49, 52
  refugees, 9, 199
  remittance flows, 45
  skilled workers, 32–5, 178
  teacher migration, 40, 45, 48, 49, 52
  United Arab Emirates, migration, 41, 42, 48, 49, 52, 124, 129, 240
  unskilled workers, 32
  women, 173, 180, 193
system theory, 220–21

Ta'iz, Yemen, 135, 168
Tabari, Khaldoun, 117
Tanta, Egypt, 89
Tanzania, 67
teacher migration, *see under* education
Temporary Migration Phenomenon, 41
temporary worker programmes, 10
terrorism, 201

third culture, 121, 126
Tokyo, Japan, 220
translocalism, 220
transnationalism 199–200, 219–20
Traoré, Lacina, 227
Trends in International Mathematics and Science Study (TIMSS), 47, 63
Trucial States (1820–1971), 112, 115–17, 122, 132
tuberculosis, 89
Tunisia
  Arab Spring (2010–11), 229, 232, 236, 244
  Qatar, migration to, 27
  sports industry, 227, 228, 230, 232
  unemployment, 193
  United Arab Emirates, migration to, 42, 124
  women, 172, 174, 190
Turkey
  Syrian refugees, 9
  United States, migration to, 108
al-Tuwal, Saudi Arabia, 133, 134, 141–2, 145, 164
Twitter, 209

Umrah, 226
unemployment, 5, 20
  and conflict, 45
  graduates, 193–4
  Jordan, 193
  Morocco, 194
  Palestinians in Lebanon, 131
  Saudi Arabia, 20–21, 140
  structural, 6
  Tunisia, 193
  Yemen, 134, 161, 165
Union of European Football Associations (UEFA), 221
United Arab Emirates (UAE), 39–63, 111–32

INDEX

Arab Spring (2011), 17, 112–13, 124, 236–45
Asian migrants, 3–4, 42, 43, 87, 122
citizenship, 14, 113, 114–15, 118, 125, 130
cosmopolitanism, 127
demographics, 171
education, 12, 39–63, 48, 49, 119, 123, 124, 126
Egyptian migrants, 41, 42, 45–6, 48, 52, 124, 239, 240
family unification, 120, 127
female migrants, 173, 181, 191, 194
financial crisis (2008), 120–21
Gaza War (2008–9), 124
Gulf War (1990–91), 112, 113, 123–4
Hadrami migrants, 81
Indian migrants, 87, 115, 239
Jordanian migrants, 41, 48, 52, 129, 190, 239, 240
kafala, 115
labour laws, 111–12, 131
Lebanese migrants, 124, 127, 129, 181–2, 187, 203, 240
Madbouh assassination (2010), 124
Maghrebi migrants, 17, 223–4, 226, 228–33
Moroccan migrants, 42, 174
nationalisation programme, 21
naturalisation, 14, 114
Palestinian migrants, 13–14, 41, 48, 111–32, 240
Qatar, migration to, 30
Red Crescent, 129
rule of law, 119
social openness, 119, 121
sports industry, 17, 217–19, 222–4, 226, 228–33
Sudanese migrants, 41, 42
Syrian migrants, 41, 48, 124, 240
third culture, 121, 126
Tunisian migrants, 42, 124
unemployment, 20
Yemeni migrants, 41, 81, 124, 240
United Arab Republic (1958–61), 42
United Kingdom (UK), 44, 112, 115–16, 122, 132
United Nations (UN), 140
  Development Programme (UNDP), 139
  Educational, Scientific and Cultural Organization (UNESCO), 40, 147
  Office for the Coordination of Humanitarian Affairs (OCHA), 160
United States (US)
  beIN Sports, 229
  female migrants, 173
  Mexican migrants, 151, 165
  Palestinian migrants, 14, 113, 114, 129–30
  Turkish migrants, 108
unskilled workers, 5, 10, 11, 14
  Asian migrants, 11, 22, 23
  Egyptian, 32, 34, 37, 180
  Kuwait, 23, 100–101, 201
  Moroccan, 174
  Qatar, 19, 32
  Saudi Arabia, 137, 148
  women, 174
urbanisation
  Kuwait, 72
  Yemen, 15, 136, 138
Viber, 209
Vora, Neha, 87, 115

wages, 19
  Asian migrants, 19, 22, 43
  Kuwait, 16, 92, 103, 104, 202–4
  nationalisation programmes, 21
  Qatar, 31
  teachers, 45, 54, 55, 56, 61, 119
  United Arab Emirates, 119, 122

311

INDEX

wasta, 75, 101, 212
welfare state, 23
West Bank, 113, 117, 119, 120, 126, 127, 128
West Indies, 130
WhatsApp, 209
Winckler, Onn, 6
women, 6, 15, 20, 169–96
   Asian, 15, 23, 169, 170, 177, 178
   Bahrain, migration to, 170, 175–8, 195
   celibacy, 172, 191
   dependants, 30–31
   education, 47–8, 49, 181–4, 193
   Egyptian, 178, 190
   Iraqi, 193
   Jordanian, 173, 180, 193, 195
   Kuwait, migration to, 170, 175–80, 195, 202–3
   Lebanese, 170, 172–4, 178, 180–8, 190–91, 193–6, 202–3
   Moroccan, 169, 172–3
   Palestinian, 173, 193
   Saudi Arabia, migration to, 173
   sex industry, 15, 169
   sexual harassment, 128
   skilled workers, 15, 23, 169–96
   Syrian, 173, 180, 193
   teacher migration, 47–8, 49
   Tunisian, 172, 174, 190
   United Arab Emirates, migration to, 173, 181, 191, 194
   United States, migration to, 173
   Yemeni, 138, 145, 147
World Anti-Doping Agency, 228
World Cup, 220, 229, 231, 232

Yemen, 3, 5, 6, 8, 12, 14–15, 65–84, 133–66
   agriculture, 15, 136–8
   Arab nationalism, 42
   Arab Spring (2011), 237
   Asian migrants, 138
   Civil War (2015–), 9, 14, 134
   education, 137, 147–8, 154, 156, 158–9, 161, 164
   Ethiopian migrants, 160
   food insecurity, 160
   Gulf War (1990–91), 8, 42, 69, 81, 83, 124, 135, 139, 140
   Hadramis, 12–13, 65–84
   and Horn of Africa, 134, 160
   manufacturing, 138
   Palestinian migrants, 131
   poverty, 139, 160, 165
   Qatar, migration to, 27, 41
   remittance flows, 14–15, 45, 69, 71, 78–9, 82–3, 137, 157–61, 165–6, 168
   Saudi Arabia, migration to, 8, 14, 81, 133–66
   socialism, 42
   Somali migrants, 160
   unemployment, 134, 161, 165
   United Arab Emirates, migration to, 41, 81, 124, 240
   urbanisation, 15, 136, 138
   women, 138, 145, 147
zakat, 128
Zayed, Emir of Abu Dhabi, 116, 129
Zayed Charitable and Humanitarian Foundation, 129
Ziani, Karim, 224